Virtual Teams: Projects, Protocols and Processes

Table of Contents

Virtual Teams: Projects, Protocols and Processes

David J. Pauleen
Victoria University of Wellington, New Zealand

IDEA GROUP PUBLISHING

Hershey • London • Melbourne • Singapore

Acquisitions Editor: Mehdi Khosrow-Pour
Senior Managing Editor: Jan Travers
Managing Editor: Amanda Appicello
Development Editor: Michele Rossi
Copy Editor: Lori Eby
Typesetter: Jennifer Wetzel
Cover Design: Lisa Tosheff
Printed at: Integrated Book Technology

Published in the United States of America by
        Idea Group Publishing (an imprint of Idea Group Inc.)
        701 E. Chocolate Avenue, Suite 200
        Hershey PA 17033
        Tel: 717-533-8845
        Fax: 717-533-8661
        E-mail: cust@idea-group.com
        Web site: http://www.idea-group.com

and in the United Kingdom by
        Idea Group Publishing (an imprint of Idea Group Inc.)
        3 Henrietta Street
        Covent Garden
        London WC2E 8LU
        Tel: 44 20 7240 0856
        Fax: 44 20 7379 3313
        Web site: http://www.eurospan.co.uk

Library of Congress Cataloging-in-Publication Data

Virtual teams : projects, protocols and processes / David Pauleen,
editor.
    p. cm.
  ISBN 1-59140-166-6 -- ISBN 1-59140-167-4 (ebook) -- ISBN 1-59140-225-5
(pbk.)
  1. Virtual work teams. 2. Teams in the workplace. I. Pauleen, David,
1957-
  HD66.V56 2003
  658.4'022--dc22
                            2003014947

Paperback ISBN 1-59140-225-5

British Cataloguing in Publication Data
A Cataloguing in Publication record for this book is available from the British Library.

All work contributed to this book is new, previously-unpublished material. The views expressed in
this book are those of the authors, but not necessarily of the publisher.

Foreword

The 17th century philosopher Thomas Hobbes described life in the state of nature as "nasty, brutish, and short." The quality of life has improved for most of us since Hobbes made his famous assertion, but our work lives still often seem frantic, frustrating, and confusing.

In large organizations, few goals can be reached solely through individual effort. The complexity of large organizations also prevents most individuals from working within a single, stable team. Our work leads each of us to be a member of multiple interlocking teams, focused on different but related goals. We seem at times to be caught in a web of organizational structure.

Many organizations adopted the concept of a "virtual team" to help deal with these challenges. The term usually refers to collections of individuals, brought together from different departments or organizations, to focus on a specific objective. The virtual team is not the organizational "home" for the participants—it is a structure they use to accomplish part of their job.

Some of these teams have long lives, existing for many years. Others may arise in response to a specific problem and dissolve quickly. Virtual teams include individuals who know each other well (for better or worse) and individuals who are strangers. Many teams are contained within a single company or organization, but increasingly, our goals span the boundaries of enterprises, with suppliers, customers, and partners working closely together.

As large organizations have become more geographically distributed, the need to work in distributed virtual teams has become commonplace. We often collaborate with team members located at another campus, in another city or country, or on another continent. Some of these team members we seldom (or never) meet in person. Along with the barrier of distance comes the barrier of time; there may be no single time of day that fits into the normal working hours of all team members.

I always found the term "virtual team" to be a misnomer. In spite of their often transitory nature, they are real teams. They face all the challenges of classic team evolution and, in fact, often face more difficult problems, because they lack the reward and authority structures that shape conventional teams. The goals set for virtual teams are often critical: responding to a crisis in the business, solving a particularly difficult problem, or bringing a highly visible project to completion.

Successful use of virtual teams requires team members with appropriate skills and behaviors, team leaders who know how to quickly assemble an effective team and manage the evolving dynamics in the group, and an organizational culture that provides the right context for the team to succeed. Lacking any one of these factors, a virtual team can easily flounder.

I recently heard a respected organizational development consultant cite research showing that it takes five to seven years to really trust a colleague. The research may well reflect a fundamental aspect of human nature, but it also is completely inconsistent with the realities of business in today's world. We need leadership approaches that develop an effective virtual team in days or weeks, not months or years.

This book is an important resource for improving the use of virtual teams. The case studies and research results presented give us new insights into the real behavior of virtual teams, facing real challenges. Our organizations can only benefit from this deeper understanding, as we use virtual teams to solve real problems.

Doug Busch
Vice President and Chief Information Officer
Intel Corporation

Preface

"Virtual teams" is one of the many hot topics in business these days. But unlike a fad, virtual teams appear to have staying power. Their use in organizations is growing in concert with globalization, the rise of the knowledge worker, the need for innovation, and the increasing use of information and communication technology (ICT). While the use of virtual teams continues to grow, our understanding of how their many unique characteristics work (or do not work) together lags far behind (Cramton & Webber, 2000). Researchers and practitioners are trying hard to correct this situation, and in this book, their best efforts are brought together.

In the 13 chapters presented here, the authors offer a well-rounded picture of the current state of virtual team practice and research; that is, what is working and what is still problematic. In addition, the chapters contain invaluable advice on how to manage the conditions that will facilitate the most effective virtual teams. Virtual team members, leaders, managers, senior executives in IT, HR, and other functional areas—as well as researchers—can all gain from a careful reading of this book.

The current notion of virtual teams has been around since the mid-1990s. First addressed by the practitioner literature (Grenier & Metes, 1995; Lipnack & Stamps, 1997; O'Hara-Devereaux & Johansen, 1994), and then by researchers investigating primarily student populations (Jarvenpaa, Knoll, & Leidner, 1998; Sahay, Sarker, & Lau, 1999; Warkenten & Beranek, 1999), research on virtual teams in organizations has only emerged in the last few years. As the reader will soon see, researchers are grappling with everything from defining what makes a virtual team virtual to all the various team, communication, and project processes and protocols that might influence how well a team works together and accomplishes its tasks, as well as the influence of organizational policies, technology, and boundary crossing on virtual team dynamics and effectiveness.

One could make the case that different forms of the virtual team have been around since the beginning of trade, with the representatives of manufacturers, agents, traders, and buyers exchanging goods and credit over distance using sophisticated protocols and available technology. (Murphy touches upon this notion in Chapter 13.) These days, organizations and management are pretty much using virtual teams by default. Global and economic pressures forced new organizations into new competitive strategies. Almost simultaneously, various ICTs were being developed (Coleman, 1997). These developments led to the use of virtual teams (Moshowitz, 1997). For the most part, these teams are thrown together, in an ad hoc fashion, often without a clear idea of how they might function effectively or how the surrounding organizations can effectively support them (Vickery, Clark, & Carlson, 1999). Meanwhile, the virtual team leaders and team members are in the thick of it, operating "from the seat of their pants," often without the virtual communication and team skills required for the virtual environment and without organizational support, and often working at odds with organizational policies that are really appropriate only for traditional organizations (Vickery et al., 1999). Significant organizational, technological, personal, and cultural barriers to the implementation of virtual teams exist (Grenier & Metes, 1995) and must be understood before organizations can make the best use of virtual teams.

This book addresses many of these issues in a practical way, supported by organizational-based research. The reader of these articles will gain a wide-ranging view of how virtual teams work (or do not work) within organizations, how members and leaders of such teams are coping (or not), and how the situation can be improved at the organizational, team, and employee levels.

The Structure of the Book

The book is divided into three sections, *Projects*, *Protocols*, and *Processes*. However, as the reader will soon see, nothing about virtual teams is so clear-cut. The issues raised in these projects, protocols, and processes sections are all closely linked, and hence, each of the chapters addresses at least two and often three of these areas.

Section 1: Projects

The first section of the book attempts to give the reader a concrete conceptualization of what virtual teams are and how they function in the "real" world of organizations. Most of the chapters in this section describe project teams and some of the key issues associated with working virtually in such project environments. These include issues such as trust and the impact of various organizational factors on virtual team project performance. Suggestions are made for improving virtual team performance.

Section 2: Protocols

The second part expands on the first section by looking at more specific ways that virtual team members, leaders, and managers can approach important virtual team concerns. The reader will find a wide range of research-based discussion of virtual team issues, such as leadership, technology, and knowledge sharing. Specific protocols for constructive responses to these issues are proposed.

Section 3: Processes

The third section investigates virtual team processes involving leadership, organizational, and employee dynamics. These chapters will help the reader gain a greater understanding of such processes with suggestions on how those involved can effectively manage them. The last chapter is a "thought" piece on the nature of virtual trust that may well challenge organizational leaders' and managers' basic assumptions of what it takes to successfully make the transition to virtual work.

Chapter Summaries

Chapter 1, "The Multifaceted Nature of Virtual Teams," serves as an excellent introduction to virtual teams. Based on an extensive review of the literature and a series of in-depth interviews with more than 40 experienced virtual team members and leaders, the authors identify the key characteristics of virtual teamwork as well as those characteristics that distinguish various virtual team configurations. They suggest that researchers must now adopt a multidimensional view of virtual teams—a view that recognizes the diversity of possible virtual team arrangements—in order to adequately compare empirical findings, build a cumulative tradition in this field of research, and provide practitioners with a framework to help them manage virtual teams effectively.

In Chapter 2, "Trust and the Trust Placement Process in Metateam Projects," an in-depth look at a virtual meta-team project is presented. A metateam is a temporary group composed of two or more geographically and interorganizationally dispersed teams, commercially linked by project-specific agreements and enabled by electronic means of communication. Metateams are largely unexplored in the IS literature, but they are economically important to major corporations and their IT vendors, as they promise to build IT solutions of high complexity, by integrating expertise from different fields and different organizations and by conquering barriers of time and space. In a global business environment that demands innovation, flexibility, and responsiveness, metateams represent a revolution in the way organizations and practitioners do IT projects. However, as discussed in the chapter, managing metateams presents unique difficulties due to conflicting demands arising from multiple realities and the way in which effectiveness of the trust placement process significantly affects project success.

In Chapter 3, "The Impact of External Factors on Virtual Teams: Comparative Cases," it is suggested that while virtual teams are powerful organizing mechanisms, practitioners and researchers need to pay attention to how corporate organizing structures impact and are impacted by virtual work environments. Reported on in this chapter are two cases where dynamics *outside* the virtual project teams powerfully affected the teams. These cases, both based on studies of real project teams operating inside corporations, highlight the desirability of understanding virtual teams in context. While external factors are not unique to teamwork, their roles have not been explored in depth in research on virtual teams. Dynamic forces outside teams seem more difficult to anticipate and identify when team members are working virtually. These powerful but invisible dynamics can be frustrating to virtual team leaders and members. Concluded in this chapter is that, contrary to initial expectations, virtual teams are not replacing traditional forms of organizing. They are coexisting with traditional forms and dynamics such as business drivers, hierarchies, departments, strategic priorities, and business needs. This coexistence can be fraught with conflict.

The final chapter of the first section takes an in-depth look at a virtual team in action. The characteristics of a project-based virtual team are described. Although there is some empirical research on virtual teams, little research has focused on describing the practical application of a virtual team in the organizational environment. Described in this chapter, titled "A Virtual Team in Action: An Illustration of a Business Development Virtual Team," are the tasks and goals of the team, how it handled virtual challenges and used information technology to bridge distance, and how it functioned within its organization. Specifically, the task of the team, team composition, team beliefs, team processes (e.g., coordination, communications, and sharing of information), organizational context, and the effectiveness of the team are described. The chapter concludes with a summary of characteristics of successful virtual teams.

Section 2 begins with the book's first chapter on virtual leadership. "Long Distance Leadership: Communicative Strategies for Leading Virtual Teams" draws on data from a series of in-depth interviews with project leaders, senior managers, and executives of six global organizations and illustrates what virtual team leaders perceive to be effective communicative tactics in virtual settings. Specifically, it explores tactics related to two leadership challenges commonly cited in the academic and popular press: overcoming virtual team members' feelings of isolation (feelings of disconnectedness, lack of cohesiveness, and limited identification with the virtual team leader or the organization); and building and maintaining trust. The chapter also presents some strategies for managing cross-cultural communication issues and offers tips on the use of communication technologies in distanced settings.

In the last decade, business processes have changed across various dimensions (e.g., flexibility, interconnectivity, coordination style, autonomy) due to market conditions, organizational models, and the usage scenarios of information systems. Virtual teams are under heavy pressure to increase time-to-market of their products and services and lower their coordination costs. In Chapter 6, "Toward Integration of Artifacts, Resources and Processes for Virtual Teams," it is argued that a fundamental need for distributed virtual teamwork is to have access to contextual information, i.e., to see a "knowledge trail" of who did what, when, how, and why. In this chapter, underlying conceptual issues are discussed, and presented in some detail is one particular implemented information system (Caramba) that supports the integration of artifacts, resources, and business processes for virtual teams.

Argued in Chapter 7, "Best Practices for Virtual Team Effectiveness" is that although working in geographically distributed teams is becoming more widespread in organizations today, how to do so effectively is not yet fully understood. The purpose of this chapter is to improve the understanding of what makes virtual teams effective. This is done by identifying the best practices that members of virtual teams should follow, the best practices for leaders and sponsors of virtual teams, and the best practices for the organizations of which the virtual teams are a part. Best practices in these categories are drawn from three major sources: empirical evidence from case studies of six existing virtual teams; the business press and academic literature related to virtual teams; and traditional team (i.e., collocated) literature and telecommuting literature (i.e., research on virtual work at the individual level). The chapter concludes with implications for organizations and potential research directions.

Provided in Chapter 8, "Varieties of Virtual Organizations and Their Knowledge Sharing Systems" is analysis of the differences between virtual teams and communities of practice. And, two growing phenomena are linked—virtual organizing and knowledge sharing (knowledge management)—based on empirical work from both fields of research. By integrating various types of virtual organizing with corresponding knowledge-sharing systems, a framework is provided in this chapter that virtual team leaders, members, and consultants can use to improve management of virtual endeavors. Suggested in this chapter is that calling nearly everything a "community of practice" creates unrealistic expectations for spontaneous organizing and knowledge sharing. The managers of virtual project teams have organizing challenges that are very different from stewardship of communities of practice. Practitioners struggling with "one-size-fits-all" prescriptions for virtual work or knowledge management can use this chapter's three generalized types to develop communications and management strategies appropriate for the unique cultures found in each of the various combinations of virtual organizing and knowledge sharing.

Section 3 begins with "Effective Virtual Teams" a chapter in which a compelling look at how employees are responding to the organizational use of virtual teams is taken. As the author points out, it is likely that employees will work on a virtual team at some point in their careers. However, the findings presented in the chapter question how effectively organizations, training, and technology support the needs of virtual teams and urge that organizations communicate what collaborative and knowledge-sharing behaviors are expected, establish reward and recognition systems that reinforce those behaviors, ensure that employees have the skills and tools required to fulfil those expectations, and develop managers that role model and reinforce the desired behaviors. Also considered is the function of technology in virtual teams, and it is concluded that collaborative technologies must also become more self-managing, provide more compelling asynchronous capabilities, and cater to individuals who may simultaneously be part of many teams.

In Chapter 10, "Prelude to Virtual Groups: Leadership and Technology in Semivirtual Groups," a study of 76 more and less virtual investment clubs examines the relationships between communication technologies used for club business (from face-to-face to more highly technologically enabled media), group leadership role behaviors, and club portfolio value. The results are interesting, with more and less virtual clubs benefiting from different forms of leadership behaviors. Clubs using fewer technologies seem to benefit from a greater focus on socioemotional role (communication) behaviors, while the opposite is found in clubs using more technologies. The effect for procedural role behaviors (agenda setting and the like) appears to run in the opposite direction: clubs using more technologies seem to benefit from a greater focus on procedural role behaviors, while the opposite is found in clubs using fewer technologies. Practitioners will need to take into account the obvious and subtle differences between groups with more and less virtual characteristics.

Chapter 11 is also presented on the theme of leadership. Findings are provided that the reader can compare and contrast with those of the proceeding chapter and Chapter 5. In "Mediating Complexity: Facilitating Relationship Building

Across Boundaries in Start-Up Virtual Teams," part of a field study of New Zealand-based virtual team leaders working with boundary spanning virtual teams is presented. Boundary-crossing issues (organizational, cultural, language, time and distance) from a team leaders' perspective are presented, and the significant way crossing boundaries can affect relationship building is reported. Then discussed are ways that virtual team leaders and organizations can improve team leaders' and members' virtual skills in mediating communication across boundaries with available ICT.

In Chapter 12, an eight-factor process model of large virtual groups is presented. In this chapter, "Factors Contributing to Knowledge Sharing and Communication in a Large Virtual Work Group," the author discusses virtual work in terms of a large work group, defined as a larger group of people more loosely connected to one another than a team by a shared work process, project, or strategic goal. The eight factors are organizational support and purpose; egalitarian structure; team culture, trust, collaboration, and relationships; people, skills, expertise, and capabilities; motivation and rewards; communication processes; communication tools; and knowledge sharing. These factors to a greater or lesser degree were shown to contribute to the effectiveness of communication in a large virtual work group during a two-phase study at Nortel Inc. Qualitative and quantitative results of this study are presented, and issues related to communication and knowledge sharing are discussed as are recommendations for successful organization and communication in large work groups.

Finally, in Chapter 13, "Trust, Rationality and the Virtual Team," an in-depth look is taken at the issue of trust in virtual teams. Virtual teams need trust in order to function, as it is an efficient way of gaining group cooperation. As the author explains, online, trust is more effective than instruction or authority or status in getting people who are strangers to work together. However, trust is not a simple quality. The kind of trust that is the cement of distance relations of a global or virtual kind is different from the type of trust that binds face-to-face interactions and from the procedural kind of trust that operates in regional or national organizations of a traditional managerial kind. In this chapter, the ways in which trust between virtual team members is generated are explored, and it is theorized that "trust between strangers" is optimally generated when persons are allowed to self-organize complex orders and create objects and processes of high quality. The kinds of personalities that are best suited to working in a virtual collaborative environment are explored, and it is concluded that persons who prefer strong social or procedural environments will be less effective in a virtual environment. In contrast, self-steering ("stoic") personality types have characteristics that are optimally suited to virtual collaboration.

As the reader will now be aware, although virtual teams are assuming a greater role in the life of organizations and employees, many critical issues and processes remain underresearched and even undiscovered, presenting practitioners and researchers with unexpected difficulties and challenges. Those working in and with virtual teams are trying to navigate new and uncharted terrain without maps and with little in the way of guidance. This book's broad-ranging discussion of key virtual team protocols and processes presented in real organizational contexts should help light the way for practitioners and researchers, hopefully ensuring a smoother trip and a more effective use of virtual teams.

References

Coleman, D. (1997). *Groupware: Collaborative Strategies for Corporate LANS and Intranets.* Upper Saddle River, NJ: Prentice Hall.

Cramton, C., & Webber, S. (2000). Attribution in distributed work groups. In P. Hinds & S. Kiesler (Eds.), *Distributed Work: New Research on Working Across Distance Using Technology* (pp. 191-212). Cambridge, MA: MIT Press.

Grenier, R., & Metes, G. (1995). *Going Virtual: Moving your Organization into the 21st Century.* Upper Saddle River, NJ: Prentice Hall PTR.

Jarvenpaa, S. L., Knoll, K., & Leidner, D. E. (1998). Is anybody out there? Antecedents of trust in global virtual teams. *Journal of Management Information Systems, 14,* 29-64.

Lipnack, J., & Stamps, J. (1997). *Virtual Teams: Reaching Across Space, Time, and Organizational Boundaries.* New York: John Wiley & Sons.

Moshowitz, A. (1997). Virtual organization. *Communications of the ACM, 40*(9), 30-37.

O'Hara-Devereaux, M., & Johansen, R. (1994). *Global Work: Bridging Distance, Culture and Time.* San Francisco, CA: Jossey-Bass Publishers.

Sahay, S., Sarker, S., & Lau, F. (1999). Understanding the process of collaboration in virtual teams: An inductive study linking micro processes of communication with macro structures of team development. *Hawaii International Conference in Systems Science,* Hawaii, USA.

Vickery, C. M., Clark, T. D., & Carlson, J. R. (1999). Virtual positions: An examination of structure and performance in ad hoc workgroups. *Information Systems Journal, 9,* 291-312.

Warkentin, M., & Beranek, P. M. (1999). Training to improve virtual team communication. *Information Systems Journal, 9,* 271-289.

Acknowledgments

The editor would like to acknowledge the help of all those involved in the collations and review process of the book, without whose support the project could not have been successfully completed. Special thanks to all the authors, most of whom also served as reviewers for articles written by other authors. A further special note of thanks goes to all the staff at Idea Group Publishing, whose contributions throughout the whole process from inception of the initial idea to final publication have been invaluable.

Section I

Projects

Chapter I

The Multifaceted Nature of Virtual Teams

Line Dubé
HEC Montréal, Canada

Guy Paré
HEC Montréal, Canada

Abstract

Despite their growing popularity in organizations, our understanding of virtual teams is still at an embryonic stage. As of today, the term "virtual team" has been loosely defined in the academic press, and empirical findings have been generalized across all types of virtual teams. Based on an extensive review of the literature and a series of in-depth interviews with more than 40 experienced virtual team members and leaders, we identified the key characteristics of virtual teamwork as well as those characteristics that distinguish among various virtual team configurations. We posit that researchers must now adopt a multidimensional view of virtual teams in order to adequately compare empirical findings, build a cumulative tradition in this field of research, and provide practitioners with a framework to help them manage virtual teams effectively. Researchers and practitioners must not only recognize the diversity of possible virtual team arrangements but also identify strategies and draw lessons that are contingent upon particular virtual team configurations.

Introduction

Today, virtual teams are considered to be the answer to many organizational problems (Duarte & Snyder, 1999; Haywood, 1998; Lipnack & Stamps, 1997). Advances in information technology, coupled with competitive pressures, led to the increasing use of virtual teams for such diverse activities as product development, customer care, systems design and programming, strategic program implementation, and building design and construction. Their growing popularity attracted the attention of researchers in information systems and organizational behavior. Despite the fact that research on this topic is blooming, our understanding of the virtual team phenomenon is still at an embryonic stage, and there is much to learn about such teams before we can fully reap their potential benefits (Bell & Kozlowski, 2002; Cramton, 2001; Furst, Blackburn, & Rosen, 1999; Saunders, 2000). Most of the early writing on virtual teams focused on their impacts, or *why* they should be used (Bell & Kozlowski, 2002; Saunders, 2000). But as organizations increasingly grasp the reasons for adopting virtual teams, the research focus must shift to issues related to *how* they can be effectively used and managed (Saunders, 2000). Because of the differences between traditional and virtual teams, what we know about managing traditional teams[2] may or may not apply to virtual ones (Saunders, 2000).

To begin looking at this issue, we conducted an extensive literature review on virtual teams. Two related problems were immediately apparent. First, we found that the term "virtual team" has been loosely defined and used by researchers in several fields of study. As an example of this, McDonough, Kahn, and Barczak (2001) defined virtual teams as "comprised of individuals who have a moderate level of physical proximity and are culturally similar" and global teams as "comprised of individuals who work and live in different countries and are culturally diverse" (p. 111). According to these authors, global teams are distinct from virtual teams. But are not global teams a particular form or configuration of virtual teams? In this chapter, we attempt to clarify this issue.

Furthermore, while several authors acknowledge that virtual teams are intrinsically different and that various virtual team configurations exist (e.g., Bell & Kozlowski, 2002; Cramton, 2001; Jackson, 1999), conclusions are commonly generalized across all types of virtual teams. For instance, Lurey and Raisinghani (2002) attempted to identify some general guidelines or best practices to assist organizations in enhancing their virtual team efforts. The virtual teams involved in this research were of different types or configurations. The authors claim their results can be generalized to a broad population of virtual teams, although they could not determine whether or not the findings were influenced by any one or a combination of distinguishing traits. Taken together, we believe these two findings raise some serious concerns about the quality and generalizability of empirical findings. Maznevski and Chudoba (2000) concurred, stating, "when added together, the conclusions from single studies do not provide a well-integrated understanding of virtual team process and performance" (p. 474).

In our view, a preliminary but necessary step is to investigate the multifaceted nature of virtual teams, so as to better define the true *object* of our investigations. A few attempts at defining different types of virtual teams have already been made. Some represent beginnings (e.g., Cramton, 2001; Jackson, 1999), but others are targeted at a certain domain (e.g., leadership), which colors the way virtual teams are conceptualized (e.g., Bell & Kozlowski, 2002). Therefore, given the actual state of our knowledge, the main purposes of this chapter are to clarify the *nature* of virtual teams and to identify the key characteristics that will allow researchers as well as practitioners to differentiate among different configurations of virtual teams. We believe such groundwork is necessary at this stage of their development and will allow for a deeper understanding of this novel form of work arrangement. In our view, researchers must now adopt a multidimensional view of virtual teams in order to compare empirical findings, accumulate knowledge, and provide practitioners with a useful framework to help them more effectively manage them.

First explored in this chapter is a basic definition of what a virtual team truly is, and then it is differentiated from other related concepts such as virtual group, virtual organization, virtual community, and telecommuting. Explained in the next section is the method used to identify the key characteristics of virtual teams. These characteristics are then explained in detail. Finally, illustrated in the last section is how different configurations of virtual teams may raise different challenges and how management strategies must be chosen accordingly to ensure success.

What is a Virtual Team?

An in-depth look at the literature reveals the confusion that exists regarding virtual teams. At present, the term is loosely defined and used. To achieve a better understanding of virtual teams, researchers must first agree on a common definition. All teams must communicate, coordinate, and collaborate to get the task or project done. However, while conventional teams accomplish this mainly through face-to-face interactions, virtual teams predominantly use information and communication technology (ICT) to communicate, collaborate, share information, and coordinate their efforts (Towsend, DeMarie, & Hendrickson, 1998). It is common knowledge that conventional teams will also use ICT to some extent to get the job done (e.g., to exchange electronic documents or schedule meetings), but *predominance* is the key word here. Virtual teams perform most of their work through ICT, while conventional teams use technology only as a punctual tool to support face-to-face work. **Working predominantly through ICT** represents the key factor that distinguishes virtual teams from traditional ones.

In several books, geographic dispersion of team members was often cited as the key criterion distinguishing virtual teams (e.g., Henry & Hartzler, 1998; Lipnack & Stamps, 1997). It was also identified as the most critical and important feature of virtual teams in research (e.g., Bell & Kozlowski, 2002). The notion of geographic dispersion has been integrated into definitions of a virtual team (e.g., Townsend et al., 1996; Henry & Hartzler, 1998; Haywood, 1998; Duarte & Snyder, 1999). Although we recognize that virtual team members are often separated by many miles or even continents (Pape, 1997; Townsend et al., 1996), they may also be situated in adjacent offices in the same facility, if they chose to communicate predominantly through ICT.[3] Similarly, distance does not play a role in virtual teams spread out in time. For instance, people could share the same physical facilities but be present at different times, creating the need to communicate through ICT. For this reason, we consider geographic dispersion to be a key feature of a virtual team's configuration but not a *defining characteristic*.

Virtual teams must also be distinguished from other related virtual entities. The literature is full of examples of misuse of the term "team" or of articles that carelessly aggregate results across many different levels of analysis. For example, Maznevski and Chudoba (2000) confusingly included all empirical studies on virtual organizations, virtual groups, and virtual teams in their literature review on "distributed teams." While integrating variables across different levels of analysis may be desirable to increase our understanding of the phenomenon, this must be done with an acute awareness of the problems caused by aggregating and disaggregating data (Morgeson & Hofmann, 1999). Virtual groups and virtual teams must also be distinguished. In this regard, we adopted Katzenbach and Smith's (1993) definition of a team: "a small number of people with complementary skills who are committed to a common purpose, set of performance goals, and approach for which they hold themselves mutually accountable" (p. 112). Sundstrom, De Meuse, and Futrell (1990) emphasized the interdependence and the shared responsibility among team members. "A small number of people" does not include communication through distribution lists to hundreds of people. It also excludes "coacting groups," where individuals report to the same manager but perform their own independent, individual tasks (Hackman, 1987). In a virtual group, performance evaluation and accountability is only at the individual level, and most interactions are with the manager (Furst et al., 1999). Thus, client service representatives working at home would qualify as a virtual group, not a virtual team. Similarly, a group of sales representatives working virtually (because they are mostly on the road visiting clients) are part of a virtual group, not a virtual team. In both examples, the group has no, or very few, common objectives, and people work independently and have few interactions. While group objectives may exist (like sales targets for a given territory), a member's major responsibility is to fulfill his personal objectives, and it is the accumulation of personal results that leads to the fulfillment of the group's aims. And, a group of people using a group decision support system (GDSS) does not qualify as a virtual team. While a GDSS *can* be used to support electronic meetings across space and work asynchronously across time (Dennis et al., 1988), GDSS sessions are usually conducted in a room where participants can see each other and communicate nonverbally, and where a leader interacts face to face with the group during a collaboration session.

Virtual teams are also frequently confused with virtual organizations and virtual communities. For example, Lewis (1998) uses the terms "virtual team" and "distributed community" interchangeably, making the object under investigation difficult to grasp. In a virtual community [also called online (e.g., Williams & Cothrel, 2000) or distributed (e.g., Wenger, McDermott, & Snyder, 2002)], people interact through ICT based upon common interests or goals (Yoo, Suh, & Lee, 2002). Participation is often voluntary and not specifically remunerated. A community's shape, membership, and objectives are fluid and often emerge through the participation process. In contrast, a virtual team is created to carry out a specific task (Brown & Duguid, 2001).

While the concept of "virtual organization" is often used, it is ill defined. Boudreau, Loch, Robey, and Straub (1998) explained that "the central feature of virtual organizations is their dependence on a federation of alliances and partnerships with other organizations" (p. 121). It is easily noticeable that the unit of analysis is very different—a whole organization rather than a small group—and that the focus is on relationships with external partners. A virtual organization may have virtual and traditional teams, and a virtual team may or may not evolve into a virtual organization. A virtual team may or may not involve members from external partners. Finally, virtual teams must also be differentiated from the concept of telecommuting (Nilles, 1994). In this regard, Bélanger, Watson-Manheim, and Jordan (2002) posited that common terms in the field of virtual work are often used interchangeably and treat virtual teams and telecommuting as similar phenomena. Because the issues faced by telecommuters are different from those faced by virtual team members, such aggregation only adds to the existing confusion. For instance, feelings of isolation and issues of personal control or work-family conflicts, to name a few, may or may not apply in the context of virtual teams, because they do not commonly work from home.

In sum, distinctions between virtual entities are essential if we are to better understand the nature of virtual teams, determine the proper unit of analysis, address the relevant issues and questions, and learn where current knowledge applies and where future research efforts are needed. In other words, the adoption of a common definition will facilitate comparisons among empirical studies (Robey & Jin, in press) and hence, enable the development of a cumulative research tradition.

Toward a Deeper Understanding of Virtual Teams

In order to provide researchers and practitioners with a deeper understanding of virtual teams, the present research adopted a two-step methodology. First, an extensive literature review was performed in order to identify the key characteristics (see Appendix A) that distinguish virtual teams from conventional ones and those that differentiate various virtual team configurations. We used the ABI/ Inform search engine to identify papers on the topic of virtual teams dating from the time the expression was first coined. To do so, we used keywords such as "virtual team" and "distributed team" and limited our search to those papers that had been published in peer-reviewed journals.[4] We also adopted the "snowball" technique to identify additional papers (going through the list of references of already identified papers). We considered only those papers that were empirical in nature (in contrast with conceptual papers) and that respected our definition of a virtual team.

A total of 49 empirical studies investigating various aspects of virtual teamwork were identified. Two types of empirical studies can be found in the literature. The first are laboratory experiments using students as subjects, while the second are studies of virtual teams in real-life organizational settings. One striking difference between the two categories of studies is that while teams in experiments totally rely on ICT to communicate and collaborate, most teams in real-life settings rely, to some extent, on face-to-face meetings to ease the process of collaboration and coordination. For this reason, studies that compare conventional and "100% virtual" teams to more "traditional" virtual teams, which rely on a mix of ICT and face-to-face meetings, should be encouraged if our goal is to better understand the dynamics of virtual teaming and success in organizational settings (see Ocker et al., 1995-1996, 1998). Finally, it should also be noted that many studies do not provide much information about the specific characteristics of the team under investigation.

As a second step, qualitative data from 41 in-depth interviews with members and leaders of 33 distinct virtual teams were collected and analyzed. Respondents were recruited using a convenient sampling method, and the sampling frame represented the researchers' personal contacts in the business milieu. These teams came from a variety of industrial sectors, including telecommunications, banking, government, consulting, IT services, and manufacturing. The empirical data were also used to look at various virtual team configurations as well as to enrich the set of key characteristics identified in Step 1. These results are presented in Appendix B. They clearly show that virtual teams come in all shapes and forms. Sizes and project/task duration varied widely. While all teams predominantly used ICT to perform their work, they relied on technology to varying degrees. Most had relatively stable membership with team members assigned either part- or full-time. Team members could be scattered around the globe or located in the same city. Finally, task interdependence and prior work experience varied widely, along with the degree of cultural diversity.

Our analysis of the literature and the empirical data revealed that there is great variation in virtual team configurations. This highlights the need for a contingency approach in research and practice. That is, researchers and practitioners must not only recognize the diversity of possible virtual team arrangements, they must also identify strategies and draw lessons that are contingent upon particular team configurations.

Key Characteristics of Virtual Teams

While the previous analysis helps us identify key characteristics that distinguish among various virtual team configurations, described in detail in the present section are the key characteristics of virtual teamwork. It should be mentioned at this stage that our goal is not to explain or predict virtual team effectiveness or to identify all the potential characteristics that could be used to describe one particular virtual team. Rather, our main intent is to identify those key characteristics that ought to be taken into consideration in order to distinguish among virtual team configurations, so that we can anticipate challenges ahead and, hence, manage these teams more effectively. As shown in Table 1, the key characteristics can be grouped into two distinct categories: the characteristics related to the basics of virtual teamwork and the characteristics that make virtual teamwork more complex. Each category is discussed in detail below.

The Characteristics Related to the Basics of Virtual Teamwork

The first category focuses on the characteristics that differentiate virtual teams from conventional ones. These characteristics are present in all virtual teams, and in a sense, they make teams virtual. All three fundamental characteristics presented below are related to the unique differentiating feature of virtual teams, namely, technological mediation.

Degree of Reliance on ICT

While a team needs to be predominantly using ICT to be called "virtual," teams use technology in different degrees. One team may use ICT 98% of the time and meet only once a year, while another virtual team may use ICT extensively but

Table 1. Key Characteristics of Virtual Teams

		DEGREE OF COMPLEXITY LOW <-----------------------------> HIGH	
The characteristics related to the basics of virtual teamwork	Degree of reliance on ICT	Low reliance	High reliance
	ICT availability	High variety	Low variety
	Members' ICT Proficiency	High	Low
Characteristics that make virtual teamwork more complex	Team size	Small	Large
	Geographic dispersion (physical proximity)	Local	Global
	Task or project duration	Long term	Short term
	Prior shared work experience	Extensive experience	No experience
	Members' assignments	Full-time	Part-time
	Membership stability	Stable membership	Fluid membership
	Task interdependence	Low interdependence	High interdependence
	Cultural diversity (national, organizational, professional)	Homogeneous	Heterogeneous

meet face-to-face every other week. In the real world, very few teams are 100% virtual. In our sample, only one virtual team (out of 33) never met face to face.[5]

The degree of reliance on ICT is fundamental, because it conditions the level of "virtuality" of a team. It is widely accepted that ICT will never be a perfect substitute for face-to-face encounters or meetings (Jackson, 1999; Roberts, Kossek, & Ozeki, 1998). Deprived of rich face-to-face contacts, especially at the beginning of a project, a virtual team may have problems or take longer to establish shared knowledge that increases the likelihood of mutual understanding (Cramton, 2001). Because communicating through ICT forces a formal structure (Qureshi, Bogenrieder, & Kumar, 2000), virtual teams may be more task-oriented. Our respondents clearly indicated that when team members are in remote locations, alignment and commitment are more difficult to generate. They consistently said that starting a new project with a face-to-face meeting is a highly useful investment. Such a meeting provides the necessary clarity of focus and direction and gives people a chance to establish relationships and develop a sense of belonging to the team (Solomon, 1995). Working almost exclusively through ICT may also make coordinating work and resolving conflicts more difficult. A higher degree of reliance on ICT will therefore make working together more complex.

ICT Availability

The type of ICT available to a team can facilitate or hinder effective communication among team members. Virtual team members can be linked through a variety of technologies, including traditional ones like phones, audioconferencing, fax machines, and e-mail, and more advanced ones such as desktop videoconferencing, collaborative software, intranets, and workflow applications. Each technology has strengths and weaknesses and its own ability to support understanding (Daft, Lengel, & Trevino, 1987). A rich media will allow feedback (immediate response), multiple cues (verbal, nonverbal, text, etc.), language variety (for example, natural language and text), and personal focus (possibility to transmit emotions) (Daft et al., 1987). Thus, the richer an ICT, the more it facilitates shared meanings, insights, and rapid understanding (Daft et al., 1987). However, it would be wrong to believe that richer is always better (McGrath & Hollingshead, 1993; Daft et al., 1987). For example, it would make no sense to individually call everybody to announce a corporate event when a simple e-mail sent in a few seconds would do the trick. While asynchronous technology gives team members more time to reflect and write their answers, it is not very effective when information is urgent, because it may cause delay (Warkentin, Sayeed, & Hightower, 1997). Furthermore, most asynchronous technologies (e.g., e-mail, group calendars, bulletin boards, workflow applications) are limited in social presence and information richness, i.e., lacking the cues that help relay meaning such as tone of voice, facial expression, and body language (Roberts et al., 1998; Sproull & Kiesler, 1986; Townsend et al., 1998), which can make interpretation difficult (Cramton, 2001). Under such circumstances, misunderstandings can result in e-mail wars (Roberts et al., 1998). Team members who have access to a large variety of ICT will be able to choose the ICT that is the most appropriate for a particular task. The mix of available ICT for a specific situation is thus critical to ensure effective communication.

Team Members' ICT Proficiency

In a virtual team, there can be wide discrepancies in the participants' technological proficiencies. Some team members might be comfortable working with groupware, whiteboards, and videoconferencing, while others might need to be taught how to attach a file to an e-mail message. For some inexperienced team members, it may be difficult to participate to their full potential because of the barrier created by technology. In one of our teams (virtual team #26), ICT proficiency was a major problem inhibiting the participation of several members. They would rely on the phone and fax instead of more appropriate and sophisticated ICT, duplicating efforts and inhibiting efficiency among team members. Members having more difficulty may also be looked down upon by more experienced users (Duarte & Snyder, 1999). Thus, while a variety of more or less sophisticated ICT may be available to a virtual team, members' abilities to use them appropriately and efficiently will facilitate or hinder the team's work.

The Characteristics that Make Virtual Teamwork More Complex

The discussion above addressed the basic characteristics of virtual teams. Now we would like to turn our attention to the underlying characteristics that distinguish alternative configurations of virtual teams. In this section, we discuss several characteristics that make virtual teamwork more complex. Although we make no claim that these characteristics are exhaustive, we believe they capture most of the diversity of different types of virtual teams. While these characteristics increase the complexity of all teams, be they virtual or conventional, they must be considered because of their amplifying effects in a virtual environment. Other characteristics, such as team members' ages, genders, and tenures, which have been shown to influence conventional team effectiveness, were omitted from this discussion, because they are not likely to have a particular effect on virtual teams.

Team Size

While some may say that an optimal virtual team size is between three and seven members (e.g., Pape, 1997), size can vary considerably. In a study of 165 project teams, Kinney and Panko (1996) found that the average team size was 7.7 members. While a large team means more resources, expertise, and ideas, it also results in greater need of coordination and may be more prone to communication breakdowns. Thus, a larger virtual team increases complexity. In addition, a large number of members means a "higher social density" that usually leads to people getting much more information than they can assimilate and respond to (Hiltz & Turoff, 1985). Increased team size may also increase the potential for free-riding and social loafing (Bettenhausen, 1991; Gallupe et al., 1992). This can be especially important on virtual teams. When virtual team members are isolated from each other, motivation may decrease, and this may increase the likelihood of social loafing (Furst et al., 1999).

Geographic Dispersion

As mentioned earlier, geographic dispersion has been widely recognized as a key criterion when characterizing virtual teams (e.g., Henry & Hartzler, 1998; Lipnack & Stamps, 1997). We found that virtual team members may be close to each other (even in the same building) or globally distributed, with members from different countries (Lipnack & Stamps, 1997). Mixed-location teams are increasingly common in organizations (Kinney & Panko, 1996). For example, in one of the software development teams in our sample (virtual team #1), a group of software engineers located in City A collaborated with a group of business analysts located in City B and a group of user representatives located in City C. Such a configuration can lead to significant challenges. For example, communication among subgroups may not be reported to the whole team, leading to unfair information sharing and creation of bad impressions or misinterpretations (Cramton, 2001). A subgroup containing more members may also have more visibility in the organization and gain all the credit for a project's successful completion.

Widely dispersed teams may also encounter a variety of challenges related to a mix of national cultures and time zone differences. Different time zones may positively affect the productivity of a virtual team by enabling work to be accomplished continually (Pape, 1997). However, they may also create delays and necessitate greater coordination (Saunders, 2000). For highly dispersed teams, synchronous communication is a scarce resource (Steinfield et al., 2001) and must be used efficiently (Lipnack & Stamps, 1997).

Task or Project Duration

A virtual team can be assembled on a temporary basis to accomplish a specific task or on a more permanent basis to tackle ongoing issues (e.g., technical service teams). In the case of temporary teams, projects may last for varying periods of time (Townsend et al., 1998; Jackson, 1999; Duarte & Snyder, 1999). When a virtual team has a short life cycle, team building can be difficult. Leaders have only a limited amount of time during which they can do this and therefore have to focus only on the most critical issues. Team members must get to know each other quickly, without time for experimentation with rules and structures (Solomon, 1995). Developing trust and cohesion and building relationships are therefore likely to be more difficult in short-duration virtual activities than in longer or more permanent ones.

Prior Shared Work Experience

Members in a virtual team may or may not have prior shared work experience. If there is a lack of common experience, the work routines of a team must be defined from scratch. Every team member joining a project comes with his or her past experiences and cultural influences (Bloor & Dawson, 1994). Team development is a complex process in which acceptable patterns are identified through discussion and trial and error and finally evolve into rules (Suchan & Hayzak, 2001). This process recurs for every aspect of team life, e.g., communication, expectations, acceptable behaviors, nature of relationships. To do this well on a virtual team, in addition to defining the team's purpose, gaining project commitment, determining project effectiveness measures, laying a foundation for trust, and establishing communication interactions and media choice patterns, requires considerable energy. A virtual team is, therefore, vulnerable to dysfunctional conflicts (Suchan & Hayzak, 2001). According to our respondents, those teams with members who have extensive shared work experience fall back on their previous successful work routines and norms and, therefore, are able to be productive very quickly compared to teams with members who are working together for the first time.

Members' Assignments

Members can be assigned to a virtual team on a full-time or part-time basis. Because the use of ICT means less travel is necessary, highly specialized people tend to be invited to participate on several teams on an *ad hoc* basis. A team member, therefore, can easily become overcommitted, being a member of too many teams at the same time (Lipnack & Stamps, 1997). This may put him or her in a complex and stressful environment (Townsend et al., 1998). Part-time assignments make managing a virtual team more complex. Different teams must fight for the same time and priorities. Concomitant peaks in several assignments will inevitably cause delays and dissatisfaction. A person who is part of many teams may have problems feeling committed to any of the project. These problems are exacerbated if a person is also part of a team that regularly meets face to face. In these cases, the person may have a much stronger sense of identification with this team than with his virtual teams (Jackson, 1999). For the team, a part-time member may not be a "real" member and may not be treated as such.

Membership Stability

Virtual teams may have relatively permanent members but can also have more fluid members who join in response to task requirements, availability, emergencies, or opportunities (Saunders, 2000). Because participation is mainly through ICT, it is easy to "connect" or "disconnect" members as required. Organizations expect teams to be productive even with this repeatedly changing membership (Townsend et al., 1998). Every time a new member joins the team, however, a complete socialization and sense-making process is triggered (Bettenhausen, 1991). Each person brings his own cultural background to a team, which is shaped by his country, his present and past organizations, his profession, and by the other teams with which he works. This will confront the values, norms, and communication patterns that the team has adopted. A learning and adaptation process on both sides then occurs and is more or less successful depending on the adaptive capacity of the parties involved. If new members join repeatedly, the life of the whole team is made more complex. If this happens frequently, considerable energy will have to be devoted to the adaptation process.

Task Interdependence

The constraining influence of task interdependence on work group structure and processes has been noted by every major literature review and theory developed in the past three decades (e.g., Bettenhausen, 1991; Kozlowski, Gully, Nason, & Smith, 1999). Task interdependence has critical implications for the structure and processes of virtual teams (Bell & Kozlowski, 2002), and research has shown that task interdependence and team complexity are positively related (e.g., Maznevski & Chudoba, 2000). While we agree that a minimum level of task interdependence should be present in all teams, the level of interdependence is likely to vary from team to team. A high degree of task interdependence requires more communication and coordination among team members. When these are made even more complex due to the intensive use of ICT, conditions are ripe for communication breakdowns.

Cultural Diversity

As a system of perceptions, meanings, values, and beliefs, culture influences all aspects of organizational life. By acting as a lens through which one interprets organizational reality, culture influences how a person thinks, feels, and acts. Three levels of cultural influence must be considered: national, organizational, and professional. First, cultural diversity in a virtual team may be created by mixing different national cultures (which is more likely to be encountered in a global virtual team). Hofstede (1993) showed how different cultures have very different conceptualizations of management, leadership, autonomy, priority and focus, decision making, and relationships between people. For example, top U.S. managers consider Norwegians to be less effective "global manager material," because Norwegian work-family values make it possible for men who have senior positions in organizations to leave at 3 p.m. to pick up their children after school (Roberts et al., 1998). Furthermore, a variety of national cultures often comes with a variety of languages, amplifying problems of communication and collaboration (Townsend et al., 1998). Halting speech, misused words, strange grammar, and mispronounced words can increase the likelihood of misunderstanding and may decrease the perceived competence of the speaker (Roberts et al., 1998).

Second, because organizations depend increasingly on strategic alliances and partnerships (Kaplan & Hurd, 2002), virtual teams may bring together different organizational cultures (Karolak, 1998). When members of different organizations are united into a single team, two or more disparate sociotechnical systems meet. For example, the culture of an organization will influence how team-related activities are valued. Faced with diverging evaluation and compensation systems, team members' motivation and behaviors may be affected (Saunders, 2000). Each member also comes to a team with taken-for-granted assumptions and expectations shaped by the culture of the member's organization (Suchan & Hayzak, 2001). Members can hold different views on the important processes of their team, such as power relationships, trust, information sharing, communication norms, level of autonomy expected, and decision making. Creating trust among partners from different organizations holding different values is, therefore, one of the potential challenges of a virtual team (Duarte & Snyder, 1999).

The third and last dimension of culture is the integration of dissimilar professional cultures,[6] usually encountered in cross-functional teams. Influenced by education and professional associations, members of a specific professional culture develop their own knowledge bases, language, specialized vocabulary, technical routines, workplace values and norms, and even dress code. Members of different professional groups can thus exhibit differing mutual knowledge, expectations, and assumptions (Cramton, 2001; Davidson, Schofield, & Stocks, 2001), and even a different code for interpreting the organizational world (Van Maanen & Barley, 1984). When unfamiliar professional cultures are united in a team, however, members may lack the shared meaning, language, pattern, and routine needed to agree on a shared purpose, goals, and priorities. They may even have problems dividing tasks, coordinating work, handling conflict, and formulating rules (Suchan & Hayzak, 2001), making working together more difficult. Engineers and software designers, for example, may have opposing views on the appropriate set of techniques for managing projects (Duarte & Snyder, 1999). An inability to break down these barriers in a single team may lead to professional prejudices and result in a workgroup of disparate people, rather than an integrated team (Moore & Dainty, 2001).

While cultural heterogeneity is an asset and brings market knowledge and a variety of perspectives to a team, it also means greater complexity (Kayworth & Leidner, 2001-2002). People tend to interpret information based on their cultural filters, leading to a potentially broad range of misinterpretations or distortions (Kayworth & Leidner, 2001-2002; Solomon, 1995). When facing such cultural disparity, it may be more difficult to establish trust, delaying the time a team requires to become effective (Jackson, 1999). With cultural diversity, many visions of reality collide. In a virtual world, it may be much more difficult to negotiate and assemble these visions into a coherent and workable one that will value diversity, teamwork, open communication, and learning (Duarte & Snyder, 1999).

The Key Characteristics in Action

Illustrated in this section, using data from two virtual teams, is how challenges and dilemmas faced by virtual team members and their leaders are contingent upon a particular team's configuration. The scenarios in this section also reveal the risks, for researchers and practitioners, of treating virtual teams as a single type. These cases also show that the various characteristics described above are highly interdependent, and that facilitating factors may compensate for more challenging ones. For instance, the increased complexity created by a highly heterogeneous group of people in a virtual team may be alleviated by the fact that it has had several months of experience successfully working together virtually.

ABC's Virtual Team Configuration

ABC[7] is a multinational organization with annual revenues of approximately US$13 billion in 2001. The company employs approximately 48,000 people and has operating facilities in 38 countries. ABC's head office is in North America, but it has major decision-making centers located in Europe and North America. ABC values integrity, accountability, trust, transparency, and teamwork, and these guide employees as well as executives in their dealings with customers, suppliers, and other stakeholders. Top management members strongly believe in leveraging the abilities of employees, suppliers, contractors, and customers through a cooperative team approach to problem solving and project implementation. Thus, interaction with other group and team members is a vital part of everyone's job at ABC.

In 1999, ABC created a global virtual team (virtual team #9) to make specific recommendations for a new security training program called "Behavior-Based Safety" or BBS. Its characteristics are depicted in Figure 1. Executives wanted precise answers to the following questions: Would this security approach further reduce the number of work accidents and deaths at ABC? Would such a program be relevant and adequate in all plants? To what extent were the company and its plants ready for such change? What would be the main implications, risks, and challenges? What would be the key constituents of a proposed implementation plan?

Team members, who had no prior shared work experience, came from around the world (Canada, United States, Scotland, Jamaica, and Germany) and were selected by top executives based on their respective expertise. All six members were considered to be the best employees in their respective sectors. Four engineers (from a variety of domains), one human resources (HR) specialist, and one marketing director constituted the global virtual team. Like many people who work in similar special assignments, the team members were assigned on a part-time basis for the duration of the project. After its recommendations were made to the CEO and the Board of Directors, 12 months later, the team dissolved.

As mentioned in the previous section, commitment and alignment around a team's purpose are best gained in a face-to-face meeting, where the team builds its own vision, and members work together to develop trust, mutual accountability, and an atmosphere of collaboration. This issue is even more critical when team members have no shared teamwork experience, as at ABC. Aware of the potential risks, top executives requested that the project start with a face-to-face kick-off meeting. This meeting, which was held in Jamaica, provided the necessary clarity of focus and direction and gave team members a chance to establish relationships and develop a sense of belonging to the team. Social activities also permitted the development of team unity, a key factor in dealing with conflicts during a project. At this meeting, team members defined a contract outlining shared values (e.g., everyone is equal in the team, tolerance and empathy in regard to cultural diversity, information transparency, etc.) as well as the roles and responsibilities of each person. The team contract included formal operating norms and key expectations, such as meeting deadlines, attendance at audioconferences, standard software packages and versions to use for collaboration purposes, standard communication platform, and honoring commitments to other team members. During this initial meeting, team members nominated the HR specialist (the only woman on the team) as leader, mainly because of her relevant domain expertise. Although some members, especially the engineers, were not convinced of the need to define a team contract at first, over the course of the project, they gradually realized how important these "soft" issues were in ensuring the team's success.

Much of the work was performed separately by each team member and then combined into a finished product, which took the form of a report and a formal presentation to the Board of Directors. Task interdependence, therefore, was low to moderate. From time to time, reports went back and forth for improvements and comments. At ABC, much of the work involved data collection and analysis by individual team members. To accommodate people from all time zones, the team met every two or three weeks in audioconferences at 5:30 a.m. eastern standard time. Audioconferences were mainly used for brainstorming and key decision-making activities. Videoconferencing was not considered because of its nonaccessibility in certain plants. Collaborative work was also done by using e-mail to communicate and pass on information (e.g., multiple

Figure 1.   Characteristics of the BBS Virtual Team at ABC

		DEGREE OF COMPLEXITY LOW <--> HIGH		
Degree of reliance on ICT	Low		X	High
ICT availability	High		X	Low
Members' ICT proficiency	High		X	Low
Team size	Small	X		Large
Geographic dispersion	Local		X	Global
Task/project duration	Long-term		X(1 year)	Short-term
Prior shared work experience	Extensive		X	None
Members' assignment	Full-time		X	Part-time
Membership stability	Stable	X		Fluid
Task interdependence	Low	X		High
Cultural diversity	Homogeneous		X	Heterogeneous

versions of a questionnaire instrument). There were wide discrepancies in the participants' technological proficiencies. Some team members were comfortable working with e-mail, while others had no prior experience with it. To address this problem, training and technical support were provided to those who needed it at their respective sites.

Cultural diversity represented another challenge for this global team. Some cultures tended to value distance in business relationships, while other cultures valued intimacy. Some cultures were neutral in terms of showing emotion, while others tended to be very expressive. Second, notions of time were also an issue at the start of the project. In some of the cultures represented, being late at a meeting is an accepted norm, while it is not acceptable in others. Third, the distribution of power and the importance of equality differed widely from culture to culture. The fact that the team was led by a woman required adjustments on the parts of some team members. Overall, however, the risks associated with such cultural diversity were minimal, due in part to the fact that all team members received a cultural training session prior to participating on the team. This training addressed several issues that could affect team performance, such as normal working hours, expected behaviors, expected levels of involvement, how decisions are made, how work must be reviewed and approved, and how to resolve conflicts. Bringing cultural issues to the surface in a positive light helped create a global virtual team that was enriched, and not paralyzed, by cultural differences.

Finally, language constituted another difficulty for the team. English is the de facto language of most linguistically diverse virtual teams. Five out of six members of this team had to speak in a foreign language. Indeed, the two team members located in Canada were French Canadians. The German member naturally spoke German as his first language, while the Jamaican member spoke a patois, which is a blend of English, Spanish, and various African languages. The person located in Scotland was born and had lived most of his life in Quebec, and French was his mother tongue. It is difficult to fully participate in an audioconference when one does not speak the language fluently. In order to give every member a chance to speak during audioconference meetings, structured communication sessions were directed by the American member of the team, whose native language was English. As mentioned earlier, tolerance and empathy were also highly valued by team members, and this encouraged equal participation. Writing minutes at the end of each oral session also helped ensure that all participants understood the same message.

In conclusion, the particular characteristics of the ABC global virtual team (e.g., geographic dispersion, lack of prior work experience, heterogeneous cultures) presented specific and difficult challenges, both human and technological. Structural characteristics (e.g., team size, team membership, electronic environment) and coping strategies and tactics (e.g., kick-off meeting, cultural training, and technical support) helped alleviate the complexity associated with the team's configuration and made a difference in the team's effectiveness.

XYZ's Virtual Team Configuration

The XYZ Consulting Group is a leader in engineering projects of all sizes and types—in fields such as building, urban infrastructures, transportation, industrial, railway engineering, environment, energy, and industrial. The multidisciplinary teams of the XYZ Consulting Group carry out projects according to professional norms, while adapting them to the needs of their clients. The firm offers a complete range of engineering services: preliminary, feasibility, and cost-benefit studies; conceptual design studies; preparation of summary plans and drawings; preparation of final plans and drawings; supervision of work; and start-up. The company has been active in the environmental sector for more than 20 years and has become the leading firm in Canada in the field of environmental site assessment.

Early in the year 2000, a multidisciplinary virtual team (virtual team #31) was created in order to design a take-off/landing runway for a major Canadian aerospace company. The key characteristics of the team are depicted in Figure 2. The initial project timeframe was four months, which is short, considering the complexity of such a project. The team was composed of eight people, all from the environment division at XYZ, including three engineers, one biologist, two cartographers, one urban development specialist, and one secretary. One of the engineers acted as project leader and was responsible for recruiting the other members on the team. Team members were selected on the basis of their respective expertise and availability. A key characteristic of this team is that all eight members used to work in the same physical facility for several years and collaborated on several projects in the past. A few weeks prior to the start of the project, the company decided to decentralize its operations, and as a result, half of the environment division staff was transferred to a new facility in a different city. The core team members (the three engineers, the two cartographers, and the secretary) were all located in the head office, while the biologist and the urban specialist were located in the newly established facilities. The physical distance between the two offices is approximately 250 km, and both cities are in the same time zone.

Because of their extensive shared work experience, team members did not consider it important to plan and organize a face-to-face kick-off meeting, even though the current project represented the company's first virtual teamwork experience. It was not seen as necessary, in part, because the major corporate values and practices of empowerment, teamwork, respect, and outcome-based evaluation had long been internalized by all team members. In addition, each participant in the team knew fairly well, through experience, the others' expectations, styles, needs, and particular requirements. Significantly, work norms had gradually been established throughout the years when team members were involved in traditional face-to-face projects. As a result, no formal team contract was developed and agreed upon at the start of the project.

Each member was primarily responsible for a segment of the project. For instance, the biologist was mainly responsible for making sure that environmental standards were respected and for minimizing the impact of the project on the environment. Despite such a pooled and additive work arrangement, some information needed to be constantly transferred between members to ensure that everyone understood certain task requirements. For instance, design plans were initially developed jointly by one of the engineers and the biologist, commented on by all team members, and revised by one of the cartographers before being submitted for final approval to the client.

Although all team members belonged to the same national culture and most of them had several years of experience within the environment division of the company, the start of the project was chaotic. It is relatively easy, according to

Figure 2.   Characteristics of the Runway Virtual Team at XYZ

		DEGREE OF COMPLEXITY LOW <----------------------------------> HIGH	
Degree of reliance on ICT	Low	X(moderate)	High
ICT availability	High	X	Low
Members' ICT proficiency	High	X	Low
Team size	Small	X	Large
Geographic dispersion	Local	X	Global
Task/project duration	Long-term	X	Short-term
Prior shared work experience	Extensive	X	None
Members' assignment	Full-time	X	Part-time
Membership stability	Stable	X	Fluid
Task interdependence	Low	X	High
Cultural diversity	Homogeneous	X	Heterogeneous

our respondents, to "forget" virtual team members who are in a different location. At XYZ, a few spontaneous meetings were organized at the head office location. These meetings involved the five local members as well as some other on-site experts. According to the project leader, these "outsiders," who were not formally involved in the project, were sporadically invited to participate in meetings to give advice and, hence, accelerate the decision-making process. The inexperienced team leader felt that having specialists at a distance slowed the project. For this reason, he requested the intervention of local experts in order to increase team effectiveness. He even tentatively transferred some of the environmental responsibilities to on-site experts. This situation created much tension and anxiety on the part of the two members who had been left out of the project. The team leader did not anticipate the impact such actions would have on the team's dynamics but soon realized how important they were for the off-site team members.

More rigorous use of communication technologies, as well as more regular face-to-face meetings, helped build and keep the momentum going. Because of the short distance separating the two sites, it was relatively easy to plan and organize face-to-face meetings in either city. In fact, after the initial chaotic period, such meetings were held about once every four weeks, mainly for brainstorming and project review purposes. Face-to-face meetings were also helpful for common design activities that are much more arduous to complete virtually. Other communication media included daily phone calls and bimonthly audioconferences. Standard documents were transferred by e-mail and fax, while legal documents were exchanged via express courier. Because both sites were located in the same time zone, all documents (both paper-based and electronic) could be easily transferred without important delays.

The team's initial experiences with audioconferencing were quite negative. All team members had been requested to participate at all phone conferences, even when the issues being discussed were specialized and did not concern everyone. As a result, there was a lot of frustration on the part of team members. With time, the team learned how to plan and organize these meetings so that they maximized everyone's time and energy.

In short, the particular configuration of the XYZ virtual team, while not as complex as that at ABC, presented specific challenges to both the team's leader and its members. Indeed, while prior shared work experience, minimal geographic dispersion, and cultural homogeneity represented key facilitating conditions, learning how to manage a project and conduct meetings in a virtual setting was essential to ensuring the project's success.

Conclusion

The main purpose of this chapter was to further our understanding of virtual teams. We identified the underlying characteristics of virtual teams that distinguish them from conventional teams and explored their different configurations. Our objective was to highlight differences in team complexity. We believe that identifying distinguishing characteristics of virtual teams will facilitate understanding of this emerging form of work arrangement.

There are several benefits of adopting of this perspective. Using and refining it will result in a clearer picture of virtual teams. It will then be easier to compare empirical findings, accumulate knowledge, and provide sound advice to practitioners. Table 1 can also be used as a diagnostic tool to help managers estimate the level of complexity of their virtual teams. Faced with a team that tends toward a high level of complexity, team leaders can then choose to reduce complexity or face it. In the first scenario, the risk involved in virtual team management can be reduced by modifying the team's configuration and moving it to the left end of the various continua. However, such an approach may increase the costs of a project, e.g., excluding an off-site expert from the team in favor of a more "local" but less knowledgeable person. In the second scenario, team managers recognize that team complexity can be a liability but also an asset to team effectiveness (Bettenhausen, 1991; Guzzo & Dickson, 1996). In our view, complexity is a characteristic that needs to be acknowledged and managed. As complexity increases, many challenges emerge, and management strategies must be carefully identified and applied in order to counteract them. As illustrated in the previous section, global virtual teams differ from and are more complex than "local" virtual teams in several respects. Because of their particular configurations, global virtual teams present significant challenges for all members of a team, especially a project leader (Dubé & Paré, 2001). Team leaders must be mindful of cultural differences, communication, language barriers, and discrepancies in technological proficiency among team members and how these make a difference in team effectiveness. Strategies must then be chosen accordingly. In our view, such a contingent perspective to virtual teams is extremely relevant and much more promising, both from a research perspective and a practical perspective, than treating virtual teams as a single type. A contingency approach to studying and managing virtual teams is also likely to help identify those issues or risk areas that deserve future attention.

Virtual teams are here to stay (Bell & Kozlowski, 2002). With this in mind, we proposed a consistent, shareable, knowledge-based approach for the study and management of virtual teams in the future. We hope this approach, along with its contingency perspective, will represent a baseline from which to proceed with the study and management of virtual teams in organizations.

References

Bal, J., & Foster, P. (2000). Managing the virtual team and controlling effectiveness. *International Journal of Production Research, 38*(17), 4019-4032.

Bélanger, F., Watson-Manheim, M. B., & Jordan, D. H. (2002). Aligning IS research and practice: A research agenda for virtual work. *Information Resources Management Journal, 15*(3), 48-70.

Bell, B. S., & Kozlowski, S. W. J. (2002). A typology of virtual teams: Implications for effective leadership. *Group & Organization Management, 27*(1), 14-49.

Bettenhausen, K. L. (1991). Five years of groups research: What have we learned and what needs to be addressed. *Journal of Management, 17*(2), 345-381.

Bloor, G., & Dawson, P. (1994). Understanding professional culture in organizational context. *Organization Studies, 15*(2), 275-295.

Boudreau, M. -C., Loch, K. D., Robey, D., & Straub, D. (1998). Going global: Using information technology to advance the competitiveness of the virtual transnational organization. *Academy of Management Executive, 12*(4), 120-128.

Boutellier, R., Gassmann, O., Macho, H., & Roux, M. (1998). Management of dispersed product development teams: The role of information technologies. *R&D Management, 28*(1), 13-25.

Brown, J. S., & Duguid, P. (1991). Organizational learning and communities-of-practice: Toward a unified view of working, learning, and innovation. *Organization Science, 2*(1), 40-57.

Burke, K., Aytes, K., Chidambaram, L., & Johnson, J. J. (1999). A study of partially distributed work groups: The impact on media, location, and time on perceptions and performance. *Small Group Research, 30*(4), 453-490.

Crampton, C. D. (2001). The mutual knowledge problem and its consequences for dispersed collaboration. *Organization Science, 12*(3), 346-371.

Daft, R. L., Lengel, R. H., & Trevino, L. K. (1987). Message equivocality, media selection, and manager performance: Implications for information systems. *MIS Quarterly, 11*(3), 355-366.

Davidson, A. L., Schofield, J., & Stocks, J. (2001). Professional cultures and collaborative efforts: A case study of technologists and educators working for change. *The Information Society, 17*, 21-32.

Dennis, A. R., George, J. F., Jessup, L. M., Nunamaker, J. F., Jr., & Vogel, D. R. (1988, December). Information technology to support electronic meetings. *MIS Quarterly*, 591-624.

Dennis, A. R., Kinney, S. T., & Hung, Y. C. (1999). Gender differences in the effects of media richness. *Small Group Research, 30*(4), 405-437.

DeSanctis, G., & Jackson, B. M. (1994). Coordination of information technology management: Team-based structures and computer-based communication systems. *Journal of Management Information Systems, 10*(4), 85-110.

DeSanctis, G., Wright, M., & Jiang, L. (2001). Building a global learning community. *Communications of the ACM, 44*(12), 80-82.

Duarte, D. L., & Snyder, N. T. (1999). *Mastering Virtual Teams*. San Francisco, CA: Jossey-Bass Publishers.

Dubé, L., & Paré, G. (2000). Global virtual teams. *Communications of the ACM, 44*(12), 71-73.

Furst, S., Blackburn, R., & Rosen, B. (1999). Virtual team effectiveness: A proposed research agenda. *Information Systems Journal, 9,* 249-269.

Galegher, J., & Kraut, R. E. (1994). Computer-mediated communication for intellectual teamwork: An experiment in group writing. *Information Systems Research, 5*(2), 110-138.

Gallupe, R. B., Dennis, A. R., Cooper, W. H., Valacich, J. S., Bastianutti, L. M., & Nunamaker, J. F. (1992). Electronic brainstorming and group size. *Academy of Management Journal, 35,* 350-369.

Guzzo, R. A., & Dickson, M. W. (1996). Teams in organizations: Recent research on performance and effectiveness. *Annual Review of Psychology, 47,* 307-338.

Hackman, J. R. (1987). The design of work team. In J. W. Lorsch (Ed.), *Handbook of Organizational Behaviour* (pp. 315-342). Englewood Cliffs, NJ: Prentice-Hall.

Haywood, M. (1998). *Managing Virtual Teams: Practical Techniques for High-Technology Project Managers*. Boston, MA: Artech House.

Henry, J. E., & Hartzler, M. (1998). *Tools for Virtual Teams: A Team Fitness Companion*. Milwaukee, WI: ASQ Quality Press.

Hiltz, S. R., & Turoff, M. (1985). Structuring computer-mediated communication systems to avoid information overload. *Communications of the ACM, 28*(7), 680-689.

Hiltz, S. R., Johnson, K., & Turoff, M. (1991). Group decision support: The effects of designated human leaders and statistical feedback in computerized conferences. *Journal of Management Information Systems, 8*(2), 81-108.

Hofstede, G. (1993). Cultural constraints in management theories. *Academy of Management Executive, 7*(1), 81-94.

Jackson, P. J. (1999). Organizational change and virtual teams: Strategic and operational integration. *Information Systems Journal, 9,* 313-332.

Jarvenpaa, S. L., & Leidner, D. E. (1999). Communication and trust in global virtual teams. *Organization Science, 10*(6), 791-815.

Jarvenpaa, S. L., Knoll, K., & Leidner, D. E. (1998). Is anybody out there? Antecedents of trust in global virtual teams. *Journal of Management Information Systems, 14*(4), 29-64.

Kaplan, N. J., & Hurd, J. (2002). Realizing the promise of partnerships. *Journal of Business Strategy, 23*(3), 38-42.

Karolak, D. W. (1998). *Global Software Development: Managing Virtual Teams and Environments.* Los Alamitos, CA: IEEE Computer Society.

Katzenback, J. R, & Smith, D. K. (1993, March/April). The Discipline of Teams. *Harvard Business Review,* 111-120.

Kayworth, T., & Leidner, D. (2000). The global virtual manager: A prescription for success. *European Management Journal, 18*(2), 183-194.

Kayworth, T., & Leidner, D. (2001-2002). Leadership effectiveness in global virtual team. *Journal of Management Information Systems, 18*(3), 7-40.

Kinney, S. T., & Panko, R. R. (1996). Project teams: Profiles and member perceptions—Implications for group support system research and products. *Proceedings of the 29th Annual Hawaii International Conference on System Sciences* (pp. 128-137).

Kozlowski, S. W. J., Gully, S. M., Nason, E. R., & Smith, E. M. (1999). Developing adaptive teams: A theory of compilation and performance across levels of time. In D. R. Ilgen & E. D. Pulakos (Eds.), *The Changing Nature of Work and Performance: Implications for Staffing, Personnel Actions, and Development* (SIOP Frontiers Series) (chap. 8, pp. 240-294). San Francisco, CA: Jossey-Bass.

Kruempel, K. (2000). Making the right (interactive) moves for knowledge-producing tasks in computer-mediated groups. *IEEE Transactions on Professional Communication, 43*(2), 185-195.

Lewis, R. (1998). Membership and management of a "virtual" team: The perspectives of a research manager. *R&D Management, 28*(1), 5-12.

Lipnack, J., & Stamps, J. (1997). *Virtual Teams: Reaching Across Space, Time, and Organizations with Technology.* New York: John Wiley & Sons.

Lurey, J. S., & Raisinghani, M. S. (2001). An empirical study of best practices in virtual teams. *Information & Management, 38,* 523-544.

Majchrzak, A., Rice, R. E., King, N., Malhotra, A., & Ba, S. (2000a). Computer-mediated inter-organizational knowledge-sharing: Insights from a virtual team innovating using a collaborative tool. *Information Resources Management Journal, 13*(1), 44-53.

Majchrzak, A., Rice, R. E., Malhotra, A., & King, N. (2000b). Technology adaptation: The case of a computer-supported inter-organizational virtual team. *MIS Quarterly, 24*(4), 569-600.

Malhotra, A., Majchrzak, A., Carman, R., & Lott, V. (2001). Radical innovation without collocation: A case study at Boeing-Rocketdyne. *MIS Quarterly, 25*(2), 229-249.

Massey, A. P., Montoya-Weiss, M., Hung, C., & Ramesh, V. (2001). Cultural perceptions of task-technology fit. *Communications of the ACM, 44*(12), 83-84.

Maznevski, M. L., & Chudoba, K. M. (2000). Bridging space over time: Global virtual team dynamics and effectiveness. *Organization Science, 11*(5), 473-492.

McDonough, E. F., III, & Cedrone, D. (2000, July/August). Meeting the challenge of global team management. *Research – Technology Management,* 12-17.

McDonough, E. F., III, Kahn, K. B., & Barczak, G. (2001). An investigation of the use of global, virtual, and collocated new production development teams. *Journal of Production Innovation Management, 18,* 110-120.

McGrath, J. E., & Hollingshead, A. B. (1993). Putting the group back in group support systems: Some theoretical issues about dynamic process in groups with technological enhancements. In L. M. Jessup & J. S. Valacich (Eds.), *Group Support Systems: New Perspectives* (pp. 93-114). Old Tappan, NJ: Macmillan.

Montoya-Weiss, M. M., Massey, A. P., & Song, M. (2001). Getting it together: Temporal coordination and conflict management in global virtual teams. *Academy of Management Journal, 44*(6), 1251-1262.

Moore, D. R., & Dainty, A. R. J. (2001). Intra-team boundaries as inhibitors of performance improvement in UK design and build projects: A call for change. *Construction Management and Economics, 19,* 559-562.

Morgeson, F. P., & Hofmann, D. A. (1999). The structure and function of collective constructs: Implications for multilevel research and theory development. *Academy of Management Review, 24*(2), 249-265.

Morris, S. A., Marshall, T. E., & Rainer, R. K., Jr. (2002). Impact of user satisfaction and trust on virtual team members. *Information Resources Management Journal, 15*(2), 23-31.

Mortensen, M., & Hinds, P. J. (2001). Conflict and shared identity in geographically distributed teams. *International Journal of Conflict Management, 12*(3), 212-238.

Nilles, J. M. (1994). *Making Telecommuting Happen: A Guide for Telemanagers and Telecommuters.* New York: Van Nostrand Reinhold.

Ocker, R., Fjermestad, J., Hiltz, S. R., & Johnson, K. (1998). Effects of four modes of group communication on the outcomes of software requirements determination. *Journal of Management Information Systems, 15*(1), 99-118.

Ocker, R., Hiltz, S. R., Turoff, M., & Fjermestad, J. (1995-1996). The effects of distributed group support and process structuring on software requirements development teams: Results on creativity and quality. *Journal of Management Information Systems, 12*(3), 127-153.

Orlikowski, W. J., & Yates, J. (1994). Genre repertoire: The structuring of communicative practices in organizations. *Administrative Science Quarterly, 39*, 541-574.

Orlikowski, W. J., Yates, J., Okamura, K., & Fujimoto, M. (1995). Shaping electronic communication: The metastructuring of technology in the context of use. *Organization Science, 6*(4), 423-444.

Pape, W. R. (1997). Group Insurance. *Inc. Tech, 2*, 29-30.

Pauleen, D. J., & Yoong, P. (2001). Relationship building and the use of ICT in boundary-crossing virtual teams: A facilitator's perspective. *Journal of Information Technology, 16*, 205-220.

Qureshi, S., & Zigurs, I. (2001). Paradoxes and prerogatives in global virtual collaboration. *Communications of the ACM, 44*(12), 85-88.

Qureshi, S., Bogenrieder, I., & Kumar, K. (2000). Managing participative diversity in virtual teams: Requirements for collaborative technology support. *Proceedings of the 33rd Hawaii International Conference on System Sciences.* Retrieved September 24, 2002, from the IEEE Xplore database.

Roberts, K., Kossek, E. E., & Ozeki, C. (1998). Managing the global workforce: Challenges and strategies. *Academy of Management Executive, 12*(4), 93-106.

Robey, D., & Jin, L. (in press). Studying virtual work in teams, organizations and communities. In M. E. Whitman & A. B. Woszczynsli (Eds.), *The*

Handbook for Information Systems Research. Hershey, PA: Idea Group Publishing.

Robey, D., Khoo, H. M., & Powers, C. (2000). Situated learning in cross-functional virtual teams. *IEEE Transactions on Professional Communication, 43*(1), 51-66.

Saunders, C. S. (2000). Virtual teams: Piecing together the puzzle. In R. W. Zmud (Ed.), *Framing the Domains of IT Management: Projecting the Future...Through the Past* (pp. 29-40). Cincinnati, OH: Pinnaflex.

Schmidt, J. B., Montoya-Weiss, M. M., & Massey, A. P. (2001). New product development decision-making effectiveness: Comparing individuals, face-to-face teams, and virtual teams. *Decision Sciences, 32*(4), 575-600.

Smith, J. Y., & Vanecek, M. T. (1990). Dispersed group decision making using nonsimultaneous computer conferencing: A report of research. *Journal of Management Information Systems, 7*(2), 71-92.

Solomon, C. M. (1995). Global teams: The ultimate collaboration. *Personnel Journal, 74*(9), 49-53.

Sproull, L., & Kiesler, S. (1986). Reducing social context cues: Electronic mail in organizational communication. *Management Science, 32*(11), 1492-1512.

Steinfield, C., Huysman, M., David, K., Jang, C. Y., Poot, J., Veld, M. H., et al. (2001). New methods for studying global virtual teams: Towards a multi-faceted approach. *Proceedings of the 34th Hawaii International Conference on System Sciences*. Retrieved September 24, 2002, from the IEEE Xplore database.

Straus, S. G. (1996). Getting a clue: The effects of communication media and information distribution on participation and performance in computer-mediated and face-to-face groups. *Small Group Research, 27*(1), 115-142.

Straus, S. G. (1999). Testing a typology of tasks: An empirical validation of McGraths's (1984) group task circumplex. *Small Group Research, 30*(2), 166-187.

Straus, S. G., & McGrath, J. E. (1994). Does the medium matter: The interaction of task and technology on group performance and member reactions. *Journal of Applied Psychology, 79*, 87-97.

Suchan, J., & Hayzak, G. (2001). The communication characteristics of virtual teams: A case study. *IEEE Transactions on Professional Communication, 44*(3), 174-186.

Sundstrom, E., De Meuse, K. P., & Futrell, D. (1990). Work teams: Applications and effectiveness. *American Psychologist, 45*(2), 120-133.

Tan, B. C. Y., Wei, K. -K., Huang, W. W., & Ng, G. -N. (2000). A dialogue technique to enhance electronic communication in virtual teams. *IEEE Transactions on Professional Communication, 43*(2), 153-165.

Townsend, A. M., DeMarie, S. M., & Hendrickson, A. R. (1998). Virtual teams: Technology and the workplace of the future. *Academy of Management Executive, 12*(3), 17-29.

Tullar, W. L., & Kaiser, P. R. (2000). The effect of process training on process and outcomes in virtual groups. *Journal of Business Communication, 37*(4), 408-427.

Van Maanen, J., & Barley, S. R. (1984). Occupational communities: Culture and control in organizations. In B. M. Staw & L. L. Cummings (Eds.), *Research in Organizational Behavior* (pp. 287-365). Greenwich, CT: JAI Press.

Vogel, D. R., Van Genuchten, M., Lou, D., Verveen, S., Van Eekout, M., & Adams, A. (2001). Exploratory research on the role of national and professional cultures in a distributed learning project. *IEEE Transactions on Professional Communication, 44*(2), 114-125.

Walden, P., & Turban, E. (2000). Working anywhere, anytime, and with anyone. *Human Systems Management, 19*, 213-222.

Walther, J. B. (1995). Relational aspects of computer-mediated communication: Experimental observations over time. *Organization Science, 6*(2), 186-203.

Walther, J. B., Slobacek, C. L., & Tidwell, L. C. (2001). Is a picture worth a thousand words? *Communication Research, 28*(1), 105-134.

Warkentin, M., & Beranek, P. M. (1999). Training to improve virtual team communication. *Information Systems Journal, 9*, 271-289.

Warkentin, M. E., Sayeed, L., & Hightower, R. (1997). Virtual teams versus face-to-face teams: An exploratory study of a web-based conference system. *Decision Sciences, 28*(4), 975-996.

Wenger, E., McDermott, R., & Snyder, W. M. (2002). *Cultivating Communities of Practice*. Boston, MA: Harvard Business School Press.

Wijayanayake, J., & Higa, K. (1999). Communication media choice by workers in distributed environment. *Information & Management, 36*, 329-338.

Williams, R. L., & Cothrel, J. (2000, Summer). Four smart ways to run online communities. *Sloan Management Review*, 81-91.

Yoo, W. -S., Suh, K. -S., & Lee, M. -B. (2002). Exploring the factors enhancing member participation in virtual communities. *Journal of Global Information Management, 10*(3), 55-71.

Yoo, Y., & Kanawattanachai, P. (2001). Developments of transactive memory systems and collective mind in virtual teams. *International Journal of Organizational Analysis, 9*(2), 187-208.

Endnotes

[1]   The Social Sciences and Humanities Research Council of Canada is gratefully acknowledged for providing financial support for this research.

[2]   "Conventional" or "traditional" is used to designate teams whose dominant mode of communication is face-to-face.

[3]   While we recognize that virtual team members can use traditional communication media such as memos/letters sent through regular or express mail, it is the more recent development and, hence, accessibility of electronic communication media that rendered virtual teamwork popular in organizations.

[4]   Conference proceedings were omitted since papers, after being presented, are usually published in journals.

[5]   Interestingly, the effectiveness of that team was not affected because extensive prior shared work experience compensated for the lack of potential benefits usually associated with face-to-face interactions.

[6]   We do not use "professional" in a rigid way, but, as in Moore and Dainty (2001), to designate "a skilful and competent individual connected with a vocation" (p. 560).

[7]   All names have been changed to assure anonymity.

Appendix A

Characteristics of Virtual Teams in the Literature

Authors	Main research method	No. of teams	Reliance on ICT	Team size	Geographic dispersion	Physical co-location	Task duration	Members' assignment	Membership stability	Task inter-dependence	Cultural diversity
Bal & Foster (2000)	Field study	2			Throughout Europe	Subgroups at diff. Loc.					Medium
Bouteillier et al. (1998)	Case study	1 org. using many virtual teams	Mix ICT and F2F	Large projects	Global					High	Medium
Burke et al. (1999)	Lab exp.	20	100%	4	Nearby	1 by himself; 3 together	4h	Full time	Permanent	Low	
Dennis et al. (1999)	Lab exp.	17	100%	2	Nearby	Separate locations	No time limit	Full time	Permanent	High	
DeSanctis & Jackson (1994)	Case study	1	ICT and monthly meetings	16			Perma-nent				Low-medium
DeSanctis et al. (2001)	Case study	24			Global						High
Dubé & Paré (2001)	Field study	18	Mostly ICT		Global						High
Cramton (2001)	Field exp.	13	100%	6		Subgroups at 2 loc.	Over 7 weeks				
Galegher & Kraut (1994)	Field exp.	67	100%	3	Nearby	Separate locations	2 tasks of 2 weeks	Part time	Permanent	low	
Hiltz et al. (1991)	Lab exp.	24	100%	5	Nearby	Separate loc.	2h	Full time	Permanent	Low	

Appendix A (continued)

Characteristics of Virtual Teams in the Literature

Authors	Main research method	No. of teams	Reliance on ICT	Team size	Geographic dispersion	Physical co-location	Task duration	Members' assignment	Membership stability	Task interdependence	Cultural diversity
Jarvenpaa et al. (1998) Jarvenpaa & Leidner (1999)	Field exp. + case study	75	100%	4-6	Global	Separate locations	Over 6 weeks	Part time	Permanent	Low	High
Kayworth & Leidner (2001-2) Kayworth & Leidner (2000)	Field exp.	12-13	100%	5-7	Global	Separate locations	Over 5 weeks	Part time	Permanent	Low	High
Kruempel (2000)	Case study	1	ICT and quarterly meetings	51	Global	Separate locations	Permanent	Part time	Rotating	High	High
Lurey & Raisinghani (2001)	Survey	67 members in 12 teams		3-15	Nearby and global		Short term to permanent				Low
Majchrzak et al. (2000a) Majchrzak et al. (2000b) Malhotra et al. (2001)	Case study	1	Mix of ICT and F2F	8	Throughout US	Subgroup of 2 in one location	10 months	Part time	Permanent	High	High

Appendix A (continued)

Characteristics of Virtual Teams in the Literature

Authors	Main research method	No. of teams	Reliance on ICT	Team size	Geographic dispersion	Physical co-location	Task duration	Members' assignment	Membership stability	Task inter-dependence	Cultural diversity
Massey et al. (2001)	Exp.	30	100%		Global	Seperate locations	Over 8 days	Part time	Permanent	High	
Maznevski & Chubdoba (2000)	Case study	3	Mix of ICT and F2F	8-12	Global	Subgroups at diff. Loc.	Perma-nent		Permanent	High	Low and high
McDonough & Cedrone (2000)	Case study	1	Mostly ICT	At least 9	Global		Perma-nent	Part time	Permanent	Medium-high	High
McDonough et al. (2001)	Survey	At least 54			Global and in one country						
Montoya-Weiss et al. (2001)	Field exp.	35	100%	5	Global	Separate locations	Over 15 days	Part time	Permanent	Low	
Morris et al. (2002)	Survey	158	Avg: 50%								
Mortensen & Hinds (2001)	Field study + survey	12		5-7	Global and domestically distributed	Separate locations		Part time			High
Ocker et al. (1995-6) Ocker et al. (1998)	Lab exp.	20	100% (10 teams); 50% (10 teams)	4-7	Nearby	Separate locations	Over 2 weeks	Part time	Permanent	Low	Low

Appendix A (continued)

Characteristics of Virtual Teams in the Literature

Authors	Main research method	No. of teams	Reliance on ICT	Team size	Geographic dispersion	Physical co-location	Task duration	Members' assignment	Membership stability	Task interdependence	Cultural diversity
Orlikowski & Yates (1994)	Field study	1	Mostly ICT (2 F2F meetings)	17 (+100 periphe-ral)	Throughout US	Subgroups at diff. loc.	2.5 years	Part time			Low
Orlikowski et al. (1995)	Case study	1	Mix ICT and F2F	9	Nearby		17 months	Part time	Permanent	Low	Low
Pauleen & Yoong (2001)	Field study	7			Mostly global (one is clearly local)						Different levels, but mostly high
Qureshi & Zigurs (2001)	Short case study	8 org.			Global						
Robey et al. (2000)	Case study	3	Mostly ICT (min quarterly meetings)		Throughout US	Subgroups at diff. loc.	Perma-nent	Part time	Permanent		High
Schmidt et al. (2001)	Lab exp.	17	100%	4-5		Separate locations	Over 7 days	Part time	Permanent	Low	Low
Smith & Vanecek (1990)	Quasi-exp.	7	100%	5	Throughout US	Separate locations	Over 2 weeks	Part time	Permanent	High	
Straus (1996)	Lab exp.	28	100%	3-4	Nearby	Seperate locations	45 min	Full time	Permanent	High	High

Appendix A (continued)

Characteristics of Virtual Teams in the Literature

Authors	Main research method	No. of teams	Reliance on ICT	Team size	Geographic dispersion	Physical co-location	Task duration	Members' assign-ment	Membership stability	Task inter-depen-dence	Cultural diversity
Straus & McGrath (1994) Straus (1999)	Lab exp.	36	100%	3	Nearby	2 people could see each other	3 tasks of 12 min	Full time	Permanent	Diff. levels	
Suchan & Hayzak (2001)	Case study	1	Kick off + ICT	31	Throughout US	Groups at diff. loc.	Permane nt	Full time	Permanent	High	Low
Tan et al. (2000)	Lab exp.	15	100%	5	Nearby	Separate locations	16h over 2 months	Part time	Permanent	Low	
Tullar & Kaiser (2000)	Lab exp.	56	100%	5-6		Separate locations	Over 1 month	Part time	Permanent	Low	
Vogel et al. (2001)	Lab exp.	10	100%	7-8	Global	2 groups in 2 locations	Over 7 weeks	Part time	Permanent	Low	
Walden & Turban (2000)	Quasi- exp.	10	100% ICT across locations	4-6	Global	2 groups in 2 locations	Over one semester	Part time	Permanent	Low	
Walther (1995)	Lab exp.	16	100%	3	Nearby	Separate locations	Over 5 weeks	Part time	Permanent	Low	
Walther et al. (2001)	Field exp.	8	100%	3	Global	2 groups at 2 locations		Full time	Permanent	Low	
Warkentin & Beranek (1999)	Field exp.	12	100%	3-4	Nearby	Separate locations	3 tasks of 2 weeks	Part time	Permanent	High	

Appendix A (continued)

Characteristics of Virtual Teams in the Literature

Authors	Main research method	No. of teams	Reliance on ICT	Team size	Geographic dispersion	Physical co-location	Task duration	Members' assign-ment	Membership stability	Task inter-depen-dence	Cultural diversity
Warkentin et al. (1997)	Lab exp.	13	100%	3	Throughout US	Separate locations	Over 3 weeks	Part time	Permanent	High	
Wijayanayake & Higa (1999)	Field study	2	100%	22-24	Throughout Japan						
Yoo & Kanawatta nachai (2001)	Quasi- exp.	38	Almost 100%	4	Global	Separate locations	Over 8 weeks	Part time	Permanent	High	

Appendix B

Data Analysis: Virtual Teams at a Glance

Team #	Reliance on ICT	Team size	Geographic dispersion	Physical co-location	Task duration (months)	Prior shared work experience	Members' assign-ment	Member-ship stability	Task interde-pendence	Organi-zational culture[1]	Profes-sional culture[1]	National culture[1]
1	High	30	2 major cities in 1 country	Large group at each site	18	Slight	Part time	Stable	Moderate	Het.	Het.	Hom.
2	High	20	2 major cities in 1 state	Large group at one site	24	Moderate	Part time	Fluid	High	Hom.	Hom.	Hom.
3	Moderate	30	2 cities in 2 countries	Small group at each site	Perma-nent	Slight	Full time	Stable	High	Hom.	Hom.	Het.
4	High	15	Global team in 3 countries	Small groups at each site	36	None	Part time	Mostly fluid	High	Hom.	Het.	Het.
5	Moderate	30	2 cities in 2 countries	Almost excl. at one site	12	Extensive	Full time	Stable	Low	Hom.	Hom.	Hom.
6	High	3	Local team in 1 city	Separate locations	1	Extensive	Part time	Stable	Moderate	Hom.	Hom.	Hom.
7	Moderate	15	Several cities in 1 country	Separate locations	4	Moderate	Full time	Stable	High	Hom.	Hom.	Hom.
8	High	6	Global team in 3 countries	Separate locations	12	None	Part time	Stable	Moderate	Hom.	Het.	Het.
9	High	6	Global team in 5 countries	Sepatate locations	12	None	Part time	Stable	Moderate	Hom.	Het.	Het.
10	High	5	Global team in 6 countries	Separate locations	12	None	Part time	Stable	Moderate	Hom.	Het.	Het.
11	High	6	Global team in 6 countries	Separate locations	12	None	Part time	Stable	Moderate	Hom.	Het.	Het.

Note 1: Het. = heterogenous; Hom. = homogeneous

Appendix B (continued)

Data Analysis: Virtual Teams at a Glance

Team #	Reliance on ICT	Team size	Geographic dispersion	Physical co-location	Task duration (months)	Prior shared work experience	Members' assignment	Membership stability	Task interdependence	Organizational culture[1]	Professional culture[1]	National culture[1]
12	High	10	Several cities in 1 country	Small group at each site	6	Slight	Part time	Fluid	Moderate	Hom.	Hom.	Hom.
13	High	10	2 cities in 1 country	Small group at each site	10	Slight	Part time	Stable	Moderate	Hom.	Hom.	Hom.
14	High	6	3 cities in 2 countries	Small group at each site	3-4	Slight	Full time	Stable	High	Hom.	Hom.	Hom.
15	High	20	Global team in 3 countries	Small group at each site	14	None	Full time	Mostly Stable	High	Het.	Het.	Hom.
16	High	15	3 cities in 1 country	Large group at one site	12	None	Part time	Mostly Stable	High	Het.	Het.	Hom.
17	High	16	4 cities in 2 countries	Large group at one site	18	None	Part time	Fluid	Moderate	Het.	Het.	Het.
18	High	6	Global team in 5 countries	Separate locations	3-4	None	Part time	Stable	Moderate	Hom.	Hom.	Het.
19	High	12	3 cities in 2 countries	Small group at each site	24	Slight	Part time	Stable	High	Het.	Hom.	Hom.
20	High	10	3 cities in 1 country	Small group at each site	24	None	Part time	Stable	Low	Hom.	Hom.	Hom.
21	Moderate	14	2 cities in 1 state	Large group in 1 city	36	None	Full time	Mostly Stable	High	Het.	Het.	Hom.
22	High (100%)	12	4 cities in 2 countries	Separate locations	Permanent	None	Full time	Stable	Low	Hom.	Hom.	Hom.
23	Moderate	10	Local team in 1 city	Small group at each site	10	Slight	Part time	Mostly Stable	Low	Hom.	Hom.	Hom.
24	High	12	4 cities in 1 country	Small group at each site	Permanent	None	Full time	Stable	Low	Hom.	Hom.	Hom.

Note 1: Het. = heterogenous; Hom = homogeneous

Appendix B (continued)

Data Analysis: Virtual Teams at a Glance

Team #	Reliance on ICT	Team size	Geographic dispersion	Physical co-location	Task duration (months)	Prior shared work experience	Members' assignment	Membership stability	Task interdependence	Organizational culture[1]	Professional culture[1]	National culture[1]
25	High	20	4 cities in 1 country	Small group at each site	18	None	Part time	Mostly Stable	Low	Hom.	Hom.	Hom.
26	Moderate	38	Global team in 3 countries	Majority located at 2 sites	Perma-nent	None	Full time	Mostly Stable	Low	Het.	Hom.	Het.
27	High	10	Global team in 3 countries	Small group at each site	3	None	Part time	Stable	High	Hom.	Hom.	Het.
28	High	40	Global team in 3 countries	Small group at each site	8	None	Full time	Stable	High	Het.	Hom.	Het.
29	High	5	4 cities in 2 countries	Separate locations	1	None	Part time	Mostly Stable	High	Het.	Hom.	Het.
30	High	12	Global team in 5 countries	Small group at each site	8	None	Part time	Mostly Stable	Moderate	Hom.	Het.	Het.
31	Moderate	8	2 cities in 1 state	Small group at each site	4	Extensive	Part time	Stable	Moderate	Hom.	Het.	Hom.
32	Moderate	6	Local team in 1 city	Separate locations	2-3	None	Part time	Stable	High	Hom.	Hom.	Hom.
33	Moderate	5	Local team in 1 city	Separate locations	12	Slight	Full time	Mostly Stable	High	Hom.	Hom.	Hom.

Note 1: Het. = heterogenous; Hom = homogeneous

Chapter II

Trust and the Trust Placement Process in Metateam Projects

Walter D. Fernández

Queensland University of Technology, Australia

Abstract

Metateams are temporary organizations composed of two or more geographically and organizationally dispersed teams that are commercially linked by project-specific agreements. In a global business environment demanding innovation, flexibility, and responsiveness, metateams represent a major change in the way organizations and practitioners conduct IT development projects. However, as we found in a recently concluded theory-building study of a real-life metateam, managing metateams presents unique difficulties due to conflicting demands arising from multiple realities. Argued in this chapter is that the effectiveness of the trust placement process (rather than just the exhibition of high levels of trust) significantly affects project success.

Introduction

Teams, or groups working toward common goals, have always existed. From the hunting and gathering days to the information revolution era, humans have been collaborating with other humans to survive, to progress, or simply to achieve temporal objectives (Roberts, 1995; West, 2001). So, why are we talking about teams again? West (2001) argued that the novelty in modern teamwork resides in the complex organizational context in which team members are embedded. Teams are the product of the context from which they emerge and, simultaneously, they help in shaping the organizational environment, by producing actions on which evolution can be based (Bandura, 2001).

During the last decade, teams working on information technology (IT) development and implementation projects experienced significant transformations. Currently, many project teams' members are working in complex and often chaotic environments. Their organizations, pushed by the competitive race and regulators, want to implement new IT solutions at frantic speeds. Teams of mere humans, interacting in a composite commercial and political milieu seeded with conflict, are in charge of delivering the wanted systems. These teams must perform at their optimum levels while interacting across departments, organizations, distances, and cultural borders. This is the world of *metateams*, where entropy reigns, and barriers to success are many and not always understood.

IT outsourcing, shorter time-to-market cycles, scarce human resources, and availability of enabling collaborative technologies are some of the factors fueling the emergence of metateams in major IT projects. A metateam is a temporary system that can be described as a loose confederation of dislocated teams linked by interdependencies and commercial agreements (Fernandez & Underwood, 2001). Within this confederation, teams are members of a *virtual team of teams*, where key teams belong to different firms, each performing well-defined functions according to their contractual roles in the alliance.[1]

Metateams are potentially powerful work structures; they can build IT solutions of high complexity by integrating expertise from different fields and organizations. With the help of communication technologies, metateams can conquer barriers of time and space, collaborating across a nation or across the globe. However, managing metateams presents unique difficulties requiring continuous resolution of conflicting demands. Achieving effective metateam collaborations is critical and difficult. Metateams are particularly exposed to the lack of common understanding of prime objectives and deficient preproject arrangements observed in traditional IS project teams (Jiang, Klein, & Means, 2000); identity issues of autostereotyping (how groups perceive themselves) and heterostereotyping (how groups perceive other groups), arising from encounters of groups exhibiting organizational or national cultural differences (Hofstede, 1997); difficulties in successfully applying "foreign" management techniques to culturally heterogeneous groups (Trompenaars & Hampden-Turner, 1998); and, goal incongruence as a product of organizational fragmentation resulting from deregulation, privatization, or outsourcing (Berggren, Soderlund, & Anderson, 2001).

This chapter aims to present significant challenges of major collaborative IT projects enacted by metateams and to suggest ways of addressing those challenges. To help illustrate the discussion, we will use observations grounded on a recently concluded theory-building study of a real-life metateam (briefly described in the next section). One of the key concepts emerging from the study is the suggestion that the effectiveness of the trust placement process, and not simply exhibition of the levels of trust, significantly impacts project success. We focus on trusting behaviors, what we *do* when we trust or distrust others. As we shall see, in our account, trust is a difficult issue with a direct impact on the *quality* and *cost* of the metateam project.

Study Background: The Project and Its Key Players

Discussed in this chapter are concepts emerging from an exploratory study of a real-life metateam project, from the perspective of a client project team interacting with other teams in a major IT project in the telecommunication industry (the SUN project). The project involved three key organizations—RedCorp, ITSP, and OSC—and dislocated teams from three countries.[2] The ITSP and RedCorp teams were based in several locations in Australia, while the OSC teams were based in the Middle East and Eastern Europe (Figure 1).

RedCorp and ITSP were partners in an IT outsourcing agreement, and OSC was an overseas-based company working in partnership with ITSP on this particular project. RedCorp, the client organization in charge of the end-to-end project, played a major and very active role in the overall project. SUN was a multimillion-dollar IT development and implementation project defined by RedCorp as "*strategic,*" a category assigned to those few projects having high priority and impact within the company. Therefore, SUN was highly visible at the top management levels in client and vendor organizations.

SUN provided a data-rich case for research. The participants were generous with their time and their disclosures. The case data included semistructured interviews, observations, and access to project documents and electronic correspondence. Interviews were conducted with all members of the RedCorp

Figure 1. SUN Key Players, their Firms, Locations and Formal Communication Channels

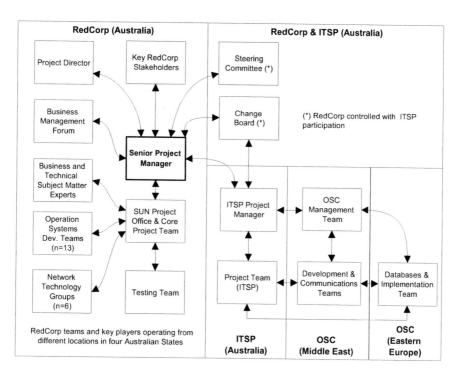

core project team. The senior project manager in charge of SUN received special attention—several interviews and many discussions were conducted with him during a two-year period. Key participating actors included the project director, senior project manager, principal communications engineer (technical leader), senior project officer, work orders manager, communication infrastructure leader, IT infrastructure leader, and testing and acceptance leader.[3]

Observing the players at work involved passive participation in project events, from formal gatherings like negotiations at the interteam management level (both face-to-face and virtual) to sharing chats in the lunchroom or "walking the floor." The project also provided rich documentary evidence, with more than 4,000 e-mails and hundreds of project documents made available for the study. Observations provided insights emerging from analyzing actions and the evidence of those actions, thereby complementing rhetorical perspectives from the actors. Grounded Theory Methodology (Eisenhardt, 1989; Glaser, 1978, 2001; Glaser & Strauss, 1967; Martin & Turner, 1986) was used to develop a conceptual account, while the software package ATLAS.ti facilitated the detailed text analysis and the gathering of research memos.

Issues, Controversies and Problems

Presented in this section are some important environmental characteristics, and discussed are aspects of trust contributing to the many issues and problems encountered in metateams. Without understanding the metateam context, it is easy to make the common mistake of overlooking the significance of organizational complexity in projects involving third parties (Berggren et al., 2001). Furthermore, we perceive trust as a necessary risk that people and organizations take, when they decide to trust others while having an imperfect knowledge of their intentions and capabilities; therefore, discussing the issues of context is paramount, as context is a critical consideration of risk analysis (Mayer, Davis, & Schoorman, 1995).

Contextual Problems

Of special interest for our discussion, are aspects of organizational fragmentation, unrealistic demands and expectations, the nature of interteam communication, the disparity of success definitions (goal incongruence), the temporary nature of project work, the type of personnel involved, and the presence and role of conflict.

Organizational Fragmentation

Organizational fragmentation constitutes a defining facet of the reality confronted by managers and members of metateams. This fragmentation restricts the types of strategies a manager could use and is a root cause of several key problems, like goal incongruence (discussed later), and different mental models of what reality is or should be. Organizational fragmentation makes coordinating interteam efforts and closely controlling activities across organizational boundaries more difficult.

Therefore, metateam managers work under increased uncertainty and are less able to implement appropriate controls to deal with that uncertainty. For example, when the SUN project manager wanted to increase controls, he had to negotiate with ITSP, and this negotiation delayed the project. This is because controls have an immediate cost, and while the client project manager had a strong interest in ensuring the quality of the system, the vendor project manager was primarily concerned with the allocation of resources, the contractual obligations to deliver by a certain date, and the cost of extra communicative actions (e.g., meetings, walkthroughs, audits). In other words, while teams are linked by interdependencies, each team has an independent role to play and potentially conflicting subgoals (goal congruence is discussed below). Consequently, ensuring fitness for the purpose of project deliverables from multiple teams to the end-to-end project, becomes challenging.

Unrealistic Demands and Expectations

To meet business objectives or regulators' demands, organizations want complex IT projects, like SUN, delivered "at Internet speed." These projects, as business sponsors would demand, "***must*** be done *on time*." Therefore, demands for timely delivery become ingrained in requests for tenders and reflected in commercial agreements. Such fixed-time agreements are highly unrealistic; they occur under conditions of uncertainty, *before* a detailed project plan has been drafted and without involving experienced project managers. However justifiable, these calls for fast deliveries often ignore significant restrictions imposed by the nature of major systems' development and implementations.

Inevitably, slack in this type of project is nonexistent (Demarco, 2001). The highly ambitious schedule forces multiple parallel activities connected by interdependencies, therefore, creating multiple critical paths and significantly increasing the risk of overrunning the schedule. The original Gantt chart for the RedCorp component of the SUN project had more than one and a half thousand tasks (and this was not at the lowest task level) to be completed in the agreed 28 weeks. Interdependencies at intra- and intercompany levels clearly indicated the fragility of the project regarding meeting its unrealistic timeframe.

The SUN project was implemented in 2002. However, reaching deployment stage took five times longer than first expected, largely because to fulfill the highly aggressive schedule, everything had to be perfect in time and quality (an unrealistic expectation even in projects of much lesser complexity), and because the agreement restricted interteam interactions, thereby causing late discovery of substantial problems and rework.

Interteam Communication

The SUN project manager perceived effective interteam communication as a key success factor. Establishing fluid communication channels was a key strategy to mitigate the risk of delivering the "wrong solution." Having experienced a multimillion-dollar loss after the total failure of a project of a similar nature to SUN, RedCorp considered this a top project risk. The client and the vendor organization and project teams were acutely aware of this fact.

Despite this, several factors restricted effective communication in the SUN project, including technical complexity, preproject agreements, different native languages, different mental models, dissonance of objectives, and personal traits. Moreover, the contact between members of different teams was infrequent, because they were working on different aspects of the systems (e.g., modifying interfaces, building telecommunication infrastructure, developing testing strategies, or developing system components). Therefore, interteam communication was restricted to interdependencies, acceptance of deliverables, or clarification of technical issues. Additionally, due to commercial reasons, ITSP mediated the communication between RedCorp and OSC technical teams; this added an extra layer to the interteam communication channel, introducing "noise" and delaying communication. Under these conditions, the interteam relationship took more time to develop, was more equivocal, and communication incidents were fewer, important, and task bounded.

At interteam level, the liaison was also shaped by the hybrid nature of the communicative events through which the relationship was enacted. Namely, (a) the use of electronic communication technology to deal with barriers of time and physical separation, thereby increasing the potential for attribution errors and misunderstandings (see also Cramton, 2002); and (b) face-to-face interactions occurring at key points in the project's life cycle, where actors are under extreme pressure to achieve their best performances in a short span of time.

In metateams, even the face-to-face component of interteam interactions are different from traditional teams (and perhaps from organizationally homogeneous virtual teams). This is due to the special conditions under which representatives from the many teams meet face to face. To illustrate this, we review the example of a key face-to-face meeting early in the SUN project. ITSP, RedCorp, and OSC conducted a joint review of specifications prepared by OSC in two overseas locations. Due to the tight schedule, the participants received electronic copies of the specifications 1 week before the meeting. The RedCorp experts were uncomfortable, believing the time assigned to go through hundreds of pages documenting complex system behavior was inappropriate, that one week was not enough to perform a quality assessment of the technical specification. Furthermore, they discovered a significant number of important issues, and they felt responsible for ensuring their resolution. During the three days of walkthrough, jetlagged OCS experts explained specifications' details to a cross-functional audience of skeptical RedCorp business and technical experts. The OSC representatives tried to understand the many issues and discuss possible solutions with the experts. The management team was trying to balance the needs to get the meeting moving, to foster common understanding, and to avoid tension escalating into hostility or disruptive adversarial positioning. The communication was entirely task-based. Even during social events, like lunch breaks and project dinners, people avoided social conversation and kept talking about project issues.

Goal (In)Congruence

The disparity of success definitions was an expensive barrier to the project. While all teams shared the distant common objective of deploying the system, what made each team successful in the eyes of their respective companies did not always align with a successful system implementation. To the RedCorp project manager, for example, success meant "implemented system *and* satisfied business customers and project sponsor." Conversely, the ITSP project manager's success was largely related to achieving contractual obligations within budget. Under these conditions, it is possible for one project manager to achieve success but not the other.

This incongruence affected perceptions of good will. Client team members believed that some of the vendor's deliveries were "what *they* thought *they* could get away with by the contractual deadline." However, the vendor's behavior was mainly a consequence of the environment constructed by the preproject agreements. The contract between RedCorp and ITSP established several penalties and rewards, which, while well intended, forced a focus on delivery and not on quality. This focus was contrary to RedCorp's fundamental business needs for system quality and performance.

Temporary Nature of Interpersonal Relationships

While projects are temporary by nature, in traditionally collocated IS projects, a significant number of people share experiences, myths, and legends as members of a reasonably homogeneous organizational culture. These people may also reasonably expect to progress as a team into the next project; therefore, while the project is definitely temporary, the relationship is less so. This is not the case of the metateam, where people are less constrained by the long-term need to "get along" with each other, and they appear to avoid acts of even superficial personal disclosure (and therefore only talk about task-related issues, as we discussed earlier).

In metateams, each new project is likely to involve unfamiliar actors with different experiences and from different cultures.[4] Thanks to organizational fragmentation, it is likely that these actors will be at different stages in their learning cycles (Berggren et al., 2001). Therefore, people would bring to the project different cognitive maps of what working in metateams actually means;

diverse, culturally induced perceptions of internal rewards (e.g., approval, esteem, love, responsiveness) (Parsons, 1951; Trompenaars & Hampden-Turner, 1998); and preconceptions about the levels of knowledge of others.[5] The extent and impact of these cognitive differences is difficult to ascertain *ex ante*.

Types of Personnel Involved

Because projects enacted by metateams exhibit complexity at managerial and technical levels and have a high corporate profile, they are likely to involve experienced professionals and top subject-matter experts (from the user community and business stakeholders).[6] The involvement of top experts presents several issues to the metateam, including the following:

1. Issues of allegiance. Most actors in the SUN project were team players and had strong identification with the team, but not all; some had stronger allegiances to their ongoing constituencies than they did to the project. Out of several factors influencing personal allegiance, we found that top technical experts value the network of like-minded people they have in the organization. In a way, these people "made" the expert; they are, simultaneously, sources of information, recognition, and pride. Therefore, it is important, from the managerial viewpoint, to identify issues that could make the top expert "protect" his or her ongoing constituency from the perceived (i.e., subjective) evils of the system under development.

2. Issues of replacement. Because of their unique expert capacity, replacing team members can be difficult and at times impossible. In projects involving complex technology, technical experts are few (i.e., in an organization like RedCorp, with tens of thousands of employees, no more than three or four people could perform the technical leader position in the SUN project). This is a limitation of metateams, due to the difficulty in selecting team members according to their psychological traits. As a senior project manager said, "in major projects we always have the best team we can have, but almost never the one we would like to have."

3. Issues of skepticism. The study suggests that veteran team members are not inclined to experience *swift trust* (Meyerson, Weick, & Kramer, 1996), a phenomena observed during experimental research on virtual teams (Jarvenpaa, Knoll, & Leidner, 1998; Jarvenpaa & Leidner, 1999; Piccoli & Ives, 2000, 2002). While some people are more willing to trust than others (Mayer et al., 1995), IT veterans are influenced by a history of project failures, which makes them more skeptical of battle cries and promises, however well intended these are. Therefore, swift trust is not just fragile

and temporal (Jarvenpaa & Leidner, 1999); it also appears as an unreliable variable for metateams. As the SUN team's most experienced member said, "trust must be earned."

Conflict

The principal type of conflict observed in the SUN project was task-related or cognitive conflict (Priem & Price, 1991). Researchers are increasingly seeing cognitive conflict as a less detrimental and even beneficial type of conflict (among others, Amason, 1996; Amason & Sapienza, 1997; DeChurch & Marks, 2001; Jehn & Mannix, 2001). Cognitive conflicts are neither good nor bad, they remain latent until becoming manifest; that is, when a party discovers that its position regarding a common issue is incompatible with the other party's position, and it engages in action to redress the situation.

Because of interdependencies, incongruent performance expectations, organizational fragmentation, different mental models, and bounded rationality, metateam projects are prolific with intrapersonal, interpersonal, intragroup, and intergroup conflicts (a typology used by Rahim, 1992). Therefore, enacting effective conflict resolution processes is essential to achieve the best possible project outcomes. Yet, as the SUN case shows, under conditions of contractual rigidity, conflict resolution becomes inefficient, time consuming, and costly, and it can have a lasting effect on the relationship.

The Risky Business of Trusting Uncontrollable Others

Undoubtedly, teamwork in major IT projects has changed considerably during the last decade. Practitioners, observing the death of the old project team and the awakening of virtual teams, are recognizing the need to evolve from previous management practices to face the new challenges (Thomsett, 1998). In his presentation at the 1998 American Programmer Summit, Rob Thomsett, a well-known Australian project management practitioner and popular presenter, recommended that because "[I]n Virtual teams, trust is replaced with contracts. Always write the relationship down." This advice contradicts the vast majority of academic research findings. Among the published research papers, only Gallivan (2001) argued that appropriate controls could replace trust in virtual organizations.

We agree by half. The need to "write the relationship down" is as unquestionable as the need to implement appropriate controls. However, we differ in something far more fundamental. We maintain that trust cannot be *totally* replaced; this is so because its replacement, total control, is a delusion in complex sociotechnical systems; and we know that contracts and specifications are inherently imperfect (Hirschheim & Newman, 1991; Rousseau, 1995). Therefore, writing the relationship down will always involve elements of risk and misinterpretation.

Organizational science scholars argued about the value of trust to interfirm relations and whether or not trust has an independent effect on the performance of interfirm alliances. Some authors suggested that organizations engaged in alliances are likely to act in self-interest (Koza & Lewin, 1998), and that trust is an outcome of well-aligned alliances (Koza & Lewin, 1998; Madhok & Tallman, 1998). Others indicate that trust is central to the effectiveness of knowledge-intensive interfirm collaborations (Powell, 1990), and that the importance of trust in interfirm relations is growing (Adler, 2001). We perceive trust as both a cause and a consequence of metateam interactions.

In our view, trust is an important variable in achieving effective metateam partnerships. This is because trust facilitates open communication, cooperative efforts, reduction of uncertainty, resolution of conflicts, common understanding, and control of transaction costs. The literature on virtual teams also considers trust an important theme (e.g., Beranek, 2000; Cascio, 2000; Evaristo & Munkvold, 2002; Gallivan, 2001; Iacono & Weisband, 1997; Jarvenpaa et al., 1998; Jarvenpaa & Leidner, 1999; Kasper-Fuehrer & Ashkanasy, 2001; Piccoli & Ives, 2002; Steinfield, 2001). This is not surprising; trust has been viewed as a lubricant to cooperation (Arrow, 1974; Misztal, 1996), as a product of cooperation (Axelrod, 1984), and as a way of dealing with imperfect knowledge and uncertainty about others' behavior (Gambetta, 2000). Therefore, we can expect trust to be relevant to those virtual team and metateam contexts exhibiting a high need for cooperation amid conditions of uncertainty.

In the SUN project, expectations of trustworthiness primarily resulted from evaluating other teams' contractual trust, competence trust, and goodwill trust.[7] In other words, are *they* going to respect the contract, do *they* have the competence to deliver as promised, and are *they* prepared to go beyond the letter of the contract to deliver on their promises? Therefore, we adopted a definition in which *trust is a psychological state reached upon an evaluation of vulnerability risks, based on expectations of the intentions, competence, or behavior of another.*[8]

In this perspective, trust and mistrust are seen as polar opposites in a conceptual continuum (a view supported by Gambetta, 2000; Giddens, 1990; and Rotter, 1967, among others). Therefore, rather than a binary state, trust is a threshold value between zero (complete mistrust) and one (complete trust). This threshold is not precise; it is a *subjective probability*, with which, according to Gambetta (2000), "an agent assesses that another agent or group of agents will perform a particular action, both *before* he can monitor such action (or independently of his capacity ever to be able to monitor it) *and* in a context in which it affects *his own action*" (p. 217). In trusting others, we take a risk because we expect certain outcomes with neither complete control of others' actions nor complete knowledge of their intentions, and because we are subject to the unforeseeable events of social reality (Lorenz, 2000; Misztal, 1996). Therefore, *trusting behavior* increases our vulnerability to another party and could make us regret our actions if that party abuses our trust (Lorenz, 2000).

Three characteristics make trust such an interesting component of metateams systems: (a) the risky nature of trusting behavior, (b) the higher conditions of uncertainty under which metateams operate, and (c) the tangible project cost of our actions and inactions. If we could totally replace trust with controls, as suggested by Gallivan's (2001) model, then we would eliminate uncertainty and reduce our vulnerability to opportunistic behaviors and late discovery of incompetence. The cost of reducing the risk would then be the cost of implementing the controls. The problem with metateams is that controls are difficult to implement (mainly due to organizational fragmentation and commercial arrangements) and are never totally effective; therefore, project managers must rely on trust and accept its intrinsic risks.[9]

Deviation-Amplifying Effect of Trust in Metateams

To make sense of how different levels of trust can affect the project, one needs to understand the role of *deviation-amplifying mutual causal processes* (Maruyama, 1963). In these interlocked processes, once an interdependent variable moves in one direction (i.e., moving toward total trust or toward total mistrust) the effect of the deviation-amplifying loop results in either virtuous or vicious circles (Weick, 1979). After each iteration, variables move increasingly closer to their extremes, and the system becomes more rigid and therefore unable to adapt. This rigidity, in the face of required changes, results in self-destruction. Systems with embedded destructive behavior can be found in nature; for example, in certain parts of Australia, ideal environmental conditions gave the koala a sense of abundance that enabled the koala population to grow rapidly; this growth continued until the food supply (forest) was destroyed, with a devastating effect on the koala population (Skelton, 2000). Similarly, the SUN study suggests that extreme levels of trust in metateams can provide a sense of being that may not have a correlation with the actual health of the project. Two opposite examples from our study explain the deviation-amplifying process.

In the presence of mistrust, the SUN project manager increased controls to monitor the project's progress and the vendors' performance. Close monitoring

Figure 2. Deviation-Amplifying Loop of Mistrust

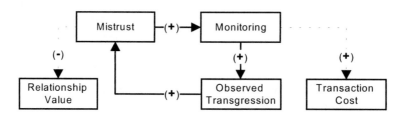

of vendors' teams and their outputs increased transaction costs, confirmed mistrust, and weakened the relationship (as suggested by Piccoli and Ives, 2000, 2002). Mistrust increased monitoring, and monitoring confirmed mistrust; this interlocked pattern created a deviation-amplifying loop that ended with the removal of the ITSP project manager from the project. This pattern is represented in Figure 2, where solid lines indicate the circular path, and signs indicate positive or negative correlation between variables.

According to Weick (1979), when left unattended, deviation-amplifying loops can only be stopped by a major environmental change, e.g., causing there to be no more eucalyptus leaves for koalas to chew or forcing the removal of the vendor project manager from the SUN project. The major change in the project's players occurred after a process of escalation, where power was exerted at various management levels simultaneously until the deadlock was solved. The extreme changes required to break the loop had an immediate cost of resolution and also a less quantifiable relationship cost for the outsourcing partners transcending the SUN project.

A second example of a deviation-amplifying loop, this time running in the direction of total trust, followed the personnel changes in the vendor team. As the level of trust of the new ITSP project manager increased, monitoring decreased, and therefore, fewer transgressions were observed, proving the correctness of trusting and inducing further reduction on monitoring, reducing transaction costs, and increasing the value of the relationship in the eyes of the SUN project manager (Figure 3). This loop ended with negative consequences when the SUN project manager, trusting the vendors' promises for delivery, publicly committed to a deployment schedule that was unachievable. *Ex post* evaluations of the actions suggest that the otherwise careful project manager should have implemented more controls; yet, the *ex ante* decision to trust the validity of the vendor's promise was "sensible," as it correlated with evidence of trustworthiness (lack of observed transgression and high level of trust), however wrong that was proven *ex post facto*.

Figure 3.   Deviation-Amplifying Loop of Trust

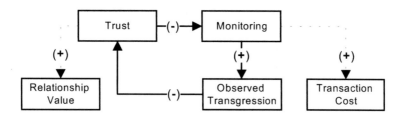

The previous two examples illustrate the risks posed by deviation-amplifying loops and how *enactment* contributes to self-fulfilling prophecies (Merton, 1948). Weick (1979) described enactment as efferent sense-making, where the actors' idea is "extended outwards, implanted, and then rediscovered as knowledge" (p. 159). To avoid the negative consequences of deviation-amplifying loops of Figures 1 and 2, project managers need to recognize and address the interrelationship among directed action, perception, and sense making that occurs over time.

Walking Along the Trust-Mistrust Tightrope

We can only assess the virtuous or vicious nature of causal loops retrospectively. For example, we will know that our high level of trust had a positive effect upon the successful completion of the project within expected cost, time, and quality. Conversely, we will know that our high level of trust was detrimental to the project when, after investing considerable funds, we realize that to implement the system, we need expensive and time-consuming modifications, therefore, running the risk of project cancellation. Therefore, while in a metateam project trust is neither good nor bad per se, trusting behavior *when well placed* (something that we will know *ex post facto*) has a direct positive effect on the cost of interteam transactions.

Many kinds of virtual teams require frequent contact among team members; in metateams, however, each team works autonomously, and interteam interactions are not as frequent. Therefore, in the SUN project, achieving a correct balance in trust placement was a difficult task, because infrequent interactions restricted the players' ability to construct informed views about other people's trustworthiness (as Misztal, 1996, observed in social contexts). The environmental conditions of our case study (described earlier) limited the rationality of the actors' trusting behavior and therefore made the effectiveness of the ongoing *trust placement process* even more important.

Two key informational sources for the trust placement process are *preproject history* and *project history*. The first refers to extant knowledge about the partner's team and, if appropriate, previous attempts to build similar information systems. Preproject history exists at organizational and individual levels. Preproject history is the collective memory of past collaborative attempts and the multitude of perceptions of those people affected by them. The second refers to knowledge generated through interactions during the life of the project; this is an evolving type of knowledge directed by personal experiences that can counteract or exacerbate some of the prejudices entrenched in preproject history.

These combined sources inform our perception and expectations of others' intentions, competency, and behaviors. Their role in trust placement is contingent on the project's stage; i.e., preproject history's highly influential role at the beginning of the project becomes progressively less relevant to trust placement, as the project unfolds, due to the continuous development of familiarity among actors.

Building familiarity is therefore an informing process, based on interactions, that improves the quality of trust placement and diminishes the role of preproject history. By building familiarity, team members develop a grounded appreciation of others' trustworthiness and can minimize attribution errors (Cramton, 2002). Observable events like project meetings, responses to deadlines, acceptance of deliverables, detected contract breaches, or joint conflict management and resolution efforts provide opportunities to build familiarity and are the basis for *ex post* assessment of the trust placement's correctness. Our study shows that when significant, these events can modify the trust threshold, resulting in a new psychological state that is used to predict future events; using the lesson learned to look ahead, perceive possible hazards, and take *ex ante* interteam hazard-mitigating actions (Williamson, 1985, 1996). Therefore, these events can either build or destroy trust. Illustrated in Figure 4 are the effects of project events on the perception of trustworthiness.

In this evolving psychological process, project managers continuously conduct post-event evaluations. Depending on the perceived importance of the event to the project's future, these evaluations will vary from a mental note to formal reviews involving many stakeholders. Trustworthiness evaluations involve an element of equivocality and nonrationality. Similar to evaluation of risks, trustworthiness assessments depend on availability of information and the belief that predictability is somehow possible (Pagden, 1988).

Achieving greater familiarity in the SUN project facilitated the actors' perceptions of hazards and the adoption of what they thought were appropriate hazard-mitigating actions. The nature of these actions (or inactions) varied depending on circumstances and the actors involved. These strategies impact on transaction costs (immediate and future) and have potential long-term effects on the

Figure 4. Effect of Project Events on Perception of Trustworthiness

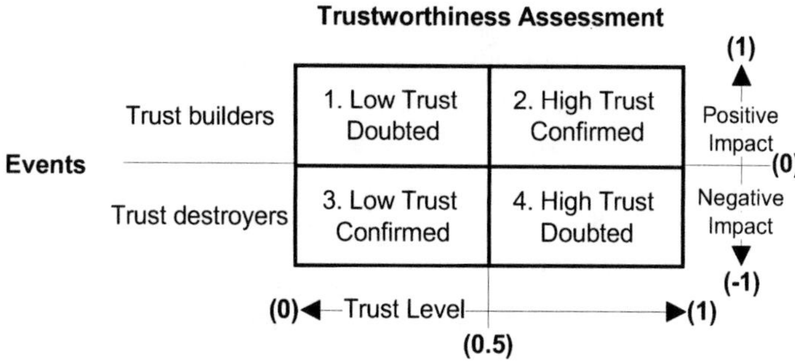

Trustworthiness Assessment

```
                              (1)
                               ▲
                               |
                 ┌───────────┬───────────┐
  Trust builders │ 1. Low Trust │ 2. High Trust │ Positive
                 │   Doubted    │  Confirmed    │ Impact
Events     ──────┼───────────┼───────────┤    ──(0)
                 │ 3. Low Trust │ 4. High Trust │ Negative
 Trust destroyers│  Confirmed   │   Doubted     │ Impact
                 └───────────┴───────────┘    ▼
                                              (-1)
        (0)◄──Trust Level────────────►(1)
                  (0.5)
```

relationship between the client and the vendor. Yet, building familiarity in metateams can be difficult, as explained in the next section.

Familiarity, Exchange, and Reciprocity in Metateams

Our notion of building familiarity as a process based on interteam interactions, aligns with Simmel's view of society as a number of individuals connected by exchange-based interaction; and that exchange and reciprocity are basic constitutive forms of relationships (Misztal, 1996). Exchange in this context is defined as "sacrifice in return for a gain" and it is "one of the functions that creates an inner bond between people—a society, in place of a mere collection of individuals" (Simmel, Bottomore, & Frisby, 1978).

We have a positive exchange when the work we do and the risks we take in trusting our partners (sacrifice) return the benefits of effective and open collaboration (gain). Conversely, the outcome of the exchange will be negative when the expected gain is (or is perceived as) not realized. Unrealistic expectations, poor understanding of structural and situational drivers, opportunism, and lack of required skills or resources are some of the factors that contribute to unrealized exchanges.

For metateams, exchanges are valuable events with potentials of creating bonds between the teams and providing the basis for mutual knowledge. At an organizational level, the relationship between teams is essentially commercial; one party sacrifices money in return for services and expects those services to be provided. At a personal level, people sacrifice time and effort (often taken away from their families or other aspects of their life) to contribute to the project outcome; in return, they expect appreciation of their effort and a comparable effort from their associates.

Because the metateam relationship is primarily task-based, the strength of the bond between teams depends on how these teams perceive the outcomes of their task-based exchanges. To expect an exchange, people in a particular team need to feel that other teams are (a) capable of doing the tasks they are contracted to do and (b) able to understand why these tasks are important in a wider context, not just for their immediate goals, and to act based on that understanding.[10] In other words, for the metateam to have successful exchanges, teams should be able not only to conduct their contractually expected actions, but also to understand the meaning of the actions' outcomes to the metateam.

We discussed interteam goal congruence earlier; it is also useful to understand issues of perceptional congruence regarding the usefulness of exchanges. It helps in explaining why the relationship between the RedCorp project manager and the initial ITSP project manager was difficult. The ITSP project manager had a self-contained objective; he knew what the ITSP team had to do, by when, and how much effort they were allowed to expend. Consequently, he did not feel a need to interact with RedCorp beyond the minimum level stipulated in the legal contract. Extra interactions could only introduce extra demands on his team, consuming time and resources and therefore increasing costs. Without a perception of potential gain, it was difficult for the ITSP project manager to accept a sacrifice (extra resources, time, and money).

Conversely, the RedCorp (SUN) project manager had a clear perception of the potential gains in interacting as "one team." In his view, the end-to-end project would benefit by allowing the early discovery and resolution of conflicts. For that to occur, fluidity and flexibility were necessary. Therefore, from RedCorp's perspective, the need for exchange was clear, because they could enable gains; like controlling the risk of "*delivering the wrong product*" (identified during a formal RedCorp-ITSP Risk Workshop, at the beginning of the project, as the major project risk). However reasonable the need for a one team approach was, it was also unrealistic; preproject agreements conditioned the relationship, causing incongruence on the perceived value of interteam exchanges at the project management level.

In Simmel's view, the preconditions for the existence of exchange are also preconditions for the existence of society, and trust is a vital condition of exchange. Without general trust among its members, "society itself would disintegrate, for very few relationships would endure if trust were not as strong as, or stronger than, rational proof or personal observation" (Simmel et al., 1978, pp. 178-179). Similarly, the SUN project manager perceived the ITSP manager's unwillingness to engage in exchanges as a pattern of "uncooperative behavior," which eventually caused distrust and harmed the relationship, precipitating the ITSP manager's replacement.

However, the collapse of the project managers' relationship enabled the parties to work on creating situations for mutual gain. This reshaped the relationship along a new nonzero sum approach and helped to resolve conflicts caused by goal incongruence. By recreating the relationship, both organizations benefited: ITSP increased its capacity to make further profits from the project and to restore the dented relationship, while RedCorp avoided sinking the multimillion dollar cost of a failed project and then having to develop an alternative solution to the original problem. The new agreement allowed the RedCorp manager to regain some degree of control over the project. It also allowed the second ITSP project manager to perceive exchange as a positive activity, allowing ITSP to fix the substantial technical problems by obtaining expert knowledge from the RedCorp team and to restore the relationship between the companies. The ability for both parties to perceive mutual gains enabled exchange, which in turn, built trust between ITSP and RedCorp.

Solutions and Recommendations

Offering quick fixes and magic recipes cannot provide valid solutions to managing complex and unique IT projects with multiple stakeholders, organizations, and teams. What we offer instead are several key areas for consideration; those involved with metateams will see how they can adapt our recommendations to their particular environments.

We propose that effective and efficient metateam systems will require appropriate controls, allow flexibility, foster cooperative conflict management, and moderate extreme values of the trust–distrust continuum. To help in fulfilling these requirements, we need to improve the effectiveness of trust placement processes by, first, increasing awareness of the metateam's challenges among the team members and their organizations and, second, addressing key environmental issues.

Furthermore, we suggest that effective metateam controls need to be entrenched in *appropriate* preproject and project agreements, and in trust, congruency, and conflict-related processes. By "appropriate," we mean agreements and controls *contributing* to the implementation of processes that are critical to issues of trust, congruency, and conflict. Shown in Figure 5 are preproject agreements influencing the interteam project agreements, which then influence trust, congruency, and conflict processes. Next, we will discuss some of these concepts.

Figure 5.   Contributors/Detractors to Effective Metateam Systems

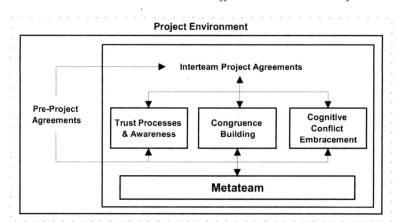

Cognitive Conflict Embracement

To embrace cognitive conflicts, we have to see them as opportunities to deliver what our customers want, to build relationships, and to develop mutual knowledge. The continuous process of discovery and resolution of conflicts allows the project to move forward. For this process to be effective, members of metateams must do the following:

1.   Share a common understanding that task conflicts will always exist in major IT projects, exhibiting task uncertainty and spanning across several organizations

2.   Exhibit a proactive and positive attitude toward conflict, where conflict discovery is recognized as a contribution to the project

3.   Trust others to report on perceived conflicts and to work collaboratively on their resolution

4.   Have the support of flexible contractual arrangements that recognize the inevitability of cognitive conflicts and bounded rationality, limit opportunistic behaviors, and foster collaboration[11]

When some or all of these basic conditions are missing, the project is likely to be jeopardized, because conflicts will remain latent until later in the project, increasing the cost of their resolution, wasting human effort, and lowering teams' morale and mutual trust. In the SUN project, late discovery of task conflicts resulted in rework (including redesign), long delays, and a significant increase in costs that almost caused the premature end of the project.

Trust Processes and Awareness

Trusting other teams to conduct their work as expected considerably reduces the *perception* of need for interteam communication and controls. When high trust is justified, the project benefits. However, high trust is a double-edged sword that could save time and money but also result in costly disappointment when high levels of trust are placed on opportunistic partners, something that can only be known *ex post*. In metateams, project managers must balance the need to capitalize on the cost-saving properties of trust and the risk of trusting others in conditions of uncertainty. As trust shapes perceptions of relationship risks in metateams, the *trust placement process* has an important role in implementing effective hazard-mitigating strategies. To enhance the effectiveness of the trust placement process, organizations must do the following:

1. Develop awareness of the trust placement process—of its nature and consequences (This awareness should help to assess trustworthiness and to generate conditions for trusting relationships.)

2. Implement strategies to help metateam project managers improve *ex ante* trust-based decisions—by structuring their project in a manner conducive to building familiarity as early in the project as possible, i.e., using mini-milestone techniques, allowing for early and frequent exchanges

Congruence Building

Because of organizational fragmentation and inappropriate preproject arrangements, the presence of a low level of goal congruence was a critical issue in the studied metateam. Congruence is something organizations need to start building during initial negotiations with their partners and to continue to develop during the project. As our study shows, in a typical cyclic fashion, the continuous resolution of conflicts and the in-built flexibility of the metateam system allow congruence building, and goal congruence facilitates conflict resolution, making the system flexible to changes. Therefore, client organizations setting up metateam projects should do so in conjunction with their partners and attempt to maximize goal congruence by paying attention to the following:

1. Ensure the correct alignment of incentives (rewards and punishments) for organizations, teams, and individuals with the project's end goals.

2. Avoid situations in which the project manager has full responsibility and accountability for the project but, due to organizational fragmentation, has no practical power to ensure the proper conduct of the project.

3. Allow the metateam to behave as "one team" by sharing risks and rewards, prioritizing effective collaboration, and making subgoals subservient to end goals.

Furthermore, severe goal incongruence born during preproject agreements has a major negative impact on project success; because incongruence, once embedded in the letter of contracts, makes it difficult and costly to resolve the many issues it creates. Therefore, to achieve congruence, appropriate agreements must exist between the organizations before the project starts, which is discussed next.

Appropriate Agreements

A key area on which to focus our attention is that of preproject agreements. Preproject agreements unavoidably condition the relationship. They set targets for the delivery of services and products and, in an indirect way, influence individual and organizational performance and behavior. Conflict, trust, and congruence processes depend on supportive preproject agreements to function efficiently and effectively.

Flexibility allows the actors to effectively and efficiently adapt to unforeseeable requirements and resolve emerging conflicts. Commercial arrangements between the parties need to reflect the critical need for flexibility and collaboration of metateam projects. To put it simply, rigid contractual agreements are major barriers to success. Flexible metateam agreements would cover the following:

1. Not force vendors to engage in minimalist approaches to tender responses, as a consequence of needing to do the following:

    a. Align their promises to the ambitious requirements of (naturally) ill-defined requests for competitive tenders

    b. Sign fixed-price/fixed-time contracts based on (naturally) an incomplete understanding of requirements[12]

2. Promote the sharing of project risks among the intervening organizations, thereby discouraging opportunistic behaviors

3. State the project in terms of desired outcomes, rather than prescribe what has to be done and set targets based on optimistic and ill-defined assumptions

4. Establish governance structures that do the following:

    a. Allow and empower project teams to collaborate in an open manner, seeking opportunities for win-win outcomes and the building of trust between the organizations

    b. Avoid problems of scope creep and "gold-plating" by centralizing the end-to-end management of the project and creating joint change control boards that are effective and represent the key stakeholders' interests

c. Institute effective control mechanisms to determine the project's continuing feasibility

d. Allow open communication at intra- and interorganizational levels

e. Monitor the conflict resolution/congruence-building processes

In the researched organization, top executives perceived fixed-price and fixed-time contracts as insurance against the common risk of IT project cost and time overruns. Undoubtedly, these contracts offer some sense of predictability and control. However, when dealing with complex projects under conditions of uncertainty, this type of control contributes to achieving an opposite result to the one intended (Bajari & Tadelis, 2001; Sadeh, Dvir, & Shenhar, 2000). Therefore, we maintain that fixed-price and fixed-time strategies, often effective in projects of lesser complexity and greater predictability, are a major barrier to success in metateam projects. In wrongly assuming certainty, the contractual rigidity of these strategies is highly likely to result in greater *ex post* costs and cause significant implementation delays.

Future Trends

Metateams offer great promises to modern corporations; yet, capitalizing on those promises seems elusive. One way of addressing this problem is by making sense of the interrelated effects of the environmental, organizational, commercial, and technological facets of metateams. In this quest for sensemaking, we align with the views of Karl Weick, to whom organizing is an imperfect, untidy, and shortsighted activity to be analyzed by observing processes, actions, and recurrent patterns (Weick, 1979, 2001).

However, sensemaking is difficult for people working in environments where the pressures to perform (and survive) are so strong (Weick, 2001). This situation presents both a problem and an opportunity for further research. By helping to make sense of what constitutes and facilitates effective metateam partnerships, researchers can contribute to organizational development and the well-being of metateam actors. Therefore, we call for further studies to investigate how we can achieve effective partnerships at organizational and project levels, including multidisciplinary research into areas such as the following:

- Development of economic models of collaboration for metateam projects that would allow organizations to engage in flexible contracting, sharing risks and benefits

- Critical success factors enabling effective and efficient metateam organizations, for example, empirical studies into areas such as governance, roles of technology, leadership, or effective knowledge management processes

- Metateam process maturity models able to assess the organizational readiness for engaging in metateams projects and to prescribe ways to continuously improve organizational metateam effectiveness

- The role and effect of preproject training, and how it can contribute to team members' awareness of trust processes and to their ability to deal with issues like conflicts, cultural barriers, incongruence, or prejudices

Conclusion

The previous sections presented key concepts emerging from our study. Central to our discourse is the continuous process of conflict discovery and resolution the metateam enacts. In this process, trust plays an important role in deciding how much others can be trusted, we make choices affecting the project's transaction cost, and therefore, we take risks. We presented contextual issues of metateams like organizational fragmentation, pressures arising from unrealistic business expectations, communication barriers, level of goal congruence, temporal nature of interpersonal relationships, type of personnel involved, and conflict inevitability, all of which must be considered when assessing project risks and strategies.

We perceive trust and distrust as opposite ends of the trust continuum. Trust has the power to shape perceptions of reality and therefore to influence the hazard-mitigating strategies actors adopt to achieve their objectives. We argued that trust is relevant to project success and that it affects the project's cost. Without trust, the interteam collaboration becomes difficult and carries a higher transaction cost due to the need to implement additional controlling processes and less efficient conflict management processes requiring frequent escalation and causing delays. However, we also alerted to the dangers of total trust in conditions of uncertainty and organizational fragmentation and proposed that a balanced system of metateams will necessarily have to alternate between tendencies toward either end of the trust continuum.

On the one hand, we believe that trust facilitates the relationship, while on the other hand, we are cautious in deriving a positive correlation between trust-based behaviors and the success of the collaborative endeavor, because *misplaced* trust is detrimental to the success of the metateam collaboration. While trust is often seen as a lubricant for cooperation (Arrow, 1974), it can also be a cause of failure in major collaborative IT projects enacted by multiple teams. As our study shows, metateams exhibit both the need for, and the risks of, trust. Acknowledging the key role this ambivalence plays is critical to our understanding of metateams. Consequently, the key issue discussed in this chapter is the risk involved in placing trust; that is, trusting others and then discovering that the trust was misplaced or, in opposition, not trusting when we should and therefore introducing costly friction. As the effectiveness of the trust placement process increases the chances for project success, we argue that more effort (in research and practice) is required to improve this process.

We also took an economist's view of trust, where the efficient building of a relationship through familiarity, exchange, and reciprocity serves the utilitarian purposes of cost minimization, effectiveness, and efficiency in major IT projects. We maintain that the economic value of creating trusting relationships outstrips the cost of doing so; consequently, we propose several areas to be considered when assembling and conducting metateam projects; including appropriate project agreements that align with critical needs for congruence building, conflict embracement, and effective trust placement.

Finally, metateams and virtual teams represent a revolution in the way we do IT projects and organize work. As the global business environment continues to demand innovation, flexibility, and responsiveness, the number of major IT projects using metateams will increase. The same demands for flexibility and responsiveness will further highlight the criticality of achieving project success; therefore, client and vendor organizations able to evolve and achieve effective metateam systems will thrive at the expense of those more inflexible and slow to adapt.

References

Adler, P. S. (2001). Market, hierarchy, and trust: The knowledge economy and the future of capitalism. *Organization Science: A Journal of the Institute of Management Sciences, 12*(2).

Amason, A. C. (1996). Distinguishing the effects of functional and dysfunctional conflict on strategic decision making. *Academy of Management Journal, 39*(1), 123–148.

Amason, A. C., & Sapienza, H. J. (1997). The effect of top management team size and interaction norms on cognitive and affective conflict. *Journal of Management, 23*(4), 495–516.

Arrow, K. J. (1974). *The Limits of Organization* (1st ed.). New York: Norton.

Axelrod, R. M. (1984). *The Evolution of Cooperation*. New York: Basic Books.

Bajari, P., & Tadelis, S. (2001). Incentives versus transaction costs: A theory of procurement contracts. *The Rand Journal of Economics, 32*(3), 387–407.

Bandura, A. (2001). Social cognitive theory: An agentic perspective. *Annual Review of Psychology, 52,* 1–26.

Beranek, P. M. (2000). *The impact of relational and trust development training on virtual teams.* Paper presented at the 33rd Hawaii International Conference on System Sciences, Hawaii, USA.

Berggren, C., Soderlund, J., & Anderson, C. (2001). Clients, contractors, and consultants: The consequences of organizational fragmentation in contemporary project environments. *Project Management Journal, 32*(3), 39–48.

Cascio, W. F. (2000). Managing a virtual workplace. *The Academy of Management Executive, 14*(3), 81–89.

Coase, R. H. (1988). *The Firm, the Market, and the Law.* Chicago, IL: University of Chicago Press.

Cramton, C. D. (2002). Attribution in distributed work groups. In P. Hinds & S. Kiesler (Eds.), *Distributed Work: New Ways of Working Across Distance and Technology.* Cambridge, MA: MIT Press.

DeChurch, L. A., & Marks, M. A. (2001). Maximizing the benefits of task conflict: The role of conflict management. *International Journal of Conflict Management, 12*(1), 4–22.

Demarco, T. (2001). *Slack: Getting Past Burnout, Busywork, and the Myth of Total Efficiency.* New York: Broadway Books.

Eisenhardt, K. M. (1989). Building theories from case study research. *Academy of Management Review, 14*(4), 532–550.

Evaristo, J. R., & Munkvold, B. E. (2002). Collaborative infrastructure formation in virtual projects. *Journal of Global Information Technology Management, 5*(2), 29–46.

Fernandez, W. D., & Underwood, A. (2001, 4–7 December). *Metateams in major IT projects: A preliminary study.* Paper presented at the Proceedings of the 12th Australasian Conference on Information Systems, Coffs Harbour, NSW, Australia.

Gallivan, M. J. (2001). Striking a balance between trust and control in a virtual organization: A content analysis of open source software case studies. *Information Systems Journal, 11*(4), 277–304.

Gambetta, D. (2000). Can we trust trust? In D. Gambetta (Ed.), *Trust: Making and Breaking Cooperative Relations, Electronic Edition* (pp. 213–237). Department of Sociology, University of Oxford.

Giddens, A. (1990). *The Consequences of Modernity*. Cambridge, UK: Polity Press, in association with Basil Blackwell, Oxford, UK.

Glaser, B. G. (1978). *Theoretical Sensitivity: Advances in the Methodology of Grounded Theory*. Mill Valley, CA: Sociology Press.

Glaser, B. G. (2001). *The Grounded Theory Perspective: Conceptualization Contrasted with Description*. Mill Valley, CA: Sociology Press.

Glaser, B. G., & Strauss, A. L. (1967). *The Discovery of Grounded Theory: Strategies for Qualitative Research*. New York: Aldine Publishing Company.

Hirschheim, R. A., & Newman, M. (1991). Symbolism and information system development: Myth, metaphor and magic. *Information Systems Research, 2*(1), 29–62.

Hofstede, G. (1997). *Cultures and Organizations: Software of the Mind* (rev. ed.). New York: McGraw-Hill.

Iacono, C. S., & Weisband, S. P. (1997). *Developing trust in virtual teams.* Paper presented at the Proceedings of the Thirtieth Hawaii International Conference on System Sciences, Los Alamitos, California, USA.

Jarvenpaa, S. L., & Leidner, D. E. (1999). Communication and trust in global virtual teams. *Organization Science: A Journal of the Institute of Management Sciences, 10*(6), 791–815.

Jarvenpaa, S. L., Knoll, K., & Leidner, D. E. (1998). Is anybody out there? Antecedents of trust in global virtual teams. *Journal of Management Information Systems, 14*(4), 29–64.

Jehn, K. A., & Mannix, E. A. (2001). The dynamic nature of conflict: A longitudinal study of intragroup conflict and group performance. *Academy of Management Journal*.

Jiang, J. J., Klein, G., & Means, T. L. (2000). Project risk impact on software development team performance. *Project Management Journal, 31*(4), 19–26.

Kasper-Fuehrer, E. C., & Ashkanasy, N. M. (2001). Communicating trustworthiness and building trust in interorganizational virtual organizations. *Journal of Management, 27*(3), 235–254.

Koza, M. P., & Lewin, A. Y. (1998). The co-evolution of strategic alliances. *Organization Science, 9*(3), 255–264.

Lorenz, E. H. (2000). Neither friends nor strangers: Informal networks of subcontracting in French industry. In D. Gambetta (Ed.), *Trust: Making and Breaking Cooperative Relations* (electronic edition) (pp. 194–210). Oxford, UK: Department of Sociology, University of Oxford.

Madhok, A., & Tallman, S. B. (1998). Resources, transactions and rents: Managing value through interfirm collaborative relationships. *Organization Science, 9*(3), p. 326.

Martin, P. Y., & Turner, B. A. (1986). Grounded theory and organizational research. *The Journal of Applied Behavioral Science, 22*(2), 141–157.

Maruyama, M. (1963). The second cybernetics: Deviation-amplifying mutual causal process. *American Scientist, 51*, 164–179.

Mayer, R. C., Davis, J. H., & Schoorman, F. D. (1995). An integrative model of organizational trust. *Academy of Management Review, 20*(3), 709–734.

Merton, R. K. (1948). The self-fulfilling prophecy. *Antioch Review, 8*, 190–210.

Meyerson, D., Weick, K. E., & Kramer, R. M. (1996). Swift trust and temporary groups. In R. M. Kramer & T. R. Tyler (Eds.), *Trust in Organizations: Frontiers in Theory and Research*. Thousand Oaks, CA: Sage Publications.

Misztal, B. A. (1996). *Trust in Modern Societies: The Search for the Bases of Social Order*. Cambridge, MA: Polity Press.

Pagden, A. (1988). The destruction of trust and its economic consequences in the case of 18th-century Naples. In D. Gambetta (Ed.), *Trust: Making and Breaking Cooperative Relations* (pp. 127–141). Oxford: Basil Blackwell Ltd.

Parsons, T. (1951). *The Social System*. New York: Free Press.

Piccoli, G., & Ives, B. (2000, December 10-13). *Virtual teams: Managerial behavior control's impact on team effectiveness*. Paper presented at the 21st International Conference on Information Systems (ICIS), Brisbane, Australia.

Piccoli, G., & Ives, B. (2002). *Trust and the unintended effects of behavior control in virtual teams*. Working paper. Cornell University.

Powell, W. W. (1990). Neither market nor hierarchy: Network forms of organizations. In B. M. Staw & L. L. Cummings (Eds.), *Research in Organizational Behavior* (vol. 12, pp. 295–336). Greenwich, CT: JAI Press.

Priem, R. L., & Price, K. H. (1991). Process and outcome expectations for the dialectical inquiry, devil's advocacy, and consensus techniques of strategic decision making. *Group and Organization Studies, 16*(2), 206–225.

Rahim, M. A. (1992). *Managing Conflict in Organizations* (2nd ed.). Westport, CT: Praeger.

Roberts, J. M. (1995). *The Penguin History of the World* (3rd ed.). London: Penguin.

Rotter, J. B. (1967). A new scale for the measurement of interpersonal trust. *Journal of Personality, 35*, 651–665.

Rousseau, D. M. (1995). *Psychological Contracts in Organizations: Understanding Written and Unwritten Agreements.* Thousand Oaks, CA: Sage Publications.

Rousseau, D. M., Sitkin, S. B., Burt, R. S., & Camerer, C. (1998). Not so different after all: A cross-discipline view of trust. *Academy of Management Review, 23*(3), 393–404.

Sadeh, A., Dvir, D., & Shenhar, A. (2000). The role of contract type in the success of R & D defense projects under increasing uncertainty. *Project Management Journal, 31*(3), 14–22.

Sako, M. (1998). Does trust improve business performance? In C. Lane & R. Bachmann (Eds.), *Trust Within and Between Organizations: Conceptual Issues and Empirical Applications* (pp. 88–117). New York: Oxford University Press.

Sauer, C., Liu, L., & Johnston, K. (2001). Where project managers are kings. *Project Management Journal, 32*(4), 39–49.

Simmel, G., Bottomore, T. B., & Frisby, D. (1978). *The Philosophy of Money.* London: Routledge and Kegan Paul.

Skelton, R. (2000, August). Can koalas survive? *National Geographic World,* 11–13.

Steinfield, C. H. M., David, K., Chyng Yang Jang, Poot, J., Huis in 't Veld, M., Mulder, I., Goodman, E., Lloyd, J., Hinds, T., Andriessen, E., Jarvis, K., van der Werff, K., Cabrera, A. (2001). *New methods for studying global virtual teams: Towards a multi-faceted approach.* Paper presented at the 34th Annual Hawaii International Conference on System Sciences, Hawaii, USA.

Thomsett, R. (1998, October). *The team is dead... long live the virtual team.* Retrieved December 11, 2000, from the World Wide Web: http://www.ozemail.com.au/~thomsett/main/articles/virtual_team_toc.htm.

Trompenaars, A., & Hampden-Turner, C. (1998). *Riding the Waves of Culture: Understanding Cultural Diversity in Global Business* (2nd. ed.). New York: McGraw-Hill.

Weick, K. E. (1979). *The Social Psychology of Organizing* (2nd ed.). Reading, MA: Addison-Wesley.

Weick, K. E. (2001). *Making Sense of the Organization* (1st ed.). Oxford, UK: Blackwell.

West, M. A. (2001). The human team: Basic motivations and innovations. In N. Anderson, D. S. Ones, H. K. Sinangil, & C. Viswesvaian (Eds.), *Handbook of Industrial, Work and Organizational Psychology* (vol. 2, pp. 270–288). London: Sage Publications.

Williamson, O. E. (1985). *The Economic Institutions of Capitalism: Firms, Markets, Relational Contracting.* New York; London: Free Press; Collier Macmillan.

Williamson, O. E. (1996). Economic organization: The case for candor. *Academy of Management Executive, 21*(1), 48–57.

Williamson, O. E., & Masten, S. E. (1995). *Transaction Cost Economics.* Aldershot, Hants, UK; Brookfield, VT: Edward Elgar.

Endnotes

[1]   Virtual teams are teams of members working from different locations, whose prime mode of communication is mediated by technology. However, the term "virtual team" is, necessarily, too broad, as it embraces many kinds of organizations involved in activities of different natures.

[2]   According to ethical and confidentiality agreements governing the research, names of people and organizations are pseudonyms.

[3]   SUN project leaders could be seen as equivalent to project managers; similarly, the senior project manager could be defined as a program manager. However, we decided not to depart from the terminology used by the actors, because it best represents the metateam organization and helps identify accountability and responsibility.

[4]   The task-based nature of the relationship among actors could have significance when the teams are from different cultural backgrounds and have different specific-diffuse and neutral-affective relational needs (Parsons, 1951; Trompenaars & Hampden-Turner, 1998).

[5]   Assumptions about others' levels of knowledge are important to our communication strategies. We tend to spend less time explaining the reasons behind a proposed line of actions if we believe the other party shares our level of understanding about those actions. We may not want to appear to be stating the obvious to the expert. Yet, in wrongly attributing a certain level of knowledge to our partner, we may equivocally conclude that we reached mutual understanding; a situation that could result in reciprocal perceptions of contract breach.

[6]   The RedCorp project director, recognizing the difficulty of the SUN project, asked the senior project manager to put together an "*A Team*" able to "*hit the ground running.*" The best and most experienced people available were recruited into the SUN RedCorp team; this required moving people working on other projects and obtaining agreement for that to occur.

[7]   Confirming Sako's (1998) assertions regarding the nature of trust in virtual teams.

[8]   Based on our data and previous definitions from Lorenz (2000) and Rousseau, Sitkin, Burt, and Camerer (1998).

[9]   Mark, the senior project manager in charge of SUN, was concerned about the risk of "*trusting each other and at the end of it not getting the project done.*" According to him, misplacement of trust could be seen as naïve—trusting too much and then causing a loss to the company and damage to one's professional reputation. Like the construction industry project managers depicted by Sauer Liu & Johnston (2001), Mark had a high desire to achieve and to enhance his reputation by being associated with successful projects. Yet, due to difficulties in exercising effective control across organizations and distance, he was confronting the fear of misplacing his trust: how much could he trust others, and how could he know *a priori* that his trust was well placed?

[10]   Expectations of exchange involve trust; without trust, we cannot expect an exchange.

[11]   Opportunism, bounded rationality, and contractual arrangement concepts in our work closely relate to those of the New Institutional Economics theory and, in particular, to transaction economics theory (Coase, 1988; Williamson, 1985; Williamson & Masten, 1995).

[12]   In this context, a minimalist approach is one that tries to do the minimum amount of effort to fulfill the cost and time requirements to produce a winning tender response.

Chapter III

The Impact of External Factors on Virtual Teams: Comparative Cases

Andrea Hornett

The Pennsylvania State University, USA

Abstract

Practitioners and researchers need to pay attention to how corporate organizing structures are impacting and are impacted by virtual work environments. Virtual teams are powerful organizing mechanisms, but they are not without limitations. This chapter reports on two cases in which dynamics outside the virtual project teams powerfully affected the teams. These cases, both based on studies of real project teams operating inside corporations, highlight the desirability of understanding virtual teams in context. While external factors are not unique to teamwork, their role has not been explored in depth in research on virtual teams. Dynamic forces outside teams seem more difficult to anticipate and to identify when team members are working virtually, and these powerful but invisible dynamics can be frustrating to virtual team leaders and members. Concluded in this chapter is that contrary to initial expectations, virtual teams are not replacing traditional forms of organizing. They are coexisting with traditional forms and dynamics, such as business drivers, hierarchies, departments, strategic priorities, and business needs. This coexistence can be fraught with conflict.

Introduction

Virtual teams are powerful organizing mechanisms (Fukuyama & Shulsky, 1997; Goldman et al., 1994; Hedberg et al., 1994; Jackson, 1999; Oravec, 1996), but they are not without limits (Hale & Whitlam, 1997). Considerable research has focused on internal virtual team communications and management for performance (Haywood, 1998; Hightower et al., 1998; Igbaria & Tan, 1998; Jarvenpaa. & Leidner, 1998; Karolak, 1998; Kayworth & Leidner, 2001; Lyons, 2000). In contrast, this chapter examines two cases where dynamics *outside* the virtual project teams affected the teams.

These cases, both based on studies of real project teams operating inside corporations, highlight the desirability of understanding virtual teams in context. In both cases, forces outside the virtual project teams (e.g., hierarchies, departmental allegiances, and rewards) were stronger than anything the teams could do. While external factors are not unique to teamwork, their role has not been explored in depth in research on virtual teams.

Dynamic forces outside teams seem more difficult to anticipate and identify when team members are working virtually, and these influential but invisible dynamics can be frustrating to virtual team leaders and members. More importantly, they raise issues for organization and management theorists and practitioners: Are corporations really ready for virtual teams? What needs to be understood to enhance performance in virtual environments? What are the key characteristics of organizational environments that permit virtual team success? This chapter only begins to try to answer these questions.

Background

Virtual teams are groups of people employed in a shared task while geographically separated and reliant on electronic forms of communication (Palmer & Speier, 1997; Palmer, 1998). As such, virtual teams represent novel structures for organizing work and new vehicles for attempting socialization. They represent a different formal approach to work and a different informal approach to communication. Consequently, research on virtual teams looks at the novelty of their geographically dispersed structures and at how distributed members communicate and cooperate.

Research on Virtual Teams

Research on virtual teams focuses on analyzing how the teams operate asynchronously, without colocation, and how they break the traditions of face-to-face communications and meetings (Ahuja & Carley, 1998; Lipnack & Stamps, 1997; Marca & Bock, 1992). Virtual teams cut across organizational boundaries (Finholt & Sproull, 1990; Mankin, Cohen, & Bikson, 1996) and change relationships (Bredin, 1996; Grenier & Metes, 1995; Zuboff, 1988). Ongoing research on virtual teams is varied but tends to focus on the dynamics inside the teams, particularly on issues of trust and socialization.

In several respects, research on virtual teams explores issues of parallel interest to researchers of teams in general. Organizational scientists investigated internal dynamics, such as the forming of teams (Banet, 1976; Hackman, 1986, 1990), productive disruptions in teams (Gersick, 1988, 1989, 1991; Gersick & Hackman, 1990a,b), learning in teams (Dechant, Marsick, & Kasl, 1993), cooperation in teams (Pinto, Pinto, & Prescott, 1993), and autonomy in teams (Wall, Kemp, Jackson, & Clegg, 1986). Accordingly, much of the advice to practitioners in virtual teams is predicated on what was learned about traditional teams (Duarte & Snyder, 2000). These findings form the basis for orientation and training of virtual team leaders and members.

This connection between research on teams and virtual teams might be comforting if management science knew all there is to know about teams. Unfortunately, teams are complex human systems defying mastery. Teams can be both production systems and learning systems (Brooks, 1994; Dechant, Marsick, & Kasl, 1993; Fisher & Fisher, 1998; Parsons, Bales, & Shils, 1953; Schwandt & Marquardt, 2000), and they form the nexus of relational issues constituting tasks, plans, coordination, and the accompanying socioemotive life of employees (Smith & Berg, 1984). Teams are dynamic organizations with members who cross boundaries into other larger organizations (Ancona [nee Gladstein], 1984, 1990; Ancona & Caldwell, 1987, 1992). Teams are, therefore, not closed systems, not entities unto themselves, but open systems involved with their organizational environments.

Open Systems

Teams are open systems (Ancona, 1990; Gersick, 1991), because they adapt to and structure themselves in accordance with environmental conditions (Lawrence & Lorsch, 1969). While traditional teams demonstrate a need for understanding their environments, because they can cross boundaries into the organization (Ancona [nee Gladstein], 1984, 1990; Ancona & Caldwell, 1987, 1992), virtual teams also do that and more. They are systems operating outside the boundaries of space and time (Lipnack & Stamps, 1997; Mankin, Cohen, & Bikson, 1996; Zuboff, 1988). They are open to information and energy from a variety of directions and must survive in dynamic environments.

Research considering traditional teams as open systems (Ancona, 1990; Ancona & Caldwell, 1992; Gersick, 1991) suggests that team environments create powerful dynamics that organize the teams. In other words, the team does not control its organization; factors and forces external to the team structure the team's internal activities and relationships. The outside can organize the inside and can also determine the team's success (Ancona & Caldwell, 1987). Some of these outside factors include reward and recognition policies (Duarte & Snyder, 1999), budgets, reporting hierarchies, and departmentalization (Hornett, 1998).

The implications of open systems theory are that virtual teams' asynchronous operations and geographically dispersed membership can blind virtual team leaders and members to signs of change, shifting political priorities, and organizational resistance. Virtual teams can experience conflicts or delays without comprehending their sources or significance, because the teams are open to all kinds of influences, pressures, and distractions from the members' geographically dispersed environments and the constant changes in any business.

The cases presented in this chapter provide empirical evidence in support of open systems theory and the role of environmental forces in structuring virtual teams. As such, these cases add to empirical work (Gorelick, 2000), suggesting the vulnerability of virtual teams, because they are open systems. Therefore, virtual team leaders and members need to manage their relationships and their tasks, *and* pay close attention to their environments.

Expectations for Virtual Teams

While open systems theory suggests that virtual teams are vulnerable to outside forces, there are expectations that virtual teams will supplant some of these forces. For example, Zuboff (1990) predicts that information processes and authority are on a collision course, because the ubiquitous nature of electronic access and information undermines traditional authority. Also, virtual teams are expected to replace other ways of working (Lipnack & Stamps, 1997) and significantly alter organizing dynamics (Duarte & Snyder, 1999; Lipnack & Stamps, 1997). Further, virtual teamwork offers potential for increasing employee participation in decision making through increased access to information (Finholt & Sproull, 1990). Because of access to information, electronic organizations are viewed as possessing potential for liberation from constricting authority and power of the status quo (Birkets, 1994; Doheny-Farina, 1996; Hiltz & Turoff, 1978; Lou, 1994; Rheingold, 1994). Schrage (1990) claimed that virtual teams' collaboration "will completely transform the organizational nervous system" (p. 150).

Schrage's optimism for the potential of electronic communication is also evident in the writings of those who develop the tools (Bullen & Bennett, 1990; Lou, 1994) and serve as an expressed goal: "We need to develop information systems that explicitly promote a sense of teamwork and cooperation" (Marca & Bock, 1992, p. 38). The expectation is that technology can empower collaboration or manufacture consent. However, the evidence of enterprise empowerment and democratic decision making through groupware are, so far, occasionally anecdotal and generally elusive.

Some empirical findings suggest that Shrage's claims may be a bit too optimistic (Brown & Duguid, 2000). In addition, Miller (1996) decried online dialogues as "banter" and lamented that society has exchanged community for jobs, while Romm (1999) found evidence that virtual communications can be dysfunctional. There is evidence that trust can be fragile and impede performance in virtual teams (Jarvenpaa & Leidner, 1998), and linkages from effort to performance may not be similar to those in traditional organizations (Ahuja & Carley, 1998).

Two Cases

While the expectations for virtual teams are mixed, it is clear that they are here to stay and can perform some things well, as these two cases illustrate. These two virtual teams struggled with the outside forces of competing strategies and priorities for their organizations, while they straddled two different businesses and covered a variety of time zones, departments, and functions.

Case 1: Conflict and Contention

The first case follows a virtual team of executives, managing a strategic project in a global, US-based, Fortune 50 corporation. This team straddled three time zones, three office buildings, four departments, and two businesses with revenues in excess of US$2 billion each. These two different businesses had different histories, different priorities, and different markets. Serious conflicts occurred between the virtual team and other parts of the organization. At the same time, the virtual team members held positions both on the team and in the traditional organization. Members of the team were leaders within departmental hierarchies that tugged at their allegiances. Perhaps it was the cross-cutting nature of the team's problem and the team's solution, but the team leader's hierarchy frequently interfered, and the team was stymied by other formal organizational functions (Barnard, 1938) holding responsibilities for technologies, budgets, or markets.

The Team

The team was composed of four executive-level members; three held positions reporting to Vice Presidents and General Managers. Two team members had been with the company less than three years, and two had more than 20 years with the company. All had more than 20 years of experience in corporate environments and held, or had held, significant management responsibilities. These team members were well informed about corporate strategy and shared a mission that provided cohesion to the team (Lipnack & Stamps, 1997). Their mission derived from a mandate from the company's Chief Executive Officer and required solving a complicated, persistent, strategic problem with a long, difficult history of resistance to a solution. The company had to achieve compatibility and coherence in a certain line of technology products employing different interface structures and different design architectures. The team was charged with designing and implementing a solution.

The virtual team in this case was distinguished from other electronic groups employed in this company for four reasons. First, this team was cross-cutting (i.e., composed of representatives from various departments), while many other virtual teams in the organization were single organizational units, reporting to one chain of command. Second, the virtual team was not the only assignment; members also held regular jobs with strategic responsibilities in addition to their virtual team project. Third, the team's purpose and the problem to be solved were exceedingly complex. And, fourth, as stated, this team was composed of executives.

The complexity of the team's organization and its assignment suggested that it was breaking down several forms of traditional organizations. At the same time, the virtual team was coexisting with ongoing structures that were a complex mixture of line and traditional staff functions (marketing, budget, etc.), chain of command, and unique staff functions involved with proprietary technologies.

This virtual team was both a different formal approach to work and a different informal approach to exchanging information. It is in this latter context, as an informal information exchange, that this virtual team created value. Unfortunately, the informal nature of the virtual team isolated it from formal resource allocations that adhered to the departmental structure of the organization. This weakened the ability of the team to move its project from the solution design stage to the solution implementation stage.

Approach

This case is based on research that employed qualitative methods (Miles & Huberman, 1994; Patton, 1990). Fieldwork included interviewing each of the members of the team three times (Seidman, 1991) during a nine month period to determine their understanding of teamwork and power. Participants were asked to recount memorable moments in their team's experience, and these stories were reviewed to identify themes and patterns. Findings were shared with participants, in an iterative fashion, for their reflections and comments. In addition, interviews were conducted with other members of the corporation to validate reports on policies toward empowerment, virtual environments, and problem solving. To further ensure trustworthiness, the interview tapes were independently transcribed, and three doctoral students independently coded items. Eighty-five percent of coded items were congruent.

It is difficult to generalize from this case, because this study focused on one virtual business team that was not colocated and included members who worked for different organizations within a very large corporation. The study necessarily employed retrospective sense making (Weick, 1979, 1995). Narrators told their own stories of their situations, involving several ambiguous phenomena (Schutz, 1973). However, this virtual team's experience is instructive.

Findings and Conclusions from Case 1

This team designed a solution but could not get it implemented. They had the CEO as a project sponsor, and they won an award for their work. However, they could not get other departments to support implementation of their solution. Their elegant systems diagram was labeled "too ambitious" and "over-reaching" by other department heads and one of the Vice Presidents.

There are three key conclusions from Case 1. The first is that virtual teams are not replacing traditional forms of organizing; they coexist with them. The second finding is that members of virtual teams are often simultaneously members of traditional organizations. Third, simultaneous virtual and traditional organizational memberships and coexistence can be fraught with conflict. Team members are torn between their identities and allegiances as members of their departments and their identities and allegiances as members of a virtual team. The coexistence of virtual and traditional organizations is filled with conflict between them as they contend for attention, priorities, resources, rewards, and recognition. In this conflict, virtual is vulnerable, because it is not visible and not an established part of hierarchies and departmentalized budgets.

Case 2: Lost Momentum

The second case involves a virtual information technology project team in a global, US-based, Fortune 100 chemical corporation. This project lost momentum when the company's strategic partner, a global engineering firm, lost interest during a decline in the chemical corporation's proposed construction activities and their related revenue for the engineering firm. The team was only able to regain momentum and produce deliverables when executives outside the team made efforts to reinvigorate the strategic partnership in conjunction with a reinvigorated construction agenda.

In this case, the purpose was to create new software that translated documents from engineering design into a corporate repository (memory bank) and back again. This system provided organizational memory for storage and retrieval of manufacturing plant designs, improvements, and modifications.

This Virtual "Site"

The eight-member virtual project team in this study was led by a manager in the Information Technology Group with responsibility for the corporation's Knowledge Management infrastructure. After its initial organization and a few meetings with company representatives from several functions and plants throughout the US, the team added a representative from the firm of the engineering subcontractor. The engineering firm was responsible for supervising the software development firm that was based in Europe, where the chemical company had several plants and the engineering firm had several offices. The team met solely electronically. All members were from different locations.

Approach

This case is based on nearly two years of research in a study that was motivated by two questions: (1) In what ways does a virtual team access organizational memory? (2) In what ways does it contribute to it? Accordingly, this study employed a qualitative methodology (Miles & Huberman, 1994; Patton, 1990) for understanding how a virtual team works from the inside and how its members make use of organizational memory. The researcher spent two years frequently interacting with the team leader face-to-face and some of the team members electronically. During the course of the study, the team evolved in its use of collaborative tools to allow members access to meetings from within and outside the firm. All of the meetings were held by teleconference and used real-time collaboration tools.

The primary data from the study come from a thorough ongoing analysis of all the documents connected with the team and its work. Document analysis involved downloading all documents from the team's Web site and tracking the progress of the team's plans and performance. The researcher analyzed all agendas and minutes of 35 meetings of the team. The researcher had regular access to the team leader and interviewed him frequently during the course of the project. Written interviews with other members of the team were conducted on a volunteer basis. Documents were analyzed for patterns in the project, particularly the use of organizational memory.

Findings and Conclusions from Case 2

The virtual team was able to effectively create an organizational capability to translate drawings and documents between the engineering vendor and the corporation and back again. They were able to agree upon a way to exchange drawings and maintain a repository and tracking system for designs and modifications. However, electronic meeting technology and sound project management could not maintain progress and momentum. Unfortunately, the engineering firm was slow to meet its project deadlines when construction activities went through a decline because of a temporary business slow down. This happened twice. Consequently, a six-month project became a two-year experience.

Demonstrated in this case is that in the presence of shared business need, projects proceed. In the absence of a compelling business need shared by all business partners, collaborative projects wane. While this is not unique to partnerships, the dispersed structure of the virtual team seems to have obscured immediate perception of these dynamics.

The engineering firm's business need, not the virtual team leader, drove the team's mission to create an organizational memory. When business need faded because of economic conditions, the team's activity level abated. They could not get access to the software developers in Europe and could not participate in the testing stages of software development. Later, when the strategic partnership between the two firms was revitalized, the project resumed. Much later, implementation at a plant was stymied by the engineering partner's failure to be responsive.

A key finding in this study is that the project was subject to the ebb and flow of the relationship between the corporation and its engineering partner and the amount of business in transaction between them during any particular period. In addition, distinct patterns of virtual team frustration emerged from analysis of this case. Team members were often frustrated trying to make sense of the delays, the members' exclusion from software testing, and the constantly changing realities of a system rollout. When the subcontractor failed to produce code on time, the virtual team struggled to ascertain why. Consequently, this case suggests that good project management and sophisticated uses of collaborative technologies are necessary but not sufficient conditions for virtual work. Further, the dispersed nature of this virtual team and its members' lack of physical proximity to the engineering firm and the corporate headquarters made for difficulty reading political cues and shifting priorities.

Analysis of Two Cases

These are only two empirical cases, and both are from studies designed to investigate different issues, but they illustrate the same problem: neither team could manage its own destiny. Both were subject to priorities and resource commitments existing outside their project team. A comparison of the two cases (Table 1) illustrates these similarities and differences.

Similarities and Differences

One similarity for the two teams is that both were dealing with compatibility issues. The first case is one of a serious product group compatibility problem that the corporation failed to resolve despite two prior attempts. The second case is one of design, storage, and retrieval compatibility, where the team was hoping to head-off a long-term incompatibility problem. In both cases, the teams were dealing with difficult issues, requiring creativity and innovation. The first team

Table 1. Comparison of the Two Cases

	Case 1: Conflicts	**Case 2: Lost Momentum**
Case time frames	1996–1997	2001–2002
Type of corporation	Global, office products; Fortune 50	Global, specialty chemicals; Fortune 100 + partner
Membership in team	Cut across two businesses, various departments	Cut across two companies; several plants, engineering, and IT
Purpose of team	Resolve serious product compatibility issue.	Create and test software to ensure transferability of documents
Size and type of team	Executive — four members from design, development, and delivery	Managerial — eight members from plants, engineering, IT (information technology); plus an outside engineering firm
Length of project	1 year	Nearly two years
Stakeholders	CEO, several VPs and GMs	Ten department heads/plant managers
Meeting technologies	Pic-Tel, face-to-face, phone	Net Meeting; intranet
Customer requirements	Understood	Understood
Design solution?	Yes	Yes
Implement solution?	No	Yes — after revision
Methods for communicating concepts	1. Selection of members of team 2. Phone calls 3. Participation in research Systems diagram	1. Team members' prior working relationships 2. Intranet site Participation in research study
Lessons we can learn from the case:	1. Resources and priorities outside a team will determine whether a team's proposal is implemented 2. Virtual team members are also members of traditional departments and may hold allegiances	1. A partner's resources and priorities may determine whether a team's work is accomplished or not 2. A virtual team may be slow to detect outside forces at work because of the distributed nature of its membership

knew of the corporation's history of failure. In contrast, the second team had no precedent for resolving the problem. The fact that both teams were able to design solutions while managing in a geographically distributed organization is remarkable and lends credence to the belief that virtual teams are useful organizing approaches.

One difference between the two cases is when they occurred: Case 1 operated in the mid-1990s, and Case 2 operated five years later. In that period of time, there was a tremendous growth in virtual meeting technologies. While the members of the virtual team in Case 1 were all technologically astute, they deliberately met face-to-face at corporate headquarters to secure political awareness of their efforts. They also used the telephone to maintain privacy when politicking. In the second case, travel was not feasible; face-to-face meetings were never even considered. The use of Net Meeting, the intranet, and stakeholder updates provided the team with its primary communication to the organization.

While the first team persisted in its systems view, the second team scrapped its systems view and went with an iterative approach. They redefined the scope and implementation schedule. All the while, they managed the stakeholders' understanding and expectations in a manner that suggested that everything was under control and any problems were minor and being solved. The first team believed that their systems view spoke for itself. While they eventually adopted an iterative, small wins approach to implementation, it was too late; they had lost organizing momentum for implementation. The corporation rewarded them for their efforts, reassigned the disruptive members of the hierarchy, forgot the whole thing, and bought another company with a better technology two years later. The second team might well have experienced a similar fate. They were fully prepared to simply shelve the project after six months. A major difference for them is the membership of plant managers on the team. These people represented both customers and stakeholders. They were going to be facing a difficult mess if the promised translation software was not eventually available. Changing the scope of the project to provide for iterative implementation, based on business need, put the customers in control of implementation and spelled eventual success for the project, despite some delays.

While the second team's project took nearly four times as long as originally estimated, this virtual team was truly empowered. There was no evidence of this team being second-guessed by hierarchies, staff functions, or management, as in the first case. In part, this is due to the lesser magnitude of the second project, and, in part, this is due to the culture of the two organizations and the managerial level at which the project was working. In Case 1, the departmental structures and leadership of the organization were being challenged by the scope of the project's solution. In Case 2, the departments were the project customers and advocates.

In both cases, the traditional organizations external to the virtual project teams held the solutions to the projects' success. In both cases, the teams were well managed and mutually supportive, but that was not sufficient to resolve the problems. In both cases, executive stakeholders outside the virtual teams had to intervene to secure the deliverables.

Conclusion

In these two cases, virtual teams deconstructed bureaucracy but did not destroy it. Both virtual teams, as new means of working, functioned in opposition to older organizational principles and processes of hierarchy, decision making, and resource allocation.

Coexistence: Virtual and Traditional

In both of these case studies, two organizing systems—the virtual and the traditional—coexist in conflict. A lesson learned here is that perhaps some of the literature (Duarte & Snyder, 1999; Lipnack & Stamps, 1997) is too optimistic about the ability of these new ways of working to supplant traditional methods. The participants in these two studies were members of traditional organizations *and* their virtual teams. Although they did not consciously acknowledge this, their allegiances were split, straddling both worlds.

The expectation that virtual ways of working will replace traditional approaches (Lipnack & Stamps, 1997) is premature. The evidence here is that the traditional departmentalized firm is not going down without a struggle, and business volume has not been eliminated as a factor. These cases provide evidence of an important role the organizational context has in setting priorities and allocating resources. These factors and forces exist outside the boundaries of virtual project teams. Policies of empowerment and good management practices inside the teams cannot prevail against certain external factors.

Organizational Impact

Another lesson learned from these cases is that corporations are not always ready for virtual teams. Much needs to be understood to enhance performance in virtual environments. Electronic networks may be useful in some contexts but not in others. Therefore, we need to understand the characteristics of these contexts and their implications for virtual team management.

These two cases illustrate what can happen when virtual structures inhibit making sense of a persistent situation. In both cases, the participants were confident about customer requirements and technologies, but they were inhibited by their lack of a permanent structure and resources for their work. They were competing for attention with other priorities, many of which they could not perceive due to their dispersed organization. In the first case, implementation of a solution could not be resourced by a virtual structure. In the second case, the fragile attachment of the engineering partner could not be secured through good virtual team dynamics.

Managing virtual teams requires understanding internal *and* external dynamics. A key to success is outside the team, in the organizing context. Understanding virtual team organizing environments presents virtual team members and researchers with a critical challenge.

Solutions and Recommendations

What can virtual team leaders, members, and consultants learn from these two cases? Members inside a team, working from different locations, departments, and time zones, must learn to identify environmental influences and devise responsive approaches. For example, the virtual team needs a specific plan for managing communications in, to, and from the team. If stakeholder management is not an explicit, detailed part of project management, they should make it so. Members should discuss the various ways in which the communications strategy for the virtual project necessarily differs from a traditional effort. They can identify the risks to the project, diagram the consequences, minimize the threats, and create opportunities for the team. By investing in a process of online and face-to-face socialization (Jarvenpaa & Leidner, 1998), a team can convey the impression of high performance (Ancona & Caldwell, 1992).

Assessing Organizational Readiness

These two cases and the literature suggest that there are four key organizational competencies for promoting positive, empowering environments for virtual teamwork. First, the organization has to have a vision of the future and awareness that new approaches to management, reward, and recognition are necessary for success (Fisher & Fisher, 1998; Crandall & Wallace, 1998). Second, the organization has to prioritize problem solving over departmentalization. Third, the organization has to be committed to a culture of collaboration. Fourth, executives need to be astute observers of markets and external environments and their implications for the organization, and they have to share that knowledge.

There are a few specific activities that virtual team leaders, members, and consultants can monitor and discuss to assess each of these four competencies. They can do this by asking and discussing specific questions among members and with stakeholders.

Competency 1: Energizing Vision

Do your customers notice the positive energy expressed by your employees? Are people attracted to the organization and glad to be working there? Do the employees understand where the organization is going and why? Do they share that view? Does the organization generally achieve its goals and sometimes exceed them? Do folks work smart (versus hard), and are they rewarded for it?

Competency 2: Empowerment

Is the reward and recognition structure built around getting work done, not protecting departments? Is everyone trained in effective teamwork, and do they practice it? Do employees feel in control of their work? Do people have the information that they need to do their jobs? Is there much re-work, or can the organization consistently get it right the first time? Do the customers agree that products and services are of quality? Do managers empower employees or is there some "second guessing"? Are projects on time and on budget? Are leaders recognized and rewarded for their abilities to empower others?

Competency 3: Collaboration

Do you have the technology you need to access and maintain knowledge as it is developed, and is everyone readily using it? Are you good at promptly and fully responding to requests from each other? Do employees respect each other and want to learn from each other? Does everyone value diversity? Are people convinced that working together produces better products and services than working alone? Are all employees recognized and rewarded for their abilities to collaborate? Do you include partners and stakeholders in your collaboration and actively solicit their feedback?

Competency 4: Environmental Understanding

Do you routinely assess whether the factors that launched the project have changed? If so, do you renegotiate the project with customers and stakeholders? Is everyone aware of and informed about the competition in a productive way? Or, is everyone oblivious; or worse, running scared? Do employees know where the business is going in the future, and is the virtual team aligned with that? Do employees have a feel for the markets, where the company is in each market, and where the company can go or is going in each? Do other companies benchmark your company? Do you revise goals when economic conditions change?

Members should discuss these questions about organizational competence and assess the answers within the team. They can report any concerns to key project stakeholders, enlisting them in actions to mitigate their concerns. For those areas in which the answers are acceptable, these are strengths; organizations can build on them. Communicate the strengths as key competencies that the organization is proud of and recognizes and rewards. Communicate "lessons learned" from this discussion of competence to participants, stakeholders, managers, and other virtual teams in the organization.

Virtual team management requires fostering a new managerial practice (Duarte & Snyder, 1999; Lipnack & Stamps, 1997). Build this new practice on those elements of strategy that virtual teams and executives share. Both want to achieve the needs of the business and anticipate market changes. Both want to satisfy the customer and be known for solid innovation. Both want to be good stewards of the organization's resources. Executive leadership, in practice and in development, tends to privilege persuasion over collaboration. Virtual teams, in contrast, can benefit from collaboration. Virtual team leaders must recognize the environment in which they work: executive suite communication or virtual team collaboration. They have to communicate well in each. Organizations need to recognize that successfully communicating beyond virtual teams to the organizational environment may require some changes in executive selection and development.

Future Trends

If virtual teams can successfully manage team dynamics and tasks and develop solutions to corporate problems, but continue to be thwarted by forces operating outside the team, what does that imply about the efficacy of the virtual workplace (Zand, 1981)? How can managers resolve conflicts or identify hazards when some of the claims on their attention are "virtually" out of sight and out of mind? Virtual teams and researchers need to pay attention to how corporate organizing structures are impacting and are impacted by virtual work environments. As teams increasingly manage tasks and tools, they will start to assess their environmental conditions for success. Organizations will want to promote and reward virtual teamwork to justify their investments in hardware and software.

Summary

These two cases, both based on studies of real project teams operating inside corporations, highlight the desirability of understanding real corporate virtual teams in context. In both cases, forces outside the teams were stronger than anything the teams could do.

Dynamic forces outside teams seem more difficult to anticipate and identify when team members are working virtually. These effective but invisible dynamics (e.g., business volume, budget processes, rewards, managerial hierarchies, departmental allegiances) can be frustrating to virtual team leaders and members. They raise issues for organization and management theorists and practitioners regarding the best ways to work in virtual teams and the best ways to develop organizational environments that appreciate virtual teamwork.

References

Ahuja, M. K., & Carley, K. M. (1998). Network structure in virtual organizations. *Journal of Computer-Mediated Communication, 3*(June), 4.

Ancona, D. G. (1984, December). Groups in context: A model of task group effectiveness. *Administrative Science Quarterly, 29*, 499–517.

Ancona, D. G. (1990). Outward bound: Strategies for team survival in an organization. *Academy of Management Journal, 33* (2), 334–365.

Ancona, D. G., & Caldwell, D. F. (1987). Management issues facing new-product teams in high-technology companies. *Advances in Industrial and Labor Relations, 4*, 199–221.

Ancona, D. G., & Caldwell, D. F. (1992). Bridging the boundary: External activity and performance in organizational teams. *Administrative Science Quarterly, 37*, 634–665.

Banet, A. G., Jr., (1976). Yin/Yang: A perspective on theories of group development. In J. W. Pfeffer & J. E. Jones (Eds.), *The 1976 Annual Handbook for Group Facilitators*. LaJolla, CA: University Associates.

Barnard, C. A. (1938, 1968). *The Functions of the Executive*. Cambridge, MA: Harvard University Press.

Birkets, S. (1994). *Gutenberg Elegies: The Fate of Reading in an Electronic Age*. New York: Fawcett Book Group.

Bredin, A. (1996). *The Virtual Office Survival Handbook*. New York: John Wiley & Sons.

Brooks, A. K. (1994). Power and production of knowledge: Collective team learning in work organizations. *Human Resource Development Quarterly, 5*(3) (Fall), 213–235.

Brown, J. S., & Duguid, P. (2000). *The Social Life of Information*. Boston, MA: Harvard Business School Press.

Bullen, C. V., & Bennett, J. L. (1990). *Groupware in practice: An interpretation of work experience*. Working paper no. 3146-90. Boston, MA: MIT, Sloan School of Management, Center for Information Systems Research.

Crandall, N. F., & Wallace, M. J., Jr. (1998). *Work & Rewards in the Virtual Workplace: A "New Deal" for Organizations & Employees*. New York: AMACOM.

Dechant, K., Marsick, V., & Kasl, E. (1993). Towards a model of team learning. *Studies in Continuing Education, 15*(1), 1–14.

Dixon, N. M. (1994). *The Organizational Learning Cycle*. London: McGraw-Hill.

Doheny-Farina, S. (1996). *The Wired Neighborhood*. New Haven, CT: Yale University Press.

Duarte, D., & Snyder, N. (1999). *Mastering Virtual Teams: Strategies, Tools and Techniques that Succeed*. San Francisco, CA: Jossey-Bass.

Finholt, T., & Sproull, L. S. (1990). Electronic groups at work. *Organization Science, 1*(1), 41–64.

Fisher, K., & Fisher, M. D. (1998). *The Distributed Mind: Achieving High Performance Through the Collective Intelligence of Knowledge Work Teams*. New York: AMACOM.

Fukuyama, F., & Shulsky, A. N. (1997). *The 'Virtual Corporation' and Army Organization*. Santa Monica, CA: Rand.

Gersick, C. J. G. (1988). Time and transition in work teams: Toward a new model of group development. *Academy of Management Journal, 31*(2, March), 9–41.

Gersick, C. J. G. (1989). Marking time: Predictable transitions in task groups. *Academy of Management Journal, 32*(June), 274–309.

Gersick, C. J. G. (1991, October). Revolutionary change theories: A multilevel exploration of the punctuated equilibrium paradigm. *The Academy of Management Review, 16*, 10–36.

Gersick, C. J. G., & Hackman, J. R. (1990). Habitual routines in task performing groups. *Organizational Behavior and Human Decision Process, 47*, 65–97.

Goldman, S., Nagel, R., & Preiss, K. (1994). *Agile Competitors and Virtual Organizations: Strategies for Enriching the Customer*. New York: Van Nostrand Reinhold.

Gorelick, C. K. (2000). *Toward an understanding of organizational learning and collaborative technology: A study of structuration and sensemaking in a virtual project team.* Doctoral dissertation. The George Washington University.

Grenier, R., & Metes, G. (1995). *Going Virtual: Moving your Organization into the 21st Century.* Upper Saddle River, NJ: Prentice Hall.

Hackman, J. R. (1986a). The design of work teams. In J. W. Lorsch (Ed.), *Handbook of Organizational Behavior.* Englewood Cliffs, NJ: Prentice-Hall.

Hackman, J. R. (1986b). The psychology of self-management in organizations. In M. S. Pallak & R. O. Perloff (Eds.), *Psychology and Work.* Hyattsville, MD: American Psychological Association

Hackman, J. R. (ed.). (1990). *Groups that Work and Those that Don't: Creating Conditions for Effective Teamwork.* San Francisco, CA: Jossey Bass.

Hale, R., & Whitlam, P. (1997). *Towards the Virtual Organization.* London: McGraw-Hill.

Haywood, M. (1998). *Managing Virtual Teams: Practical Techniques for High-Technology Project Management.* Boston, MA: ARTECH House.

Hedberg, B., Dahlgren, G., Hansson, J., & Olve, N. (1994). *Virtual Organizations and Beyond: Discover Imaginary Systems.* New York: John Wiley & Sons.

Hightower, R.T., Sayeed, L., Warkentin, M. E., & McHaney, R. (1998). Information exchange in virtual work groups. In M. Igbaria & M. Tan (Eds.), *The Virtual Workplace.* Hershey, PA: Idea Group Publishing.

Hiltz, S. R., & Turoff, M. (1978, 1993). *The Network Nation: Human Connection Via Computer.* Cambridge, MA: The MIT Press.

Hornett, A. (1998). *Power and a virtual team: Modern and postmodern interpretations.* Doctoral dissertation. The George Washington University.

Igbaria, M., & Tan, M. (eds.). (1998). *The Virtual Workplace.* Hershey, PA: Idea Group Publishing.

Jackson, P. (ed.). (1999). *Virtual Working: Social and Organizational Dynamics.* London: Routledge.

Jarvenpaa, S. L., & Leidner, D. E. (1998). Communication and trust in global virtual teams. *Journal of Computer-Mediated Communication 3(4),* June.

Karolak, D. W. (1998). *Global Software Development: Managing Virtual Teams and Environments.* Los Alamitos, CA: IEEE Computer Society.

Kayworth, T. R., & Leidner, D. E. (2001). Leadership effectiveness in global virtual teams. *Journal of Management Information Systems 18*(3), 7–40.

Lawrence, P., & Lorsch, J. (1969). *Organization and Environment.* Cambridge, MA: Harvard University Press.

Lipnack, J., & Stamps, J. (1997). *Virtual Teams: Reaching Across Space, Time, and Organizations with Technology.* New York: John Wiley & Sons.

Lou, H. (1994). Groupware at work: User's experience with lotus notes. *Journal of End-User Computing, 6*(3), 12–19, Summer.

Lyons, K. L. (2000). Using patterns to capture tacit knowledge and enhance knowledge transfer in virtual teams. In Y. Malhotra (Ed.), *Knowledge Management and Virtual Organizations.* Hershey, PA: Idea Group Publishing.

Malhotra, Y. (ed.). (2000). *Knowledge Management and Virtual Organizations.* Hershey, PA: Idea Group Publishing.

Mankin, D., Cohen, S. G., & Bikson, T. K. (1996). *Teams and Technology: Fulfilling the Promise of the New Organization.* Boston, MA: Harvard Business School Press.

Marca, D., & Bock, G. (1992). *Groupware: Software for Computer-Supported Cooperative Work.* Los Alamitos, CA: IEEE Computer Society Press.

Miles, M. B., & Huberman, A. M. (1994). *Qualitative Data Analysis.* Thousand Oaks, CA: Sage Publications.

Miller, S. E. (1996). *Civilizing Cyberspace: Policy, Power and the Information Superhighway.* Reading, MA: Addison-Wesley.

Oravec, J. (1996). *Virtual Individuals, Virtual Groups: Human Dimensions of Groupware and Computer Networking.* Cambridge, UK: Cambridge University Press.

Palmer, J. W. (1998). The use of information technology in virtual organizations. In M. Igbaria & M. Tan (Eds.), *The Virtual Workplace.* Hershey, PA: Idea Group Publishing.

Palmer, J. W., & Speier, C. (1997). *A typology of virtual organizations: An empirical study.* http://hsb.baylor.edu/ramsower/ais.ac97/papers/palm_spe.htm. Retrieved February 1999.

Parsons, T., Bales, R., & Shils, E. A. (1953). *Working Papers in the Theory of Action.* Glencoe, IL: The Free Press.

Patton, M. Q. (1990). *Qualitative Evaluation and Research Methods.* Newbury Park, CA: Sage Publications.

Pinto, M. B., Pinto, J. K., & Prescott, J. E. (1993). Antecedents and consequences of project team cross-functional cooperation. *Management Science, 39*(10), 1281–1297.

Rheingold, H. (1994). *The Virtual Community: Homesteading on the Electronic Frontier.* New York: Harper Perennial, Harper Collins.

Romm, C. T. (1999). *Virtual Politicking: Playing Politics in Electronically Linked Organizations.* Cresskill, NJ: Hampton Press.

Schrage, M. (1990). *Shared Minds: The New Technologies of Collaboration.* New York: Random House.

Schutz, A. (1973). *The structure of the life-world [by] Alfred Schutz and Thomas Luckman.* Translated by R. M. Zaner, & H. T. Engelhardt, Jr., Evanston, IL: Northwestern University Press.

Schwandt, D., & Marquardt, M. J. (2000). *Organizational Learning: From World-Class Theories to Global Best Practices.* Washington, DC: St. Lucie Press.

Seidman, I. E. (1991). *Interviewing as Qualitative Research: A Guide for Researchers in Education and the Social Sciences.* New York: Teachers College Press, Columbia University.

Smith, K. K., & Berg, D. N. (1987). *Paradoxes of Group Life: Understanding Conflict, Paralysis and Movement in Group Dynamics.* San Francisco, CA: Jossey Bass.

Wall, T. D., Kemp, N. J., Jackson, P. R., & Clegg, C. W. (1986). Outcomes of autonomous workgroups: A long-term field experiment. *Academy of Management Journal 29*(2), 280–304.

Weick, K. E. (1979). *Social Psychology of Organizing* (2nd ed.). New York: Random House.

Weick, K. E. (1995). *Sensemaking in Organizations.* Thousand Oaks, CA: Sage.

Zand, D. E. (1981). *Information, Organization, and Power: Effective Management in the Knowledge Society.* New York: McGraw Hill.

Zuboff, S. (1988). *In the Age of the Smart Machine: The Future of Work and Power.* New York: Harper Collins, Basic Books.

Chapter IV

A Virtual Team in Action: An Illustration of a Business Development Virtual Team

Ian K. Wong
Queen's University, Canada

D. Sandy Staples
Queen's University, Canada

Abstract

Examined in this chapter are the characteristics of a project-based virtual team. Although there is some empirical research on virtual teams, little research has focused on describing the practical application of a virtual team in the organizational environment. Described in the chapter are the task and goals of the team, how it handled virtual challenges and used information technology to bridge distance, and how it functioned within its organization. Specifically, the task of the team, team composition, team beliefs, team processes, organizational context, and the effectiveness of the team are described. The chapter is concluded with a summary of characteristics of successful virtual teams.

Introduction

Virtual teamwork is a new approach for people in organizations working together on projects and in research. New pressures facing organizations have led many to use virtual teams (Montoya-Weiss, Massey, & Song, 2001). The need to compete in a rapidly changing, hypercompetitive, and global marketplace is prompting many organizations to transform their organizational structures from large, hierarchical structures to agile, flexible, new structures (Morris, Marshall, & Rainer, 2001). These teams, in which team members work together from dispersed locations, are appearing in all types of organizations in various sectors. There is some empirical research on virtual teams, however, little research has focused on describing the practical application of a virtual team in the organizational environment. Therefore, it is the goal of this chapter to examine and describe the characteristics of one such project-based virtual team. Described in this chapter are the task and goals of the team, how it handled virtual challenges, and how it functioned within its organization.

The content in this chapter is taken from interviews with team members of the virtual team and their business sponsor. Team members were interviewed, either face-to-face or via the telephone using a semistructured interview method that typically lasted 1.5 h each. The company in which the illustrated virtual team operates is part of a large worldwide manufacturing organization with many locations, and all team members are employees of that organization. Therefore, this team is a geographically distributed intraorganizational (virtual) team.

The team was structured in such a way that there were two separate groups within the team. The first group (three people), called the leadership team, met regularly to discuss project progress, financial issues, etc. The second group, referred to as the project team, was made up of the rest of the team (five people) who were in the manufacturing, trials, and R&D functional areas. The entire team, therefore, had eight team members, with one external business sponsor. The team was dispersed across the Eastern part of North America, with the distance between the farthest two locations being approximately 2300 km. Two people were located in each of the first three of the locations, and one person was located in each of the last two (see Figure 1). The locations were diversified in terms of the functional area of the organization. Leadership team members were located at Site 3 and Site 5. Several options existed for communicating with the team, including telephone and teleconferencing systems, e-mail, sharing information on electronic databases (i.e., Lotus Notes), and face-to-face meetings. Communication patterns are more fully described in the section, "Team Processes."

The rest of this chapter describes characteristics of the team's situation and identifies strengths and weaknesses that readers can use to inform their own design and operations of effective virtual teams. Cohen's (1994) model of team effectiveness was used as an organizing framework for the chapter. Characteristics of the team's situation such as the design of the team's task, the characteristics of the members of the team, the processes used by the team, and the organizational context in which the team operates potentially affect how successful the team will be at meeting its task [as per traditional team research findings (e.g., Bettenhausen, 1991; Cohen, 1994; Cohen & Bailey, 1997; Goodman, Ravlin, & Schminke, 1987)], and are, therefore, worthy of examination. Accordingly, the task of the team is described in the next section. In the following section is a description of the characteristics of the team, in terms of team composition and team beliefs. Then, the team's processes in terms of coordination, communications, and sharing of information are described. In the next section, the organizational context that the team operated in is described, followed by discussion about various indications of the effectiveness of the team in the next section. Presented in the last section is a summary of characteristics of successful virtual teams, based on ideas from the team members interviewed in this study, followed by concluding remarks.

Task of the Team

Appropriate task design can be a powerful motivator (Cohen, 1994). Job characteristics theory (e.g., Hackman & Oldman, 1976, 1980) and sociotechnical theory (e.g., Cummings, 1978; Pasmore, 1988) suggest that group task design is critical for employee motivation, satisfaction, and performance. Both theories suggest that to positively impact performance and attitudes, the task should be designed so that the following take place:

- To complete the task, a variety of skills are required

- To see the outcome of their efforts, members should be assigned a task that is a whole and identifiable piece of work

- To add meaning, the task should be perceived to have significant impact on the lives of other people

- To be most effective, the team should have considerable autonomy and independence in determining how the work will be done

- To ensure that the team can understand how it is performing, regular and accurate feedback should be provided

Job characteristics theory, which has fairly strong empirical support, suggests that task attributes influence effectiveness through their impact on critical psychological states such as motivation and satisfaction with the work. Positive motivation and satisfaction levels have a positive effect on the quality of the work and overall productivity of the team (i.e., an indirect effect potentially exists between task design and productivity and quality) (Cohen, 1994). Below, we first generally describe the task of the team and then examine it with respect to the task design variables listed above.

The team's task was to adapt an existing material, that the organization owned, for use in a new market and new application, and turn the new product line into a viable, commercial business. The existing material had some unique properties that could provide some significant benefits and opportunities over current products in the market. The task involved many aspects, including research and development, field testing, manufacturing, and marketing, as well as finance and general project management.

Almost everyone on the team felt the project was quite complex. In addition to facing the challenge of developing the product into a viable commercial market, other factors added to the project's difficulty. The new product was being developed for use in the agricultural industry. When working with agricultural products, many other variables can come into play, such as weather and crop physiology. These things can hamper field trial progress and render results unreliable. Furthermore, the company had never done business in this specific area, so the team faced such challenges as deciding what market strategy to deploy in order to get the product to market (i.e., picking which channel mechanism or combination of channels to use).

Most of the team members felt they were under severe time pressure, and some expressed concern that things might be moving too fast. At the time of the interviews, the project was in the precommercial stage. The target approximately 16 months in the future was to establish if this is a feasible business or not. There was a long-term (i.e., 10-year) vision of where the product line should go generally. For the immediate three to four years, there were more detailed plans and a number of steps defined that must be taken to demonstrate if the product was commercially viable (e.g., start with small trials and increase the size of the trials each year).

Variety of Skills Needed so that Team Members Rely on Each Other

Of the skills required for effective performance, team members identified a wide variety of needed skills. These included leadership skills, technical skills (in each of the functional areas mentioned above), and communication skills. Given the wide variety of areas of expertise required, it is not surprising that team members felt that they had high levels of interdependence on each other. Team members described the high interdependencies as follows:

> *"They're [the components of the task] very interdependent. We have a manufacturing component that has to develop and manufacture the actual devices or else it can't be tested in the field."*

> *"If we make the system this way it's going to affect the manufacturing. So again there's a lot of interrelation between what you design, and the manufacturing you do and how you would sell the system...and the performance and perception of that in the marketplace."*

Seeing the Whole Task

Defining the task so that people saw it as an entire whole and understood how their parts fit together was a challenge that took time to overcome. One person was designated as team leader, and he spent a great deal of time with planning and coordination functions. Information technology tools played a significant role in enabling this. One of the things he did was use a Lotus Notes database to help structure tasks and responsibilities and share knowledge. To implement structure into the team, there was a work plan that worked backwards from the timing targets. Each person in the team had different items assigned to him or her that were indicated in the database. Project management tools such as Microsoft Project were also used to facilitate scheduling and coordination. Milestones and deliverables were specified. The members of the team placed documents in the Notes database, and all members used it fairly regularly. The general consensus was that the information technology tools were very useful in managing the coordination of this dispersed team and helped people understand more fully how their pieces of the task fit with and affected other members of the team.

Significance of the Task

Helping people understand the potential impact of their work is an important part of the task design. The project sponsor (i.e., the senior manager that the team reported to) felt that establishing a cause and a passion within a team was critical for team success. He explained:

> *"If you can create a cause around something you usually get passion for it...[You] can create this passion by gathering the stakeholders together...the business team participants all together*

in one place and allow them to see the direct impact of their project...Can also have passion when the management can demonstrate how the project will result in significant outcomes for the [team members] themselves because they will grow with this business opportunity. They will get to do things that they never thought they were going to do before."

The team spent several days at a potential future customer's site working with the product, and it was felt that after that experience, each team member truly understood the high potential impact of the product. Consistent with this, everyone on the team felt the team's task had high significance, in terms of potential impact on future customers and society. The average response to a question asking how significant their work was on a 1 to 7 scale, with 7 being very high, was 6.75. By showing the team what the product could potentially do, passion and motivation were created. Also, as mentioned by the project sponsor, the opportunity to create a new business line within the organization was an unusual and highly visible opportunity, so people also felt that they were being given exceptional opportunities for personal career growth (in addition to the opportunity to develop an important product). When asked about their level of motivation with the team's work (again on a 1 to 7 scale), the average response was 6.4, and many of the comments explaining the high satisfaction levels reflected the high perceived significance of the project.

Autonomy and Independence Provided to the Team

Most team members felt that the team had a fair amount of autonomy (i.e., freedom) to set the direction of the project. One team member explained:

"I think we have a lot of autonomy...it's up to us really to figure out how to make it work and we're not being told by anybody how to do that. They [senior management] are basically coming to us and saying, hey you guys know lots about this or know people who know lots about this...go do it."

Within each individual's area of expertise, everyone felt they had considerable autonomy to make their own decisions. However, at the team level, some people felt that they had less input than desired into the overall direction of the team and its task. As previously mentioned, there were two subgroups within the team: the leadership and the project groups. Many members of the project subgroup felt that they were not involved in setting the direction of the project, and that this was largely decided for them by the leadership group. The person who felt most strongly about this also had the lowest levels of motivation and satisfaction with being part of the team, supporting the importance of having high team autonomy and independence (and the negative impact of not having this).

Feedback

As discussed above, high levels of feedback play a role in increasing the level of team performance. In the team, feedback mechanisms were largely informal, and the team leader played a key role in providing feedback. Bimonthly conference calls and quarterly to semiannual face-to-face meetings were held for the project team. The leadership team met about monthly, usually face-to-face (members of the project team attended as needed). Feedback from senior management was usually provided through the team leader. Team members felt this was useful; however, more feedback would have been welcomed by some of the team members. Feedback was also provided by upper management in terms of their continuing approval for project funding. Unfortunately, some members were concerned with the frequency and consistency of the feedback. One member noted, "Some informal feedback is provided and this is valuable, but not everybody gets this as not everybody is interacting with senior management."

Overall, as summarized in Table 1, the design of the task for this team had some strengths and weaknesses. On the positive side, a wide variety of skills were required so that team members were interdependent on each other, the task was an identifiable whole, and the task was perceived to be very important by all team members. However, autonomy for each member of the team was perhaps perceived to be less than ideal due to the two-tier structure within the team, and feedback to the members of the project team could have potentially been increased.

Characteristics of the Team: Composition and Beliefs

The composition of the team, in terms of the size and stability of the team, the skills of the team members, and the location of the team members (i.e., the team's virtualness), along with the beliefs the team members hold about their ability to function, all potentially impact the effectiveness of the team (Cohen, 1994). Each of these team characteristics will be described more fully below.

Table 1.   A Summary of the Design of the Team's Task

Variety of skills required?	Identifiable piece of work?	Task significant?	Team given autonomy?	Feedback?
High	Yes, outcomes visible	Highly	For members of the leadership team, yes. Members of the project team perceived having less autonomy.	Mostly informal and/or through the team leader. Potential existed to improve feedback to the entire team from senior management.

Size of the Team

The size of the team can affect the ability of the team to do its task (Cohen, 1994; Guzzo & Dickson, 1996). If it is too big, higher coordination costs result. If the team size is too small, it will not have the resources needed to complete its work, and team members will be less likely to be committed to the team.

As previously mentioned, the team had eight team members with one external business sponsor. Team members felt that currently the team was about the right size for the task, but many mentioned that in the future it would have to grow, or existing team members would have to take on a larger time commitment to it (i.e., the ones that were currently assigned to the team on a part-time basis). At the time of the interviews, only three people felt they were currently working full time on the project. Other team members worked on a part-time basis, ranging from 20% to 85% of their time. Overall, it was felt that more resources would be needed in the future as the product moved from a design stage into a manufacturing stage.

Stability of the Team

Stability of team membership is also an important factor, because familiarity among team members has been found to be linked to performance (Guzzo & Dickson, 1996). If turnover is high, time and effort will be spent orientating new members, performance norms will not develop, and performance will suffer. However, some turnover can be beneficial, in that it could revitalize a stagnant team and enhance creativity (Cohen, 1994).

Since the initial development of the idea for the product, there were changes in the members of the team and its size. It grew naturally as it moved from the idea stage to the precommercialization stage (i.e., more people with various functional skill sets were brought on board). Some members had come and gone throughout the project. The departures from the team created some challenges over the course of the project. For example, the inventor of the product left the team, creating a loss of expertise. A part-time person took over the position, but it took some time to get up to speed. Furthermore, a new person joined the team in the role of team manager, whose vision was somewhat different than the previous team manager, which also created additional challenges. As new members arrived to the team, introductions were made typically via teleconference calls. There had been no particular time that everyone got together face-to-face to start the project (since it evolved slowly over the last three years). Most of the team members knew at least one other member from previous interactions. Some of the team members knew several of the others from previous projects. For the last year, team membership was stable, and it was anticipated to remain that way for the foreseeable future.

Skills of the Team

The collective knowledge and skills of a team will impact the team's ability to carry out its task (Cohen, 1994; Guzzo & Dickson, 1996). This includes functional expertise and skills, information systems (IS) skills, and interpersonal skills. Information systems skills are needed so that people can effectively use the information technology systems that played a key role in the communication and sharing of information within the team.

One of the goals in designing the team was to bring people onto the team that could contribute a unique skill set in one area or another, because this makes efficient use of resources and enhances the interdependence and importance of each other's role. Therefore, most people brought unique sets of technical skills such that they could complete their function roles. The only skill set that most of the team felt was lacking was specific knowledge related to the area of application for the new product and that marketplace. It was a complex market, and the team members thought that it would be useful to have an expert that understood issues particular to the area.

Other than functional skills, general communication skills seemed to be of high importance to the team members. According to one team member, "It is very important to use time effectively. Communication skills are important to enable this to happen, so that time isn't wasted with duplication." Furthermore, team members noted that in addition to having solid face-to-face communication skills, team members needed to know how to write clearly over e-mail and communicate effectively using the phone. These skills were important, because communication technologies such as e-mail and telephone were most frequently used by team members to communicate with other members. There were some concerns about communication skills, as it was suggested that the competence varied among the team members. This should be a cause for concern, because effective communication skills among team members are vital to the effectiveness of a virtual team (Grenier & Metes, 1995). It was interesting that all of the members of the leadership team felt communications were good within the team; however, several members of the project team felt that communications could be improved.

Several team members also commented that the level of interpersonal skills varied widely among individuals within the team. Specific problem areas mentioned were listening skills and the need to strengthen interactions between the technical team members and the marketing-focused team members such that plans and promises made to customers would be realistic.

The levels of skills with the information and communication technology tools appeared to be adequate. All team members felt that their capabilities and those of their teammates were adequate. Lotus Notes was adopted by the company three years prior to the time of the interviews, and new people were trained in how to use it. Lotus Notes was used as the e-mail platform and to share documents and materials (i.e., as a collaborative tool). Lotus Notes databases, e-mail, and teleconferencing were extensively used. MS Project was used for scheduling and project planning, mostly by the project leader. NetMeeting was used once with marginal results. One person commented on this and implied that the document-sharing features of NetMeeting were not required by the team, because their Lotus Notes systems provided sharing capabilities and were used by those that needed access to various documents.

Geographical Distribution of the Team (Degree of Virtualness)

There has been limited empirical evidence to suggest that greater geographic distribution of a team leads to lower levels of performance (Cramton & Webber, 1999). This is presumably due to reduced face-to-face contact, reduced opportunities to build social relationships, and difficulties in communicating and coordinating virtually using communication technology rather than face-to-face communication. This implies that higher virtuality could be negatively related to team performance and satisfaction with the work and the team.

Overall, the team was geographically dispersed but in the same time zone, and the entire team had face-to-face interactions about every quarter of a year. Therefore, the degree of virtuality can be thought of as medium. Team members were spread among five locations in Eastern North America, as illustrated in Figure 1. Two people were located in each of three of the locations. The locations were logical in terms of providing the required diversity of expertise and resources to the team, which is what made it necessary for this team to be virtual. For example, two people worked at the site where the product was manufac-

Figure 1. The Location of Team Members and Numbers of Members at Each Site

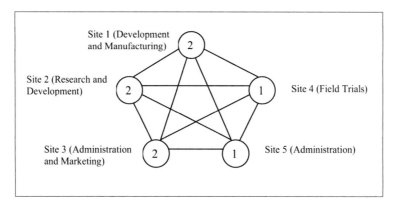

tured, one person worked where the basic research was done, and two worked near the administrative headquarters of the group to which the team reported. Although the geographic spread was large (ranging from the southern United States to Canada), it was largely North to South, such that everyone was usually in the same time zone. At the time of the interviews, the frequency of face-to-face meetings declined due to budget cuts. It was expected that, typically, the entire team would meet face-to-face every quarter of a year, as had been happening for the previous several months. The three members of the leadership team were within a 3 to 4 h automobile drive of each other, so they would typically meet face-to-face on a monthly basis.

Team Beliefs

Team performance beliefs have been found to be a strong predictor of group effectiveness in previous research (Cohen, 1994). In this study, team beliefs were assessed via a concept called group potency. Group potency captures efficacy beliefs at the group level. Group potency (sometimes referred to as group efficacy) is "a collective belief in the capability of the group to meet a task objective" (Gibson, Randel, & Earley, 2000, p. 71). The group potency scale developed by Guzzo, Yost, Campbell, and Shea (1993) was used in this study, because it had established reliability and validity characteristics to assess general team efficacy (Gibson et al., 2000). Respondents were asked to indicate how accurately, on a 1 to 10 scale (10 = high agreement), a series of eight statements described their team. The statements dealt with issues of confidence, the ability to produce high-quality work, the ability to be a high-performing team, the ability to deal with problems, and the ability to be productive.

Table 2.   A Summary of the Characteristics of the Team

Size of team?	Stability of the team?	Team skills?	Degree of virtualness?	Team beliefs?
About right but will need to grow in the future.	Has been some turnover, but the team has been stable for the last year.	Missing one set of technical skills. Interpersonal skills and communication skills could be improved.	Appropriate diversity of skills and resources achieved via the virtual distribution of the team. Although face-to-face contact was quarterly or more frequent, people felt more would help team communications.	Moderately positive belief in the abilities of the team.

The average score was 7.2, reflecting moderately positive beliefs in the team's ability. The average for the leadership team was somewhat higher than that for the project team. For the entire team, individual assessments of team potency varied from a low of 6.0 to a high of 8.9. The two team members with the lowest potency scores had relatively low perceptions of team effectiveness and performance and relatively low team satisfaction levels, supporting the importance of having strong beliefs in the team's abilities.

Summarized in Table 2 are the characteristics of the team. The size and the current stability of the team were generally positive. Diversity of functional skills was appropriate, with one exception, and the team was aware of this need. At the time of the interviews, the team was actively looking for external resources to provide the missing skill set. The main reason that this expertise set was not part of the team was that it did not exist internally. Interpersonal and communications skills were problematic, indicating that improvements could be made in these areas, through things like training and coaching. A moderately positive belief in the abilities of the team existed, possibly somewhat low due to the communications problems and lack of one skill set. Addressing both of these things could potentially increase the team's efficacy, which could have a positive impact on the effectiveness of the team (Cohen, 1994).

Team Processes

Several variables pertaining to team process were examined: coordination, caring (i.e., team spirit), sharing of expertise, and effectiveness of communications. These are important things to examine, because good coordination among team members leads to working together without duplication and wasted efforts. Caring about each other implies working together with energy and team spirit. Sharing and benefiting from others' knowledge and expertise is important to support effective cross training and decision making and to fulfill interdependencies. Good communications are required in order to make this possible. These team process variables are part of most models of team effectiveness and have been found to be associated with group effectiveness in previous research (Cohen, 1994).

Coordination

How team members coordinate is an important characteristic of a team (Cohen & Bailey, 1997). In this team, there were mixed opinions about the quality of coordination. Most members felt the coordination to be reasonable, although several said it could be better. One person specifically mentioned the use of the Notes database as a coordination mechanism. In terms of being a coordination mechanism, Lotus Notes helped store meetings and documents and was used for online discussion. However, this person suggested that it was poorly organized, such that it was hard to find information or that sometimes material was posted without informing others where to find it. Most team members felt that there had been little duplication (duplication can be an indicator of poor coordination); however, two teams members said they observed some duplication of efforts that could have been avoided with better coordination and communication.

Team Spirit

Everyone felt that team spirit existed, but some felt it was stronger with some segments of the team than others (i.e., higher at the project team level than at the leadership team level):

> "There are pockets of team spirit, but not cohesively throughout the group due to interpersonal barriers. There are subgroups that work well together."

The virtual nature of the team and the part-time commitment of some members also had negative impacts on team spirit, according to two people. For example, one person felt:

> "However, the people on the team are not full-time on the team (i.e., dedicated 100% of their time to this project)....Given the part-time situation of members of the team, it is not as natural to pick up things that crop up. When everyone is together, there is a spirit of teamwork. You see each other working on things. There is more of a sense of commitment. In a virtual team, you can't see the work and efforts so it [team spirit] is not visible as quickly."

Sharing Information

Most high-performing teams are teams in which members are comfortable sharing information and communicate well (Cohen, 1994). In this team, the majority of members felt that there was a high level of comfort with the sharing of information in person and electronically. People were generally comfortable relying on others so long as the giver of information was speaking from their area of expertise. However, some people felt that information sharing was not always as open as it might be, and one person said that this could be caused by having the leadership and project subteams (i.e., the split functions and people).

Communication Patterns

This team relied heavily on information and communication technologies to function. In order to share information and to communicate, most communications were done via e-mail (often daily with other interdependent team members) or telephone. About twice per month, a team teleconference call took place, which typically lasted for about 2 h. A Lotus Notes database was also used to help members communicate. It was used to document meetings, store documents, and have online discussions. The discussion thread feature within Lotus Notes was used. One team member summarized communications as follows:

> "On a quarterly basis, there is a joint project/leadership face-to-face meeting. This is often combined with a face-to-face project meeting (i.e., match up with that timing so extra travel is not required). This joint meeting usually runs one day for the project group and one day for the joint meeting. We do this at places/ points of significance. For example...we had a session at a trade show where we focused on the finished product."

Another member pointed out that communications was structured and broken down by subteam:

> "The team has had to evolve a very disciplined method of communicating just because of the challenging diversity of the team members....[There is] a weekly technical conference call...then we have a bi- or every two or three weeks we have a leadership team meeting...and then we have a once a quarterly face-to-face meeting and then we may have more frequent interaction if we need to."

Table 3. A Summary of Team Processes

Coordination?	Team Spirit?	Information Sharing?	Communications?
Coordination was reasonable but there was potential to improve it.	Team spirit was stronger within the project team than the leadership team.	Fairly open. Some felt the two team structure hurt open sharing.	Fairly structured communication patterns were used to create the coordination between the dispersed team members.

Overall, it was suggested by more than one person that communications could be improved. Members attributed the communication and coordination problems to how geographically remote the team was. To solve this problem, it was suggested by some members that there should be more face-to-face meetings:

> *"I think that we have a general communication problem and it's because everybody's geographically remote and so coordination I think suffers. I don't think it's a lack of will or desire, it's just, you know, geography kind of gets in the way and people get overlooked and forgotten so I think communication is an issue. But there's no resolution to it. I mean we have to keep working at making it better given what we have. Because obviously we're not all going to move to live in one city together."*

As summarized in Table 3, the team processes led to relatively good coordination and information sharing, largely through structured, frequent communications and the use of IT tools. There are indications that the subgroup structure of the team was creating some coordination and information-sharing problems and creating different levels of team spirit. This would be consistent with previous research on in-groups and out-groups. Members of their own subgroups tend to evaluate their members and the subgroup more positively and identify more strongly with them (Ashforth & Mael, 1989).

Organizational Context

The organizational context that a team works in can create the environmental factors that can help a team to be successful or to fail (Cohen, 1994; Cohen & Bailey, 1997). The team with the best internal processes may still perform poorly if it lacks the resources or information needed to do its task. A team will not be able to make good decisions without proper information, without sufficient training, and without adequate resources. Therefore, a series of organizational

Table 4.   A Summary of the Organizational Context

HR Structure and Policies?	Training?	Management Support?	Power structure?	Access to required information and resources?
Generally supportive of team efforts.	Training was available.	Supportive, in terms of funding and providing autonomy to the team.	The two tier power structure within the team appeared to hurt the cohesiveness and perceived autonomy.	Access was seen as quite good.

context variables were examined (Table 4). These variables potentially interact to create an environment in which the employee wants to be involved and can participate to complete their tasks effectively. Specific variables examined were human resource policies and the reward system (it should be designed so it is tied to performance and development of capability and contributions to the team); availability of training (it should be available to enable employees to develop the skills and knowledge required to complete their tasks); management support and the power structure in place affecting the team; and access to needed information (without this, employees will not be able to effectively complete their tasks) and resources, including information technology infrastructure to communicate and share information electronically in the virtual setting (adequate resources are needed to enable employees to complete their tasks).

Policies and Human Resources Structure

According to Duarte and Snyder (2001), human resource policies must be designed and integrated in such a way that virtual team members are recognized, supported, and rewarded for their work. Cohen, Ledford, and Spreitzer (1996) found that management recognition was positively associated with team ratings of performance, trust in management, organizational commitment, and satisfaction for self-directed and traditionally managed groups in organizations. As such, it is important that an effective reward system with performance measures be in place to reward results. Grenier and Metes (1995) and Lurey and Raisinghani (2001) also suggested that it is important for the organization to reward high levels of team performance. Within the organization being described, there was a rewards initiative, where people were recognized and given small monetary rewards for performance beyond the norm that reflected values consistent with the organization's mission. Several of the team members were recognized under this program and won financial rewards. Peer recognition rewards were also possible within the organization, where an individual would nominate his or her peer for an extraordinary effort or contribution. If the nomination was successful, the person nominated would get recognition and a small financial award. Last, recognition awards were possible for the entire team as well, but this had yet to happen for the team being described. The main reward system was the salary system at the individual level. The individual set initial objectives with their direct supervisor, and meeting the objectives affected salaries. The team leader could also get involved at this stage so that there were no surprises in terms of commitment to the project and to make sure that members were rewarded for their efforts.

Training

It is important that team members have access to continual online training and technical support (Duarte & Snyder, 2001; O'Hara-Devereaux & Johansen, 1994). Training and team building are important, because they ensure that employees develop the knowledge required to contribute to organizational performance (Cohen, 1994). Team members on the project team felt that training was readily available and supported. However, the individual was largely responsible for taking the initiative to identify when and what training was needed. In this case, the economy had not been strong, and employees were encouraged to be more selective in terms of which training programs they chose to participate in. In these times, the organization did not cut training altogether, but it wanted employees to get trained in the areas most relevant and useful to their work.

Management Support

Team members felt that management support was good, and a key thing almost everyone identified was that management generally left the team alone to meet their own goals and objectives. It was also agreed that the management helped to protect the team from the rest of the corporation. Without management's support, there would be a great deal of demand and pressure on the team to deliver the commercial product. Management also ensured that the team remained well budgeted and well resourced. Overall, the general feeling was that management was effectively supporting the team; however, areas of improvement existed. Some team members felt that management fell short in terms of giving feedback of their expectations and where they thought the team should be going. Also, team members wanted to see more encouragement; team members wanted not only to see monetary encouragement, but symbolic gestures, like a "pat on the back" or verbal communication that the team was doing a good job. The team's business sponsor played a key role in supporting the team and in providing some direction. One person explained this key role:

> *"[Our] director provides overall guidance for these teams and his involvement or lack thereof is key...in this case he's not been involved very much with this team and I think it's given the team a real sense of ownership. However, while he's hands-off, he also believes in teams. He expects us to work in teams and he trusts...he trusts the team decisions. But he has certain expectations...whereas, some of the teams I've been involved with before, you might have a very overbearing manager that wants to manage the team or manage certain members of the team and that can be a problem."*

Power Structure

All members of the team said the team was a self-managed team. Within the team, however, as previously mentioned, there was a subteam called the leadership team that did much of the coordination and liaison with senior management. This subteam also made most of the high-level decisions for most of the team. Having the subteam make most of the major high-level decisions caused some friction in the team, because some of the team members outside of the leadership subteam felt they had little autonomy at a high level. This behavior would not be considered to be effective according to virtual team literature; to be successful in virtual groups, the team members must have independence and decision-making capabilities (Lipnack & Stamps, 1997). Also, according to Cohen and Bailey (1997), an organization needs to give members of work teams autonomy in their work. Worker autonomy has been shown to have clear benefits; it enhances worker attitudes, behaviors, and performances (whether measured objectively or rated subjectively by team members).

Access to Information and Resources

With respect to information access, team members felt that most of the information they needed was held by themselves or other team members. Several individuals mentioned that they also had to access information and expertise from colleagues outside the team. Getting market information from potential customers was more problematic, because not all customers shared information freely, and sometimes the challenge was identifying whom to ask. In terms of availability of resources, most team members did not have any issues, although several members mentioned that a larger budget would be an asset to the team's efforts. Overall, the company provided good information technology tools and infrastructure to support electronic communication. One member, who was working from a remote location, felt that geographic location hindered access to resources. Because this particular member was not located in the organization center, the member felt that others had better access to databases and internal support. Another member felt that due to the nature of virtual work, members missed out on the advantages of day-to-day contact. For instance, in general, many good ideas are shared and generated in social settings such as coffee breaks. This type of contact is not available to individuals working in virtual teams.

Overall, the organizational context was supportive for the virtual team and its efforts. The team was resourced at a reasonable level, reward systems were in place to recognize team achievements, and access for most of the team members to required information and resources was good. When considering the power structure within the team and the organization, it appeared that the organization overall provided the team with a bit of autonomy, but that this autonomy and responsibility for the team were not equally shared within the team. The leadership subgroup had more power than the project group.

Team Effectiveness

Perceived assessments of the productivity of the team and attitudes of the team members were used to help understand how effective the team was overall. Half of the team felt the team was very effective in terms of getting things done and meeting timelines. According to one team member, 80% to 90% of planned tasks got done on time, which is very good compared to the other projects within the organization. Some people commented that they perceived the team was more effective recently than it had been in the past. However, some people believed that there was room for the team to be more effective. One person commented that the team was not effective, due to communication problems caused by the virtual nature of the team. Suggestions about how to better communication included having more face-to-face meetings. Other ideas to make the team more effective included being given more financial resources, filling the need for technical expertise in the one area missing within the team, developing a stronger awareness of how the various components of the project fit together and how one person's actions impact another person's efforts, and allowing for more involvement of the project team members with decision making. Individually, there were somewhat mixed feelings about how the team was performing. One member noted, "It's functioning but not happily. Not everybody has an interest if it fails." Whereas another member, who was more positive about the team's performance, commented: "We've basically accomplished all of our objectives. We could have exceeded them further of course but I think we've done a very good job."

In terms of the commitment of team members, most members felt there were few problems with absenteeism or withdrawal of efforts by team members. There was the belief in the team that everyone was involved, and that the team members were engaged. This could be attributed to the idea that most of the people involved in the project looked at the project as something unique and fairly interesting, not to mention significant to society. As a result, there were high levels of interest and commitment in making the project work. The only concern with respect to commitment was with the part-time allocation of most members. Most members had work to do on other projects and usually had other tasks assigned. This created difficulties, because there was a sense of a gap or absence in the team when other duties took people away.

The motivation to succeed on the project was also high in the team. Many felt the project was interesting and wanted to see it succeed. One major reason for this is the high level of personal significance and social significance of the project; if the project succeeded, there was the potential for tremendous impact on society at large and on the organization's bottom line. Last, although the team members were generally highly motivated and committed, they expressed lower levels of satisfaction with their work, with the team, and with the company. Dissatisfaction from some people appeared to stem from the existence of the two subgroups. Not surprisingly, most of the negative comments regarding this came from members of the low-power project subgroup. Members of the high-power subgroup, the leadership team, saw few problems caused by this. Another general complaint that was suggested to be a cause of lower levels of satisfaction was that a bit of time spent in processes, procedures, and politics was not very productive.

Conclusion: Characteristics of High- and Low-Performing Virtual Teams

To summarize this chapter, characteristics of high- and low-performing virtual teams were identified. The ideas presented in this section were taken from interviews with team members. Members expressed their views, based on their experience working on the team that has been described and teams with which they worked in the past.

The following findings from the team members' experiences are valuable and relevant for managers and practitioners. Managers of virtual teams can use this information to assess how their team is progressing. By having a clear knowledge of some of the characteristics of high- and low-performing teams, managers will know how to make their teams more effective and how to recognize when their teams are going in the wrong directions.

According to team members, the following is a summary of the characteristics of high-performing virtual teams. How the team attempted to achieve this is indicated below each point:

- Have a clear vision for the team; one that is passionately pursued and can be articulated for the team members:

  - The team sponsor made sure that the team members knew how important the product was to their future customers and that team members appreciated the opportunity they were being given for personal development and career growth.

- Have clear goals and objectives at the individual team member level that align with the overall team direction:

  - The team used IT tools such as Lotus Notes and Gantt chart schedules to make everyone aware of the various components of the project and how their pieces all fit together.

- Set timelines for objectives, and ensure that they get done on time:

  - The project management software aided in this, as did the coordination efforts of the team leader and others on the team.

- Have individuals on a team who are highly motivated:

  - Team members were highly motivated, stimulated by the high potential impact that product could have for their customers.

- Select a leader who plays a role in generating motivation and enthusiasm, in developing the shared vision, and in getting management support:

  - The team sponsor played a key role in doing this, and the team leader (a member of the team) played an important role in developing shared visions and goals within the team.

- Have members on the team who have few interpersonal problems:

  - Team members were selected for the technical skills they brought to the task, not for their interpersonal skills. Some interpersonal problems were evident that reduced the effectiveness of the team and satisfaction of some of the team members.

- Have members who are team players and have a positive attitude about working in a group:

  - It is not clear how successful the team was in this regard or if this was considered when choosing team members.

- Have team members who have the ability to recognize when they need help and where to find it:

  - The roles of the various team members were clear so that the team members knew who to turn to for needed information and advice.

- Have a good composition of team members in terms of the collective skill set and knowledge:

  - The team was made up of people with the required skills, with one set of skills missing (this was identified, and steps were being made to fill this need).

- Have team members with strong technical skills:

  - Team members had strong technical skills and were well respected by each other.

Conversely, the following is a summary of the characteristics of low-performing virtual teams:

- Have a team leader who has an autocratic style:

  - Although the project sponsor was supportive and was definitely not autocratic, the creation of the leadership subgroup made the project subteam feel that they had less input into decisions and autonomy than they would have desired. Some members of the project subteam felt that the leadership subteam acted in an autocratic fashion sometimes.

- Have poor communication between team members, either in terms of quality or frequency, or both:

  - It was necessary for this company to create a virtual team in order to get the required diversity of skills on the team. The resulting geographical distribution limited face-to-face interaction and made communications challenging. Regular electronic communication channels were maintained. More open communications between the leadership subgroup and the project subgroup were desired by members of the project subgroup.

- Lack shared purpose and goals:

  - Overall goals for the team were shared.

- Have overlapping responsibilities:

  - This did not appear to be a significant problem.

- Have the wrong people on the team, in terms of background or training:

  - There did not appear to be any problems in this area.

- Lack a shared sense of success (individuals want to work independently or want the rewards individually):

  - No indications of problems here.

Overall, this team faced many challenges in terms of having an ambitious project to work on, and having people from different functional areas within their company on the team. Making progress on the tasks for an individual team member was highly interdependent on the progress of other team members. Relatively effective coordination was achieved across the geographic distances through the use of structured communication and electronic communication and information-sharing tools. However, as noted above, there were areas for improvement within the team, particularly with respect to splitting the team into two subgroups. It is hoped that the description of how this team tried to cope with some of the difficulties of working virtually, along with their suggestions for how to design highly effective virtual teams, will help organizations design future teams and associated processes so that they can enjoy the full potential of working virtually.

References

Ashforth, B. E., & Mael, F. (1989). Social identity theory and the organization. *Academy of Management Review, 14*(1), 20–39.

Bettenhausen, K. L. (1991). Five years of group research: What we have learned and what needs to be addressed. *Journal of Management, 17*(2), 345–381.

Cohen, S. G. (1994). Designing effective self-managing work teams. In M. M. Beyerlein, D. A. Johnson, & S. T. Beyerlein (Eds.), *Advances in Interdisciplinary Studies of Work Teams, Vol. 1, Series of Self-Managed Work Teams.* Greenwich, CT: JAI Press.

Cohen, S. G., & Bailey, D. E. (1997). What makes teams work: Group effectiveness research from the shop floor to the executive suite. *Journal of Management, 23*(3), 239–290.

Cohen, S. G., Ledford, G. E. Jr., & Spreitzer, G. M. (1996). A predictive model of self-managing work team effectiveness. *Human Relations, 49*(5), 643–676.

Cramton, C. D., & Webber, S. S. (1999). Modeling the impact of geographic dispersion on work teams. Working paper. George Mason University.

Cummings, T. G. (1978). Self-regulating work groups: A sociotechnical synthesis. *Academy of Management Review, 3*(3), 625–634.

Duarte, D. L., & Snyder, N. T. (2001). *Mastering Virtual Teams: Strategies, Tools, and Techniques that Succeed.* San Francisco, CA: Jossey-Bass Inc.

Gibson, B. G., Randel, A. E., & Earley, P. C. (2000). Understanding group efficacy: An empirical test of multiple assessment methods. *Group & Organizational Management, 25*(1), 67–97.

Goodman, P. S., Ravlin, E., & Schminke, M. (1987). Understanding groups in organizations. In *Research in Organizational Behavior, 9*, 121–173.

Grenier, R., & Metes, M. (1995). *Going Virtual.* Upper Saddle River, NJ: Prentice Hall.

Guzzo, R. A., & Dickson, M. W. (1996). Teams in organizations: Recent research on performance and effectiveness. *Annual Review Psychology, 47*, 307–338.

Guzzo, R. A., Yost, P. R., Campbell, R. J., & Shea, G. P. (1993). Potency in groups: Articulating a construct. *British Journal of Social Psychology, 32*, 87–106.

Hackman, J. R., & Oldman, G. R. (1976). Motivation through the design of work: Test of a theory. *Organizational Behavior and Human Performance, 16*, 250–279.

Hackman, J. R., & Oldman, G. R. (1980). *Work Redesign.* Reading, MA: Addison-Wesley.

Lipnack, J., & Stamps, J. (1997). *Virtual Teams: Reaching Across Space, Time, and Organizations with Technology.* New York: John Wiley & Sons.

Lurey, J., & Raisinghani, M. (2001). An empirical study of best practices in virtual teams. *Information & Management, 38*(8), 523–544.

Montoya-Weiss, M., Massey, A., & Song, M. (2001). Getting it together: Temporal coordination and conflict management in global virtual teams. *Academy of Management Journal, 44*(6), 1251–1262.

Morris, S., Marshall, T., & Rainer, R. (2001). Impact of user satisfaction and trust on virtual team members. *Information Resources Management Journal, 15*(2), 22–30.

O'Hara-Devereaux, M., & Johansen, R. (1994). *Global Work: Bridging Distance, Culture & Time.* San Francisco, CA: Jossey-Bass.

Pasmore, W. A. (1988). *Designing Effective Organizations: The Sociotechnical Systems Perspective.* New York: John Wiley & Sons.

Section II

Protocols

Chapter V

Long Distance Leadership: Communicative Strategies for Leading Virtual Teams

Stacey L. Connaughton
Rutgers University, USA

John A. Daly
The University of Texas at Austin, USA

Abstract

Because virtual teams are becoming more common in global organizations, research that explicates issues related to this emergent organizational phenomenon is necessary. One major topic is the leadership of virtual teams. Drawing on data from a series of in-depth interviews with project leaders, senior managers, and executives of six global organizations, in this chapter, what virtual team leaders perceive to be effective communicative tactics in virtual settings will be illustrated. Specifically, tactics related to two leadership challenges commonly cited in the academic and popular press are explored: (a) overcoming virtual team members' feelings of isolation—feelings of disconnectedness, lack of cohesiveness, and limited identification with the virtual team leader and the organization; and (b) building and maintaining trust. Also presented in the chapter are some strategies for managing cross-cultural communication issues, and tips are offered on the use of communication technologies in distanced settings.

Introduction

The globalization of business as well as recent patterns in corporate restructuring demand that more organizations utilize geographically dispersed work groups and use advanced technologies to communicate with them (Benson-Armer & Hsieh, 1997; Hymowitz, 1999; Townsend, DeMarie, & Hendrickson, 1998; Van Aken, Hop, & Post, 1998). Organizations such as IBM, Hewlett-Packard, GE, AT&T, and Proctor & Gamble, for instance, incorporated various degrees of virtuality into their operations (Davenport & Pearlson, 1998). Some firms employ "telecommuting," in which members may work at home, on the road, or at the office (Hymowitz, 1999). Other companies enjoy operations that are globally dispersed. Leaders in organizations that have adopted this extreme form of "operational virtuality" (Van Aken, Hop, & Post, 1998) face the complex task of leading people who are often thousands of miles away from their home organizations. A manager in Austin, Texas, for example, may be responsible for coordinating employees in Ireland, Malaysia, and Brazil. In this chapter, we use the term "long-distance leadership" to refer to leadership in globally dispersed organizations.

Popular press writers caution long-distance leaders against assuming that geographically dispersed operations foster the same level of coordination among, and productivity from, individuals as among members who are geographically proximate (see Handy, 1995; Upton & McAfee, 1996). This emergent brand of leadership is, in fact, not easy. In a recent survey of 500 virtual managers, 90% believed that managing over distance was more difficult than managing face to face, and 40% held that individuals produced less when they were geographically distant from their managers (Hymowitz, 1999).

In this chapter, we review what is known about the challenges inherent in long-distance leadership and offer practical recommendations for meeting these challenges. To do so, we first illuminate tactics for dealing with two specific leadership challenges: virtual team members' feelings of isolation—perceptions of disconnectedness, lack of cohesiveness, and limited identification with the virtual team leader and the organization; and building and maintaining trust among virtual team members. Second, we introduce an additional challenge—cross-cultural communication differences—and offer our perspectives on how this dimension relates to the others. Third, we present advice to distanced leaders on ways to use communication technologies to achieve objectives. We conclude by discussing projected research trends in this area and drawing conclusions from our research.[1]

Background

Although leading from afar is becoming more common, we have a limited understanding of it. To be sure, training and development journals (e.g., Geber, 1995; Nelson, 1998) as well as weekly periodicals (e.g., *Fortune* and *Business Week*) have, in the last five years, devoted several feature articles to describing the emergence and uniqueness of leading from afar. Additionally, popular management books (e.g., Duarte & Snyder, 1999; Fisher & Fisher, 2001; Haywood, 1998; Lipnack & Stamps, 1997; O'Hara-Devereaux & Johansen, 1998) highlight several challenges to leading over distance. These works, however, do not systematically pinpoint the critical dimensions of long-distance leadership, and they do not document specific communication tactics that people employ to effectively lead across time and space.

Popular press writers have not been the only ones remiss in articulating the complexities of long-distance leadership. Scholars have yet to diagnose effective leadership strategies for these unique organizational relationships. Previous empirical studies uncovered the "best practices" for *designing* effective virtual teams (Lowry, 1998; Lurey, 1998), praised the positive outcomes of virtual teams (higher flexibility, lower costs, and improved resource utilization, see Mowshowitz, 1997; Snow, Snell, & Davison, 1996), and revealed the relationship between virtual team structures and the use and adaptation of technology in attaining goals (Majchrazak, Rice, Malhotra, King, & Ba, 2000). Some scholars focused on issues of trust in virtual teams (Jarvenpaa, Knoll, & Leidner, 1998), while others examined the use of communication technologies in virtual teams (Pauleen & Yoong, 2001; Scott, Frank, Cornetto, Sullivan, & Forster, 1999). In a field study of New Zealand-based virtual team facilitators who worked with virtual teams across organizations, Pauleen and Yoong (2001) found that boundary-crossing issues (organizational, cultural, language, time, and distance) can profoundly affect the facilitator's ability to build relationships with team members. And, Kayworth and Leidner (2002) noted the managerial behaviors of leaders in global virtual teams. But, scholars have not examined how issues such as isolation, trust, cross-cultural differences, and communication technology relate to one another, specifically in terms of leading distanced teams. Our chapter begins to fill this void.

Challenges to Leading from Afar: Isolation, Trust and Cross-Cultural Communication

The challenges inherent in long-distance leadership become apparent when we acknowledge the advantages of physically proximate offices. Traditional office settings provide more opportunities for organizational members to communicate frequently and spontaneously with each other; the potential to interact immediately for troubleshooting; a forum in which to directly access information; and the chance to develop and maintain relationships (Davenport & Pearlson, 1998). Often, leaders develop and energize relationships with their employees through informal as well as formal interactions with organizational members. Yet in globally dispersed organizations, fewer opportunities to incorporate that informal communicative component exist. Distanced employees often feel isolated from their leaders and from events that take place at the central organization (Fisher & Fisher, 2001; Van Aken, Hop, & Post, 1998; Wiesenfeld, Raghuram, & Garud, 1998).

The consequences of isolation are typically negative. Feelings of disconnectedness adversely affect distanced employees' morale (Van Aken, Hop, & Post, 1998; Wiesenfeld, Rahuram, & Garud, 1998), their commitment to the organization (Staples, 1996), their communication satisfaction with distanced leaders, and their perceptions of team cohesion (Warkentin, Sayeed, & Hightower, 1997). For organizational leaders, this lack of cohesiveness is cause for concern, because high degrees of group cohesion and agreement on organizational goals have been shown to yield greater performance levels (Yukl, 1989).

We contend that isolation is only part of the issue. What exacerbates this physical isolation is the potential for decreased trust, and more frequent misunderstandings because of cultural differences. These issues pose challenges for long-distance leaders when building connectedness.

Trust

Trust between leaders and organizational members is critical to effective long-distance leadership (Lipnack & Stamps, 1997; Nilles, 1998; O'Hara-Devereaux & Johansen, 1994) and to successful virtual teams (Jarvenpaa, Knoll, & Leidner,

1998; Jarvenpaa & Leidner, 1998). Across time and space, however, trust is often precarious, swift, and temporal (Geber, 1995; Jarvenpaa, Knoll, & Leidner, 1998; Jarvenpaa & Leidner, 1998).[2] That is because facilitators of trust in face-to-face contexts, such as shared norms and experiences (Bradach & Eccles, 1989), and the anticipation of future interactions (Powell, 1990; Walther, 1994) are often unavailable to leaders and members over distance. Misunderstandings that would be resolved quickly in face-to-face environments may fester when people are distant from one another; perceived nonresponsiveness due to time zone differences may lead people to think that commitments are not being honored; hurried mandates without thorough explanations may be seen as dictatorial admonishments; and, a sense that some people are privy to information while others are not may generate suspicions of favoritism and inequity. In short, long-distance leaders face the difficult challenge of building and maintaining trust in what is often an inherently isolating context.

Cross-Cultural Communication

Feelings of isolation and distrust can be amplified in long-distance contexts due, in part, to cross-cultural communication differences. As organizations become more globally dispersed, their members also become more diverse, representing different national and cultural backgrounds. Cascio (1999) addressed the cross-cultural challenges of distance leadership by positing that individuals raised in low-context cultures experience more satisfaction and productivity in virtual teams than those raised in high-context cultures. The former might depend more on precise language; the latter on nonverbal and contextual cues that would be unavailable to them in a virtual environment.

Beyond coping with cultural differences concerning the ways people frame their worlds, long-distance leaders face more mundane cultural challenges—working hours and habits may be different; what counts as holidays and as "perks" may vary; what norms exist for appearance, for entertainment, even for ethical decisions may differ; how important status is and how decisions get made often vary across national cultures. The combination of language differences, national cultural diversity, and varied communication norms presents major challenges to long-distance leaders. Making a mistake on any of these can easily foster misunderstandings and, consequently, distrust. And, even without an overt error, all of these differences can result in a sense of isolation for people who do not believe their cultural norms are understood or valued.

In sum, connectedness and trust are significant ingredients in the long-distance leadership recipe. Whereas others examined them independently, we contend that these factors are interdependent. Trust begets a sense of connectedness; feelings of isolation may exacerbate distrust. Complicating the mixture are cross-cultural communication differences. Following Pauleen and Yoong (2001), we argue that time, space, national cultures, and technology *have the potential* to limit the tacit binds that often allow groups to cohere.

Meeting the Challenges: Tactics for Leading from Afar

Given the challenges inherent in distanced work settings—isolation, trust, cultural differences—what tactics do leaders find useful in facilitating employees' sense of connection? To answer this question, we interviewed 21 leaders in geographically dispersed global organizations and asked them to discuss their "best practices" for leading from afar. All of the respondents worked for large worldwide organizations. All were able to travel when necessary, had easy access to various communication technologies, and had high levels of education and training. All had led distanced teams before and had led teams that were colocated. In organizing their responses, we used the conceptual framework described in the previous section.

Combating Perceived Isolation

Unlike leaders of copresent teams, who can have casual conversations with employees many times each day, long-distance leaders have fewer opportunities to interact with their team members. Consequently, they may be tempted to communicate only about task-related topics when they interact with their distanced employees (Scott et al., 1999). But, that often creates more problems than it solves. Our respondents believe that *nontask-related interactions must take place with geographically distanced individuals*. One leader put it this way:

> *There's a different dynamic in terms of allocation of time when you are managing locally versus managing from afar. Locally, I have one staff meeting a week and I have hallway conversations. I spend probably 15% to 20% of my time doing [nontask] "interaction"...When you are remote, it's really 50% interaction time. The more separated your people are, the more time [nontask] interaction takes up. Locally, when you manage, "interaction" is an afterthought. (Worldwide Marketing Director, Technology Sales Organization)*

In face-to-face settings, nontask interactions often occur in unscheduled ways. But when leading those who are geographically separated, our respondents note the importance of *establishing regular interaction times*. Otherwise, these interactions might not happen. One leader explained:

> *You don't get to see them face to face. They don't hang around with you, they don't get to go to lunch with you; they don't get to have the more relaxed hallway conversations that come out of "how ya doing this morning?" The "how's the wife?" "how are the kids?" None of that happens with them. One of the things that is critical is establishing the relationship. I believe in one-on-ones with your people, but I don't normally schedule them with people I have that are local. I have time to catch them and they can catch me when we need to have one-on-one conversations. But that dynamic is missing in worldwide settings. You need to schedule one-on-one phone calls to get it going. (Director of Worldwide Process Technologies, Technology Sales Organization)*

A concern raised by some leaders with establishing these weekly, planned, structured conversation times with long-distance employees is that there will be nothing to talk about, and hence, both parties will lose valuable business time. Our interviewees emphasize the value of these conversations. In the words of one long-distance leader:

> *The response that I get from people at a distance [to the idea of having set times for phone calls] is "what are we going to talk about?" And this is from people who are management on the other side of the world, who know "one-on-one's" and the value of them. But I always just tell them, "we're going to talk about whatever. If we have nothing to talk about, we'll hang up the phone." We never hang up the phone. We've always got at least 15-30 minutes of stuff to talk about. And many times, the phone calls start out, "I don't have much to talk about today, but..." And, then inevitably, the phone call will go over time because we have things to talk about. (Worldwide Product Marketing Manager, Technology Sales Organization)*

One type of interaction that is vital for the maintenance of all relationships (Knapp & Vangelisti, 2000) is "small talk." Yet small talk can easily be forgotten in distanced relationships. The distanced leaders we interviewed make it a point to *engage in, and encourage, small talk*. In the words of one informant:

Over distance you have a complete void of frequent interactions with people. You are missing one of your fundamental tools. Somehow you've got to overcome that. And that's where the one-on-one calls come in, because you really have to have meaningful interaction with these people somehow. So, during the calls I spend time trying to get to know the person well, not just the work stuff. For example, I know that our engineering manager over in Europe likes to go sailing on his vacations and I know the way he manages his day, and I know when I can catch him and when I can't, and I know what worries him. (Product Engineering Manager, Semi-Conductor Manufacturer)

Our leaders report using small talk, or what one interviewee calls "free-flow chatter," in many different ways. One interviewee begins his monthly videoconference meeting with long-distance individuals asking questions such as "How have you been since the last time we talked?" or "Did you go skiing like you had been talking about last time?" While the nature of their answers is important, it is the conversations, initiated by these questions, that are perceived to bind individuals together.

In addition to adopting a regular communication pattern and encouraging small talk, many of our respondents build connections by *personalizing their interactions with distanced employees*. One leader, for instance, not only has group pictures of himself and his regional teams displayed on his office wall, but he also maintains a "log" of remote individuals' interests and their family members' names. Two interviewees specify receiving what they felt was a positive response from distanced individuals when they address them by their nicknames, know their likes and dislikes, and can name members of their families and inquire about their lives. One interviewee illustrated:

One of the ladies that I work with internationally, is Rosalyn. I picked up on the fact that people call her "Roz." Everytime I talk to her, I call her Roz. When you work with them on a daily basis, trust and respect are the core of motivation. You have to pick up on things that help to establish a connection with them. Roz has a husband, David. So, when I pick up the telephone, I ask, "How is David?" These are things that you do in the hallway in the U.S. When you are interacting internationally, you don't have the opportunity to do that unless you make it. (Senior Project Manager, Technology Hardware Organization)

Another long-distance leader electronically sends a personal story, along with a weekly business update, each week. When he encounters an employee in the hallway during a visit to an international location, the employee and he have something to chat about apart from work. His hope is that these *narratives will bridge the distance between him and those at remote sites*, bonding him with them as well as offering them insights into his world (Browning, 1992).

Our long-distance leaders also indicate that building and maintaining connection involves establishing mechanisms that ensure a constant flow of information both to and from remote sites. In the process of doing this, our interviewees say they follow a few "ground rules." First, some leaders *ensure that all employees— distant and local—hear the same messages at the same time.* For example, they try not to let local people hear about a new policy, initiative, or agenda before distanced individuals. Otherwise, the local group might attain a favored "in" position, creating implied status differences between those working near and far. One interviewee noted:

> *Distanced contexts require just as much, if not more, interaction as local environments. It is easy to under-communicate outside of your immediate sphere of contact everyday. And that means that people feel lost and disconnected. When they hear about something that everyone back here [headquarters] knew for weeks was coming and nobody told them they feel they have wasted time, effort, and personal investment. That's a real problem. (Worldwide Sales and Marketing Manager, Technology Sales Organization)*

Our respondents also *intentionally distribute information not directly or even obviously relevant to employees' job responsibilities.* This aids employees in understanding the organization and seeing their roles within the collective. Employees who are proximate to their "home" office may informally acquire this sort of information. But distanced employees often have little sense of the "big picture," unless there is a concerted attempt to inform them. For example, one corporation's Chief Information Officer disseminates to all employees daily, over e-mail, a summary of key events, financial achievements, and corporate developments. Another leader uses the Internet to post a company "newsletter," updating individuals in remote sites not only about developments in their functional division but also in other divisions.

In addition, many of these leaders try to *ensure that job-related information is readily available to long-distance employees.* This "knowledge management" task is especially critical, the informants tell us, when individuals are spread across the globe. Much of this information is easily accessible when working face to face, but distance presents a challenge. For example, one leader created a Web site where project managers post their "lessons learned" and share best practices with other organizational leaders. Another leader uses an electronic forum to advertise what "works" in the regions and to propagate those ideas to headquarters and other remote sites. And, one leader developed an internal electronic bulletin board, where project leaders can ask questions and receive suggestions from other project leaders.

Our leaders believe that techniques such as these assist them in minimizing distanced employees' sense of isolation. Previous research suggests that this isolation may be exacerbated by the fragile nature of trust in dispersed contexts (Jarvenpaa, Knoll, & Leidner, 1998; Jarvenpaa & Leidner, 1998). How managers build and maintain trust in an isolating environment is the topic of the next section.

Building and Maintaining Trust over Distance

To build trust with those they lead from afar, our long-distance leaders report that they *must first quickly create a strong personal relationship between themselves and geographically distant others*. As one respondent advised:

> *However you can form the personal relationship, whether that's through phone calls or traveling and being there, if you don't have a personal relationship with those people that you are managing remotely, it just isn't going to work. It doesn't have to be a friendship necessarily, but it has to be personal contact. It's got to have the ability for openness and you have to establish trust. You've got to show trust. If you can't do those things, you are going to fail. (Director of Platform Development, Technology Sales Organization)*

Although computer-mediated communication makes leading from a distance possible, our respondents overwhelmingly emphasize the importance of *building these relationships through face-to-face communication initially and then using telephone and electronic channels to maintain relationships*. They attribute the necessity of face-to-face communication to their belief that trust is built with an individual they met in person, not with a voice on a phone or with an author of an e-mail. Two interviewees articulated this notion:

> *When I took over the role, I went to the different locations in Europe. It made me see people on a personal level. I think when you see each other face-to-face you don't start to wonder what the agenda is. You see each other face-to-face and you can talk through it. I think I was able to demonstrate that I was going to listen to what was going on. I need to see what contexts they work in. I think that in order to be accepted, I need to show my willingness to come on their turf. And, I need to get to know them*

on a personal level. A lot is happening in technology where you can do videoconferencing. I do a lot of teleconferencing with [one site]. But, there's nothing that replaces face-to-face. (Director of Worldwide Training, Technology Sales Organization)

In managing from afar, before you can effectively use certain tools like e-mail and telephone you need to be able to build trust. The only way to build that trust is verbal communication and acknowledgment of goals and objectives. Once you have that trust and understand those goals and objectives, then e-mail works well. When someone sends an e-mail, they know you are going to read it, they know you are going to respond and take action. Until you have that agreement and trust, those things can't happen. (Director of Worldwide Compensation, Technology Sales Organization)

Beyond initial face-to-face meetings, many interviewees feel that one of the most important tactical and symbolic steps leaders can take to build and maintain trust is to *make regular personal visits to the remote sites*. Practically, these personal visits function to increase the long-distance leader's understanding of the remote employees' points of view. For example, one executive reports how visiting a remote site was imperative to help site members refocus on issues critical to the company's performance goals:

The reality is that when I went down there [Brazil] a month and a half ago they were still working all the wrong issues. So, I had to intervene and had to learn and listen and talk to people. I had to go to the location and get blown off by the customs guy there. I had to experience that for half a day. It's the most frustrating thing, it's such a waste of time, but yet, if you don't understand the subtleties of what exactly that means, then you can't help them deal with it. After being down there 10 days we can provide them different resources, different ways to work on it. (Vice President of Worldwide Operations, Technology Sales Organization)

Face-to-face visits also offer symbolic value. Our respondents suggest that long-distance leaders *must be willing to go to remote sites whenever they are needed, even without prior notice*. The interviewees believe that doing so sends a powerful message of dedication and can enhance remote employees' motivation. One interviewee gave this advice:

Sometimes the politics of e-mail and telephone discussions get you nowhere. Be willing to drop what you are doing and get on a plane and go wherever you need to go. If for no other reason

then that act in and of itself can be very impressive to the
individual you are talking to. You thought it was important
enough to come talk. It may be their problem. It may have no
severe adverse effect on you, but it's very important to them. You
have to be willing to recognize that and say, "I'll be right there.
This is important." (Reserve Unit Captain, U.S. Military Unit)

Hence, our respondents seem to believe that trust is built through a developed
personal relationship and face-to-face contact, especially through spontaneous
and planned personal visits to remote sites. Although communication technologies enable interaction, the interviewees do not see them as substitutes for face-
to-face interaction. Whether interacting in person or through mediated means,
our respondents note cross-cultural communication issues that affect these long-
distance relationships.

Enhancing Cross-Cultural Communication over Distance

One of the benefits to global organizations engaging in operational virtuality is the
availability of talented people who reside in various countries. Cross-cultural
communication challenges, however, accompany the move to this organizational
form. As one interviewee described:

Misinterpretation gets ten times worse when you go around
world. You not only have the different work cultures in the
company that you are in, but you've got a new business culture
in the country that you are trying to work in. And, you probably
don't understand it like you should. (Human Resources Director,
Technology Sales Organization)

Our interviewees attribute these communication challenges to differences in
communication norms, cultural norms, and business norms. One interviewee
points to divergent public communication norms in the United States and some
Asian cultures:

You might be communicating something with a lot of emotion,
passion, you might be angry or you might be really seriously
concerned about something. It is not a part of some Asian
cultures—out of respect for individuals and their bosses—to push
back or to openly disagree. They might just say "okay" and
kindly absorb it. You don't really know what they are feeling

> *which may cause a high level of frustration. It is not in their*
> *nature to push back at you. That is due more to cultural norms*
> *than to specific words. (Vice President of Worldwide Procurement,*
> *Technology Sales Organization)*

One manager who long worked with Asian teams in Japan noted that he tries to understand Japanese indirectness. For example, when a Japanese manager responds to his request by saying, "That will be very difficult," our respondent says the manager means that it will never happen. Inexperienced leaders raised in the United States, he says, often take statements like that and interpret them literally as a challenge, responding with phrases such as "Well, if we work hard, we can make it happen." According to this interviewee, they are then surprised when nothing happens.

Our interviewees also reveal differences across cultures in the use of communication technologies, complementing previous research in this area (see Rice, D'Ambra, & More, 1998). One participant noted that when he electronically sends a list of issues for his Asian counterparts to consider, they will not respond to any of the issues until they have a response for *all* of the issues. He related the following:

> *This may be a cultural issue. When you do a 12 to 13 hour time*
> *zone difference, sometimes it is more convenient to collect a*
> *whole set of issues in one big e-mail. Well, the Taiwanese style of*
> *doing things has been that they won't answer anything until*
> *they've answered everything. It's a very long delay for an*
> *answer. We would prefer that they would answer the ones they*
> *can answer and get back to us on the others. (Worldwide Sales*
> *and Marketing Manager, Technology Sales Organization)*

In addition to varied interaction norms, our long-distance leaders report encountering distinct and often unfamiliar cultural norms during their conversations with those from other countries. One technology leader says that when she calls Europe, she sometimes can "hear cans being popped open…and they aren't soda cans! [beer] But, that's a cultural norm for them and that's okay," (Senior Project Manager, Technology Hardware Organization). A female executive (Vice President of Worldwide Procurement, Technology Sales Organization) who leads people over distance disclosed an additional cultural norm related to influence and gender. She noted that, in attempting to lead some Asian and Middle Eastern nationals who are located in their home countries, it is necessary to lead through a "third party," a male leader who may have lower status in the company yet who is seen as more credible as a leader because of his sex. In addition to gender, other national cultural norms related to appearance, holidays, and religious observations might differ between leader and long-distance employees, potentially causing leadership challenges if those norms are unrecognized.

Similarly, long-distance leaders' communication with those they lead from afar is complicated by differences in the ways business is conducted across cultures. One interviewee noted:

> *"When you are designing something, you need to have urgency so that you can own the marketplace. Some countries don't feel that urgency. They think about it for awhile, they are more reflective" (Senior Project Manager, Technology Hardware Organization).*

To unravel a culture's norms, the interviewees advise *taking the time to learn as much as one can before going in-country and to adapt communicative behaviors accordingly.* As one individual recalled:

> *We had the opportunity to take classes to learn about the culture and to learn about various business practices. I've watched some ugly Americans when they've engaged on a global basis. We seem to be more insensitive to it than people I've worked with from other countries. (Director of Worldwide Training, Technology Sales Organization)*

Another interviewee said that in order to deal with this difference, he adjusted when he initiates conversations with his French colleagues:

> *I don't ask the people I work with in France to do an 8 a.m. [France time]) conference call. If I do, I send the message that I don't understand when they do business. I try to do it later in the day or in the early evening because they are much more open to evenings than they are to mornings. (Worldwide Marketing Director, Technology Sales Organization)*

Along with different communication and business norms across cultures, long-distance leaders may interact with individuals whose first language is not English and with individuals from cultures that have different interpretations of nonverbal cues. For example, one interviewee remarked that Americans speak with many colloquialisms that do not translate (e.g., "Are we straight on that?" "I'm fixin' to begin work on the project tomorrow."). Misinterpretations may also be amplified across cultures when leaders do not convey their messages explicitly. People from other cultures may not pick up on the implicit meanings in U.S. leaders' messages, as exemplified in one interviewee's comments:

Once when we were working with the Irish, we said, "Here is an idea that you might think of implementing in your area." What we meant was, "Here's something I'd like to get your buy-in on because you really ought to do it." We were giving the Irish the soft sell. The Irish read our statement as "You're giving me an option." It went from a standard that they needed to implement to something that was an option simply by the way we chose the words. (Manager of Worldwide Operations, Technology Sales Organization)

The interviewees pointed out that long-distance leaders should *strive to understand what constitutes acceptable interaction in business contexts* and should pay careful attention to how the receiver might be interpreting the message. One interviewee cautioned:

Be very very careful that you are sure your words mean what you think they mean. Part of dealing with another country is knowing that what we see as healthy aggression may be construed as rudeness. (Senior Project Manager, Technology Hardware Organization)

Another interviewee provided an example of how that rudeness can be manifested in conversation:

In Japan, you really want to avoid saying things like, "No, we're not going to do that." The assertive, negative way of saying "No" is shocking to them. They don't do that. You have to find ways of saying "No" in a nice way. Or, to say that it is better for the business. (Director of Platform Development, Technology Sales Organization)

Some exchanges actually create humorous misunderstandings. One U.S. manager described driving a British colleague home after a party. The British engineer, visiting his team near London, at one point exclaimed to the U.S. manager that he was "really pissed." The manager, worried about what he might have said, stayed quiet for the rest of the trip. Only later did he learn that in the U.K., "pissed" is a slang word for having too much to drink.

Nonverbal cues may have different meanings across cultures. The interviewees noted the complexities of some nonverbal cues by offering two examples:

A nod has a different meaning across cultures than it does in the U.S. It could be "confusion"; it could be "I have no idea." International people do it because you don't put them on the spot anymore once you see them nodding. (Product Engineering Manager, Semi-Conductor Manufacturer)

When someone from Japan, for example, says "yes" and they physically bow, that means acknowledgment. Acknowledgment doesn't necessarily mean agreement. I learned that the hard way. You need to ask the question in a different way. Over e-mail, you can never quite understand if there's agreement unless you ask, "Are you going to do this tomorrow?" That's where the cultural differences come in. (Director of Worldwide Compensation, Technology Sales Organization)

The interviewees suggest *constantly seeking clarification* to help combat differences in language and in interpretations of nonverbal cues. And they advise that it is important to *clarify the other's answers to questions*. One interviewee offered: "Being able to 'play back' what people from another culture said, especially if English is not their first language, is really important. Saying 'this is what I think I heard you saying' is critical." In communicating across cultures, our leaders reported *using multiple examples to convey their ideas*. Offering only one example may foster misunderstanding.

Using Communication Technologies

The long-distance leaders we talked to prefer *using face-to-face communication to set vision, to reach policy decisions, and to begin to build relationships*. The interviewees overwhelmingly choose face-to-face communication as the most effective medium for shaping vision. They indicate various reasons for this, including the following:

- Face-to-face interaction accommodates leaders' needs to read body language in order to see if remote employees are buying into ideas.

- It enables remote employees to ask timely procedural questions.

- It allows leaders to immediately respond to remote employees' reactions.

  For vision and goals, there needs to be more of an exchange of understanding. Most of the people that we have worldwide have been here less than a year, so we wanted to give them a really good common level of understanding of [company's] vision. The best way to do that is get them together and let them say, 'I understand how we are doing this, but here are some of the concerns I have in the Asia-Pacific.' Face-to-face is critical. (Director of Worldwide Process Technologies, Technology Sales Organization)

Additionally, many of our respondents reported using face-to-face communication when major policy decisions must be made. Here, they indicated that the need for efficient conversation, for quickly exchanging pertinent data, and for negotiating power issues among relevant actors contribute to their desire for face-to-face interaction.

> *For decision making, face-to-face is absolutely critical. There are so many layers of decisions such as the immediate issue at hand, the other agendas that are involved in the decision, and the interpersonal stakeholders. There's data on both sides and it's really important to have a really efficient conversation. There's nothing more efficient than face-to-face. There's also the interpersonal stuff, the power stuff. People will demonize other people the further they are from them. The closer they are to them, the more they tend to see in almost all cases, there's a good intention there. When people don't talk to each other first face-to-face, they assign all kinds of negative attributions to the opponent. (Manager of Materials Engineering Technology, Technology Sales Organization)*

These long-distance leaders *use regularly scheduled telephone calls to exchange important task-related information, to maintain relationships, to appraise performance, and to coordinate teams.* Because leaders cannot always travel to regional sites, the telephone provides another rich medium through which to communicate. Not only does the telephone allow for quick exchange, but the respondents reported that it also allows them to maintain the relationship. They also noted the importance of paying attention to paralanguage in order to make assessments about their remote employees' affective sentiments. Along these lines, one interviewee underscored the role that telephone conversations play:

> *A good example would be you can't, over e-mail, understand somebody's mood. You can't hear the tone of their voice. For example, there was the recent earthquake in Taiwan. The guy who works for me there is a volunteer for the International Red Cross. I didn't realize that before he started working for me. At first, I didn't realize that he was pulling people out of buildings everyday and it wasn't until I talked to him on the phone, the Monday morning after the earthquake, that I really realized it because the guy sounded like he had been hit by a truck. And I said, "What's going on? Are you feeling all right?" That's when all of this stuff comes out. If it was just e-mail back and forth, I wouldn't have*

known. I wouldn't have known that he needed to get a lot of slack cut for him because he was working two jobs. (Director of Platform Development, Technology Sales Organization)

These experienced long-distance leaders *find the telephone more effective than e-mail to provide performance feedback and to coordinate teams.* They suggest that in order to perform both of these responsibilities successfully, leaders must allow for questions, feedback, and real-time exchange. For example, research shows that performance feedback, especially areas of improvement, should be given in a private, one-on-one setting, where the appraisee has the opportunity to respond and ask questions (Lee & Jablin, 1995). The telephone allows for that immediate exchange when face-to-face interaction is impossible, according to our respondents.

Another leader highlighted the advantages of telephone over less rich media, such as e-mail, by claiming that using the telephone results in greater interactivity and vocality. He noted:

You get some sense of how things are and instant feedback of how things are being interpreted. That very basic communication skill of playing back, "this is what I think I heard you say." You can do that regularly. And that's very important with people from different cultures. You need that to get to real communication. It [telephone] is two-way. E-mail seems two way, but it's not really two-way communication. (Vice President of Human Resources, Technology Sales Organization)

One challenge with using the telephone is different time zones. When it is 3 p.m. in Dallas, Texas, it is 5 a.m. in Tokyo and 10 p.m. in Frankfurt. Conference calls across long distances are problematic. Consequently, leaders often opt for e-mail. While it cannot replace face-to-face and the telephone for some functions, long-distance leaders report *successfully using e-mail to exchange technical information, to give specific directions, to update interested parties, and to maintain relationships.* One interviewee found e-mail to be particularly good at sending technical directions when all recipients of the message understand the overall objective. Several interviewees advise being as detailed and specific with directions as possible to minimize the potential for misinterpretation. Moreover, with individuals who speak different languages, the respondents articulate that *communication is more efficacious when the communicator uses multiple examples and literally over-communicates.* E-mail messages are also sometimes better understood than oral communication, because most people have better skills at reading a language such as English than they have in understanding oral delivery of messages.

Interviewees also remark that e-mail is an efficient way to update team members. For example, when a European manufacturer gives information about when a shipment will be going out, the leader at corporate headquarters will "fan" their e-mail to everyone involved with that project. Everyone wants to know that information, and e-mail is an efficient means by which to share it. One interviewee shares that his geographically dispersed team uses e-mail after face-to-face or computer-mediated meetings in order to brainstorm action items for their next face-to-face or virtual meeting. Yet several of our respondents caution against relying solely on e-mail to send important, detailed information. They recommend *a follow-up telephone call to ensure that these messages were acknowledged.* This relates to why they found e-mail to be a successful tool for monitoring and assessing performance:

> *To monitor and assess effectively, you need to know lots of things. It's not simply "how many did you build today?" It's "how can we build that many?" What I have found is that when it is simply a matter of facts, personal interactions can be less efficient, because you end up talking about stuff that is off the point. You get everything about "how's your weekend?" if the answer is longer than "fine." Finding time when we can meet can delay things. In monitoring and assessing, you don't want to delay. (Supply Manager, Technology Hardware Organization)*

E-mail is a suitable tool for maintaining relationships, according to our informants. One interviewee commented on using e-mail to fill the social void of "you never write, you never call" (Manager of Materials Engineering Technology, Energy Company).

Incorporating brief relational messages such as "how was your daughter's football tournament?" into an e-mail, every so often, helps *create the social presence that is taken for granted in traditional offices.*

> *I think for executives especially, that have eight to 10 meetings per day, are working six to seven days a week, get 100 e-mails a day, always on airplanes, even scheduling a 15 minute phone call is tough. This is a quick way to let someone know that you thought of them during the day. That's a positive. (Director of Technical Support Services, Technology Sales Organization)*

But initiating the relationship is only part of the long-distance leadership puzzle. Our leaders reported tactics they use in order to nurture the relationship. E-mail and other computer-mediated communication channels are efficient tools, but, according to the interviewees, these media are more effective after a relationship has been established:

> *E-mail is a wonderful communication efficiency tool when it is used on top of an established relationship, but it is a lousy tool at establishing a good relationship. The relationship doesn't get built there. E-mail builds on top of a relationship to make things more efficient. (Director of Worldwide Process Technologies, Technology Sales Organization)*

Yet several interviewees *caution against using e-mail to handle emotionally charged relationship issues*. For instance, some interviewees note that they find conflict is handled best through a channel other than e-mail. These informants found that individuals will react more strongly to e-mail that they perceive negatively than they will to a message delivered over the phone or in person:

> *It is very difficult with tone in e-mail. So, when things are off track or off expectation, people personalize e-mail frequently. So, they'll read something into it that you didn't mean. You have to be very careful with that. You start to see defensive behavior. On the phone, if you sense that is happening, you have a chance to meet. (Technical Manager of Research & Development, Energy Company)*

One interviewee comments that when people are upset, they tend to read into the written text based on their own perspectives. This attribution serves to augment conflict instead of rectify it. Not only do emotions flare, individuals also may forward that e-mail to others in the organization, thereby intensifying the disagreement further. Conflict, and other emotionally charged issues, should not, according to the interviewees, be dealt with over e-mail. And, as one interviewee reported, e-mail can delay progress:

> *Typically, we abuse e-mail. People have the feeling that when they hit the "enter" key, they are done. People don't know how to use "reply," "reply all," "cc." So you've got all this traffic flying around and it lengthens the cycle. Asia is 13 hours away from us. You could send out an e-mail and because it was so poorly written, what you get back are questions or statements of misunderstandings. The cycle time for resolution of the problem grows. (Worldwide Systems Manager, Technology Sales Organization)*

Future Trends

As business becomes more global, as talent becomes more dispersed, and as technology enables people to do far more from afar, the challenges of leading from a distance will only increase. Highlighted in this chapter are many of the issues distance leaders face and hinted at are some possible solutions. Our objectives for this chapter were to explicate what organizational leaders do to overcome the inherent isolation of distanced work relationships (see Appendix for Checklist of Distanced Leadership "Do's" and "Don't's"). We argued that distanced relationships exacerbate feelings of isolation and distrust. We contended further that these feelings are amplified by cultural differences and technology that may or may not restrict communication.

To make sense of this complex leadership process, we advance a stage model of distance leadership (see Figure 1). In the "initial" stage, face-to-face communication is important, particularly for building trust. Face-to-face communication is also critical because it allows all parties to come to understand the various nuances of one another. In the "maintenance" stage, continued communication is necessary. Communication technologies are useful here and can be the predominant channel of communication. But, even after leaders and followers established relationships, occasional face-to-face communication remains critical.[3]

In reflecting on our findings, it is possible that trust is experienced differently in global, virtual organizations than it is in geographically proximate settings. For instance, perhaps instead of emerging from personal relationships as it often does in geographically proximate contexts, trust in some virtual organizations (especially those with finite life spans) may emanate from people's shared goals or deadlines. When project teams are under strict timelines, trust must get built quickly or it does not get built at all. This notion, explicated in the theory of "swift

Figure 1.   Stage Model of Long-Distance Leadership

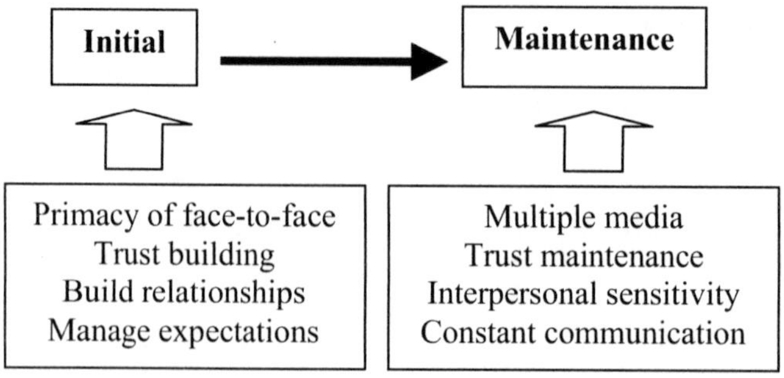

Initial	→	Maintenance

Primacy of face-to-face Trust building Build relationships Manage expectations	Multiple media Trust maintenance Interpersonal sensitivity Constant communication

trust" (Meyerson, Weick, & Kramer, 1996), applies to teams with members who have a limited history of working together and are unlikely to work together in the future, yet share an impending deadline that requires their coordination. The challenge is that in situations calling for "swift trust," members make attributions about behaviors based on stereotypes (Meyerson et al., 1996), attributions that could be dangerous in cross-cultural contexts, where interactants may have limited or even inaccurate perceptions of the "other" culture, and where the opportunities for deep face-to-face interactions are lacking. Whereas traditional theories of trust focus on the construct's interpersonal and relational dimensions, the realities of some global virtual organizations may call on leaders, as Jarvenpaa and Leidner (1998) suggest, to thoughtfully wrestle with slightly different conceptualizations of trust. Future research should focus on the critical place of routines in distanced relationships, the importance of systems that enhance coordination when working from afar, and the centrality of focused goals for trust in dispersed workforces.

An agenda for future scholarship would also include the development of theoretical models of distanced leadership as well as stronger empirical work on the suggestions we make in this chapter. Conceptually, the study of distanced leadership lacks an integrative theoretical model. Some of the issues we highlight in this chapter may serve as constituent elements of such a theory. For instance, when it comes to scope conditions for a theory, it is important to understand that physical distance *per se* does not define a virtual relationship. Instead, it is *physical distance* and *access* that together create a distanced relationship. Additionally, we argue that any distanced relationship faces, as primary challenges, isolation and trust. The sense of isolation combined with threats to trust creates opportunities for conflict, poor communication, and a lack of identification with teams.

One important theoretical issue is the presumption made by many that distanced teams have more difficulty than face-to-face teams. That may or may not be true. Throughout our research, the interviewees were insistent that face-to-face exchanges offer them the optimal medium for communication. E-mail and telephone calls were regarded as necessary and helpful, but for some important leadership challenges, not preferred. No leader in our study saw mediated technologies as optimal for personnel issues, conflicts, and relational development. These responses may be tied to experience, training, and generational differences. It is possible that as people become wiser about using various technologies for communication that the presumed primacy of face-to-face interactions may fade. In fact, some people prefer mediated technologies today for some leadership functions (e.g., scheduling). It will be interesting, as new technologies blossom and people's comfort and familiarity with them increases, to see whether the universal preference of managers for face-to-face exchanges remains.

In this project, we focused on what people assigned to manage and lead virtual teams do to successfully accomplish their leadership goals. In many cases, virtual teams also develop informal leaders. It would be interesting to examine how these emergent leaders operate and how their emergence shapes team activities. One thing that is clear in the research we conducted is that you cannot manage a distanced team the same ways you manage a face-to-face team. The opportunities for communication, for monitoring, for feedback, and for just about every other leadership function, are limited in distanced settings. In addition, there are probably teams where there is no reporting relationship between members and an assigned leader. Future research should look at these sorts of teams and their dynamics.

Additionally, the evidence for what we discussed in this chapter came from a series of interviews with people one might consider experts. All participants had experience leading distanced teams. Their ideas and anecdotes offered insights into both the challenges and possible solutions for successfully leading distanced teams. What remains is for larger, more data-based studies to probe whether the issues and suggestions summarized in this chapter are valid.

Conclusion

Our results allow us to make two general conclusions about long-distance leadership. First, successful long-distance leaders internalize the importance of initially building relationships. The centrality of building relationships also means that communication is at the heart of leading over distance. The difference seems to be, however, that in distanced settings, the communication needed for leaders to build and maintain relationships has to be planned, programmatic, and consciously built into the leader's routine. Through the programmatic use of tactics such as organizational stories and other corporate cultural tools, leaders enhance distanced employees' mental pictures of the organization, and in the process, minimize the isolation and distrust that those at a distance sometimes feel.

Second, in order to execute leadership functions successfully, leaders must choose the appropriate communication channel. New communication technologies make leading over distance possible. They are not a panacea, however. As this study has shown, certain leadership objectives require some degree of face-to-face communication. Results of our study also reveal that social/relational communication plays a critical role in executing leadership tasks over distance, especially in preventing feelings of isolation. This finding suggests that long-distance leaders should integrate relational communication into their mediated and face-to-face interactions with distanced employees.

References

Bell, R., & Daly, J. A. (1984). The affinity seeking function of communication. *Communication Monographs, 51,* 91–115.

Benson-Armer, R., & Hsieh, T. (1997). Teamwork across time and space. *The McKinsey Quarterly, 4,* 18–27.

Bradach, J. L., & Eccles, R. G. (1989). Price, authority, and trust: From ideal types to plural forms. *Annual Review of Sociology, 15,* 97–118.

Browning, L. D. (1992). Lists and stories as organizational communication. *Communication Theory, 2,* 281–302.

Cascio, W. F. (1999). Virtual workplaces: Implications for organizational behavior. In C. L. Cooper & D. M. Rousseau (Eds.), *Trends in Organizational Behavior* (pp. 1–14). Chichester: John Wiley & Sons.

Cummings, L. L., & Bromiley, P. (1996). The organizational trust inventory (OTI): Development and validation. In R. M. Kramer & T. R. Tyler (Eds.), *Trust in Organizations: Frontiers of Theory and Research* (pp. 302–330). Thousand Oaks, CA: Sage.

Dainton, M., & Stafford, L. (1993). Routine maintenance behaviors: A comparison of relationship type, partner similarity, and sex differences. *Journal of Social and Personal Relationships, 10,* 255–271.

Davenport, T. H., & Pearlson, K. (1998). Two cheers for the virtual office. *Sloan Management Review, 39,* 51–65.

Duarte, D. L., & Snyder, N. T. (1999). *Mastering Virtual Teams: Strategies, Tools, and Techniques that Succeed.* San Francisco, CA: Jossey-Bass.

Fisher, K., & Fisher, M. D. (2001). *The Distance Manager: A Hands-On Guide to Managing Off-Site Employees and Virtual Teams.* New York: McGraw-Hill.

Geber, B. (1995). Virtual teams. *Training, 32*(4), 36–40.

Handy, C. (1995, May–June). Trust and the virtual organization. *Harvard Business Review,* 40–50.

Haywood, M. (1998). *Managing Virtual Teams: Practical Techniques for High-Technology Project Managers.* Boston, MA: Artech House.

Hymowitz, C. (1999, 6 April). Remote managers find ways to narrow the distance gap. *The Wall Street Journal*, p. B1.

Jarvenpaa, S., & Leidner, D. E. (1998). Communication and trust in global virtual teams. *Journal of Computer-Mediated Communication, 3.*

Jarvenpaa, S., Knoll, K., & Leidner, D. E. (1998). Is anybody out there? Antecedents of trust in global virtual teams. *Journal of Management Systems, 14,* 29–64.

Kayworth, T. R., & Leidner, D. E. (2002). Leadership effectiveness in global virtual teams. *Journal of Management Information Systems, 18,* 7–40.

Knapp, M. L., & Vangelisti, A. L. (2000). *Interpersonal Communication and Human Relationships* (4th ed.). Boston, MA: Allyn & Bacon.

Lee, J., & Jablin, F. M. (1995). Maintenance communication in superior–subordinate work relationships. *Human Communication Research, 22,* 220–257.

Lipnack, J., & Stamps, J. (1997). *Virtual Teams: Reaching Across Space, Time, and Organizations with Technology.* New York: John Wiley & Sons.

Lowry, J. S. (1998). *Alternative work arrangements: The effects of distance and media use on the supervisor–subordinate relationship.* Unpublished doctoral dissertation, Rice University.

Lurey, J. S. (1998). *A study of best practices in designing and supporting effective virtual teams.* Unpublished doctoral dissertation, California School of Professional Psychology–Los Angeles.

Majchrzak, A., Rice, R. E., Malhotra, A., & King, N. (2000). Technology adaptation: The case of a computer-supported inter-organizational virtual team. *MIS Quarterly, 24,* 569–600.

Meyerson, D., Weick, K. E., & Kramer, R. M. (1996). Swift trust and temporary groups. In R. M. Kramer & T. R. Tyler (Eds.), *Trust in Organizations: Frontiers of Theory and Research* (pp. 166–195). Thousand Oaks, CA: Sage.

Mowshowitz, A. (1997). Virtual organization. *Communications of the ACM, 40,* 30–37.

Nelson, B. (1998). Recognizing employees from a distance. *Manage, 50*(1), 8–9.

Nilles, J. M. (1998). *Managing Telework: Strategies for Managing the Virtual Workforce.* New York: John Wiley & Sons.

O'Hara-Devereaux, M., & Johansen, R. (1994). *Global Work: Bridging Distance, Culture, & Time.* San Francisco, CA: Jossey-Bass.

Pauleen, D., & Yoong, P. (2001). Relationship building and the use of ICT in boundary-crossing virtual teams: A facilitator's perspective. *Journal of Information Technology, 16,* 205–220.

Powell, W. W. (1990). Neither market nor hierarchy: Network forms of organizations. *Research in Organizational Behavior, 12,* 295–336.

Rice, R. E., D'Ambra, J., & More, E. (1998, Summer). Cross-cultural comparison of organizational media evaluation and media choice. *Journal of Communication,* 3–26.

Scott, C. R., Frank, V., Cornetto, K. M., Sullivan, C., & Forster, B. (1999). *Communication technology use and key outcomes in novice groups: A comparison of site and virtual teams.* Paper presented at the Annual Conference of the National Communication Association, Chicago, Illinois, USA.

Snow, C. C., Snell, S. A., & Davison, S. C. (1996). Use transnational teams to globalize your company. *Organizational Dynamics, 24,* 50–67.

Staples, D. S. (1996). *An investigation of some key information technology-enabled remote management and remote work issues.* Conference proceedings of the Australasian Conference on Information Systems. University of Tasmania, Hobart, Australia.

Tepper, B. J. (1995). Upward maintenance tactics in supervisory mentoring and nonmentoring relationships. *Academy of Management Journal, 38,* 1191–1205.

Townsend, A. M., DeMarie, S. M., & Hendrickson, A. R. (1998). Virtual teams: Technology and the workplace of the future. *Academy of Management Executive, 12,* 17–29.

Upton, D. M., & McAfee, A. (1996, July–August). The real factory. *Harvard Business Review,* 123–133.

Van Aken, J. E., Hop, L., & Post, G. J. J. (1998). The virtual organization: A special mode of strong interorganizational cooperation. In M. A. Hitt, J. E. Ricart, I. Costa, & R. D. Nixon (Eds.), *Managing Strategically in an Interconnected World.* Chichester, UK: John Wiley & Sons.

Walther, J. B. (1994). Anticipated ongoing interaction versus channel effects on relational communication in computer-mediated interaction. *Human Communication Research, 20,* 473–501.

Warkentin, M. E., Sayeed, L., & Hightower, R. (1997). Virtual teams versus face-to-face teams: An exploratory study of a web-based conference system. *Decision Sciences, 28,* 975–996.

Wiesenfeld, B. M., Raghuram, S., & Garud, R. (1999). Communication patterns as determinants of identification in a virtual organization. *Organization Science, 10,* 777–790.

Yukl, G. (1989). Managerial leadership: A review of theory and research. *Journal of Management, 15,* 251–289.

Endnotes

[1]   The data for this chapter come from semistructured, extended interviews conducted with organizational leaders who frequently lead from afar. Twenty-one leaders with global responsibilities in technology organizations were interviewed. All participants were executives or divisional directors who were at the time leading globally remote employees. We conceive of "remote workers" as those organizational members located in a different building than their leader or manager. Under this definition, remote workers could be across the city, state, or country from their leader. In this chapter, we focus on instances where the remote workers are located across the globe. The organizations included a large hardware manufacturer, an integrated computer company, an energy company, two semiconductor manufacturers, and a military unit.

[2]   Following Jarvenpaa and Leidner (1998) and Cummings and Bromiley (1996), we conceptualize trust between a long-distance organizational member and leader as the belief that the other individual is genuinely trying to follow through on their commitments; the assumption that the other individual is being honest; and the faith that one person will not take advantage of the other when the opportunity arises.

[3]   The model resembles, conceptually, work in interpersonal communication that suggests that romantic relationships move from an affinity development stage (Bell & Daly, 1984) to more of a maintenance stage (Dainton & Stafford, 1993) as well as work done on various interpersonal relationships in organizations, such as mentoring (Tepper, 1995) and supervisor-subordinate interactions (Lee & Jablin, 1995), which both highlight the importance of maintenance behaviors.

Appendix

Discipline of Distanced Leadership Checklist

Long-Distance Leaders Should:

- Devote time to building and maintaining relationships with those they lead over distance
- Communicate face to face at the beginning of a relationship
- Make periodic planned and spontaneous visits to remote sites
- Provide opportunities for representatives of remote sites to visit headquarters periodically
- Engage in small talk with distanced individuals in face-to-face settings *and* in computer-mediated exchanges when appropriate
- Regularly distribute company-wide information to remote employees (e.g., a virtual newsletter)
- Notify long-distance employees of news that affects them at the same time as local employees receive the news
- Match the appropriate communication technology to the desired leadership objective
- Be specific and detailed with directions given over e-mail
- Initiate follow-up phone calls to important e-mail messages
- Forward e-mail messages only to relevant parties
- Delete unnecessary parts of a previous message when forwarding or replying
- Be cautious of the use of "reply"—are you replying to one individual or a list?

Long-Distance Leaders Should Not:

- Deliver bad news through an e-mail
- Use American colloquialisms with foreign nationals, especially in e-mail
- Use e-mail to discuss emotionally charged issues (e.g., disagreements, conflict)
- Assume that once an e-mail message is sent, it will be read and understood
- Relate information only one time and in only one way

- Always travel to remote sites or expect remote individuals to always travel to headquarters
- Disclose pertinent information to local individuals before distanced individuals
- Assume that meanings are shared
- Allow e-mail interaction to completely replace telephone/teleconference interaction

Chapter VI

Toward Integration of Artifacts, Resources and Processes for Virtual Teams

Schahram Dustdar
Vienna University of Technology, Austria

Abstract

Over the last years most business processes changed in various dimensions (e.g., flexibility, interconnectivity, coordination style, autonomy) due to market conditions, organizational models, and usage scenarios of information systems. Virtual teams are under heavy pressure to increase time-to-market of their products and services and lower their coordination costs. A fundamental need for distributed virtual teamwork is to have access to contextual information, i.e., to see a "knowledge trail" of who did what, when, how, and why. In this chapter, we discuss underlying conceptual issues and one implemented information system (Caramba®) to support the integration of artifacts, resources, and business processes for virtual teams.

Introduction

Over the last years, most business processes changed in various dimensions (e.g., flexibility, interconnectivity, coordination style, autonomy) (e.g., Zeng et al., 2001) due to market conditions, organizational models, and usage scenarios of information systems. Generally, one can witness a trend toward decreasing hierarchical organizational forms and moving to flatter organizational structures. The question of the "right" organizational form and the appropriate information systems support remains of paramount importance and still constitutes a challenge for virtually all organizations, regardless of industrial background. Organizations distribute their required work activities among a group of people (teams), with teams constituting the main building block for implementing the work (tasks). In most cases, team members are organized as "virtual (project) teams." These teams are under heavy pressure to increase time-to-market of their products and services and lower their coordination costs. Some characteristics of distributed virtual teams are that team (member) configurations change frequently and that team members report to different managers, maybe even of different organizations. From an information systems' point of view, distributed virtual teams are often self-configuring networks of mobile and "fixed" people, devices, as well as applications. A newly emerging requirement is to facilitate not just mobility of content (i.e., to support a multitude of devices and connectivity modes) to team members, but also to provide contextual information on work activities to all distributed virtual team members (Dustdar, 2002a, b, c).

By context, we mean traceable and continuous views of associations (relationships) between artifacts (e.g., documents, database records), resources (e.g., people, roles, skills), and business processes. Context is composed of information on the "who, when, how, and why." In order to illustrate the lack of context in information systems currently in use by virtual teams, consider an "Explorer"-like view on a file system. This view allows the person to see documents (artifacts) stored inside folders. The names of such folders might reflect project names. The mentioned view on these documents does not contain further contextual information on what any virtual team member actually has to do (did) with it (e.g., create another document, send an e-mail to a customer, call a partner organization, etc.). For example, if the team member in the above example needs to see who received a document stored in any given (project) folder, he is required to manually retrieve his e-mail box in order to find this information. This simple example shows that relationships (links) between artifacts, such as documents or database information, and work activities performed by team members are usually not stored in groupware, project management, or workflow management systems. However, this linkage is of paramount importance for knowledge-intense business processes of virtual teams, in order to provide contextual information on knowledge artifacts for processes such as new product development, which cannot be modeled using a traditional workflow management system.

The remainder of this chapter is organized as follows: the next section provides an overview of related work on classification systems of collaborative systems and provides an overview on evaluation aspects of current collaborative systems for virtual teamwork. Discussed in the third section are some issues and problems related to the integration of artifacts, resources, and processes. In the fourth section, one proposed solution is presented. Finally, in the last section, some future trends are discussed and the chapter is concluded.

Functional Classification of Collaborative Systems

There has been a lot of work on classification models for collaborative systems. However, there is no "one and agreed upon" taxonomy of analyzing and understanding collaborative systems. Academia and industry suggest various classification schemes. In industry, for example, people frequently use the term e-mail and groupware interchangeably. More generally, there is the tendency to classify categories of collaborative systems by naming a product (e.g., many use the term Lotus Notes® and groupware interchangeably). Academic research has suggested many different classification models. For a recent survey of collaborative application taxonomies, see Bafoutsou and Mentzas (2002). DeSanctis and Gallupe (1987), Ellis, Gibbs, and Rein (1991), and Johansen (1988) suggested a two-dimensional matrix based on time and place, where they differentiate between systems' usage at the same place/same time (e.g., electronic meeting rooms), the same place/different time (e.g., newsgroups), a different place/different time (e.g., workflow, e-mail), and a different place/same time (audio/videoconferencing, shared editors). This classification model helps us to easily analyze many tools on the market today; however, it fails to provide detailed insights on collaborative work activities as well as their relationships to business processes. Ellis (2000) provided a functionally oriented taxonomy of collaborative systems, which assists in understanding the integration issues of workflow and groupware systems and is shown in Table 1.

The classification system of Ellis (2000) provides a framework with which to understand the characteristics of collaborative systems and their technical implementations. The first category (Keepers) provides those functionalities related to storage and access to shared data (persistency). The metaphor used

Table 1.   Collaborative Systems Taxonomy

Taxonomy	Metaphor	Characteristics
Keepers	Shared Workspace, Database	Access control, artifacts versioning, backup, recovery, and concurrency control.
Communicators	Messaging (point-to-point)	Supports explicit communications between participants.
Coordinators	Coordination and Organizational Model	Handles the ordering and synchronization of activities.
Team-Agents	Agent (Application or User-Interface agents)	Provide domain-specific functionalities, such as a meeting scheduler.

for systems based on this category is a "shared workspace." A shared workspace is basically a central repository where all team members put (upload) shared artifacts (in most cases, documents) and share those among the team members. Technical characteristics of "keepers" include database features, access control, versioning, and backup and recovery control. Popular systems examples include BSCW (Bentley et al., 1997), IBM®/Lotus® TeamRoom (IBM, 2002) and the Peer-to-Peer workspace system GROOVE® (Groove, 2002).

The second category (Communicators) groups all functionality related to explicit communications among team members. Basically, this boils down to messaging systems (e-mail). Its fundamental nature is a point-to-point interaction model, where team members are identified only by their names (e-mail address) and not by other means (e.g., by skills, roles, or other constructs, as in some advanced workflow systems). The third category (Coordinators) is related to ordering and synchronizing individual activities that make up a whole process. Examples of Coordinator systems include workflow management systems. Finally, the fourth category (Team-Agents,) refers to (semi)intelligent software components that perform domain-specific functions and thereby help the group dynamics. An example for this category is a meeting scheduler agent. Most systems in this category are not off-the-shelf standard software.

Both evaluation models presented above provide guidance to virtual teams on how to evaluate products based on the frameworks. Current systems for virtual teamwork have their strengths in one or two categories of Ellis' framework. Most systems on the market today provide features for *Keepers* and *Communicators* support or are solely *Coordinator* systems (e.g., Workflow Management Systems) or are *Team-Agents*. To the best of our knowledge, there is no system in which at least three of the above categories are integrated in one system. In the following section, we evaluate current collaborative systems categories for their usage in virtual teams and summarize their shortcomings in respect to the requirement for virtual teamwork.

Evaluation of Collaborative Systems for Virtual Teamwork

Cooperative tasks in virtual teams are increasing, and as a consequence, the use of collaborative systems is becoming more pervasive. In recent years, it has become increasingly difficult to categorize systems according to the frameworks discussed above, because systems boundaries have become increasingly fuzzy and because of recent requirements for virtual teamwork. Traditional systems in the area of interest to virtual teamwork are groupware, project management (PM), and workflow management systems (WfMS). The mentioned systems categories are based on different "metaphors." Groupware systems can mainly be categorized along two lines (metaphors), namely, the *communications* or *workspace* metaphor.

Communications-oriented groupware supports unstructured work activities using communications as the underlying interaction pattern. One popular instance of communications-oriented groupware is e-mail. When e-mail is used as the main medium for virtual teams (as in most cases), data and associated information (such as attachments) remain on central mail servers or in personal in-boxes without any *contextual* information on which those e-mail communications were used (involved business processes, performed activities, created artifacts, as described above). Enterprise groupware systems are generally focused on enterprise-wide messaging and discussion databases and do not support organizational components and structures, such as people and their associated roles, groups, tasks, skills, etc. This leads to "organizationally unaware" systems treating all messages alike (semantically), without any awareness of underlying business processes, which are essential for efficient collaboration in project teams.

Workspace-oriented groupware, on the other hand, allows team members to upload and download artifacts using files and folders to organize their work. Groupware, as indicated above, usually does not implement an underlying organizational model (i.e., providing information on the structure of a team such as team members and their roles, skills, tasks, and responsibilities). The lack of explicit organizational "structuring" is a disadvantage as well as an advantage. It is disadvantageous because traditional groupware has no "hooks" for integrating business process information, which is important in order to integrate artifacts, resources, and processes. This will be discussed in more depth in the next section. The advantage of the lack of explicit organizational structure information is the fact that such systems may be used in all organizational settings without much prior configuration efforts, and second, this leads to increased personal flexibility, as the proliferation of e-mail systems in teamwork demonstrates.

The second category, which we will briefly investigate in this section includes *project management systems*. As stated above, virtual teamwork is in most cases organized as project work. Projects have well-defined goals and are defined by their *begin* and *end* dates as well as by the required resources and their tasks (work breakdown structure). It is interesting to note, however, that PM systems traditionally support the work of the project manger as the main (and only) user of the PM system. They do not support dynamic interaction (instantiation) of processes. More recently, project management systems combine with information-sharing tools (shared workspaces) to provide a persistent storage for artifacts. The enactment of the task by team members, as being defined by the project manager, is not supported by PM systems. In other words, we can conclude that PM systems are not geared toward virtual teamwork but are focused more on the planning aspect. They provide "static" snapshots (usually in the form of Gannt charts) of projects and how they "should" be. There is no support for the work activities performed by the virtual team members.

The purpose of *workflow management systems* is to support the notion of processes within, and in some cases between, organizations (Aalst & Kumar, 2001; Bolcer, 2000; Bussler, 1999). However, WfMS requires that a model of a business process (build time) first be created and then this model should be enacted (run time). This leads to substantial inflexibility (Ellis, Keddara, & Rozenberg 1995) for virtual teams. In business, "exceptions are the rule"; therefore, modeling a process (project) is often not possible for creative,

Table 2. Evaluation of Collaborative Systems

	Requirements for Virtual Teams			
Current Technology Support	Device Independence (Content Adaptation)	Process-Awareness: Traceability of Work Activities	Integration of Artifacts, Resources, Processes	Organizational Awareness
Synchronous Communications (e.g., audio/videoconferencing)	2	1	1	1
Asynchronous Communications (e.g., e-mail messaging)	5	4	1	1
Synchronous Collaboration (e.g., shared editing groupware)	3	1	1	1
Asynchronous Collaboration (e.g., workspace groupware)	3	2	2	2
Asynchronous Coordination (e.g., workflow systems)	4	4 (modeled processes)	2	5

Legend: Scale on 1 to 5 with 5 indicating full support and 1 no support for the analyzed requirement

innovative virtual teams of knowledge workers, such as in product development or consulting teams. A business process can be unstructured (ad hoc), semistructured, or highly structured (modeled). For example, a business process such as "customer order entry" can be modeled using a traditional WfMS. However, *highly structured* processes can only be enacted (instantiated) as they were designed. If an exception occurs, a workflow administrator needs to remodel the process before the execution can continue. This limits the usability of WfMS in a world where constant adaptation to new situations is necessary, and where teams are increasingly mobile and distributed. An example of an ad hoc process is discussion of a project's design review using Groupware. A *semistructured* process consists of groups of activities, which are modeled; however, in contrast to a structured (modeled) process, it may also consist of activities, which are not predefined. A process is semistructured when there might be one or more activities between already modeled activities such as *assign process*, which are not known beforehand and therefore cannot be modeled in advance.

In Table 2, we combine the two classification systems (discussed in the second section) and provide an example for each category based on our experience and evaluation of how virtual teams work. The columns depict those requirements we consider essential for virtual teams. It is important to note that requirements for virtual teamwork do not follow the traditional boundaries of systems presented above. We summarize our evaluation of technologies supporting virtual teamwork in a classification matrix using a simple scale from 1 to 5 indicating no support (1) or full support (5) for the requirements we consider essential for virtual teams. Basically, we differentiate between synchronous and asynchronous technologies for teamwork support. For each category, we provide a well-known example system. During our case study requirements analysis, we came to the conclusion that distributed product development in virtual communities requires a blend of synchronous and asynchronous systems support for communications, as well as basic support for asynchronous coordination of team members and their activities.

To summarize, the requirements for virtual teams cannot simply be met by using a combination of traditional synchronous and asynchronous systems, because the criteria for successful systems in this area differ substantially compared to traditional "enterprise information systems." We identified and implemented (see the fourth section) four fundamental feature sets for our virtual team software (device independence; process awareness; integration of artifacts, resources, and processes; organizational awareness). Most systems on the market do not cater to the requirements of virtual teams, namely, *dynamic views of relationships* between artifacts, resources, and process awareness are vital to the work organization of virtual teamwork.

On the Integration of Artifacts, Resources and Processes

Organizations increasingly define the work activities to be fulfilled in "virtual teams," where team members from within the organization cooperate (communicate and coordinate work activities) with outside experts and therefore form virtual teams, which in many cases operate as geographically dispersed teams. In fact, team members work on business processes; however, in many instances, team members view their works as a "project" and not necessarily as part of a larger business process fulfilling a business goal in a larger context. The work of virtual team members often results in artifacts (e.g., documents) that need to be shared among virtual team members.

The underlying assumption of this chapter is that *process awareness* is increasingly important to virtual teams. Teamwork is a fundamental property of many business processes. Business processes have well-defined inputs and outputs and serve meaningful purposes within or between organizations. Business processes in general and their corresponding workflows in particular exist as logical models (e.g., weighted directed graphs). When business process models are executed, they have specific instances. A business process consists of a sequence of work activities. An activity is a distinct process step and may be performed by a human agent or by a machine (or software). A workflow management system enacts the real-world business process for each process instance (Craven & Mahling, 1995; Dayal et al., 2001; Schal, 1996). Any activity may consist of one or more tasks. A set of tasks to be worked on by a user (human agent or machine) is called a work list. The work list is managed by the WfMS. The WfMC (WfMC, 1995) calls the individual task on the work list a work item. Software systems for workflow management, Groupware, process modeling (e.g., Puustjärvi & Laine, 2001), and project management were used to automate or to augment business processes in organizations (Casati, Sayal, & Shan, 2001; Hausleitner & Dustdar, 1999).

Workflow management systems were defined as "technology based systems that define, manage, and execute workflow processes through the execution of software whose order of execution is driven by a computer representation of the workflow process logic" (WfMC, 1995). Workflow systems generally aim at helping organizations' team members to communicate, coordinate, and collaborate effectively as well as efficiently. Therefore, WfMS possess temporal aspects such as activity sequencing, deadlines, routing conditions, and schedules. WfMS are typically "organizationally aware," because they contain explicit representations of organizational processes (process model). However, traditional WfMS present a rigid work environment consisting of *roles* and their associated *activities and applications*. In this context, they do not provide support for virtual teams, such as frequently changing process participants, ad hoc formation of groups collaborating on a business process, and device-independent support of group activities.

Unfortunately, today's WfMS assume that each *work item* is executed by a *single* worker (Aalst & Kumar, 2001). Most WfMS focus on automating structured (modeled) intraorganizational business processes. Groupware, on the other hand, typically does not contain any knowledge or representation of the *goals* or underlying business *processes* of the group. Table 3 depicts results from a recent study on virtual teamwork (Akademie für Führungskräfte, 2002), where problems associated with virtual teamwork were identified. The authors interviewed 376 team members of various industrial backgrounds on their experiences in virtual teamwork. Current collaborative systems such as Groupware, PM, and WfMS do not cater for the requirements that virtual teams are challenged with, as mentioned in Table 3.

We argue that, considering the top three problems occurring in virtual teamwork (Table 3), increasing contextual information in the form of building *relationships between artifacts, resources, and business processes* solves the fundamental problems and, as an implication, the most dominant problems such as "difficulties in team communications" and "unclear work activities." Our approach for integration of artifacts, resources, and processes is comprised of a communications and coordination building block, where team members exchange "enriched" messages. Workflow research has shown that modeling organizational structures has substantial benefits for business processes. Therefore, we allow modeling of organizational constructs such as groups, roles, skills, and organizational units. Each team member can be associated to those constructs, as shown

Table 3.   Problems in Virtual Teamwork

Problems	Occurrence in %
Difficulties in team communications	97.0
Unclear work activities	94.3
Lack of collaborative culture	91.0
Implicit team conflicts	90.2
Lack of trust	90.2
Power struggles	87.8
Inefficient team meetings	84.8
No team calendar	79.6
Dominating personal interests	69.2
Unclear organizational hierarchies	56.9
Open conflicts	52.9
Lack of time	47.8

in the fourth section. Furthermore, an integrated database allows for database objects to be attached to the communications and coordination activities of virtual team members, enabling integration of resources (organizational constructs) and artifacts. The process modeling component allows directed graphs consisting of tasks and their relationships with organizational constructs to be created. The next section, therefore, discusses implementation issues on how to make context information (e.g., information about process instances, the team configuration); (i.e., participants and their roles), their associated artifacts, and connectivity modes of group members (such as fixed, mobile, or ad hoc) accessible to all virtual team members.

The Case of an Integrated Interaction Management System for Virtual Teams

In the following section, we will provide an overview of integration issues we are concerned with while designing an integrated system for virtual teams called *Caramba*® (Caramba Labs, 2002). An in-depth presentation of the architecture or the components is beyond the scope and focus of this chapter and can be found in the literature (Dustdar, 2002a, 2002b, 2002c; Hausleitner & Dustdar, 1999).

The Caramba® software architecture is composed of multiple layers: middleware, client suite, and a persistence store. Objects and services are accessed through the Transparent Access Layer (TAL) from the CarambaSpace platform (middleware). Depending on access mechanisms and the requested services (e.g., via Java client with RMI protocol or via Web browser with http), Caramba provides a unique way to handle requests using a metamodel framework to describe content and separating presentation, logic, and data. This model permits high flexibility, enables customization and extensions, as well as allows for the adoption of new devices or technologies. The goal of this layer is to offer transparent access to a CarambaSpace. The TAL utilizes various services to transform, describe, manipulate, and observe objects. All objects managed through a CarambaSpace are well described using a metamodel description framework. Objects can be customized in their structure (e.g., adding columns to tables, adding relations to objects) and their presentation by adopting their metamodel descriptions. Any changes are dynamically reflected by client components. Based on the metamodel description framework, Caramba® enables various options to customize data and content and to integrate data from different resources (e.g., corporate databases). This layer also provides facilities for fine-grained object notification services and the implementation of customized services based on object observers. The middleware does not manage states and persistence of objects. Objects are stored, manipulated, and retrieved via the Persistence Layer (PEL). Caramba leverages and adopts standard Java-based technologies (e.g., JDBC, JNDI, HTTP, etc.) to access and integrate data.

An overall conceptual overview of how Caramba® implements the requirements and how a work scenario of virtual teamwork may look is depicted in Figure 1. Virtual teams have one or more project managers and several resources (people) with various skill sets and professional backgrounds as well as possibly different organizational affiliations. The daily teamwork schedule consists of meetings, (exchange of) documents, and many communications (tasks, e-mails) being sent back and forth. For each project (business process), there are meetings and the exchange of documents and communications, and the trail of communications and interactions is depicted as lines between the team members. Without appropriate virtual team software, the relationships between artifacts, resources, and business processes are only available in the "heads" of the team members. For example, each team member has to remember *when* a particular document was sent to *whom* (e.g., a customer) and *why* (i.e., as part of a particular business process). The goal of virtual team software should be to explicitly provide this relationship information to all team members based on their views and interests.

In order to provide an example of what an implementation looks like, we present the Caramba® components. The ObjectCenter component provides mechanisms with which to link activities with artifacts. Based on a metamodel, Caramba®

Figure 1.   Conceptual View on Virtual Team Software Support

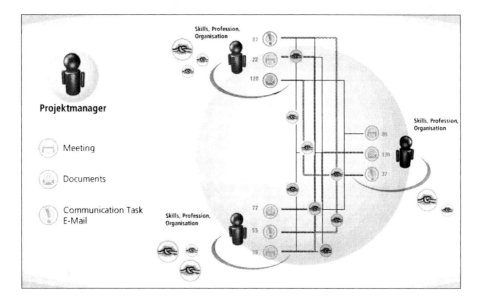

provides a set of organizational objects: Persons, Roles, Groups, Skills, Units, Organizations, Tasks, and Documents (i.e., Templates). Utilizing these organizational constructs, an administrator is able to model any organizational structure, such as hierarchical, flat, or matrix. Each object class consists of attributes describing the object. The object class Persons contains attributes about the person, such as name, address, etc. The object class Roles allows definition of organizational roles, such as "Head of IT." The object class Group defines project settings, such as "Product Team IT-Solutions." Skills enables the definition of required skill sets, such as "Certified Java Developer." Units describe permanent departments, such as "Marketing." The ObjectCenter provides means (by drag and drop) to link the rows of object classes with each other, as depicted in Figure 2. It allows users to view relationships between who (organizational constructs) is performing which activities (Tasks) and using what (Documents). A business process modeler component enables a project manager to model a process template, which may be instantiated later using the built-in Workflow engine. Exceptions to the model are possible without the need to remodel the process template, by choosing the communications (coordination) partner (from the ObjectCenter). The receiving end can read the appropriate message in his inbox.

Figure 2. Modeling Organizational Resources and Processes

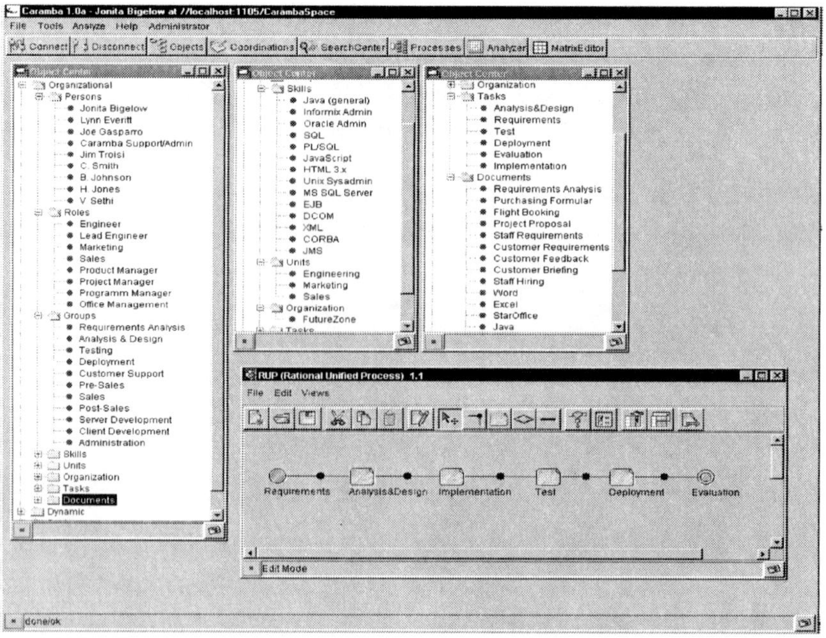

Conclusion

During the last few years, virtually all business processes changed regarding their requirements for flexibility, interconnectivity, and coordination styles. Most business processes are based on teamwork. Most teams are organized as virtual teams, with team members coming from different organizations. In this chapter, we discussed the requirements of modern virtual teamwork and the problems associated with using traditional groupware, project-, and workflow management systems for virtual teamwork. A fundamental need for distributed virtual teamwork is to have access to contextual information, i.e., to see a "knowledge trail" of who did what, when, how, and why. We presented the underlying conceptual issues and one implemented information system (Caramba®) to support the integration of artifacts, resources, and business processes for virtual teams. Future virtual team systems should provide mechanisms for the integration of organizational models with artifacts and business processes in loosely coupled information systems. In our future work, we plan to design and implement support for definition, configuration, and composition of processes for virtual teams based on Web services.

A Web service is an interface that describes a collection of operations that are network accessible through standardized XML messaging using Web servers or Application servers. A Web service is described using a standard, formal XML notion, called its service description. It can be published and found by other Web services. To summarize our recommendations and lessons learned, depending on the team configuration and project content, we suggest that decision makers evaluate the tool support according to Table 2. We think that for typical mid-size (e.g., 15 persons) virtual teams (geographically dispersed), process awareness, organizational awareness, and the integration of artifacts, resources, and processes are crucial. In most cases, we found that asynchronous systems support was of paramount importance the more team members a virtual team has and the more work across different time zones occurs.

Acknowledgments

The author thanks all team members of Caramba® Labs Software AG for the fruitful and constructive discussions.

References

Aalst, W. M. P., & Kumar, A. (2001). A reference model for team-enabled workflow management systems. *Data & Knowledge Engineering, 38,* 335–363.

Akademie für Führungskräfte. (2002). Probleme bei der Teamarbeit (Report), Germany.

Bafoutsou, G., & Mentzsa, G. (2002). Review and functional classification of collaborative systems. *International Journal of Information Management, 22,* 281–305.

Bentley, R., Appelt, W., Busbach, U., Hinrichs, E., Kerr, D., Sikkel, K., Trevor, J., & Woetzel, G. (1997). Basic support for cooperative work on the World Wide Web. *International Journal of Human–Computer Studies, 46,* 827–846.

Bolcer, G. A. (2000). Magi: An architecture for mobile and disconnected Workflow. *IEEE Internet Computing,* (May/June), 46–54.

Bussler, C. (1999). Enterprise-wide workflow management. *IEEE Concurrency, 7*(3), 32–43.

Caramba Labs Software AG. (2002). Retrieved January 15, 2002, from the World Wide Web: http://www.CarambaLabs.com.

Casati, F., Sayal, M., & Shan, M. C. (2001). Developing e-services for composing e-services. In *Proceedings CaiSE 2001* (pp. 171–186). Computer Science Lecture Notes. Heidelberg: Springer Verlag.

Craven, N., & Mahling, D. E. (1995). Goals and processes: A task basis for projects and workflows. In *Proceedings COOCS International Conference,* Milpitas, California, USA.

Dayal, U., Hsu, M., & Ladin, R. (2001). Business process coordination: State of the art, trends, and open issues. In *Proceedings of the 27th VLDB Conference,* Roma, Italy.

DeSanctis, G., & Gallupe, R. B. (1987). A foundation study of group decision support systems. *Management Science, 23*(5), 589–609.

Dustdar, S. (2002a). Mobility of context for project teams. *Proceedings of the International Workshop on Mobile Teamwork at the 22nd International Conference on Distributed Computing Systems (ICDCS 2002),* (July). IEEE Computer Society Press.

Dustdar, S. (2002b). Collaborative knowledge flow — improving process-awareness and traceability of work activities. *4th International Conference on Practical Aspects of Knowledge Management (PAKM 2002),* (December). Springer LNCS.

Dustdar, S. (2002c). Reconciling knowledge management and workflow management: The activity-based knowledge management approach. In H. Nemati, P. Palvia, & R. Ajami (Eds.), *Global Knowledge Management: Challenges and Opportunities*. Hershey, PA: Idea Group Publishing.

Ellis, C. A. (2000). An evaluation framework for collaborative systems. University of Colorado at Boulder Technical Report CU-CS-9001-00.

Ellis, C. A., Gibbs, S. J., & Rein, G. L. (1991). Groupware: Some issues and experiences. *Communications of the ACM, 34*(1).

Ellis, C. A., Keddara, K., & Rozenberg, G. (1995). Dynamic change within workflow systems. In *Proceedings COOCS International Conference*, Milpitas, California, USA.

GROOVE®. (2002). http://www.groove.net.

Hausleitner, A., & Dustdar, S. (1999). Caramba — Ein Java basiertes Multimedia Koordinationssystem. In Silvano Maffeis et al. (Eds.), *Erfahrungen mit Java. Projekte aus Industrie und Hochschule*. Heidelberg: Springer Verlag.

IBM. (2002). http://www.ibm.com.

Johansen, R. (1988). *Groupware. Computer-Support for Business Teams*. New York: The Free Press.

Puustjärvi, J., & Laine, H. (2001). Supporting cooperative inter-organizational business transactions. In *Proceedings DEXA 2001* (pp. 836–845). Computer Science Lecture Notes. Heidelberg: Springer Verlag.

Schal, T. (1996). *Workflow Management Systems for Process Organizations*. New York: Springer.

WfMC. (1995). Workflow Management Coalition — Workflow management specification. Retrieved January 15, 2002, from the Web: http://www.wfmc.org/standards/docs/tc003v11.pdf.

Workflow Management Coalition (WfMC). (1995). Workflow management specification glossary. On the Web: http://www.wfmc.org.

Zeng, L., Benatallah, B., & Ngu, A. H. H. (2001). On demand business-to-business integration. In *Proceedings CoopIS 2001* (pp. 403–714). Computer Science Lecture Notes. Heidelberg: Springer.

Chapter VII

Best Practices for Virtual Team Effectiveness

D. Sandy Staples
Queen's University, Canada

Ian K. Wong
Queen's University, Canada

Ann Frances Cameron
Queen's University, Canada

Abstract

The purpose of this chapter is to improve the understanding of what makes virtual teams effective. This is done by identifying the best practices for individual team members, the best practices for leaders and sponsors of virtual teams, and the best practices for the organizations that the virtual teams are a part of. Best practices in these categories were identified from: (1) empirical evidence from case studies of six existing virtual teams; (2) the existing literature related to virtual teams; and, (3) traditional team (i.e., collocated) and telework literature. The chapter concludes with implications for organizations and potential research directions.

Introduction

The use of teams as fundamental building blocks in organizations is growing (Furst, Blackburn, & Rosen, 1999), as is the frequency of teams to be distributed geographically (which we call virtual teams). Virtual teams are now being used by many organizations to enhance the productivity of their employees and to reach a diversity of skills and resources. Virtual teams are groups of individuals who work on interdependent tasks, who share responsibility for outcomes, and who work together from different locations. Information technology can support their activities by reducing travel costs, enabling expertise to be captured where it is located, and speeding up team communication and coordination processes. Unfortunately, these distributed teams are not always productive. For example, team members may have difficulties in coordinating work with their remote colleagues, or they may not be comfortable using the technology.

Although working in geographically distributed teams is becoming more wide-spread in organizations today, how to do it effectively is not fully understood. The purpose of this chapter is to improve our understanding of what makes virtual teams effective. This will be done by identifying the best practices that individuals on virtual teams should follow (i.e., the team members), the best practices for leaders and sponsors of virtual teams, and the best practices for the organizations of which the virtual teams are a part.

Ideas for best practice were identified from three major sources:

1. Ideas were gathered from case studies of existing virtual teams.

2. The business press and academic literature related to virtual teams were reviewed for best practice ideas.

3. We examined literature from two other areas related to virtual teams. Specifically, these were traditional team (i.e., collocated) literature and telecommuting literature (i.e., research on virtual work at the individual level).

We suggest that there is value in combining the best practice perspectives from the multiple sources. A synthesis of ideas from the tradition team literature, individual-level virtual work literature, virtual team literature, and our own empirical research can potentially offer a relatively complete picture of virtual team best practices.

Our chapter is organized as follows. The chapter presents more background on the sources of the best practices. The best practices are presented in the following sections: "Organizational Best Practices", "Management and Team Leader Best Practices", and "Team Member Best Practices". Presented in the last section is a summary of the findings and concluding remarks.

Background on the Sources for the Best Practices

As mentioned above, the ideas for best practices were identified from case studies of existing virtual teams and from reviews of various bodies of literature. This section provides more background on the teams that were part of the case studies so that readers can understand the contexts in which the teams were operating and provides background on the approaches used for the literature reviews.

Background of the Case Studies of Virtual Teams

Six existing virtual teams were studied. The six teams were from three different companies in different industries (i.e., high-tech, manufacturing, and consulting). All participants were active members of virtual teams working on real projects.

Because there can be some ambiguity in the way the term "virtual" is used, it is important to clearly define how this term will be used in the following discussion. Virtual is defined in the dictionary as "Existing or resulting in essence or effect though not in actual fact, form, or name." So, to what does the *virtual* in virtual work, teamwork, and organizations refer? Three major dimensions have been used in the literature: time, place, and organizational membership. Teams can vary in the length of time they exist, ranging from a very short time (i.e., a temporary team) to a more or less permanent ongoing team. Place refers to the degree of geographic dispersion (i.e., a lack of physical presence). The last dimension is organizational membership. A virtual team can be made up of members from different organizations or from the same organization. The focus of the case studies reported in this chapter was on teams that were geographically distributed, that existed for a relatively long period of time (i.e., not short-term teams assembled for a study), and that worked for the same organization (i.e., to control for the effect of different organizational cultures).

In Table 1 are short descriptions of each team, describing the nature of the task, the type of team, and the degree of virtuality present (i.e., how geographically distributed the team was). To protect confidentiality and anonymity, the identities of the companies and team members are disguised. A total of 39 team members were interviewed, either face-to-face or via the telephone. Each semistructured interview typically lasted 1.5 h. Team members were asked about possible best practices for virtual team members and the challenges and rewards of working as part of a virtual team. Although not the prime focus of this chapter, additional questions were asked about the team's task, the team's characteristics, the organizational environment, the supervisor and business sponsor's involvement,

Table 1. Characteristics of the Virtual Team Case Studies

Team	Nature of the Task	Duration of the Team	Technology Used	Virtuality	Reporting Structure
A	Developing new product lines. Complex task, high interdependence among team members.	Long-term project team	Heavy use of teleconferencing and e-mail. Lotus Notes databases used fairly heavily to collect and share information.	Multiple cities in NE North America. Face-to-face (FTF) meetings a few times per year.	Self-managed team. Report to business director. High autonomy given to the team.
B	Developing new product lines. Complex task, high interdependence among team members.	Long-term project team	Heavy use of teleconferencing and e-mail. Lotus Notes used fairly heavily.	Multiple cities in Eastern North America. FTF meetings a few times per year.	Self-managed team. Report to business director. Fairly high autonomy given to the team.
C	Developing new product features for an existing product. Fairly complex task, high interdependence among team.	Medium-term project team (approximately nine months)	Heavy use of teleconferencing and e-mail. An intranet system was also used fairly heavily to share documents.	Multiple cities in North America plus one member in India. Met once FTF.	Self-managed team. Report to a panel of business sponsors. High autonomy given to the team.
D	Developing new product features for an existing product. Fairly complex task, fairly high interdependence.	Medium-term project team (approximately nine months)	Heavy use of teleconferencing and e-mail. An internal intranet system was also used to share documents.	Multiple cities in North America. Never met FTF.	Self-managed team. Report to a team of business sponsors. Fairly high autonomy given to the team.
E	Providing products to internal service groups. Relatively routine tasks with relatively low dependence on other team members.	Permanent team	Heavy use of teleconferencing, instant messaging and e-mail. Lotus Notes used fairly heavily.	Team members in North America, Europe and Asia. Meet FTF roughly once per year.	Direct reporting relationship to team manager. Autonomy limited, as the work is fairly structured.
F	Providing products to internal service groups. Relatively routine tasks with relatively low dependence on other team members.	Permanent team	Heavy use of teleconferencing, instant messaging and e-mail. Lotus Notes used fairly heavily.	Team members in North America, Europe and Asia. Meet FTF roughly once per year.	Direct reporting relationship to team manager. Autonomy relatively limited, as the work is fairly structured.

the performance of the team, and the team member's attitudes toward the team. Insights learned from these questions are included in the chapter, where they add to our understanding of the findings and issues. In addition to the team members, the managers and business sponsors of each team were interviewed to learn their perspectives on the effectiveness of the teams. Most interviews were taped on audiotape (some participants did not allow this). Transcripts were prepared from the interviews and entered into a qualitative analysis software package (N6® from QSR International). Analysis was done to identify best practices for the individual team members, the management, and the organization overall, from the perspective of making the individual team member an effective member of his or her team.

It is worth pointing out that by several indicators, all the teams were relatively effective. They have been mostly successful in meeting their objectives. The managers of all the teams felt they were effective. Team members rated the performance of their own teams on a 1 to 7 scale, with 7 being very high, at values of 5.2, 5.5, 6.0, 5.2, 5.6, and 6.0, again indicating that the teams were fairly effective. Therefore, it appears reasonable to conclude that the members of these teams are members of successful virtual teams, and hence, their ideas for what it takes to make virtual teams and virtual team members effective have validity.

Background of the Literature Reviews

There exist several "how-to" books on virtual teamwork. We reviewed six of these to identify best practices (Duarte & Snyder, 2001; Fisher & Fisher, 2001; Grenier & Metes, 1995; Haywood, 1998; Lipnack & Stamps, 1997; O'Hara-Devereaux & Johansen, 1994). We also searched the academic literature for articles that dealt with best practices for virtual teams. Two articles were found (Leidner & Kayworth, 2001; Lurey & Raisinghani, 2001), and these were included in our review.

Groups in organizations have been formally studied for over half a century, resulting in thousands of studies and a huge body of literature (Guzzo & Shea, 1992). Fortunately, several reviews of the knowledge in this field already exist (e.g., Bettenhausen, 1991; Cohen, 1994; Cohen & Bailey, 1997; Goodman, Ravlin, & Schminke, 1987; Guzzo & Shea, 1992; Holland, Gaston, & Gomes, 2000), and these reviews will be used as the basis for our understanding of traditional team best practices.

Most of the individual-level (i.e., nonteam) research on virtual work examined the practice of telecommuting or telework (generally in home settings). Research on individuals telecommuting began in the 1980s, and summaries of this body of knowledge exist (e.g., Belanger & Collins, 1998; McCloskey & Igbaria, 1998; Pinsonneault & Boisvert, 2001; Switzer, 1997). In this chapter, we draw on Pinsonneault and Boisvert's (2001) recent review of the empirical and anecdotal telecommuting literature.

Organizational Best Practices

Contained in this section is a description of the practices that organizations need to follow to create, develop, and support successfully virtual teams. Discussion is organized around six general organizational-level topics: selecting appropriate team members, providing resources and support, having appropriate human resource policies, giving the team autonomy, using standard procedures, and having an organizational culture that encourages sharing and communication.

Carefully Selecting the Team Members so They Have Appropriate Diversity for the Required Task

More than half of the interviewees in the case studies of the existing virtual teams revealed that diversity was important to the success of a virtual team and one of the main advantages of virtual teams (see Appendix A for a table of how many participants identified the various best practice ideas). One business sponsor felt that his virtual team was successful because the company actively sought diversity in their project teams. Other interviewees saw diversity as one of the major benefits of virtual teams. Working in a virtual team can produce a diversity of backgrounds, experiences, ideas, thoughts, competencies, perspectives, and views. Virtual teams might also involve employees from different functional areas. As one member described it, "if the people who are geographically dispersed are near to customers, or near to manufacturing, or near to the power center or the power structure, that's a benefit." By involving those individuals who are closer to the action, virtual team structures allow the team to hear "the real line rather than just the official line." Several of the team members also mentioned that the diversity stimulated interest and made it more rewarding and fun to work on virtual teams, because they got the opportunity to learn about new cultures and interact with people beyond their own work location. Therefore, organizations should assemble appropriately diverse teams when team selection is made.

The importance of creating teams with the appropriate mix of skills and individual traits (discussed below in the section on individual best practices) has also been identified in the traditional (i.e., collocated) team literature. Virtually all team models of effectiveness include team composition as an important input variable (e.g., Bettenhausen, 1991; Cohen, 1994). The collective knowledge and skills of a team will impact the team's ability to carry out its task.

Supplying Sufficient Resources and Support

Fifty-three percent of team members interviewed stated that organizations have to supply virtual teams with sufficient resources. These resources include such things as financial resources, time, facilities, hardware, software, communication channels, technical equipment, and proper training. In a virtual team, several of these resources are key to the actual operation of day-to-day activities. One interviewee claimed, "If we didn't have access to the technology [working in a virtual team] would just not be feasible."

Given the need to communicate electronically, it is essential that virtual team members be provided the technical resources and support for working virtually. Policies should be in place to provide the virtual team with technical support, and all members should have access to electronic communication and collaboration technology (Duarte & Snyder, 2001). Fisher and Fisher (2001) also agreed that virtual team members need good information and communication systems to interact effectively with the team leader and each other. The virtual work (i.e., telecommuting) literature reinforces the importance of having good information technology (IT) support. Organizations should supply appropriate IT equipment and provide support and training in using IT for managers and telecommuting employees (Pinsonneault & Boisvert, 2001). In addition to simply having systems to facilitate collaboration, communication, and information sharing, the right conditions have to exist to facilitate use. The system has to fit with the strategy, structure, culture, processes, and IS infrastructure (e.g., training and support), implying that the organizational context has to support the use of the systems.

In addition to having the IT systems available, it is important that team members have access to continual online training and technical support so that they develop the ability to use the systems effectively (Duarte & Snyder, 2001; O'Hara-Devereaux & Johansen, 1994). Continual training and learning can be accomplished through the use of shared lessons, databases, knowledge repositories, and chat rooms. Organizations must ensure that virtual team members are capable of facilitating meetings using technical and nontechnical methods (Duarte & Snyder, 2001). Furthermore, O'Hara-Devereaux and Johansen (1994) believe that IT training is much more than simply teaching users to use applications. It means continually supporting users as applications evolve, grow in functional complexity, become integrated with other applications, and as cross-platform problems are resolved. Users need to understand and accept the new work processes.

IT training by itself is not enough. Organizations also need to provide adequate training for how to work in teams and provide team-building activities for team members. According to Nykodym, Rund, and Liverpool's (1987) study of collocated quality circles, providing transactional analysis training prior to implementing a quality circle program improved perceived coworker communication and interaction in a prepost, control-group study of office workers. A three-day team development workshop significantly improved teamwork, conflict handling, and information sharing in seven Israeli combat command teams, compared to nine control groups (Eden, 1986). Training and team building are important, because they ensure that employees develop the knowledge required to contribute to organizational performance (Cohen, 1994).

Another way an organization influences the resources a virtual team has is by controlling the number of people that are on the team. Case study participants identified the importance of having an adequate number of team members on the team so that they had the resources needed to accomplish their tasks. In situations where the team leader decides team selection, organizations should provide the resources necessary for that team leader to select the best possible team members with the appropriate levels of diversity of skills and access to resources.

Supporting the case study participants' comments, the potential for the size of the team to affect the ability of the team to do its task was also found in collocated team research (e.g., Cohen, 1994). If it is too big, higher coordination costs result. If the team size is too small, it will not have the resources needed to complete its work, and team members will be less likely to be committed to the team. In addition to simply the number of team members, the stability of team membership is also an important factor. If turnover is high, time and effort will be spent orientating new members, performance norms will not develop, and performance will suffer. However, some turnover can be beneficial, in that it could revitalize a stagnant team and enhance creativity.

Develop Human Resource Policies that Stimulate High Virtual Team Performance

The impact of the organizational context on team effectiveness was identified in collocated (e.g., Cohen, 1994) and virtual team research (e.g., Duarte & Snyder, 2001), although it did not explicitly surface in the suggestions from participants in the virtual team case studies. Organizational human resource policies (i.e., those with reward structures for team activities) can positively affect collocated team cohesion, motivation, and effectiveness (Cohen, 1994). With respect to traditional teams, several studies found positive relationships between providing rewards to team members and some measure of team effectiveness. Cohen, Ledford, and Spreitzer (1996) found that management recognition was positively associated with team ratings of performance, trust in management, organizational commitment, and satisfaction for self-directed and traditionally managed groups in a telecommunications firm. Lawler (1986, 1992) suggested that the organization should provide employees with rewards that are tied to performance results, the development of capability, and contributions. This motivates employees to achieve their performance goals.

In addition to providing rewards, the design of the reward system also has an effect on team performance. In Wageman's study (1995), it was found that the highest performing collocated maintenance technician groups were those in which the structure of the task matched the design of the reward system. Group rewards were put in place to motivate tasks that were interdependent, while individual rewards motivated individual independent tasks. This illustrates the importance of designing reward systems that are linked to the nature of the task.

The virtual team literature also suggests that organizational practices and policies shape the effectiveness of virtual teams. At the organizational level, supportive and well-designed human resource policies are key to a virtual team's success. According to Duarte and Snyder (2001), human resource policies must be designed and integrated in such a way that virtual team members are recognized, supported, and rewarded for their work. As such, it is important that an effective reward system with performance measures be in place to reward results. Grenier and Metes (1995) and Lurey and Raisinghani (2001) also suggest that it is important for the organization to reward high levels of team performance. Furthermore, special career development opportunities should be created for virtual team members. Because virtual team members are not seen every day in the office, it is possible that they may be overlooked for promotional opportunities (Duarte & Snyder, 2001). Telecommuters also identified that lack of equitable rewards and career advancement opportunities (Pinsonneault & Boisvert, 2001) can be a serious issue that organizations must address so that the "out of sight, out of mind" phenomenon does not occur. This phenomenon can result in local employees being favored over remote employees. A results-based assessment system is required to support and equitably recognize teleworkers' activities.

Provide Appropriate Autonomy to the Team

While organizations are encouraged to supply appropriate resources, they are also encouraged to leave decision making to the team leader and team members. A few interviewees felt that senior management involvement demonstrated a healthy interest in the team's activities. However, over one-third of team members interviewed in the case studies suggested that lack of involvement from senior management was usually preferable, as long as the organization still provided the funds and resources necessary. As one interviewee bluntly put it, senior management and organizations can support virtual teams best if they provide the team with resources and then just "leave us alone."

This is consistent with research findings on effective collocated teams. According to Cohen and Bailey (1997), the organization needs to give team members autonomy in their work. Worker autonomy is shown to have clear benefits; it enhances worker attitudes, behaviors, and performance (whether measured objectively or rated subjectively by team members). Organizations should give team members the power to take action and make decisions about work and business performance (Cohen, 1994). The organization needs to share information with team members about processes, quality, customer feedback, business results, competitor performance, and organizational changes. If team members are given team-based rewards but do not have the autonomy needed to influence performance, then money will be wasted. Teams would have been offered a reward that they do not have the power, information, or knowledge necessary to work toward.

Use Standard Processes and Procedures

Another practice an organization can adopt to improve virtual team effectiveness is to use standard processes and planning procedures. For example, one of the case study teams had standard processes in place, and many of the team members felt that this contributed to high levels of coordination and project success.

Support for the importance of standard processes and practices can be found in the virtual team literature. The use of standard processes can reduce the time needed for team startup and may eliminate the need for unnecessary reinvention of operating practices every time a new team is needed (Duarte & Snyder, 2001). Common standard technical processes include definitions of requirements, estimates of costs, procurement, team charters, project planning, documentation, reporting, and controlling. Standard communication procedures and policies may also improve a virtual team's ability to perform (Duarte & Snyder, 2001; Fisher & Fisher, 2001; Grenier & Metes, 1995). Fisher and Fisher (2001) suggested that a good face-to-face startup may help create bonds between team members and develop agreements on how members are going to work together. This time can also be spent on team-building activities such as developing goals, creating measures, and clarifying roles and responsibilities.

Develop an Organizational Culture that Stimulates the Sharing of Information

The organizational culture plays a large role in determining how well a virtual team functions within the organization, because it influences how individuals in an organization behave. Although this issue did not explicitly surface during the case study interviews, it is evident in the virtual and traditional team literature.

In the virtual team literature, one key issue is how willing an organization is to share information not only with its employees but also with external partners. Grenier and Metes (1995) suggested that value is realized by sharing information with others who need to know what is going on. Conversely, treating partners as less than equal, hoarding information, forgetting to share data or results in a timely manner, and using competitive or proprietary information inappropriately can erode trust quickly (Duarte & Snyder, 2001). Therefore, organizations should work to build within their organization culture norms and values that promote communication and the sharing of information.

The traditional team research also identified the importance of having a supportive culture. Organizations should strive to ensure that there exists a cooperative work environment where norms are established that reinforce and support team behaviors, such as sharing information, responding appropriately to team members, and cooperating (Bettenhausen, 1991). This has been found to be critical for effective team performance. For instance, utility companies from an engineering consulting firm that believed their goals were cooperatively attained, interacted effectively, made progress on their tasks, and strengthened their work relationships (Tjosvold, 1988).

Management and Team Leader Best Practices

Summarized in this section are best practices ideas relating to the leadership and management of the team. For self-managed teams, some of these activities may come from within the team and some may come from the business sponsor they report to, or both. For teams that have a clear, more formal team manager (either internal or external to the team), then the activities would largely fall on his or her shoulders. It was interesting to find that some of the practices that are appropriate for organizations are not appropriate for team managers or team leaders. For example, an organization's senior management should use a hands-off approach, while team leaders are sometimes expected to do the opposite, in order to provide necessary structure and direction. This section is organized around seven general team leader best practices: setting goals and direction, providing feedback, building trust, empowering team members, motivating team members, having appropriate leadership styles, and developing self-control mechanisms in team members.

Setting Goals and Establishing Direction

Many case study participants stated that managers and team leaders should not take a hands-off approach when it comes to setting the team's objectives and goals. Sixty-four percent of team members recognized the need to carefully set realistic, clear goals and timelines. One manager suggested that to be successful, virtual teams must "find common ground to work towards." Further, the team leader must clearly define the direction, goals, and objectives of the team in relation to the external world. Only then will team members "know what they are working against." To accomplish this, management and team leaders can develop a "roadmap" with realistic time lines that are compatible with the expectations of senior management. Next, the critical path through the project should be identified. Based on this path, major milestones should be set. Whether or not it affects them directly, all team members should be constantly reminded of the next milestone. Focusing on milestones and deliverable dates will help members keep the big picture in mind when working on their individual tasks. Successful virtual teams are those that, with the help of a focused manager, are consistently able to meet these milestones within the allotted time. Those teams that do not meet the deadlines may have had unrealistic expectations or were not focusing their efforts on the right tasks. Case study participants suggested that good project management skills would be valuable to facilitate these practices.

Case study participants also identified the importance of having clear roles. Team members and managers in the case studies felt that by clearly defining goals, paths, and objectives (as suggested above), the individual roles and responsibilities of each member would be better understood. One individual suggested that the "mapping of individual goals with the team goals" would make the definition for each role and responsibility apparent.

The literature on virtual teams also emphasizes the importance of setting clear goals and establishing clear roles and clear responsibilities (Fisher & Fisher, 2001; Grenier & Metes, 1995; O'Hara-Devereaux & Johansen, 1994). Goals must be clear so that virtual team members know what the objectives are and how they are to work. Defining team roles and responsibilities should also be given special attention. Once in agreement on common areas of responsibility, individual roles should be defined. It may also be useful to identify the degree to which members need to learn one another's roles for backup or development (O'Hara-Devereaux & Johansen, 1994). Definition of roles reduces the ambiguity in responsibilities between team members. This will reduce the chance of work being duplicated or work being left undone.

The telecommuting literature also reinforces the importance of having clear goals in a virtual work environment. Teleworkers' objectives and goals should be clearly articulated so that it is clear what is expected and on what the individual will be assessed (Pinsonneault & Boisvert, 2001).

In order to set goals, the overall purpose of the team must be clear. The virtual team literature strongly suggests that effective leaders understand the importance of defining a vision for the virtual team (Fisher & Fisher, 2001; Grenier & Metes, 1995; Lipnack & Stamps, 1997; O'Hara-Devereaux & Johansen, 1994).

According to Lipnack and Stamps (1997), a predictor of virtual team success is the clarity of its purpose and vision. Purpose and vision generate the internal spark of life for task-oriented, boundary-crossing virtual teams. To succeed, teams must turn their purpose and vision into action (e.g., by setting goals, roles, and responsibilities), using it to help design their work and processes (Lipnack & Stamps, 1997).

Provide Feedback via Effective Coaching and Modeling

Effective coaching is something team leaders can provide to team members to help them work more effectively. It helps members ensure that their activities and goals are in line with the team's overall goals. In terms of individual coaching, team leaders need to provide members with timely feedback about their performance so that team members know what they can do to continuously improve their performances (Duarte & Snyder, 2001). In virtual teams, this might require getting informal input from various people who interact with team members within and outside of the organization. It can also include formal communication with vested parties about the performances of team members.

Simply providing feedback however is not enough; virtual leaders also need to teach and model how to give and receive feedback (Fisher & Fisher, 2001). In addition to providing feedback, effective virtual leaders should demonstrate a mentoring quality characterized by concern for members, understanding, and empathy (Leidner & Kayworth, 2001). Staples' (2001) empirical study of remote workers and their managers' activities supports the importance of regular feedback and communication. The manager's ability to provide remote employees with advice and help was significantly related to the effectiveness of the remote employees. The modeling of appropriate virtual work habits by managers was also found to positively affect a remote employee's perceived ability to work remotely and their effectiveness (Staples, Hulland, & Higgins, 1999). Pinsonneault and Boisvert (2001) identified several aspects of the interactions between managers and employees that could potentially affect task performance. These included managers keeping remote employees well informed of organizational activities, providing regular feedback on performance and progress (and receiving regular feedback from their employees), establishing well-structured and constant communications, and being available at hours that fit with teleworkers' work routines.

Build Trust Through Open Communication and Honest Behavior and by Delivering on Commitments

According to authors of the virtual team literature, one of the most important things that team leaders need to do is to build trust between themselves and the team and within the team (Duarte & Snyder, 2001; Fisher & Fisher, 2001; O'Hara-Devereaux & Johansen, 1994). Fisher and Fisher (2001) suggested that without trust, productivity suffers, as team members play politics and spend time covering themselves instead of working on real issues that affect customers. To build trust, it is important for team leaders to communicate openly and frequently with team members. Furthermore, in order to gain trust of team members, team leaders must set the example and learn to give trust. Waiting to give trust to employees until they earn it is not as effective as assuming they are trustworthy until they prove otherwise (Fisher & Fisher, 2001). Perhaps the single most important variable that affects trust is honesty. Leaders who demonstrate openness about their actions will find that members respond with sincerity. Furthermore, team leaders will make mistakes. These mistakes should be admitted instead of covered up. Leaders should do what they say they will do and make their actions visible. Visibly keeping commitments increases trust, whereas breaking promises diminishes it (Fisher & Fisher, 2001).

The traditional team research also identified the importance of team leaders effectively communicating with their team members. How a leader listens and communicates with his or her team members is very much related to team effectiveness (Cohen & Bailey, 1997). Leaders who show high consideration actively listen to team members' inputs, whereas leaders who show low consideration listen without comment. Team members have higher perceptions of fairness and higher commitments toward the recommendations of the team leader in the group with high levels of communication. Team member attachment and trust in the leaders increases under high consideration and decreases under low consideration.

Empower the Team

While a manager or team leader is expected to set guidelines, milestones, and goals, they should still give the team members the power to decide how to reach these goals. Although only a few of the team members mentioned this issue, almost all of the team managers and sponsors believe that empowered virtual teams perform better. While overbearing and dictatorial managers can be problems, leaders who trust in team decisions can give the members a sense of ownership. A virtual team manager may define the task objectives but allow the team to decide how to reach these objectives. One team sponsor felt so strongly about team empowerment that he stated, "I don't like the word 'manager' period." Another team leader felt that this hands-off approach is particularly important in a virtual team environment, where geographic separation makes micromanagement impractical. This best practice is related to the organizational practice of more generally providing autonomy to teams. At a lower level, team leaders also have to provide the appropriate level of autonomy, setting overall team goals and establishing direction, while allowing individual team members to decide how they carry out their specific tasks.

Motivate the Team

In some cases, a particular practice may exist on the management and individual levels. As described below, motivation is a quality necessary for the individual team member. However, motivating is also an activity that can be performed by team leaders. In a virtual team environment where tasks may appear unconnected, the big picture is not always easy to visualize, and it may be difficult for employees to remain committed to the project. Thus, team leaders can play a key role in helping virtual team members maintain motivation. One business sponsor interviewed in the case studies had a strong vision of what it took to get his virtual team motivated. He believed that "if you can create a cause around something you usually get passion for it," and that this passion creates motivation. This individual gathered all the project stakeholders together at a customer's site and allowed them to see the direct impact their product could have. By identifying the importance of their work, he provided the team members with the motivation needed to successfully complete the project.

Demonstrating how the project will result in significant outcomes for the individual team members can also foster motivation. One of the case study team leaders felt that it was important that team members see that "they will grow with this business opportunity. They will get to do things that they never thought they were going to do before." By linking team success to individual success and opportunities, team members were highly motivated to succeed on the project.

Leadership Style

Over a quarter of case study team members reported that appropriate leadership at the *appropriate time* was one of the key elements of a successful virtual team. During the initial phases of the project, the appropriate leader is one who can "whip up enthusiasm" and motivate the team. During the later stages, the effective leader is someone who is "getting the right people together and keeping everybody on task and keeping everything going." Therefore, the styles and activities of team leaders have to be appropriate for the stage the team is currently at and the needs at that particular time.

Develop Self-Control Mechanisms in the Team

According to Cohen (1994): "Employee behaviour is determined by internal control systems, and organizational control systems work only to the degree that they influence the employees' self-regulating systems. A leader's role in a self-management system is to facilitate the development of employee self-controls, so that they can lead themselves."

Therefore, self-leadership directly affects performance outcomes, because team members will be encouraged to perform behaviors that improve their performance. The following are encouraging behaviors that leaders can perform to help improve a team's performance (Cohen, 1994):

- Encourage self-observation/self-evaluation so that the team gathers information and monitors and evaluates performances.

- Encourage self-goal-setting so that the team sets performance goals.

- Encourage self-reinforcement so that the team recognizes and reinforces good performance within the team.

- Encourage self-criticism so that the team recognizes and deals appropriately with poor team performance.

- Encourage self-expectation management so that the team has appropriately high expectations for team performance.

- Encourage rehearsal so that the team plans and practices an activity before actually performing the activity.

Team Member Best Practices

Suggestions for what makes individuals effective members of virtual teams included specific behaviors as well as attitudes and beliefs that individuals should have. Five general characteristics of effective members of virtual teams are communicating effectively, having appropriate skills, being motivated, being supportive of other team members, and being action oriented.

Communicate Effectively

Eighty-four percent of team members interviewed in the case studies recognized the importance of effective communication in building a successful team. Communication involves transferring ideas, sharing information, listening and internalizing the ideas of others, and notifying team members of any problems or issues. As one team member saw it, "If there's any information that comes your way that could help the team, you share it as soon as possible." Others took a more limited approach, suggesting that not all information has equal significance, and detailed information should only be shared when it is essential to other members of the team. One team manager noted that while he is frequently copied on e-mails, he would rather just be told when a decision has been reached. He had no "need to hear or read the back and forth."

Effective communication is challenging in a virtual team, where face-to-face communication and impromptu meetings are infrequent, if not impossible. One team member described the typical hallway conversations of collocated teams as "priceless," and another stated, "Nothing replaces face-to-face interaction." In an attempt to solve this problem, virtual team members suggest working hard to keep lines of communication open. One way to accomplish this is to develop or find the right communications tools that make up for the loss of face-to-face time and provide for informal interactions. In addition, team members have to be responsive, quickly returning telephone calls and responding to e-mails, even if it is just to say, "I don't have time right now but I'll get back to you in two days with the answer." Two virtual team managers also suggested that the recipient should confirm that the message was received and ensure that the major points in the message were understood. Setting communication norms such as these, helps to avoid misinterpreting situations or behaviors.

The virtual team literature echoes the case study findings. Virtual work depends on a high level of communications and trust. Teams must develop the capabilities to work with information and communication technologies in stressful situations, with a variety of competencies in people from several locations and organizations (Grenier & Metes, 1995). With respect to the process of continuous and effective communication, virtual team members should communicate when in doubt. Contrary to the manager above who did not want to be copied on e-mails, the literature suggests that team members should not worry if they have nothing in particular to say; communication builds the ability to communicate. An informal e-mail to another team member strengthens the social network, which increases the ability to respond when important problems or questions arise. Communication builds trust, which in turn, builds better communication; this is a positive feedback loop that virtual teams want to feed, not constrain (Grenier & Metes, 1995). The ability to communicate effectively has also been found to be a critical skill for telecommuters, remote workers, and managers of remote workers (Pinsonneault & Boisvert, 2001; Staples, 2001).

In addition to communicating within a team, traditional team research also found that team members' external communication was related to a team's effectiveness (Cohen & Bailey, 1997). It was suggested that communication with managers above the team in the organizational hierarchy leads to higher team performance, as these communication activities usually involve lobbying management for resources and seeking protection and support. Furthermore, communication that is conducted laterally across the organization to coordinate technical or design issues has also been found to increase team effectiveness.

Have the Necessary Skill Sets

Over half of the interviewees believed that several sets of skills were important for a successful virtual team member. In addition to the communication skills mentioned above, virtual team members in the case studies reported that team members should have the ability to organize effectively, a strong competency in an individual's functional area of responsibility, adequate technical skills to use the information and technology tools available, and good time management skills.

The ability to use time effectively was also identified as a key ability for remote employees to have (Staples, 2001). This includes being able to prioritize daily tasks and completing the high-priority tasks. Being able to manage one's own workload and priorities well is also identified in the virtual team literature as important personal workload management skills that a virtual team member needs to develop. A virtual team member should have the ability to communicate to management when he or she is overloaded. Also, members should develop a sense of "appropriate reaction times"; members should not accept another's sense of urgency unless norms have been established. Members should not hesitate to ask the team for help (reinforcing the importance of supporting fellow team members), and they should get issues on the table (i.e., be able to communicate openly) (Grenier & Metes, 1995).

Traditional team literature also identifies the importance of individual skills. The effectiveness of a team depends on the collective knowledge and skills of its members. In order to make good decisions, people in teams who have the authority to collectively make decisions about how they do their tasks need the appropriate knowledge and skills (Cohen, 1994). Team members need interpersonal skills to work together effectively. Further, research has found that team members are more satisfied with their interpersonal relationships and the team when team members have good interpersonal skills. If team members do not have the technical skills required to collectively carry out the various components of the task, the effectiveness of the team will be limited.

The virtual team literature and the telecommuting literature also identify the importance of having skilled team members. People should first know how to use the electronic communication tools they have available and then be able to use an electronic social network to build and sustain team-wide relationships, develop skills in using virtual tools, and maintain cross-cultural dialogue. Specific social skills may involve learning how to negotiate creatively, mediating online disputes, and making new members of the team feel included (Grenier & Metes, 1995). To communicate, team members should create an electronic social network as soon as possible using e-mail. E-mail is the backbone for global-work, which represents an infrastructure on which more sophisticated systems can be built. Team members should also use e-mail to function as a "virtual coffee pot or water cooler," around which personal conversations can occur. Such social uses of e-mail or other electronic media (e.g., instant messaging) can promote a team spirit and corporate culture and improve overall communications (O'Hara-Devereaux & Johansen, 1994).

Be Highly Motivated

Almost three-quarters of the case study participants interviewed noted the importance of individual commitment to the project. Individuals should be motivated, willing to get involved, interested, feel individual responsibility, take initiative, and be prepared to "work like hell" on the assigned task. In a virtual team environment where tasks may appear unconnected, the big picture is not always easy to visualize, and it may be difficult for employees to maintain commitment. The ability to self-motivate is important, because virtual team members are often working far apart from their other team members.

The virtual team literature also identifies the importance of team members being self-motivated. To a significant degree, virtual teams are self-managing. To be successful in virtual groups, the team members must be able to work independently and be motivated to make appropriate decisions. This is made possible by having clear goals and responsibilities and having high personal commitment and motivation to the team, along with having the resources and information needed to do the job (as previously mentioned) (Lipnack & Stamps, 1997).

The telecommuting literature also identifies the importance of self-motivation for remote workers. Individual factors that affect telecommuting effectiveness include being self-motivated and self-disciplined, because these enable effective work with little supervision. Remote workers should have a preference or need for little social interaction or have the ability to fulfil this need outside of the work environment, because their work environment (i.e., usually working at home) results in significant isolation (Pinsonneault & Boisvert, 2001).

Be Supportive of Other Team Members

Thirty-nine percent of team members in the case studies believed that a supportive team environment was key for a successful virtual team. Several dimensions of a supportive team emerged during the interviews. First, team members felt that it was important to recognize when someone else did a good job and to congratulate or thank them accordingly. Such recognition does not have to come from management or have a monetary basis; even verbal encouragement from peers is appreciated. Also of importance is how the team reacts to failure or a mistake. Recalling one successful virtual team experience, an interviewee remembered, "You weren't at each other's throat saying 'You screwed up'." Instead of dwelling on the mistake or making it into a big issue, team members should help fix the mistake, learn from it, and move on.

Second, interviewees sought a respectful team environment where members were not afraid to openly discuss ideas. "Everyone on the team has to be able to ... or [is] required to take a leadership role so that they should speak up and not feel that their opinion is not valued." Another member suggested that unsuccessful teams are those with "idea killers." Idea killers were suggested to be outspoken individuals who were negative and pessimistic and continually critical of the ideas of others.

A third dimension of being supportive is the ability to get along with others. Several individuals felt that the ability to get along with other team members was an essential quality for an effective virtual team member. However, one of the managers disagreed, suggesting that liking is not necessary, it is respect that is important.

Research on collocated teams supports the importance of being supportive within the team. The way in which team members interact with each other has an effect on team effectiveness (Cohen, 1994). Coordination and caring involves working together without duplication or wasted efforts. It also involves working together with a sense of energy and team spirit. With self-managing teams, self-management depends upon effective coordination, and team spirit can be contagious and can foster a "can do" attitude (group self-efficacy) that can eventually translate into higher performance.

Part of being supportive is being willing to share ideas and expertise to help others. Traditional team research (e.g., Cohen, 1994) found that team members can also improve their team's performance if they interact and share their expertise. Sharing of expertise means that team members share as well as listen to other's knowledge and expertise. The sharing of expertise is critical to support effective cross-training and decision making, which will add to a team's knowledge base.

Be Action-Oriented and Use Time Effectively

A "doer," "proactive," "uses an entrepreneurial approach," and "looks for solutions." These are all phrases that case study members of one team used to describe a top-performing virtual team member. Interviewees felt that an action-oriented approach was key when participating in a virtual team. Successful virtual team members "organize their thoughts into actions or proposals that get a good buy" or influence the rest of the group. Telecommuting research also suggests that virtual workers have to be self-disciplined and be able to work on their own to get their tasks done (Pinsonneault & Boisvert, 2001).

Summary and Conclusion

The recommendations for virtual team best practices identified in the sections above are briefly summarized in Appendix B, broken down by the source of the idea. A brief recap of the main themes in the best practices is listed below:

- Organizations must provide a supportive environment for the team, in terms of providing necessary resources, autonomy to the team, and recognition and reward systems that are tied to the results that the team and individuals achieve.

- Organizations must design teams that have the necessary diversity, in terms of skills, access to knowledge and resources, and backgrounds.

- Team leaders of virtual teams have to establish clear goals and expectations such that a team can have a focus and a direction to pursue. If possible, building passion for a cause can be a powerful stimulus for everyone on the team to pull together in the same direction.

- Individuals need certain skills to be effective members of virtual teams. Required skills include technical skills to carry out assigned parts of the team's task, interpersonal skills, teaming skills, and skills to use electronic communication and information-sharing tools.

- Individuals have to be motivated and self-disciplined so that they can manage themselves and their time effectively.

While this chapter attempted to identify the best practices for members of virtual teams, leaders of virtual teams, and the organizations that virtual teams work in, it has not identified which are most important. In other words, some of the practices may have a stronger influence on team success than others. Some questions that future research should address include:

- Which of the best practices are most critical for team effectiveness?
- Does the impact of certain practices on effectiveness vary depending on the task and the organizational context?
- Does one set of practices (i.e., individual, managerial, or organizational) take precedence, such that those practices have to be in place before the other practices have a positive effect?

Understanding what practices are important leads to other questions, such as:

- How does an organization ensure that best practices are followed?
- Can training programs be developed for managers and leaders and for members of virtual teams? What should be in these training programs, and how should they be delivered?
- Can policies be developed and norms established in organizations such that supportive practices, which research suggests leads to effective virtual work, are followed? How can this be done most effectively?

The answer to some of the questions above is undoubtedly "yes," but there are many questions remaining as to "how." There are many opportunities for future research in this area. The findings from this research could help organizations create and maintain more effective virtual teams. Given the growing use of virtual teams in organizations today, the need for more understanding of how to make virtual teams work well is great. We hope this chapter has made a contribution in that direction, and we look forward to other researchers and practitioners answering some of the questions posed above.

References

Belanger, F., & Collins, R. W. (1998). Distributed work arrangements: A research framework. *Information Society, 14*(2), 137–152.

Bettenhausen, K. L. (1991). Five years of group research: What we have learned and what needs to be addressed. *Journal of Management, 17*(2), 345–381.

Cohen, S. G. (1994). Designing effective self-managing work teams. In M. M. Beyerlein, D. A. Johnson, & S. T. Beyerlein (Eds.), *Advances in Interdisciplinary Studies of Work Teams, Volume 1, Series of Self-Managed Work Teams.* Greenwich, CT: JAI Press.

Cohen, S. G., & Bailey, D. E. (1997). What makes teams work: Group effectiveness research from the shop floor to the executive suite. *Journal of Management, 23*(3), 239–290.

Cohen, S. G., Ledford, G. E., & Spreitzer, G. M. (1996). A predictive model of self-managing work team effectiveness. *Human Relations, 49*(5), 643–676.

Duarte, D. L., & Snyder, N. T. (2001). *Mastering Virtual Teams: Strategies, Tools, and Techniques that Succeed.* San Francisco, CA: Jossey-Bass.

Eden, D. (1986). Team development: Quasi-experimental confirmation among combat companies. *Group and Organization Studies, 11*, 133–146.

Fisher, K., & Fisher, M. D. (2001). *The Distance Manager: A Hands on Guide to Managing Off-Site Employees and Virtual Teams.* New York: McGraw-Hill.

Furst, S., Blackburn, R., & Rosen, B. (1999, August). *Virtual teams: A proposed research agenda.* Paper presented at the Academy of Management Conference, Chicago, Illinois, USA.

Goodman, P. S., Ravlin, E., & Schminke, M. (1987). Understanding groups in organizations. *Research in Organizational Behavior, 9*, 121–173.

Grenier, R., & Metes, M. (1995). *Going Virtual.* Upper Saddle River, NJ: Prentice Hall.

Guzzo, R. A., & Shea, G. P. (1992). Group performance and intergroup relations in organizations. In M. D. Dunnette & L. M. Hough (Eds.), *Handbook of Industrial and Organizational Psychology* (2nd ed., Vol. 3, pp. 269–313). Palo Alto, CA: Consulting Psychologists Press.

Haywood, M. (1998). *Managing Virtual Teams: Practical Techniques for High-Technology Project Managers.* Boston, MA: Artech House.

Hinds, P., & Kiesler, S. (eds.) (2002). *Distributed Work.* Cambridge, MA: MIT Press.

Holland, S., Gaston, K., & Gomes, J. (2000). Critical success factors for cross-functional teamwork in new product development. *International Journal of Management Reviews, 2*(3), 231–259.

Lawler, E. E. (1986). *High-Involvement Management: Participative Strategies for Improving Organizational Performance.* San Francisco, CA: Jossey-Bass.

Lawler, E. E. (1992). *The Ultimate Advantage: Creating the High Involvement Organization*. San Francisco, CA: Jossey-Bass.

Leidner, D., & Kayworth T. (2001). Leadership effectiveness in global virtual teams. *Journal of Management Information Systems, 18*(3), 7–40.

Lipnack, J., & Stamps, J. (1997). *Virtual Teams: Reaching Across Space, Time, and Organizations with Technology*. New York: John Wiley & Sons.

Lurey, J., & Raisinghani, M. (2001). An empirical study of best practices in virtual teams. *Information & Management, 38*(8), 523–544.

McCloskey, D. W., & Igbaria, M. (1998). A review of the empirical research on telecommuting and directions for future research. In M. Igbaria & M. Tan (Eds.), *The Virtual Workplace* (pp. 338–358). Hershey, PA: Idea Group Publishing.

Nykodym, N., Ruud, W. N., & Liverpool, P. R. (1987). TA: Can it improve worker satisfaction with organizational decision-making? *Journal of Systems Management, 38*(5), 18–21.

O'Hara-Devereaux, M., & Johansen, R. (1994). *Global Work: Bridging Distance, Culture & Time*. San Francisco, CA: Jossey-Bass.

Pinsonneault, A., & Boisvert, M. (2001). The impacts of telecommuting on organizations and individuals: A review of the literature. In N. J. Johnson (Ed.), *Telecommuting and Virtual Offices: Issues & Opportunities* (pp. 163–185). Hershey, PA: Idea Group Publishing.

Staples, D. S. (2001). Making remote workers effective. In N. J. Johnson (Ed.), *Telecommuting and Virtual Offices: Issues & Opportunities* (Chap. 11, pp. 186–212). Hershey, PA: Idea Group Publishing.

Staples, D. S., Hulland, J. S., & Higgins, C. A. (1999). A self-efficacy theory explanation for the management of remote workers in virtual organizations. *Organization Science, 10*(6), 758–776.

Switzer, T. R. (1997). *Telecommuters, the Workforce of the Twenty-First Century: An Annotated Bibliography*. Lanham, MD: Scarecrow Press.

Tjosvold, D. (1988). *Working Together to Get Things Done: Managing for Organizational Productivity*. Lexington, MA: Lexington Books.

Wageman, R. (1995). Interdependence and group effectiveness. *Administrative Science Quarterly, 40*, 145–180.

Appendix A

Frequency of Best Practice Ideas Mentioned by Virtual Team Members*

Best Practices	Team A 8 people	Team B 9 people	Team C 7 people	Team D 6 people	Team E 8 people	Team F 7 people	Total	Proportion Out of 45
Organizational Practice								
Seek Diverse Team Members	6	2	4	4	6	4	26	58%
Supply Sufficient Resources & Support	3	6	6	5	4	1	25	56%
Provide Appropriate Level of Autonomy	5	4	3	3	1	0	16	36%
Team Leader Practice								
Set Goals and Establish Direction	5	8	6	5	2	3	29	64%
Empower the Team	2	4	1	2	0	0	9	20%
Appropriate Leadership Style	0	2	4	2	3	1	12	27%
Team Member Practice								
Communicate Effectively	7	7	6	3	8	7	38	84%
Have Necessary Skill Sets	3	4	5	1	7	6	26	58%
Be Highly Motivated	5	8	2	6	6	6	33	73%
Be Supportive of Other Team Members	5	6	0	0	4	2	17	38%
Be Action-Oriented	5	4	0	0	2	2	13	29%

* the number of people in the team includes the team manager/business sponsor

Appendix B

A Summary of Best Practices and Their Source(s)

	From Virtual Team Members	From Virtual Team Literature	From Traditional Team Literature	From Non-Team Virtual Literature
Organizational Best Practices				
Carefully select team members for diversity	X		X	
Supply sufficient resources and support	X	X	X	X
Develop human resource policies that stimulate virtual team performance		X	X	X
Provide appropriate autonomy to the team	X		X	
Use standard process and procedures	X	X		
Develop an organizational culture that stimulates information sharing		X	X	
Management & Team Leader Best Practices				
Set goals and establish direction	X	X		X
Provide feedback via coaching and modelling		X		X
Build trust through open communication, honest behaviour, and delivering on commitments		X	X	
Empower the team	X			
Motivate the team	X			
Use appropriate leadership style at appropriate time	X			
Develop self-control mechanisms in team			X	
Team Member Best Practices				
Communicate effectively	X	X	X	X
Have necessary skill sets	X	X	X	X
Be highly motivated	X	X		X
Be supportive of other team members	X		X	
Be action-oriented	X			X

Chapter VIII

Varieties of Virtual Organizations and Their Knowledge Sharing Systems

Andrea Hornett

The Pennsylvania State University, USA

Abstract

Provided in this chapter is an analysis of the differences between virtual teams and communities of practice. The chapter links two growing phenomena: virtual organizing and knowledge sharing (knowledge management), based on empirical work from both fields of research. By integrating various types of virtual organizing with corresponding knowledge-sharing systems, the author provides a framework that virtual team leaders, members, and consultants can use to improve management of virtual endeavors. This chapter suggests that calling nearly everything a "Community of Practice" creates unrealistic expectations for spontaneous organizing and knowledge sharing. Indeed, the managers of Virtual Project Teams have organizing challenges that are very different from stewards of Communities of Practice. Practitioners struggling with "one-

size-fits-all" prescriptions for virtual work or knowledge management can use this chapter's three generalized types to develop communications and management styles appropriate for the unique cultures found in each of the various combinations of virtual organizing and knowledge sharing.

Introduction

Virtual organizations are varied in their designs, memberships, purposes, and uses of technology. Each variation has different reasons and methods for exchanging information and sharing knowledge. Integrated in this chapter are these various types of virtual organizing with corresponding knowledge-sharing systems. The result is a framework that identifies three generalized types of knowledge sharing, each indicative of certain types of virtual organizing. With awareness of the differences in these types, virtual team leaders, members, and consultants can improve communication and management of virtual endeavors by clarifying the goals and purposes of their various organizing activities and related knowledge-sharing systems.

Each of these types poses unique challenges to practitioners for managing and communicating in virtual environments. Practitioners struggling with "one-size-fits-all" prescriptions for virtual work or knowledge management can use these three generalized types to appreciate the reciprocal dynamics of virtual organizing and knowledge sharing and address the needs of both. Each type suggests that calling nearly everything a "Community of Practice" creates unrealistic expectations for spontaneous organizing and knowledge sharing. The managers of Virtual Project Teams have organizing challenges that are very different from those facing stewards of Communities of Practice. Provided in this chapter are analyses of the differences between virtual teams and communities of practice, and linked are two growing phenomena: virtual organizing and knowledge sharing (knowledge management), based on empirical work from both fields of research.

In the first of the three types of virtual organization, including Communities of Practice, knowledge sharing is the main purpose of the organization, and communications are driven by a need to make information available. In this type, the culture is primarily egalitarian. In contrast, the second type, which includes Virtual Project Teams, occurs where organizing is driven by project deadlines or individual agendas. Here, knowledge sharing requires extraction or release of information. The corresponding management culture is directive, and the organizing structure is purposeful. A third type, including joint ventures, favors a direct exchange of information for mutual benefit. Here, the culture is primarily utilitarian, and the organizing structure enables exchange. These three types each include a variety of subtypes and are evidence of the burgeoning growth of virtual endeavors and the compelling need to share knowledge in complex, dispersed organizations. In practice, organizations employ all these types and their variations. Therefore, awareness of their differences in culture and knowledge sharing helps leaders, members, and consultants to focus their efforts productively, with realistic expectations for performance.

Background and Purpose

Virtual organizations arrived on the scene, replacing other forms of working (Fisher & Fisher, 1998; Grenier & Metes, 1995; Lipnack & Stamps, 1997); while, from a different route, knowledge management emerged as an organizing strategy (Brown & Duguid, 2000; Davenport & Prusak, 1998; *Harvard Business Review*, 1998; Wenger, 1998). These two streams of organizing converge at the nexus of learning and performing. Virtual organizing offers structures for performing, while knowledge management offers strategies for sharing knowledge and learning in the organization.

Virtual Organizations

Virtual organizations are geographically dispersed groups of people who communicate from different locations (Palmer & Speier, 1997; Palmer, 1998). They may replace other forms of organization (Lipnack & Stamps, 1997), because they can accomplish work and enhance competitive advantage through speed and agility. Virtual organizations are recommended as new ways of working (Grenier & Metes, 1995), and there is an expectation that they will require new approaches to organizational management (Duarte & Snyder, 1999; Fisher & Fisher, 1998; Grenier & Metes, 1995; Igbaria & Tan, 1998; Lipnack & Stamps, 1997).

Initially, virtual organizations were defined as temporal, even ephemeral. They were "virtual," because they were dynamic, evolving, continuously innovating organizing strategies (Hale & Whitlam, 1997). Later, virtual organizations were considered a more permanent fixture in the organizing toolkit.

Virtual team management is of interest to organization scientists (Igbaria & Tan, 1998), information scientists (Jarvanpaa & Leidner, 1998; Liebowitz, 2000; Palmer, 1998; Palmer & Speier, 1997), and communications theorists (Robins & Webster, 1999; Romm, 1999); and there have been several attempts to improve their organization and management by categorizing different types of teams and their organizing mechanisms (Duarte & Snyder, 1999; Grenier & Metes, 1995; Hedberg et al., 1994; Lipnack & Stamps, 1997; Palmer & Speier, 1997). This chapter builds on those efforts.

Knowledge Sharing and Virtual Organizing

Knowledge sharing is an organizing function and the essence of knowledge work (Fisher & Fisher, 1998). It can occur at several levels—individual, team or group, organizational, industrial, and societal—and can be as mechanical as data exchange, as social as information exchange, and as organic as competency development and strategy execution. It can even be self-organizing or a combination of self-organizing and "husbanded" (Brown & Duguid, 2000).

Knowledge sharing is an aspect of knowledge management (Davenport & Prusak, 1998; Liebowitz, 2000; Nonaka & Takeuchi, 1995) that occurs when knowledge—actionable information (Tiwana, 2001)—leaks into, or is imported into, or exchanged within a system and adds value. Knowledge sharing can exist solely within face-to-face interactions and physical libraries; however, considerable aspects of communication and coordination rely on electronic means (Davidow & Malone, 1992; Svelby, 1997) or define knowledge management as using technology to enable sharing through access and relevance (Brown & Duguid, 2000). Therefore, knowledge sharing often relies on virtual forms of organizing and communicating, particularly in geographically distributed forms of human endeavor.

Role of Knowledge Sharing

Knowledge sharing affects learning (Olivera & Argote, 1999) and performance (Fisher & Fisher, 1998), because knowledge is a "matter of competence with respect to valued enterprise" (Wenger, 1998, p. 4). Knowledge sharing offers potential for increasing competency (Broad, 2000) by having the information needed to make decisions, by improving coordination of performance through shared information and meaning, by employing best practices widely to the benefit of the organization, by efficiently accessing help and information, by improving time to market, by improving customer satisfaction with products or services, and by learning and innovating products and services. Knowledge sharing includes document management (Collins, 1997; Lyons, 2000) plus "capturing," "organizing," "accessing," and "using" information and expertise (Uschold & Jasper, 2001). Examples of knowledge sharing are not exclusively virtual or physical. They illustrate businesses combining face-to-face opportunities with electronic means of connecting with information and ideas in places such as Ameritech (Klein, 1998), British Petroleum, Chevron, Ford, Lockheed Martin, Motorola (Dixon, 2001), 3-M, NEC, BP Exploration (Davenport & Prusak, 1998), Buckman Labs, Dow Chemical, Ericsson, HP Consulting, and IBM (Harryson, 2000), to name a few of the companies that pioneered knowledge management.

Under New Management

Knowledge sharing is revolutionizing management theory and practice (Crandall & Wallace, 1998; Evans & Wurster, 2000; Fisher & Fisher, 1998; Goldman et al., 1994; Hackett, 2000; Harryson, 2000; Martin, 1996; Myers, 1996; Savage, 1996; Snowden, 2002), because knowledge does not respond to traditional management theories of resource allocation or command and control. Knowledge can be sticky (Brown & Duguid, 2000) and unresponsive to strategies to transfer it; and it can be leaky (Brown & Duguid, 2000) and end up in unintended destinations. By linking knowledge sharing with virtual organizing, this chapter opens a door for developing new theories of managing in virtual environments and sharing knowledge in dispersed situations.

The Linking Framework

Integrating categories of knowledge sharing with types of virtual organizing is problematic. The literature on virtual organizing is focused on the characteristics of organizing and tends to ignore the details of what knowledge was shared how, where, when, and for whom. Likewise, the knowledge management literature is focused on characteristics of knowledge management and tends to lack sufficient description of the virtual nature of any organizing approaches involved. The variety and strategic nature of knowledge sharing make for idiosyncratic evidence of knowledge sharing at work, and this makes categorization difficult, whether the examples used are from studies by information scientists (Borghoff & Pareschi, 1998; Roy, 2001; Thierauf, 1999) or organization scientists (Davenport & Prusak, 1998; Dixon, 2001; Ruggles, 1997). Nevertheless, there have been several efforts to link the two constructs (Jackson, 1999; Malhotra, 2000; Oravec, 1996; Schrage, 1990). The framework presented here builds upon these other efforts to link virtual organizing and knowledge sharing.

The method employed in developing this framework was to review the literature and identify cases of virtual organizing with corresponding knowledge-sharing activities or cases of knowledge sharing with corresponding virtual organizing. Then, these examples, cases, and references were laid out in patterns based on shared organizing characteristics and organizing purposes. These patterns were given general descriptions and definitions.

Types of Virtual Organizing

Palmer and Speier's (1997) early study of 55 virtual organizations built on information from the field and identified four types: the unit, which includes the telecommuter (Crandall & Wallace, 1998); the project team (Lipnack & Stamps, 1997; Haywood, 1998); and temporary and permanent joint ventures (Grenier & Metes, 1995). These four types are encompassed by a different, although compatible, classification developed by Duarte and Snyder (1999). To these four, add professional collaborations known as Communities of Practice (Wenger, 1998), and information or chat groups known as Communities of Interest (Brown & Duguid, 2000; Fisher & Fisher, 2000), for a total of six types of virtual organizing. A seventh type, Communities of Passion, entered the language of Lotus Notes users, but this type is really a subtype of Communities of Interest. These six types of virtual organizing span a variety of business purposes, organizational designs, and cultures. Each has unique socialization, communications, and performance management strategies, because each has a different focus, scope, life cycle, and use of technology.

Some virtual forms of organizing exist primarily to get work done (Lipnack & Stamps, 1997), and some spring from a need to transfer information and knowledge (Wenger, 1998; Brown & Duguid, 2000). Some share tips, coordinate expertise, or troubleshoot; some exchange ideas; and some serve as conversations online. Some forms appear to be spontaneously self-organizing (Communities of Practice and Interest), and some are organized when management creates them to do work (e-commerce and Virtual Project Teams). Some are composed primarily of members within an organization (Duarte & Snyder, 1999; Lipnack & Stamps, 1997), and some forms are recommended for their ability to move across organizational boundaries and form new, virtual entities (Grenier & Metes, 1995). These varieties are more evident when each type is examined in detail.

The Virtual Unit

The Virtual Unit is the most commonly understood or recognized form of virtual organizing. Also known as home-based entrepreneurs, telecommuters (Bredin, 1996), teleworkers (Nilles, 1998), or computer-mediated work groups, these units operate primarily within an organization and engage in work that is continuous in nature. Virtual Units are independent operators (organizations of one with no chain of command), or they are out-stationed employees who share the same chain of command while doing the same or similar jobs in different locations. Some examples of this type are sales representatives and manufacturers' representatives, but the type may also include office workers who are working from home temporarily or permanently. They may employ "hot desking" or "hoteling" at the central office location as at IBM and Digital Equipment Corporation, where there is no permanent office for any employee (Hale & Whitlam, 1997).

The knowledge-sharing challenge for the Virtual Unit is to communicate priorities and best practices so that knowledge is extended within a region or group and consistency is maintained. This type of knowledge sharing is called "serial transfer" (Dixon, 2001). There can also be "near transfer," when separated units develop new business practices based on interpretations and applications of the experience of other units that posted this information electronically as, for example, the case of Ford Vehicle Operations (Dixon, 2001).

Community of Practice

The Community of Practice is perhaps the most popular form of virtual organization and receives considerable attention as group chat on the Internet or in corporations, because it is recommended as a tool for knowledge sharing. Wenger's (1998) foundational description of these communities appreciates the social aspects of learning and the self-organizing production of knowledge. Communities of Practice can be face-to-face or electronic. They can organize members within and without a specific organization. Their only limits are the nature of the topic and access to communications. A primary example of a Community of Practice is the Xerox repairmen, who used their interactions with each other in the employees' break room to diagnose and troubleshoot problems and develop best practices (Brown & Duguid, 2000). Their knowledge-sharing challenge is pertinence. When members find information and exchange useful, they participate; if not, they do not.

Companies are investing in the hardware and software that will enable these communities, and they are struggling with how to "manage" to make them happen, because, paradoxically, they seem most viable when they are spontaneous and self-organizing.

Knowledge sharing outside these communities to the rest of the organization is problematic (Wenger, 1998) when participation in these communities suffers from a lack of full participation by everyone (marginalities of competence) or failure to remember learning or apply lessons learned (marginalities of experience). While vendors of electronic groupware state that their products enable electronic collaboration, organizations cannot seem to control knowledge sharing in virtual environments, despite attempts to create sharing cultures.

The Virtual Project Team

The Virtual Project Team is recommended (Duarte & Snyder, 1999; Lipnack & Stamps, 1997) for its ability to transcend the barriers of space and time that are confronted by globally distributed cross-functional teams. Sometimes called networked teams (Duarte & Snyder, 1999), these cross-cutting groups are primarily internal to a business but may include suppliers and customers. They are similar to the virtual learning groups that professors establish in distance classes, where they must balance task performance and electronic socialization to achieve high performance (Jarvenpaa & Leidner, 1998). Their most obvious use is in global software development (Haywood, 1998; Karolak, 1998), where teams involve several businesses, time zones, and cultures. Virtual Project Teams often equip employees with home offices, as Hewlett-Packard did for new product design team members (Fisher & Fisher, 1998).

This organizing mechanism is focused on a project and is united by commitment to the project's purpose. Virtual Project Teams are temporary in nature, dispersing when the project ends. As learning and performing systems, they prioritize performance over learning. They are driven by deadlines and are challenged when they need to share their learning outside the team's boundaries (Brown & Duguid, 2000; Hornett, 1998).

Virtual Project Teams can engage in "near transfer" (Dixon, 2001), a type of explicit knowledge sharing, where the receiving team is engaged in a project or tasks similar to the source team. If they devise operating procedures or process norms that can be applied to future project teams, these forms of knowledge can be shared as accepted approaches or project models, a concept called "far transfer" (Dixon, 2001). This form of organizing also achieves "strategic transfer" (Dixon, 2001) when the impact is great and the larger organization learns and adopts new approaches. There is a difference between knowledge sharing within the teams and knowledge sharing throughout the organization (Olivera & Argote, 1999). Team knowledge can get embedded in the context of a specific project and resist transfer to other contexts, or strong team boundaries can prevent knowledge from leaking into the rest of the organization.

Communities of Interest

Communities of Interest most commonly occur on the Internet and involve people who do not share a profession or an employer. Inside companies, these communities may be constrained by the Information Technology Department's audits of computer use and Internet or intranet activities. In popular parlance, these Communities of Interest often call themselves Communities of Practice, adding to the confusion about how to operate in these organizations or how to operate them on behalf of an organization. Communities of Interest are similar to Communities of Practice; however, the members do not share a profession or an allegiance. Members of these list serves or chat rooms (e.g., Yahoo® Groups; Groove® Networks) share an interest in an event, an issue, a cluster of issues, or an idea. They are not necessarily organizing for any collective learning or action. They are accessing or providing information or comment. Sometimes, they may post a calendar or notices of upcoming events, but collective action is not deliberately coordinated. Knowledge sharing in these groups is primarily information and idea exchange. Action is dependent on an individual member's level of interest. The knowledge-sharing challenge in this type of virtual organization is to extend the reach of information sharing, to expand involvement and awareness.

Temporary Virtual Organizations

Temporary Virtual Organizations are referred to as new venture development and also as networked teams (Duarte & Snyder, 1999). Their purpose is to explore the feasibility of joint ventures (Grenier & Metes, 1995). The Temporary Virtual Organization shares the project-based life cycle of the Virtual Project Team, but its focus is to span organizations and produce a joint effort. Consequently, the membership of these organizations is external to any one organization and may include employees of several organizations who are not usually in an ongoing business relationship. The performance challenge for this organization is whether ongoing business can be developed. The knowledge-sharing process is a "near transfer" (Dixon, 2001), with an exchange of explicit information.

At the point where the exchange concludes with a deal, the Temporary Virtual Organization changes (morphs) into another form of organizing that may or may not be virtual. This process can include strategic transfers of knowledge, where collective knowledge accomplishes an infrequent, nonroutine task of importance to an entire organization (Dixon, 2001). This form poses considerable challenge for knowledge-sharing students, because the members of the Temporary Virtual Organization represent various organizing cultures and business functions and do not necessarily share an organizational allegiance, culture, schema, or value system. They exchange data or information without sharing contextual appreciation.

Permanent Virtual Organizations

This type represents the *modus vivendi* of the virtual enterprise (Hale & Whitlam, 1997). While first introduced in the literature as a vehicle for ongoing joint ventures such as Ameritech's cellular services (Grenier & Metes, 1995) or Sun Micro Systems and Alpha Laval Agri (Hedberg et al., 1994), this business model has changed over time into three distinct varieties, or clusters, of organizing types.

One cluster includes the essence of e-commerce and employs six different organizing models for virtual electronic business: a Web presence, partnerships, star alliances that are coordinated networks of relationships, value chain or supply chain models, market alliances such as Amazon.com, and virtual brokers (Burn & Ash, 2000). Another cluster of this permanently virtual type focuses on creating agility (Goldman et al., 1994; Savage, 1996) and is an organizing model that forms in response to market opportunities. This type ranges from a fragile "dot-com" business model to the heartier dot-com or a model of low overhead with contracted relationships and services such as those commonly found in the magazine publishing business. The third cluster is what Jones (1999) calls a network of experts who organize quickly to design and produce a product or service while retaining their individual corporate affiliations and legal identities. The boundaries established in these low-overhead ventures, where considerable work is contracted out, provide barriers to collective learning. Indeed, these forms of organizing are often created to avoid learning. For example, a Web-based bookseller may deliberately choose to *not* learn product delivery and therefore contract out for this service.

There is a lack of information on the relative "virtualness" of documented success in knowledge sharing through these joint ventures; for example, IBM Japan collaborating with NTT (Badaracco, 1996) to develop capabilities with large-scale computer networks. The same is true for IBM's work with Mitsubishi to create a joint satellite communications service, and, in the United States, with MCI to get a stake in the telecommunications business (Badaracco, 1996).

Types of Knowledge Sharing

Each of these six types of virtual organizations fits into three distinct types based on its purpose and strategy for performance (Table 1). Type 1 exists to share;

Table 1.   Types of Virtual Organizing and Their Knowledge-Sharing Systems

Organizing Strategy:	Type One: Exist to Share	Type Two: Event-Driven	Type Three: Transaction-Driven
Types of Virtual Organizations:	Virtual Units	Virtual Project Teams	Temporary Virtual Organizations
	Communities of Practice	Communities of Interest	Permanent Virtual Organizations
Culture / Values:	Social learning	Hierarchies of expertise	Utilitarian
Knowledge Sharing:	Meaning is negotiated. Potential is there for shared schema.	Explicit Tacit may develop over time with enough experience to create shared schema.	None. Serve to exchange data or information. Learning may occur but it is not an objective.
Type of Knowledge Sharing System:	**Cooperative**	**Competitive**	**Exchange**

Type 2 is driven by events, and Type 3 exists to make transactions. These organizing strategies result in different knowledge-sharing strategies. For example, knowledge sharing drives the Communities of Practice and the Virtual Units that share information to achieve a commonly held purpose. The members engage in social learning, where meaning is negotiated. These are cooperative systems. In contrast, the Virtual Project Teams and the Communities of Interest extract information to achieve a specific purpose to which members may be directly or tangentially connected. This focus on purpose develops hierarchies of expertise in which ideas compete for value. These are competitive knowledge-sharing systems, where learning is primarily explicit. The third type, Temporary and Permanent Virtual Organizations, exchange information to execute a business operation that is delineated, not shared. Their culture is utilitarian. In these exchange systems, knowledge sharing is not a goal.

In these three distinct ways, knowledge-sharing strategies vary with type and purpose of virtual organization. Additional research may determine how these differences in approach—sharing, extracting, or exchanging affect theorizing about organizing cultures, performance, learning, knowledge management, and change management. The need to manage each type differently becomes apparent when comparing them.

Type 1: Exist to Share—Cooperative Systems

Both Virtual Units and Communities of Practice are driven by a need to share. They are organized for purposes of sharing information and engage in benchmarking best practices and exchanging tips. These two types rely on peer-to-peer transfer of information and create cultures of uncompetitive information sharing, where meaning is negotiated through a social learning process (Wenger, 1998). For the Virtual Unit, this is encouraged when all members report to the same management. For the Community of Practice, peers may or may not report to the same management, but their knowledge sharing is an expression of collegiality, wherein the members share a profession, a practice.

In both of these cases, the communal bond is a tacit one. Members share a profession and, therefore, a mental schema (Bartunek et al., 1992), a way of thinking or problem solving. Explicit knowledge may be encapsulated in insider language, lingo, or acronyms. Managers of these groups promote and reward cooperation.

Type 2: Event Driven—Competitive

In contrast to Virtual Units and Communities of Practice, Communities of Interest and Virtual Project Teams are both driven by events. Their needs for information revolve around who knows what or who can do what when. Project needs, deadlines, individual interests, or agendas drive the action to extract information. These organizations form and disband around events and tend to have limited life spans, unlike Virtual Units and Communities of Practice.

In Virtual Project Teams and Communities of Interest, members use queries, database searches, expert locators, e-mails, list serves, groupware, and chat rooms in order to access knowledge. They may have team leaders or discussion leaders that control use of these tools. There may be a social hierarchy within these groups based on apparent expertise or ability to secure useful information quickly. Consequently, the cultures of these groups can be relatively less collegial than the cultures of Virtual Units or Communities of Practice. Managers of these groups promote and reward timeliness, pertinence, and usefulness.

Explicit information may form the basis of knowledge sharing unless and until the members know each other. Tacit information is extremely hard to share in these organizations, because the members do not necessarily share a mental schema (Bartunek et al., 1992) or professional association. The culture is competitive: ideas compete for value and use.

Type 3: Exchange Systems

Temporary and Permanent Virtual Organizations exchange information pertinent to their business transactions. While electronic exchanges may be enhanced by socialization and sharing of expertise, such exchanges are ancillary to the purposes of these organizations. Knowledge sharing is the least social in these two types and is closer to information or data exchange and explicit document management than in the other four types of virtual organization. Managers of these groups value ease of access and completion of transactions.

As depicted in Table 1, virtual organizations are varied in their design, membership, purpose, and exchange of information. Each has different reasons and methods for sharing knowledge, and these create unique cultures. Virtual team leaders, members, and consultants can improve communication and management of virtual endeavors by focusing on the type of organization they are involved in, its purpose, and the nature of its knowledge-sharing system.

Discussion of Implications

There are several implications from linking knowledge sharing and virtual organizing for managers and members of these systems. Leaders and members of Virtual Units can benefit from efforts toward socialization and sharing. However, the Virtual Project Team leader who is devoting time to socialization and sharing may experience diminishing returns and a loss of performance on deadline (Jarvenpaa & Leidner, 1998). Likewise, stewards of Communities of Practice will want to foster sharing toward learning for advancement of the practice, while stewards of Communities of Interest will hold more value for volume of interest and individual access to and use of information. In these ways, one size does not fit all; each virtual type requires pertinent management. Because practitioners in many organizations are simultaneously members of several of these types of groups, it is helpful to distinguish behaviors in accordance with context.

Implications for Virtual Project Teams

Virtual Project Teams have membership from a variety of functions. It is this cross-cutting nature coupled with geographic dispersion that makes management of virtual projects even more of a challenge. Members of Virtual Units may be involved in projects too. However, they do not face the barriers of cross-functional team membership that make developing a shared understanding so difficult.

Managers and members of Virtual Project Teams have been given good advice (Hayward, 1998; Kayworth & Leidner, 2001), and there is evidence of best practices (Pauleen & Yoong, 2001a, 2001b). They need to place a premium on communication, shared files, and well-planned meetings. They need to ensure that customers and stakeholders are understood and understand. They need to communicate progress. They need to engage and make extra efforts to ensure that the project is in tune with the priorities of the larger organization. Virtual Project Team leaders will want to mix asynchronous communications for efficiency with synchronous opportunities to improve understanding and develop some shared perspective to enable effective coordination.

Team leaders in these environments need to recognize the value of hierarchies of expertise to assist them in structuring the work in accordance with business need and value added. They need to understand that knowledge sharing needs to be explicit and take time to make that possible and useful to the members. They need to use the event-driven, deadline-driven nature of projects as an asset, not a hammer. Most of all, they need to recognize that working virtually may jeopardize their ability to take in and analyze political undercurrents and environmental factors. They should openly consider this disability as part of project planning and execution. "Virtual" is a vehicle for communication, a nontraditional way of organizing work and power. Therefore, virtual teams are vulnerable to the impacts of traditional ways of organizing work and power.

Virtual Project Teams face additional challenges when team membership crosses boundaries into other businesses, for example, suppliers and vendors. In these situations, members do not share organizational allegiance, and they do not share a profession. Therefore, their challenge to communicate clearly and coordinate actions is particularly difficult. Members of these teams are distracted by the physicality of their home-based environments and have difficulty responding to the demands of their virtual teamwork. Team leaders can find reward and punish management systems relatively useless in a virtual work environment, where the team leader does not control or influence the reward and punishment structure or policies of the team members' environments. In addition, when the work is done, Virtual Project Teams disband. Any fealty or goodwill based on virtual social exchange may not apply in the next project that has team members who may be of a different composition.

Implications for Research

Each of the knowledge-sharing challenges of various virtual forms of organizing indicates a need for focused research on that type. If virtual organizing requires new forms of management, as most authors suggest, then those forms and theories also need to reflect the diversity of knowledge-sharing systems and related cultures. Further, researchers need to address the feasibility of extending traditional theories to virtual environments when virtual environments show evidence of being more complex and less capable of learning. Permanent virtual organizations may be designed to avoid learning activities and functions not considered to be core strategic competencies.

Increased Complexity

One company may simultaneously engage in many, if not all, of these forms of organizing, providing its members with a cacophony of organizing types and knowledge-sharing strategies. To those managers schooled in traditional management, virtual organizations can seem complex and difficult. Virtual environments lack some of the traditional efficiencies of span of control and chain of command hierarchies (Czernaiwska & Potter, 2001). Sharing knowledge in a distributed organization is more difficult (Burn & Ash, 2000). Virtual communication lacks rich context and can be fraught with more misunderstandings and unexamined assumptions than face-to-face environments (Hightower et al., 1998). This relatively impoverished context of virtual communication necessarily limits the social aspect of learning (Brown & Duguid, 2000).

Not Designed for Learning

The leaky and sticky nature of knowledge (Brown & Duguid, 2000) suggests that managers of virtual enterprises will be challenged to implement communications, socialization, and performance strategies that can simultaneously encompass the ambiguous nature of virtual organizing and the ephemeral characteristics of knowledge sharing. There is little evidence that these virtual organizations are designed for individual, group, or organizational learning. Each is designed to transcend physical and temporal limitations and achieve some purpose, and these designs may impoverish learning through asynchronicity and considerable reliance on text-based communications.

Analysis of Implications

The potential for collective learning when both virtual organizing and knowledge sharing are combined is weakened by diminished socialization and impoverished information exchange. There is some evidence that virtual organizations can perform well (Jarvenpaa & Leidner, 1998). However, most of the recommendations for knowledge sharing involve actions and interactions of people in physical space (Davenport & Prusak, 1998; Mankin, et al., 1996), not cyberspace. For example, at British Petroleum (Davenport & Prusak, 1998), face-to-face moments were more memorable (Gorelick, 2000) for the virtual knowledge management team.

The evidence that virtual organizing supports knowledge sharing is mixed. The evidence that they are combined in practice is strong and suggests that more work needs to be done in order to understand how these phenomena can achieve synergies.

The future will be challenging. While new ways of organizing should alter the individualistic and hierarchical nature of compensation systems (Crandall & Wallace, 1998; Hollensbe & Guthrie, 2000), electronic organizing and communicating may contribute to dysfunction and lack of consensus building (Romm, 1999). Further, the virtual nature of organizing may thwart learning. While new ways of organizing and learning provide foundations for successful strategies (Schwandt & Marquardt, 2000), they often require collective enterprises (Brooks, 1994; Jones, 1995; Mankin, Cohen, & Bikson, 1996; Schrage, 1990; Thompson, Levine, & Messick, 1999) that employ knowledge-sharing processes that are primarily social (Brown & Duguid, 2000) and work to eliminate hierarchies (Fukuyama & Shulsky, 1997). Accordingly, knowledge management requires problem-centered managers, not territory-centered (Zand, 1981). To date, reward and recognition systems tend to value territory or departments over problem solving.

The expectation is that managers and organizations will structure and communicate differently in virtual environments (Hedberg et al., 1994), but we have little evidence of the nature of knowledge sharing in those environments in the absence of an integration of research on virtual organizing and knowledge sharing. This chapter adds to that effort by alerting practitioners to the need for integration and by suggesting to researchers that there is much more work to do.

Conclusion

An integrated framework linking virtual organizing and knowledge sharing assists those researching and teaching management, leadership, information technologies, organization theory, and organization learning, and those attempting to operate virtual knowledge-based enterprises, to connect the disparate managerial approaches currently offered by the information sciences and the organizational sciences for virtual work and knowledge management. A framework of types of virtual endeavors, with corresponding knowledge-sharing strategies, provides a foundation for discussion of the managerial, cultural, and organizational issues affecting knowledge sharing (Borghoff & Pareschi, 1998). This framework's evidence of specific types of virtual organizing and knowledge sharing contributes to the broader body of knowledge enterprise literature (Davidow & Malone, 1992; Fisher & Fisher, 1998; Leonard, 1998; Shapiro & Varian, 1999) and supports the growing recognition that new ways of working are emerging in response to technological developments and the quest for global markets.

The resulting paradigm shift for management and organization theory is that knowledge originates in people and creates networks, communities, and routines with life spans that transcend the tenure of individual members (Czerniawska & Potter, 2001; Leibowitz, 2000). Thus, theories of management and organization are refocused from people to processes.

Researchers from sociotechnical systems theory, organizational learning, culture theory, and information sciences can begin to develop effective virtual management models with corresponding knowledge-sharing practices. Meanwhile, practitioners should question recipes that transfer what is known from physical work environments to prescriptions for virtual ones. Instead, they should focus on the purpose and culture of their virtual organization and communicate and manage that in support of a value for appropriate knowledge sharing. In these ways, practitioners in Virtual Project Teams face unique challenges in this regard, as they must add to their project management competencies the additional demands for electronic communication and performance management at a distance. The framework provided by this chapter helps to clarify the differences between collaborative organizations (e.g., Virtual Units, Communities of Practice) and cross-cutting project teams. Virtual Project Teams are bounded by the traditional constraints of time, scope, quality, and budget, *plus* the communication and knowledge-sharing challenges of cross-cutting and geographically dispersed memberships. Therefore, Virtual Project Teams deserve special attention and support, not advice derived from traditional work or ideas better suited to other forms of virtual work.

References

Badaracco, J. (1996). Knowledge links. In P. S. Myers (Ed.), *Knowledge Management and Organizational Design.* Boston, MA: Butterworth-Heinemann.

Bartunek, J. M., Lacey, C. A., & Wood, D. R. (1992). Social cognition in organizational change: An insider-outsider approach. *Journal of Applied Behavioral Science, 28*(2), 204–233.

Borghoff, U. M., & Pareschi, R. (eds.). (1998). *Information Technology for Knowledge Management.* Heidelberg: Springer.

Bredin, A. (1996). *The Virtual Office Survival Handbook*. New York: John Wiley & Sons.

Broad, M. (2000). Managing the organizational learning transfer system: A model and case study. In E. F. Holton, III, T. T. Baldwin, & S. S. Naquin (Eds.), *Advances in Developing Human Resources* (8). Baton Rouge, LA: Academy of Human Resource Development.

Brooks, A. K. (1994). Power and production of knowledge: Collective team learning in work organizations. *Human Resource Development Quarterly, 5*(3) (Fall), 213–235.

Brown, J. S., & Duguid, P. (2000). *The Social Life of Information*. Boston, MA: Harvard Business School Press.

Burn, J. M., & Ash, C. (2000). Managing knowledge for strategic advantage in the virtual organization. In Y. Malhotra (Ed.), *Knowledge Management and Virtual Organizations*. Hershey, PA: Idea Group Publishing.

Collins, H. M. (1997). Humans, machines, and the structure of knowledge. In R. L. Ruggles, III (Ed.), *Knowledge Management Tools*. Boston, MA: Butterworth-Heineman.

Crandall, N. F., & Wallace, M. J., Jr. (1998). *Work & Rewards in the Virtual Workplace: A "New Deal" for Organizations & Employees*. New York: AMACOM.

Czerniawska, F., & Potter, G. (2001). *Business in a Virtual World: Exploiting Information for Competitive Advantage*. West Lafayette, IN: Purdue University Press, Ichor Business Books.

Davenport, T. H., & Prusak, L. (1998). *Working Knowledge: How Organizations Manage What They Know*. Boston, MA: Harvard Business School Press.

Davidow, W. H., & Malone, M. S. (1992). *The Virtual Corporation: Structuring and Revitalizing the Corporation for the 21st Century*. New York: Harper Business.

Dixon, N. (2000). *Common Knowledge: How Companies Thrive by Sharing What They Know*. Boston, MA: Harvard Business School Press.

Duarte, D., & Snyder, N. (1999). *Mastering Virtual Teams: Strategies, Tools and Techniques that Succeed*. San Francisco, CA: Jossey-Bass.

Evans, P., & Wurster, T. S. (2000). *Blown to Bits: How the New Economics of Information Transforms Strategy*. Boston, MA: Harvard Business School Press.

Fisher, K., & Fisher, M. D. (1998). *The Distributed Mind: Achieving High Performance Through the Collective Intelligence of Knowledge Work Teams*. New York: AMACOM.

Fukuyama, F., & Shulsky, A. N. (1997). *The 'Virtual Corporation' and Army Organization.* Santa Monica, CA: Rand.

Goldman, S., Nagel, R., & Preiss, K. (1994). *Agile Competitors and Virtual Organizations: Strategies for Enriching the Customer.* New York: Van Nostrand Reinhold.

Gorelick, C. K. (2000). *Toward an understanding of organizational learning and collaborative technology: A case study of structuration and sensemaking in a virtual project team.* Doctoral dissertation, George Washington University, Washington, DC.

Grenier, R., & Metes, G. (1995). *Going Virtual: Moving Your Organization into the 21st Century.* Upper Saddle River, NJ: Prentice Hall.

Hackett, B. (2000). *Beyond Knowledge Management: New Ways to Work and Learn.* New York: The Conference Board.

Hale, R., & Whitlam, P. (1997). *Towards the Virtual Organization.* London: McGraw-Hill.

Harryson, S. J. (2000). *Managing Know-Who Based Companies: A Multinetworked Approach to Knowledge and Innovation Management.* Cheltenham, UK: Edward Elgar.

Harvard Business Review on Knowledge Management. (1998). Boston, MA: Harvard Business School Press.

Haywood, M. (1998). *Managing Virtual Teams: Practical Techniques for High-Technology Project Management.* Boston, MA: ARTECH House.

Hedberg, B., Dahlgren, G., Hansson, J., & Olve, N. (1994). *Virtual Organizations and Beyond: Discover Imaginary Systems.* New York: John Wiley & Sons.

Hightower, R. T., Sayeed, L., Warkentin, M. E., & McHaney, R. (1998). Information exchange in virtual work groups. In M. Igbaria, & M. Tan. (1998). *The Virtual Workplace.* Hershey, PA: Idea Group Publishing.

Hollensbe, E. C., & Guthrie, J. P. (2000). Group pay-for-performance plans: The role of spontaneous goal-setting. *Academy of Management Review, 25*(4), 864–872.

Igbaria, M., & Tan, M. (Eds.). (1998). *The Virtual Workplace.* Hershey, PA: Idea Group Publishing.

Jackson, P. (ed.) (1999). *Virtual Working: Social and Organizational Dynamics.* London: Routledge.

Jarvenpaa, S. L., & Leidner, D. E. (1998). Communication and trust in global virtual teams. *Journal of Computer-Mediated Communication, 3*(4), June.

Jones, J. W. (1999). *The Virtual Entrepreneur: Electronic Commerce in the 21ˢᵗ Century*. Arlington Heights, IL: Business Psychology Research Institute.

Jones, S. G. (ed.). (1995). *Cybersociety: Computer-Mediated Communication and Community*. Thousand Oaks, CA: Sage.

Karolak, D. W. (1998). *Global Software Development: Managing Virtual Teams and Environments*. Los Alamitos, CA: IEEE Computer Society.

Kayworth, T. R., & Leidner, D. E. (2001). Leadership effectiveness in global virtual teams. *Journal of Management Information Systems, 18*(3), 7–40.

Klein, D. A. (ed.). (1998). *The Strategic Management of Intellectual Capital*. Boston, MA: Butterworth-Heinemann.

Leonard, D. (1995). *Wellsprings of Knowledge: Building and Sustaining the Sources of Innovation*. Boston, MA: Harvard Business School Press.

Liebowitz, J. (2000). *Building Organizational Intelligence: A Knowledge Management Primer*. Boca Raton, FL: CRC Press.

Lipnack, J., & Stamps, J. (1997). *Virtual Teams: Reaching Across Space, Time, and Organizations with Technology*. New York: John Wiley & Sons.

Lyons, K. L. (2000). Using patterns to capture tacit knowledge and enhance knowledge transfer in virtual teams. In Y. Malhotra (Ed.), *Knowledge Management and Virtual Organizations*. Hershey, PA: Idea Group Publishing.

Malhotra, Y. (Ed.). (2000). *Knowledge Management and Virtual Organizations*. Hershey, PA: Idea Group Publishing.

Mankin, D., Cohen, S. G., & Bikson, T. K. (1996). *Teams and Technology: Fulfilling the Promise of the New Organization*. Boston, MA: Harvard Business School Press.

Martin, J. (1996). *Cybercorp: The New Business Revolution*. New York: AMACOM.

Myers, P. S. (ed.). (1996). *Knowledge Management and Organizational Design*. Boston, MA: Butterworth-Heinemann.

Nilles, J. M. (1998). *Managing Telework: Strategies for Managing the Virtual Workforce*. New York: John Wiley & Sons.

Nonaka, I., & Takeuchi, H. (1995). *The Knowledge-Creating Company*. New York: Oxford University Press.

Olivera, F., & Argote, L. (1999). Organizational learning and new product development: CORE processes. In L. Thompson et al. (Eds.), *Shared*

Cognition in Organizations. Mahwah, NJ: Lawrence Erlbaum Associates.

Oravec, J. (1996). *Virtual Individuals, Virtual Groups: Human Dimensions of Groupware and Computer Networking.* Cambridge, UK: Cambridge University Press.

Palmer, J. W. (1998). The use of information technology in virtual organizations. In M. Igbaria, & M. Tan (Eds.), *The Virtual Workplace.* Hershey, PA: Idea Group Publishing.

Palmer, J. W., & Speier, C. (1997). *A typology of virtual organizations: An empirical study.* On the Web: http://hsb.baylor.edu/ramsower/ais.ac97/papers/palm_spe.htm. Retrieved February 1999.

Pauleen, D. F., & Yoong, P. (2001a). Facilitating virtual team relationship via Internet and conventional communication channels. *Internet Research: Electronic networking applications and policy, 11*(3), 190–202.

Pauleen D. F., & Yoong, P. (2001b). Relationship building and the use of ICT in boundary-crossing virtual teams: A facilitator's perspective. *Journal of Information Technology, 16*(4), 205–220.

Robins, K., & Webster, F. (1999). *Times of the Technoculture: From the Information Society to the Virtual Life.* New York: Routledge.

Romm, C. T. (1999). *Virtual Politicking: Playing Politics in Electronically Linked Organizations.* Cresskill, NJ: Hampton Press.

Roy, R. (ed.). (2001). *Industrial Knowledge Management: A Micro-Level Approach.* London: Springer.

Ruggles, R. L. (ed.). (1997). *Knowledge Management Tools.* Boston, MA: Butterworth-Heinemann.

Savage, C. M. (1996). *Fifth Generation Management: Co-Creating Through Virtual Enterprising, Dynamic Teaming, and Knowledge Networking.* Boston, MA: Butterworth-Heineman.

Schrage, M. (1990). *Shared Minds: The New Technologies of Collaboration.* New York: Random House.

Schwandt, D. R., & Marquardt, M. J. (2000). *Organizational Learning: From World-Class Theories to Global Best Practices.* Washington, DC: St. Lucie Press.

Shapiro, C., & Varian, H. R. (1999). *Information Rules: A Strategic Guide to the Network Economy.* Boston, MA: Harvard Business School Press.

Snowden, D. (2002). *Complex acts of knowing — paradox and descriptive self-awareness,* IBM Global Services white paper. Also published in *Journal of Knowledge Management, 6,* 2 (May).

Svelby, K. E. (1997). *The New Organizational Wealth: Managing and Measuring Knowledge-Based Assets*. San Francisco, CA: Barrett-Koehler.

Thierauf, R. J. (1999). *Knowledge Management Systems for Business*. Westport, CT: Quorum Books.

Thompson, L. L., Levine, J. M., & Messick, D. M. (eds.). (1999). *Shared Cognition in Organizations*. Mahwah, NJ: Lawrence Erlbaum Associates.

Tiwana, A. (2001). *The Essential Guide to Knowledge Management: E-Business and CRM Applications*. Upper Saddle River, NJ: Prentice Hall.

Uschold, M., & Jasper, R. (2001). Ontologies for knowledge management. In R. Roy (Ed.), *Industrial Knowledge Management*. London: Springer.

Wenger, E. (1998). *Communities of Practice: Learning, Meaning and Identity*. Cambridge, UK: Cambridge University Press.

Zand, D. E. (1981). *Information, Organization, and Power: Effective Management in the Knowledge Society*. New York: McGraw-Hill.

Section III

Processes

Chapter IX

Effective
Virtual Teams

Tammie D. Hertel
TeamAbilities, USA

Abstract

It is likely that employees will work on a virtual team at some point in their careers. However, it is questionable how effectively organizations, training, and technology support the needs of virtual teams. Organizations must communicate what collaborative and knowledge-sharing behaviors are expected, establish reward and recognition systems that reinforce those behaviors, ensure that employees have the skills and tools required to fulfill those expectations, and develop managers that role model and reinforce the desired behaviors. Collaborative technologies must also become more self-managing, provide more compelling asynchronous capabilities, and consider that individuals may be part of many teams, thereby requiring better data aggregation and visualization.

Introduction

The days of frequent face-to-face interaction appear to be a thing of the past. The notion of proximal teams and real-time interaction may no longer always be an option or be desired. As such, it is more likely that employees will work on a virtual team at some point in their careers. Yet, how well do organizations really support virtual team effectiveness? How well skilled are employees at working and building relationships virtually? How well do our virtual team leaders really lead? Does technology really support the way teams work or support the socioemotional needs of virtual teams?

Effectiveness can vary greatly from team to team. When there is no consistent and cohesive mechanism for driving practices, setting expectations, measuring performance, and developing and selecting technologies, teams find it difficult to function effectively as they work across organizations or in other boundary-spanning scenarios. Unless team members are intrinsically motivated to over-come challenges that inhibit effectiveness, they either continue with extremely frustrating experiences or function unproductively. Virtual teams need motivation, incentive, and the reduction of existing demotivating factors. Corporations that attempt to implement a virtual environment without understanding the drastically different context in which teams must exist will likely suffer frustration rather than reap the benefits virtuality can afford (Piccoli, 1999).

Being equipped with even the most advanced technologies is not enough to make a virtual team effective. Much attention must be paid to the overall introduction of the concept of virtual teams and the tools, processes, and organizational systems that support them (Boyett & Boyett, 2000; Hertel, 2002; Joinson, 2002; Lurey & Raisinghani, 2001; Piccoli, 1999). For example, information technology (IT) should not focus on designing or deploying collaborative technologies without understanding the various needs of teams and how they work (Bruck, 2000b; Jackson, 1999; Robb, 2002). Technologists should also place more focus on enabling more compelling asynchronous (different time/different place) interactions. As corporations become more global and the number of available synchronous time slots decrease, work and life balance issues will increase unless corporations start to make the shift to asynchronous work. Another significant area where focus is necessary in collaboration technologies is the need for seamless integration of key collaborative capabilities beyond the traditional portal paradigm. Technologies must consider that individuals may be part of many teams. Individuals need technologies that can help them manage their responsibilities and commitments to all teams from one place, which provides activity coherence and aggregation of data from a variety of sources.

Training should not focus only on how to use the features and functions (mechanics) of collaborative tools but should also include cognitive and social processes, as well as individualized coaching that helps teams make the connection between the tools, techniques, and their practical application within an individual's own work context. The objectives of this chapter are to provide insight to virtual team challenges; illustrate how even with appropriate use of technology, training, best practices, and coaching, teams continue to be ineffective; identify socialization aspects that inhibit virtual teams from being effective; and identify technology issues that hinder virtual team performance.

Background

In the winter of 2000, a study was launched to determine the causes of Simcon's[1] virtual team ineffectiveness. Simcon is a highly dispersed corporation that almost exclusively leverages virtual meetings to bring teams together to get work done. Simcon's teams form dynamically and frequently span departmental structures. Because team members come from different reporting hierarchies, Simcon's teams operate with a great deal of autonomy. Teams typically solve their own problems, set their own objectives, and hold themselves accountable for completing work. Management sponsors or champions are assigned, but they have little involvement with team activities. Teams are periodically expected to review progress, status, or help needed with their sponsors. However, sponsors typically only act as sounding boards, ensuring the team's work is on track, and may sometimes be asked to remove barriers beyond a team's span of control.

Old norms provided the flexibility and luxury of frequent travel to meet face to face. Employees did not have to invest time in learning new skills required in distributed team situations. However, as travel budgets became limited, teams increasingly struggled to accomplish tasks and meet deliverables. The corporation no longer had the ability to compensate for the lack of skills by traveling to meet face to face.

The Working Closer Team

The Working Closer team was formed to identify the root causes of Simcon's virtual team ineffectiveness and develop solutions to those problems. The Working Closer team was named appropriately, signifying the desire to have teams function as though they were physically located together. The Working Closer team, with the assistance of researchers at University of California, Irvine, authored a survey instrument and a series of follow-up interview questions to probe into the effectiveness of Simcon's distributed teams. The corporation leveraged electronic and collaborative capabilities to help gather information and recruit teams from across the organization, and globe, to participate.

Methodology

The Working Closer study was part of a larger study of distributed team performance, and data gathered were analyzed along with data gathered during an additional internal study conducted by Kleinhanns and Klein (2001). Twenty-nine teams were identified in the organization that met the criteria of having well-defined team membership, a minimum number of regularly scheduled meetings, geographic dispersion, and willingness to participate in the study. The teams were placed into three different groups and were observed for six months. The first group was an observation-only group. This group was given no information, no training, and no tools; their behaviors and processes were observed and documented. This group was established to help determine whether behaviors would change due to the teams knowing they were being observed. The second group was observed and provided with a website that contained a wealth of detailed information about effective virtual team processes and techniques. The objective was to observe what would get implemented without any additional intervention. The third group was observed and provided the website and appropriate technology. Additionally, these teams were given a coach to help apply the concepts.

A Web link to a 72-question survey was e-mailed to every team member before and after the intervention. Examples of team tasks included a project team designed to develop relocation policies, a taskforce established to standardize hazardous waste removal practices across manufacturing sites, and a knowledge management team established to share "lessons learned" associated with troubleshooting production technology at different manufacturing sites. The coached teams were also interviewed at different times throughout the study.

What Makes Virtual Teams Effective?

Virtual team challenges can stem from the fact that there is little ability to get to know one another or socialize as in face-to-face environments, and that the processes and techniques for doing so are unfamiliar and different from what teams have been trained to do in face-to-face settings (Bruck, 2000b). The concept of virtual teams can be viewed as individual pieces that must work together and be orchestrated synergistically. To be effective requires not only technologies and collaborative capabilities but also the development of new skills, processes, and behaviors (Joinson, 2002; Lurey & Raisinghani, 2001; Piccoli, 1999), as well as the establishment of new norms and the communication of expectations along with changes to reward systems. The Working Closer study found that without motivators, employees (and management) did not invest the time necessary to increase effectiveness.

Motivators

Corporations must begin to define a new or enhanced set of expectations along with new structures, policies, and processes. This is not to suggest that a corporation needs to completely change its culture. Instead, corporations need to work with the strengths of the existing culture and add elements and new methodologies that support the shifts to globalization and virtuality. Additionally, if we consider that performance management and reward systems can influence effectiveness, then measurement against expectations must be developed (Boyett & Boyett, 2000; Nucifora, 2001). Simcon currently has corporate values, but none are specifically related to behaviors, norms, or expectations associated with virtuality or establishment of a collaborative, knowledge-sharing culture; hence, there is no real measurement of performance. This presented a challenge in the Working Closer efforts, because there was no corporate support to drive and reward the right behaviors and actions. At the conclusion of the study, it was hypothesized that this represented the single largest reason for lack of change after a variety of interventions.

There are many organizational variables that affect virtual team effectiveness and collaborative behaviors, such as group dynamics, education and training, reward systems, leadership styles, communication patterns, and performance reviews (Lurey & Raisinghani, 2001; Warkentin & Lee, 1999). Developing these appropriately can build the foundation for the necessary motivators that can be catalysts for change.

Measurement

Measurement is always a tricky task; however, measuring effectiveness is extremely difficult, because there are many variables that contribute to or inhibit it, and the variables are extremely hard to isolate. Handy (1995) suggested that team members that fail to uphold their team responsibilities should be confronted if their behaviors continue. This approach was recommended to the teams in the Working Closer study and was also included in Simcon's effective virtual teams classes. The feedback received from team leaders and team members was that they did not feel comfortable confronting others about performance issues, especially when the team member was not a direct report. Simcon often forms teams using matrix resources. Additionally, team members felt uncomfortable pointing to the team leader as a source of the team's ineffectiveness, although team members from one specific team requested private interviews to discuss their challenges with the team leader. Some of the reasons cited for virtual team ineffectiveness were lack of accountability, no reward for performance, no consequence for nonperformance, no established expectations to be measured against fairly, no ground rules, and no documented roles and responsibilities.

Another study (Lurey & Raisinghani, 2001) suggested that performance could be measured by monitoring output, processes for conducting the work, how well team members were enabled to work together interdependently in the future, and level of member satisfaction. However, the Working Closer study revealed that this approach did not work. Lurey and Raisinghani considered team members' impressions a conclusive account of how well a team would perform. Although it is true that participants are central to the work and can directly influence productivity and satisfaction, the question remains, what if team members do not know what they do not know? In the Working Closer study, teams initially ranked themselves much higher in effectiveness than an external researcher would have ranked them. Upon a series of direct observations, researchers found a great deal of discrepancy between the survey data and actuality. One issue was that the teams were not given a baseline of how they should be performing if they were effective, so they had nothing to compare themselves against. For example, not one of the teams used an electronic workspace, provided by Simcon, that would have been conducive to their activities. Some teams did not take meeting minutes, almost all teams used e-mail as their exclusive form of communication for everything, and a percentage of teams experienced frequent team member changes. None of the teams had a process for integrating new members, a team history, or a visibly documented charter. In most cases, roles and responsibilities were not clearly defined, and in one particular case, the team members did not even have the skills required to complete the tasks they were being assigned. During the study, it became clear that teams had no idea how much their performance could have improved. Organizational leaders can be catalysts by establishing benchmarks by which teams can measure themselves; by guiding employees to appropriate resources; and by role modeling, rewarding, and recognizing the behaviors and mindsets that build a collaborative culture.

Reward and Recognition

Employees can be given the best tools and the best training, yet still be hindered by the lack of organizational support systems. If employee reviews continue to focus on the individual and ignore team contributions, employees will focus their energies on their individual efforts (Boyett & Boyett, 2000). If there is no reward for being a role model or exhibiting effective virtual team behaviors and no consequences for nonperformance or lack of discipline, an environment is created where there is no priority to be effective, and any activities related to improving effectiveness are viewed as having little value and not worth the extra time investment.

Boyett and Boyett (2000) compiled tips, tricks, and techniques for team success from several prominent virtual team experts, such as Lawler (1997) and Smith and Katzenbach (1993). There is a strong case for redesigning compensation systems, as current systems reward people for developing skills that help them get promoted versus skills that expand team capabilities or that contribute significantly to a positive change in organizational culture. For example, those that role model working collaboratively and sharing knowledge and encouraging others to do the same make significant contributions to the long-term success of global corporations, yet compensation systems do not reward this effort, most likely because the result is not immediately tangible. Suggestions for improving compensation systems included paying for knowledge rather than position, delivering pay raises as additional skills are acquired, or offering one-time lump sum payments when new skills are developed. The lump sum payments would work well where the skills are either required for a temporary or short-term basis, when a salary is already high, or when the corporation does not want the burden of an ongoing cost. Corporations should be revisiting compensations systems and ensuring that there is some form of incentive and recognition of the value of team contribution, knowledge sharing, cultural awareness, team effectiveness, and performance that goes beyond the traditional reward for completing tasks or other tangible deliverables.

Demotivators

During the Working Closer study, teams had many opportunities to express their frustrations with their processes, their tools, and their working relationships, among other things. Key findings were related to feelings of exclusion, frustrations due to lack of commitment and discipline, not having the right tools, needing to make decisions on which tools to use based on cost not productivity, and not having enough time to really do things right.

Establishing a Level Playing Field

Organizations need to understand the things that make remote members feel isolated from their teams and establish processes that prevent this sense of isolation from occurring. However, observations and interviews showed that team members were not conscious of how other team members feel. A typical example that happened too frequently was that collocated team members would gather in a conference room, while others joined remotely. This action immediately placed the remote members at a disadvantage, because the people located in the conference room typically engaged in side conversations or had issues being heard due to the positioning of a speakerphone. It was also typical that someone would start illustrating something on a whiteboard or flipchart that the remote members could not see, and at times, collocated members even performed inclusion activities that completely excluded the remote participants. The Working Closer recommendation suggested that if there was a mixture of remote and collocated team members that all members should participate in the same manner, which typically translated to everyone participating from their own desks via an audioconference.

Building Relationships Virtually

You can build very close virtual relationships, and teams should take the time to invest in the human and social sides of people, not just the part they play as a team member or business associate. Studies show that trust and respect will be developed when you provide the opportunity to share experiences, bond, and deliver on commitments. Taking time for small talk helps put aside formal roles and mentalities and can help the team become more cohesive faster (Lipnack & Stamps, 1997; Tan et al., 1999; Warkentin, Sayeed, & Hightower, 1997). However, when time constrained, positive social and relational aspects are ignored (Kleinhanns & Klein, 2001; Walther, Slovacek, & Tidwell, 2001). Only one team in the Working Closer study had team building as a regular agenda item. This was primarily due to inclusion and team building being perceived as taking time away from work. Organizations can improve this situation by making inclusion part of its standard meeting process. For example, agenda templates can be prepopulated to encourage and remind teams to take time to conduct relationship-building activities.

Discipline

For all that can be done to improve virtual team effectiveness, there is little that can be done to instill discipline, yet today's tools force the use of manual processes that require discipline. Nucifora (2001) stated:

> *Successful virtual teaming takes more than bonding and consensus. It also requires a rigorous mindset. Applied discipline*

and virtual teaming delivers speed, innovation, competitive advantage and a synergism that can be achieved with maximum efficiency and at a minimum cost. (p. 9)

When a team consists of members that lack discipline, are unprepared, or do not contribute, team members that exhibit discipline will become unwilling to devote time and effort, because they lack the trust in other team members that they will do the same. If this type of behavior is not addressed, it can diminish the performance of the entire team. A laissez-faire attitude toward commitments will lead to frustration and undermine trust (Kleinhanns & Klein, 2001). When there is a common belief that others will make good-faith efforts to behave in accordance with commitments (explicit or implicit) and act honestly in negotiation of those commitments, trust begins to be established among team members (Galvin, 1999). The teams observed during the Working Closer study exhibited an extreme lack of discipline. All too frequently, team members would hear comments such as "I know you can't see this, but …", or "I'm not connected right now, I'll just listen." These types of scenarios were caused by the lack of preparation and appropriate planning. Meeting materials were often posted to a team workspace at the last minute or were e-mailed just prior to the meeting start time. This lack of discipline penalized team members who did not have the convenience of multiple connections that allowed simultaneous use of voice and data, placing them at a significant disadvantage. People need time to prepare, read, and absorb; yet this preparation was viewed as added work (Kleinhanns & Klein, 2001). These behaviors were extremely demotivating for the team members who were consistently disciplined, because they felt their time was being wasted. There was also a frustration that ineffectiveness due to lack of discipline was not being addressed and therefore would not improve. By measuring performance against expectations, organizations can begin to address performance issues, especially those related to lack of discipline, that contribute to the ineffectiveness of an entire team.

Lack of Effective Facilitation

Because the virtual environment can be very complex, facilitators become key players in developing and implementing processes that hold the virtual team together. Facilitators are responsible for ensuring appropriate levels of participation, keeping electronic workspaces clean and organized, and for making team activities easy for people to accomplish, among other things. Challenges such as disambiguation; establishment of group cohesion; conflict management; remote management; and challenges with time zones, cultures, and other motivational factors force facilitators to be well skilled in addressing these challenges. Each additional challenge a facilitator must deal with adds to the cognitive load and amount of time required to effectively facilitate (Lopez, Booker, Shkarayeva, Briggs, & Nunamaker, 2002). Trained facilitators will be required until collaborative environments become more self-managing and compelling. The facilitator role did not formally exist in any of the teams in the Working Closer study. The observations found that team leaders tried to perform the responsibilities of both roles and ultimately did not perform either of the roles effectively. Consequently, team workspaces were not well organized and were cumbersome to navigate. Team members could not find what they were looking for and they could not find information on what they were expected to do, which resulted in excuses for why work was not completed. This greatly hindered the ability of the teams to make forward progress from week to week. When team members do not have discipline, facilitators must work hard to garner participation until good habits are established. Organizations should recognize the additional overhead required of the facilitator roles, recognize the value, and reward them appropriately for their extra efforts. Special recognition should be given to those facilitators who make positive improvements in team performance.

Making the Investment

For virtual teams to work efficiently and effectively, organizations need to invest in appropriate virtual team training. This can include cultural awareness, creating common understanding, developing team processes, developing relationships, and influencing technology direction to efficiently enable these activities. It is not achieved overnight. The social, cultural, behavioral, and cognitive processes take time to develop (Jackson, 1999; Kleinhanns & Klein, 2001). The point is that organizations need to start viewing these activities as investments and not expenses (Kleinhanns & Klein, 2001). This investment provides payback in the long run, even though the investment may cause an initial decline in effectiveness. Research shows that organizations that invest the time in various forms of process, communication, and technology training, produce effective virtual teams that catch up and outperform those that do not (Chidambaram, 1996; Tan, Wei, Huang, & Ng, 2000; Warkentin & Beranek, 1999). Lipnack and Stamps (1997) also stressed the need for greater socialization efforts among virtual team members. These efforts can also be supported by the organization through communicating what collaborative and knowledge-sharing behaviors are expected, establishing reward and recognition systems that reinforce those behaviors, ensuring that employees have the skills and tools necessary to fulfill behavioral expectations, and developing managers that role model and reinforce the desired behaviors.

The Working Closer study only addressed the aspects of providing appropriate technology, tool training, and coaching on techniques and behaviors, but there was nothing done to move the teams into long-term or repeated actions. After the study was over, the results showed that there was little increase in overall virtual team effectiveness, regardless of the approach used (observation only, Web only, or coached). Qualitative data from the study clearly indicated that teams felt there was too much overhead involved in changing processes, learning new tools, and addressing root causes or performance problems. Despite the fact that teams were frustrated with their inefficiencies, not a single one was willing to invest the time in making long-lasting changes, even though they had the authority and ability to do so. In one case, a team leader expressed that all the recommendations she was given were valuable and would no doubt improve effectiveness, but she would not entertain implementing any of them, because addressing the root causes of some of her problems was "too hard" and would "take too much time." Because there was no measurement, focus, or value placed on the effectiveness of her team by her management, she had no reason to make changes, and she was not internally motivated to do so.

Training

Skills and techniques are very different from those of the face-to-face environment (Bruck, 2000a). It is critical to develop training and awareness programs that go beyond the use of collaborative tools. Individuals must learn to apply tools and behave in ways that will instill trust and accountability among team members. Simcon provided employees with skill-based training on the tools being used, training on concepts and techniques related to working virtually, awareness of expectations and performance requirements, cultural and global awareness, and coaching to help transfer what was learned in theory and mechanics to practical application in the employee's own work setting. Overall, Simcon has a comprehensive program. However, publishing materials (such as best-known methods or even a detailed website) without other intervention proved to be ineffective in the absence of other motivators. Additionally, even though Simcon's training program appeared to be addressing all the right things, long term, it still did not motivate employees to action. The key lesson learned was that training alone, even a comprehensive program, did not solve the problems. It was only part of a bigger picture that should have also been implemented at the same time. Illustrated in Figure 1 are the elements identified during the Working Closer study that must be synergistically present in order for change to occur.

Technology

Technology is not a solution in itself; it is an enabler. However, if the appropriate technologies and capabilities are not available, it can greatly hinder a team's

Figure 1.   Illustration of Inputs Required to Establish an Effective Virtual Team Environment (Individuals may then reuse what they learned in other teams and thereby permeate the organization with effective behaviors.)

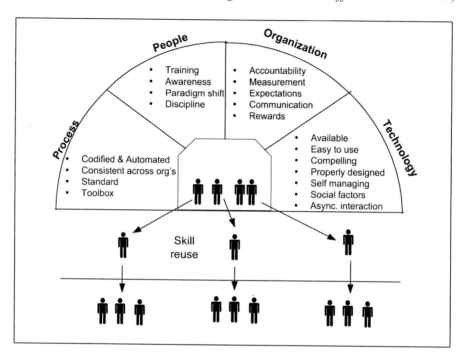

performance. The Working Closer study identified several key areas where technology gaps inhibited team and individual performances. The underlying premise is that before any IT solution is designed, implemented, or deployed, IT must first understand the complexities of how teams work before trying to prescribe a solution. Simcon is expert at deploying tools but not at understanding the problems the tools should solve. It is natural for technically minded groups to develop solutions based on technical requirements, but without input from individuals who understand team processes, human dynamics, human factors, and usability issues, systems can be delivered that do not meet the needs, and consequently, will not be adopted or bring the desired productivity improvements (Bruck, 2000b; Jackson, 1999; Robb, 2002). Furthermore, research on virtual teams and their technology usage has not delved deeply enough into how effectively technologies enable specific interactions. Often, questions are asked about what tools are used, how often they are used, and why they were selected, but the answers to these questions do not yield results that will help software developers and technologists build better capabilities. One study currently being conducted (Majchrzak & Malhotra, 2002) addresses much more specific questioning on how well IT supports a variety of interactions. The findings will be of great interest to Simcon and other organizations.

Simcon's IT environment is complex. At times, teams are either unaware of all the choices in collaborative technologies or they are unable to make the right choices due to a lack of understanding of what they need or of a tool's capabilities. To further exacerbate the situation, sometimes a single tool does not provide all the necessary capabilities, causing confusion about how to combine tools to get the right solution set. When individuals participate on multiple teams, there is no guarantee that the same tools were selected, which forces individuals to learn multiple tools and manage multiple, disconnected workspaces. Current tools in the marketplace also present some significant gaps for highly dynamic organizations such as Simcon that have self-forming teams, cross-functional teams, and individuals who participate on many teams. During the Working Closer study, technology was viewed as an inhibitor in several areas. The general opinion was that using technology effectively (including processes and techniques) required more overhead and time than team members were willing or able to give (see Table 1 for a summary of the technology issues encountered during the study).

The Multiteam Scenario

The collaborative tools available today help teams to be more effective…if a person only works on a single team. At Simcon, it is more likely for an individual to be part of many teams than it is for them to participate in only one focused set of team activities. Future technologies need to provide stronger and more seamless integrations of key collaborative capabilities, beyond the traditional portal paradigm, including better visualization and representation of data, alerting, and other visual cues in the user-interface design. Technologies must consider that individuals may be part of many teams, which requires capabilities that help individuals manage their responsibilities and commitments to all teams from one place. Without activity coherence and aggregation of data from a variety of sources, manageability quickly becomes a personal productivity issue.

Manageability was a big problem for Simcon's teams, because their technologies did not provide a consolidated view of all team activities across teams. Although team workspaces may help a team, they can be detrimental to the individual if they are implemented as silos. Because activities were too cumbersome to manage, individual contribution and participation suffered, and consequently, so did the performance of the teams with which the individual was associated. Having separate and disparate workspaces also created a great deal of redundancy, because the same information would often need to be placed in multiple workspaces, and there was no way to link teams that had needs for similar

Table 1. Summarization of Technology Issues

Issue	Challenge/Consequence	Solution
Individuals are part of many teams	• Current technology assumes an individual has a single focus and only requires one team workspace • Lack of manageability of activities across all teams • Loss of individual productivity • Difficult to find information • Data redundancy	Develop a user interface that integrates key collaboration components that provides aggregation of data from multiple sources into a single, visual view.
Difficult to share socio-emotional cues	• Rich media is too cumbersome and bandwidth intensive • Expects a real-time interaction that is not always possible in global environments • Lack of trust, respect, and cohesion	Develop technologies that can support visual representations of people, their bios, and other indicators that raise cultural awareness and sensitivity.
Asynchronous work is not considered part of the job	• Low participation • Excuses for why the work is not getting completed • Loss of productivity due to lack of focus and time to work on activities	Deliver content to the end user in a visual, aggregated way instead of requiring the end user to check multiple workspaces for activity. Tie asynchronous activities to electronic calendars to establish the work as part of the normal workday.
Asynchronous capabilities require too much overhead	• Requires discipline to schedule work and check multiple workspaces for activity • Low participation • Puts too much emphasis on live meeting time which affects work/life balance	Develop technologies that facilitate a continuous flow of information that can support both synchronous and asynchronous scenarios. Capabilities should become more self-managing and self-monitoring to reduce administrative overhead.

information. Maintenance of the content also became a burden that caused the information to become outdated.

Socioemotional Cues

Too many approaches to virtual teams concentrate on how well technology can substitute for face-to-face interaction, when what really should be considered is how well the overall environment (not just the technology) enables teams to work together in ways that are just as good as face-to-face interactions (Jackson, 1999; Lipnack & Stamps, 1997; Warkentin & Lee, 1999). The key is not in media-richness alone but in the opportunity to engage in many different forms of communication and social interactions that help clarify roles and responsibilities, help team members to get to know each other better, and help with other teamwork processes, such as effective meeting practices, development of strong foundational elements, and content and information sharing (Jackson, 1999). Expressivity (conveyance of vocal inflections, body language, facial gestures, receptivity, etc.) is also missing in current technologies but will become increasingly important (Devine & Filos, 2000). Globalization introduces the need for other visual indicators, such as mapping and location of team members, a world view, time zone indicators, and potentially other country information, in order to heighten cultural sensitivity and awareness. Future virtual environments should also include visual indicators that check for participant pulse when working synchronously (e.g., speaking too fast, speaking too slow, cannot hear, do not understand, have a question). Providing such visual mechanisms can allow less disruptive feedback than today's method of having to abruptly interrupt conversation in order to gain attention. This may also allow contributions from introverted individuals or those whose culture may not be comfortable interrupting others to have their voices be heard.

Simcon focused on developing virtual inclusion activities, virtual bonding and team-building exercises, and the use of still pictures to help team members associate names with faces, because videoconferencing was much too cumbersome. When introducing the idea of using photos and biographical information of team members, issues were experienced with the lack of a central repository for photos, the need for photos to be placed in multiple team workspaces, individuals not feeling comfortable sharing their photo with others, HR feeling that photos could be used for discriminatory purposes, and the time it takes to make the effort (especially when it has to be done for multiple teams) and team members being skeptical of the value.

Asynchronous Capabilities

How does deep dialog happen in the virtual environment? At Simcon, it occurs by using audioconference calls, videoconferencing, instant messaging, or chat, but these are only effective when time zones allow everyone to be available at the same time. In highly geographically dispersed organizations, teams would benefit by leveraging asynchronous capabilities to share thoughts or ideas and continuing to work across the globe, regardless of the time of day or the availability of others (Devine & Filos, 2000; Eom & Lee, 1999; Kleinhanns & Klein, 2001; Walther et al., 2001). The problem is that one of the mechanisms that has the most potential for boosting performance and productivity also requires more discipline than people are willing (or have time) to give. Any tool that allows asynchronous work to be conducted can be a powerful tool in a virtual environment, but Simcon's teams are uncertain and sometimes uncomfortable with shifting from working synchronously to asynchronously. This is not to say that one replaces the other. On the contrary; some of the best results can be achieved by combining both. It is important to strike the right balance of face-to-face, real-time, and asynchronous interactions (Devine & Filos, 2000). The struggle Simcon is currently facing is understanding how to recondition employees to think about separating what work really needs to be conducted with live interaction and what work can be done on one's own schedule.

One of the greatest frustrations heard during the study was that with existing technologies, individuals must remember to check for activity or be disciplined enough to pay attention to e-mail reminders or schedule time within their day to participate and contribute to asynchronous activities. Even when an individual exhibits commitment to the task(s), he or she is faced with an additional burden of having to monitor and manage links to multiple workspaces if he or she is in a multiteam scenario. Asynchronous capabilities are not compelling enough or easy enough to access and cause asynchronous activities to be viewed as separate from the job and, therefore, as extra work (Kleinhanns & Klein, 2001).

Another ongoing challenge is that teams are not always skilled in the art of online conversation and dialog (Tan et al., 2000). There are definitely clear techniques for structuring good discussions or the generation of ideas, but many are not skilled or experienced enough to do it. At Simcon, the concept of threaded discussions is relatively new to many. It has been typical for work to happen during meetings, and many things that could have been reviewed beforehand were reviewed with everyone on the conference call. Too much time was spent on merely sharing information in meetings rather than doing truly collaborative work. With limited time and multiple priorities, it is difficult to get team member focus except during the team meetings (Kleinhanns & Klein, 2001). Although teams tend to understand there is value in working asynchronously, many lack the discipline and comfort with technology required to actually work in that manner. Team leaders play a significant role in guiding teams and removing barriers in the shift to asynchronous work.

The Need for New Asynchronous Tools

Collaborative technologies must begin to focus attention on asynchronous capabilities and start bringing the content and the activity to the individual versus the individual remembering to go to the content. Team activities must become part of the workday and can potentially be resolved by automatically scheduling asynchronous work on electronic calendars. Because it is difficult to instill discipline, technology must provide ways to embed this interaction with little thought on the individual's part. Asynchronous technology must be able to reach across team workspaces and present all asynchronous interactions in a single, visually engaging, always-present view. Special alerting and presence detection mechanisms (beyond e-mail as a delivery channel) can help indicate where there is increased activity or where other team members may be present and actively contributing to an activity. Providing such visual cues and easy access, will keep asynchronous work at the heart of the workday and will keep participants easily apprised of any changes or activity. Lopez et al. (2002) suggested that the development of tools designed to listen and watch for behaviors based on user input could significantly improve the quality and process of virtual group systems.

Based on the findings of the Working Closer study, Simcon established a collaboration research team tasked with influencing the development of an immersive, intelligent collaborative environment in which asynchronous interaction, global tools, user interfaces, expressivity, and intelligent calendaring are key areas of focus. Provided in Figure 2 is one idea for visually representing asynchronous work.

This illustration represents a visualization that might be found within a user's collaborative environment, always active, always present. In this illustration, we see an individual who is part of many teams where asynchronous work was assigned. The hub and spoke model represents the asynchronous theme and can support the monitoring of and access to any number of asynchronous activities. All activities are presented in a single view, regardless of where the content resides. When changes occur, the spoke can provide several visual cues, such as changing color, to indicate a new submission or to indicate that something is due. To further the richness of the information, the spoke can display a count of new items added and include images to represent presence in a given workspace. By providing such visual cues, the individual is aware of the exact level of participation and activity without having to think about it. Additionally, the individual may be drawn to a particular spoke if a count gets high or when there are a large number of images representing presence.

Figure 2.   Asynchronous Visualization Example Showing a Consolidated View of all Asynchronous Activities

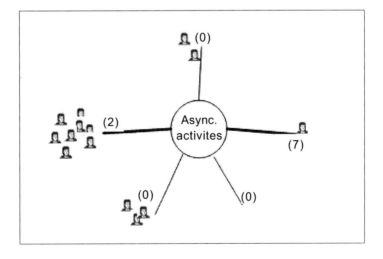

Solutions and Recommendations

There are many methods that can be implemented to improve virtual team effectiveness. However, it is of utmost importance to view the concept of virtual teams holistically before trying to implement a solution. Launching a corporately sanctioned program that leverages the strengths of departments such as IT, OD, HR, and Training will provide tremendous benefits. HR and OD should work to establish new norms and expectations that can help motivate and instill discipline and accountability, while training programs address helping employees to perform in order to meet expectations. Ensure that reward and recognition systems encourage the right behaviors and actions.

Implement more than just a list of best-known methods. Employees need specific how-to information and coaching, because virtual skills are still unfamiliar. Include a toolkit that provides detailed information on effective virtual team techniques, processes, and concepts to be used whenever it is needed. However, do not use this as a replacement for comprehensive training and development. Consider the implementation of change agents that can work with employees to apply the concepts and techniques to their own work contexts.

Standardize key technologies and core capabilities to reduce the amount of time team members spend on learning multiple tools and managing multiple workspaces. Do not prescribe IT-based solutions without understanding the complexities of how teams work. Teams will end up with tools that do not meet needs and will never be adopted or built into the team's work practices. Include process in technology design. Concentrate on the user interface, and establish an environment that is intelligent and integrated versus a series of disconnected tools presented in a portal interface. Make sure the system design codifies and automates business processes wherever possible to increase the likelihood that processes will be used. Tools and processes can be tightly connected and could potentially increase effectiveness if this is true (Robb, 2002). Technology must explicitly, yet transparently, embody cognitive and social processes. Develop self-managing environments using intelligent agents or other technologies (Lopez et al., 1997), and focus a great deal of energy on enabling more effective asynchronous work from technological and organizational perspectives. Set expectations that asynchronous work is part of the job and part of the normal workday. Make workspaces more manageable for the individual by considering the multiteam scenario, and provide compelling visualization that aggregates activities and other information from across team workspaces, regardless of where the content resides.

Future Trends

The Working Closer study was only the beginning of Simcon's virtual team research. The study provided clear direction on other areas that need to be considered and to be additionally researched. One key area is the shift to asynchronous work, which includes automation of facilitation tasks, along with self-managing collaborative environments, user interface design, and the development of more compelling technologies that increase participation and remove the need for so much discipline. Simcon also requires more data that firmly establish whether reward systems, accountability, and measurement of performance against expectations influences performance.

Conclusion

Kerry Johnson, Ph.D., Chief Research Officer at InsightShare (2002), stated:

> *Relationships, once based on proximity and chance now extend to a web of people and informal networks, many of whom never meet face to face. This fundamental shift in work has left teams without comprehensive tools that mirror the way they now must work to create business results. (p. 1)*

Because of this, a team's effectiveness heavily depends on the creation of processes that make up for gaps in other aspects of the overall environment. In order for teams to work effectively and efficiently, an investment of time and effort must be made. It takes time to establish shared understanding, to establish appropriate team processes, to set rules for participation, and to develop activities that foster the building of relationships. Factors such as social presence, balanced composition, training, and trust were shown to have a greater influence on outcomes than technological factors (Warkentin & Lee, 1999), although it can be argued that identified gaps inhibit performance. Keep in mind that effectiveness does not happen overnight or without time-consuming effort, and accept it. Do not look for the quick fix; one does not exist. The social, cultural, behavioral, and cognitive processes all take time to develop. Corporations must begin preparing and supporting effective virtual teams as an investment rather than an expense. There is no silver bullet, becoming more collaborative in a virtual environment is a significant paradigm shift that must be addressed holistically. Of course, this is easier said than done. Moving to action will require a number of catalysts, such as setting and communicating new expectations, holding individuals accountable for performing to those expectations, and ensuring that technologies and training programs support and enable collaborative work to be completed efficiently. If effective virtual teaming is not a priority among other things, it will always fall to the bottom of the list and never happen.

Currently, there is too much focus on real-time collaborative capabilities and not enough on establishing compelling asynchronous capabilities. As corporations continue to become more global, there are limited hours in a day that team members can meet synchronously. If teams do not start to embrace asynchronous work and technologies continue not to support it effectively, global corporations will be faced with serious work and life balance issues.

References

Boyett, J. H., & Boyett, J. T. (2000). *Tips, tricks, and techniques for team success.* Retrieved on September 30, 2002 from: http://www.jboyett.com/tips&.htm.

Bruck, B. (2000a, May 8). *How companies work. Creating distributed teams online.* A Caucus Systems White Paper retrieved from: http://www.caucus.com.

Bruck, B. (2000b, November 16). *How companies collaborate. Sharing work online.* A Caucus Systems White Paper retrieved from: www.caucus.com.

Chidambaram, L. (1996). Relational development in computer supported groups. *Management Information Systems Quarterly, 20,* 142–165.

Devine, M., & Filos, E. (2000). Virtual teams and the organizational grapevine. In L. Camarinha-Matos, H. Afsarmanesh, & R. Rabelo (Eds.), *E-Business and Virtual Enterprises*: *Managing Business-to-Business Cooperation* (pp. 414–424). Boston/Dordrecht/London: Kluwer Academic Publishers.

Eom, S. B., & Lee, C. K. (1999). Inevitable vs. evitable: An approach to the better situation for virtual teams. In D. Haseman & D. Nazareth (Eds.), *Proceedings of the 5th Americas Conference* (pp. 292–294).

Galvin, J. E. (1999). The effect of trust on team cooperation: A longitudinal view. In D. Haseman & D. Nazareth (Eds.), *Proceedings of the 5th Americas Conference* (pp. 975–977).

Handy (1995). Trust and the virtual organization. *Harvard Business Review,* (May/June), 40–50.

Hertel, T. (2002). [Virtual team effectiveness, Working Closer team study]. Unpublished raw data.

Jackson, P. J. (1999). Organizational change and virtual teams: Strategic and operational integration. *Information Systems Journal, 9*, 313–332.

Johnson, K. (2002, Fall). Team work: Cognitive and social process. *InsightShare Quarterly,* 1–2.

Joinson, C. (2002, June). Managing virtual teams. *HR Magazine, 47*(6), 68–73.

Katzenbach, J. R., & Smith, D. K. (1993). *The Wisdom of Teams: Creating the High-Performance Organization.* Boston, MA: Harvard Business School Press.

Kleinhanns, A., & Klein, J. (2001). Maximizing the contribution of diverse voices in virtual teams. Working paper WP01-3 available from the clearinghouse program on negotiation at Harvard Law School at: http://www.pon.org/product.cfm?productid=wp01-3.

Lawler, E. (1997). *Strategic Pay: Aligning Organizational Strategies and Pay Systems.* San Francisco, CA: Jossey-Bass.

Lipnack, J., & Stamps, J. (1997) *Virtual Teams.* New York: John Wiley & Sons.

Lopez, A., Booker, Q., Shkarayeva, S., Briggs, R., & Nunamaker, J. (2002). Embedding facilitation in group support systems to manage distributed group behavior. *Proceedings of the 35th Hawaii International Conference on System Sciences (HICSS-35).*

Lurey, J. S., & Raisinghani, M. S. (2001). An empirical study of best practices in virtual teams. *Information & Management 38*, 523–544.

Majchrzak, A., & Malhotra, A. (2002, April 26). *Creation of intellectual capital in "far-flung" virtual teams.* Presentation at the MIT Conference on Virtual Teams.

Nucifora, A. (2001, December 18). Teamwork goes virtual. *Business News New Jersey, 14*(51), 9.

Piccoli, G. (1999). Assessing managerial impact in virtual teams: Possible directions for future research. In D. Haseman & D. Nazareth (Eds.), *Proceedings of the 5th Americas Conference* (pp. 7–9).

Robb, D. (2002, June). Virtual workplace. *HR Magazine, 47*(6), 105–110.

Tan, B. C. Y., Wei, K., Huang, W., & Ng, G. (2000, June). A dialog technique to enhance electronic communication in virtual teams. *IEEE Transactions on Professional Communication, 43*(2), 153–165.

Walther, J. B., Slovacek, C. L., & Tidwell, L. C. (2001). Is a picture worth a thousand words. *Communication Research.*

Warkentin, M., & Beranek, P. (October, 1999). Training to improve virtual team communication. *Information Systems Journal, 9*(4), 271–289.

Warkentin, M., & Lee, Y. (1999). The impact of information quality on perceptions and outcomes of computer-mediated communication. In D. Haseman & D. Nazareth (Eds.), *Proceedings of the 5th Americas Conference* (pp. 367–368).

Warkentin, M., Sayeed, L., & Hightower, R. (1997). Virtual teams versus face-to-face teams; an exploratory study of a web-based conference system. *Decision Sciences, 29,* 975–996.

Endnotes

[1]   Simcon is a fictitious name used to maintain anonymity.

Chapter X

Prelude to Virtual Groups: Leadership and Technology in Semivirtual Groups

Terri L. Griffith
Santa Clara University, USA

David K. Meader
University of Arizona, USA

Abstract

A study of 76 more and less virtual investment clubs examines the relationships between communication technologies used for club business (from face-to-face to more highly technologically enabled), group leadership role behaviors, and club portfolio value. The results are interesting, with more and less virtual clubs benefiting from different forms of leadership behaviors. Clubs using fewer technologies seem to benefit from a greater focus on socioemotional role (communication) behaviors, while the opposite is found in clubs using more technologies. The effect for procedural role behaviors (agenda setting and the like) appears to run in the opposite direction: clubs using more technologies seem to benefit from a greater focus on procedural role behaviors, while the opposite is found in clubs using fewer technologies. Managers take into account obvious and subtle differences between more and less virtual groups.

Introduction

Virtual groups, groups that use technology to navigate the physical or temporal separation of their members, are expected to increase as markets expand globally and communication technologies proliferate. However, research on virtual groups is still in its infancy (e.g., see the brief reviews in Griffith & Neale, 2001; Warkentin, Sayeed, & Hightower, 1997), even though almost one third of 100 sampled Fortune 500 firms report they have virtual work in place (Davenport & Pearlson, 1998). Not surprisingly, of this same sample of Fortune 500 firms, only a "few" addressed the skills needed for managing in a more virtual environment.

In the last few years, the research landscape has begun to change. Across the range of traditional and more virtual groups, there are theoretical considerations of information processing (Griffith & Neale, 2001), group identification (Pratt, Fuller, & Northcraft, 2000), and conflict management (Mannix, Griffith, & Neale, 2002). There is also empirical work focused on trust (Jarvenpaa & Leidner, 1999), the formation of group norms (Postmes, Spears, & Lea, 2000), communication dynamics (Tidwell & Walther, 2002), and the development of relationships (Walther, 1995). However, field-based research (versus laboratory, often student-based research) forms the minority of the empirical studies (though see Gibson & Cohen, 2003; Hinds & Kiesler, 2002; Majchrzak, Rice, Malhotra, King, & Ba, 2000; Maznevski & Chudoba, 2000, for some current examples of field-based research). Our purpose in this chapter is to examine, in the field, the most prevalent form of work group—semivirtual groups—to describe certain important leadership dynamics in these groups. In particular, we aim to answer these questions:

- What role does leadership play in the success of more virtual groups?

- Which leadership behaviors have which impacts?

- Why do these behaviors have the impacts they do?

We draw the answers from a study of investment clubs that vary in their internal communications across the continuum of traditional interaction (face-to-face) to semivirtual interaction (both face-to-face and electronically mediated interaction; Wiberg & Ljungberg, 2001). These clubs allow their members to pool their money, expertise, and efforts for the purposes of investment success, and to a greater or lesser degree, financial education and social interaction. As of 1998, there were over 36,000 of these clubs in existence, and their numbers were growing at a rate of 40 a day (Kadlec, 1998).

In the sections to follow, we present background information on semivirtual teams and leadership role behaviors. The background information is followed by a discussion of how the need for various leadership role behaviors may vary in semivirtual teams. We then present the description of our investment club study followed by an overview of the study's results and our subsequent recommendations. We conclude with suggestions for how managers and researchers can learn more about the obvious and subtle differences across the full range of group contexts.

Background

Traditional, Semivirtual, and Pure Virtual Groups

There is no real reason that groups must work face to face. Classic characteristics of a "group" include interaction, interdependence, mutual awareness, a past, and an anticipated future (McGrath, 1984, p. 6). Being a group means that group members must communicate, directly (perhaps through electronic media[1]) or indirectly (e.g., by passing along different stages of completed work), in order to complete the group's work and to develop a sense of being a group. Purely virtual groups, then, are groups that work without any face-to-face contact. However, precisely what the structure of a virtual group is remains tough to pin down. Researchers use the term "virtual group" to mean different things, with no one definition universally accepted (Mowshowitz, 1997). Many take it to mean, simply, geographically or temporally distributed (Nunamaker, Briggs, Romano, & Mittleman, 1998; Warkentin et al., 1997), while others focus on qualities that make virtual groups different from face-to-face groups. Turoff (1997) focused on the adaptability and resiliency of virtual teams to meet unanticipated needs. Others discussed the need for multiple media to support group member interaction (Nunamaker et al., 1998), while still others focused on the global and intercultural natures of many of these groups (e.g., Maznevski & Chudoba, 2000). We acknowledge the value of these dimensions but believe at this stage of our understanding that we should focus on the variety of technologies used in the group's work. This approach is then applicable to groups a world or a cubicle apart, culturally heterogeneous or homogeneous, synchronous or asynchronous, linguistically familiar or different.

We see virtualness more as a continuum of context rather than a discrete differentiation of face-to-face and virtual [at the higher level of virtual organization, Venkatramen (1998) argued for a similar view]. While the bulk of computer-mediated communication research focuses on the dichotomy of face-to-face versus virtual (such as media richness theories), the existence of semivirtual groups, groups that meet face to face as well as virtually, seems to predominate the industrial scene (Griffith, in press; Nunamaker, 1998; Warkentin, 1997; Zigurs, 2003). We suggest that managers can fruitfully consider two dimensions of virtualness in designing and managing such groups: level of face-to-face interaction and variety of technological support. Within these dimensions, we see three categories of groups. Members of traditional groups perform group activities only face-to-face and without technology support. Members of pure virtual groups perform their activities completely apart, though generally with varying amounts and types of technology support (such as e-mail, videoconferencing, or knowledge management systems). Members of semivirtual groups probably make up the majority of all groups in businesses. These groups interact over time, according to the needs of the moment, and use a variety of technological tools. While we reserve the term "pure virtual" for groups that never work face to face, we propose that this two-dimensional approach to the

Figure 1.   Two-Dimensional Model of Virtual Groups (Adapted from Griffith & Neale, 2001)

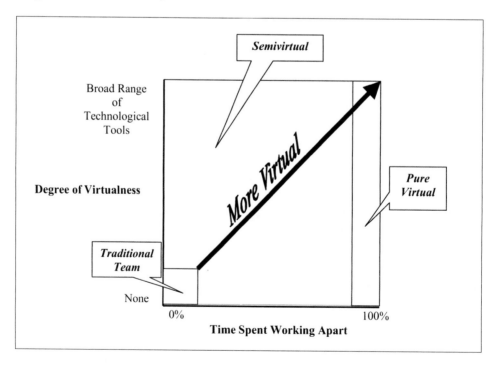

range of virtualness will help managers plan for and run productive groups across the range of virtualness likely to be seen in organizations. Illustrated in Figure 1 is this perspective, though it is beyond the scope of this chapter to examine the framework in detail.

In our field study of investment clubs, we adopt this emerging view of varying degrees of virtualness, rather than a simple dichotomy between face-to-face and virtual. Virtualness means the degree to which group members use a variety of communication technologies for their interaction. High virtualness means extensive use, and low virtualness means minimal use. However, we have had to exclude purely virtual groups in the current field study based on the limited availability of such investment clubs (only two such clubs were identified at the time of our study). So, in this chapter, we look at the range of traditional and semivirtual groups. Situations where face-to-face communication never occurs are left for future work. This approach lets us consider the most common parts of the continuum (semivirtual groups), while also letting us focus our analyses on the technology dimension of virtualness.

What We Know about Leadership Roles in Groups

We look at the dynamics of virtual groups from the perspective of how virtualness and leadership roles work together in groups. We examine groups on a continuum based on the variety of technology used for communicating about club business. Below we present background on group leadership roles, and then in the next section make the link: How do degree of virtualness and leadership behaviors work together to determine a group's success?

Leadership behaviors are important in organizations generally, and in groups specifically. The study of leadership has an extensive background in the social sciences, and specific leadership roles that people play are useful for understanding how technologically enabled groups perform (e.g., Zigurs & Kozar, 1994). Groups need people who can do the task, people who can organize the task, and people who can motivate the members to participate (Steiner, 1972). Certain combinations of these observable behaviors constitute leadership *roles*. However, in this line of thinking, any member of a group can demonstrate leadership behaviors at various times and situations—leadership then is not restricted to just one person, even the "official" leader. The key is that someone performs a specific behavior, and this action provides structure for the group's functioning. We chose to study group leadership role behaviors (versus other leadership topics such as information processing, conflict management, leader identification, leader style, etc.), because they provide an effective and basic lens through which we can see the structure and dynamics of semivirtual groups. Without the presence of these roles, it is difficult for a group to succeed.

Current research describes task, procedural, and socioemotional leadership roles. Ketrow (1991) summarized the different leadership role categories as follows:

- The **task leadership role** (also sometimes called the analytical role) deals with the generation and evaluation of information necessary to the goal of the group.

- The **procedural leadership role** deals with directing the group's actions.

- The **socioemotional leadership role** deals with the activities that motivate contribution and cooperation within the group.

What We Need to Know

Group Leadership Roles and Technology

What we know about the different communication technologies provides mixed insight into how group leadership roles will function in semivirtual groups. Most studies focus on e-mail, chat rooms, bulletin boards, and videoconferencing, but do not consider these activities under the lens of leadership role behaviors. For example, communication in media with fewer social context cues is more likely to result in uninhibited communication (Sproull & Kiesler, 1986), yet in some circumstances may also lead to more personal relationships than communication through media with more social context cues (Walther, 1995). Computer-mediated work is likely to be more task focused (Jarvenpaa, Rao, & Huber, 1988) and direct (Tidwell & Walther, 2002), yet people may be less likely to notice the passage of time (Webster, Trevino, & Ryan, 1993). Sproull and Kiesler (1991) noted that electronic communication creates situations where "People don't establish or enforce deadlines; they lack norms for smooth teamwork; they fail to resolve inefficient or inequitable time demands" (p. 53). Broadly, semivirtual teams may experience more and different types of conflict than traditional teams, resulting in undesirable outcomes, unless team processes are effectively managed (Mannix et al., 2002). Leadership role behaviors are key to this management.

When group leadership role behaviors and degree of virtualness are considered together, moderated effects may surface—that is, both the type of behavior exhibited and the type of group (more or less virtual) may matter to the outcome. For example, groups further toward the pure virtual end of the continuum may perform their tasks in enriched information contexts (if they are using a broad range of technologies) and so will have to manage the additional complexities presented by using these multiple technologies before they can gain any benefit of the enrichment. Let us look at the investment club field study to investigate these issues in a real-world context.

Field Study

Our field study of investment clubs lets us examine the relationships between three factors: the variety of communication technologies used for club business (from traditional to semivirtual settings), group leadership role behaviors, and club portfolio value. These results generalize to a broader range of public and private groups that function in semivirtual settings, given that we are looking at these issues within the context of functioning groups with real money on the line. As we noted earlier, investment clubs are comprised of groups of people who combine their money, efforts, and expertise to make pooled stock market investments. As of January 2003, investment clubs had more than $125 billion (USD) invested (http://www.better-investing.org/about/fact.html).

All of the clubs in this study met once a month to share their investment research and to make group investment decisions. These clubs vary in whether and how they communicate the rest of the month. The traditional clubs have limited interactions and rely on their monthly face-to-face meetings to exchange information. The semivirtual clubs interact to varying degrees over varying technologies over the course of the month.

In the sections below, we provide a full description of the hypotheses and analysis. This is a relatively "academic" section. If this is not your interest, we suggest going directly to the "Overview of Results," "Recommendations," and "Conclusions," sections, where we present the results in context with the implications for management.

Hypotheses

Socioemotional Leadership Role Behaviors

Socioemotional leadership role behaviors affect the management of contributions and cooperation within the group. In particular, the goal of socioemotional leadership role behaviors is to make the information stored within the members of the group available for the use of the group as a whole. That is, get people to engage themselves in the work. There are two ways to explain how the degree of virtualness will interact with socioemotional leadership role behaviors. The first is that more socioemotional leadership role behaviors may be needed to manage members' communications and contributions effectively in context with more virtualness. Communication may be electronic (e-mail, fax, etc.), reducing the availability of visual, nonverbal cues (Sproull & Kiesler, 1986). Members may have to deal with information from a variety of sources, each with different perceived media richness (Carlson & Zmud, 1999).

The second argument is that socioemotional leadership role behaviors are actually less necessary in groups with more virtualness. There are two components to this argument. First, the more complex technological context may reduce the socioemotional expectations for the group, and so less socioemotional effort is necessary. This latter contrast is similar to Locke's (1976) range-of-affect argument for job satisfaction (i.e., level of satisfaction is a function of what is expected, what is received, and how important the issue is overall). Group members in settings with high virtualness may understand and expect that various technologies will likely filter the leadership behaviors for contribution and cooperation and so will take more individual responsibility to perform as needed. That is, group members may structure their social and technical interactions to incorporate this understanding (e.g., DeSanctis & Poole, 1994). The second component of this argument is that a broader range of technological tools may provide more opportunities to communicate over time as well as greater ability to document and maintain access to information that is communicated. In essence, the technology may be performing socioemotional leadership role behaviors by enabling enhanced communication within the group (though prior research suggests that the group members will not perceive the role of the technology in this way) (Zigurs & Kozar, 1994).

To summarize these two arguments:

1. The successful performance of these leadership behaviors is important to the group's performance, yet these behaviors will be harder to pull off in groups with more virtualness.

2. Groups understand that socioemotional leadership role behaviors will be harder to pull off in groups with higher virtualness; however, as a result, these group members may have reduced expectations regarding the performance of these role behaviors and may be motivated to contribute anyway because of their expectations and through the opportunities provided by the technology.

Indeed, if group members in highly virtual groups perceive high levels of socioemotional leadership behaviors occurring, then these behaviors may be occurring at a level that is actually harmful to the group's performance. Both of these arguments suggest that the degree of virtualness will moderate the effect of socioemotional leadership role behaviors, though prior research does not provide much evidence for the direction of this moderation. In summary:

H1: The effect of socioemotional leadership role behaviors on group outcomes will be moderated by degree of virtualness.

Procedural Leadership Role Behaviors

Procedural leadership role behaviors, in general, affect how the group does its work. We expect virtualness to increase a group's procedural complexity; that is, make it more complex to do their task. More virtual groups have to manage more information, more information sources, and more communication media than do less virtual groups. Groups adopt technology tools, because they provide increased capability or other relative advantages, such as speed of communication, ability to work around time zones, etc. (e.g., Igbaria, Zinatelli, Cragg, & Cavaye, 1997). However, these benefits only come to fruition if the group manages the technology effectively (e.g., DeSanctis & Poole, 1994). The greater the variety of procedural leadership role behaviors, the better the group may manage their increased capabilities for the benefit of the groups' outcomes.

H2: The effect of procedural leadership role behaviors on group outcomes will be positively moderated by degree of virtualness.

Task Leadership Role Behaviors

Task leadership role behaviors, in general, affect the generation and evaluation of ideas relating to the group's goals. Here, we expect the impacts of task leadership role behaviors to be moderated by degree of virtualness, the degree of reliance on technology tools. People become more task focused in computer contexts in general, and in successful virtual teams, more specifically (Jarvenpaa, Knoll, & Leidner, 1998). This research finding is also supported by Walther's (1995) study of face-to-face versus purely computer-mediated virtual groups. If teams with higher virtualness are already task focused (perhaps an implicit focus on evaluation of ideas), we believe that group members may actually hurt, or at least offer no improvement, if they perform task leadership role behaviors (such as additional explicit evaluation of ideas).

H3: The effect of task leadership role behaviors on group outcomes will be negatively moderated by degree of virtualness.

Finally, we must also acknowledge that the relationship between leadership role behaviors and degree of virtualness is more complex than we will look at here. The nature of the task is clearly an additional moderator of technology and group outcomes (e.g., McGrath & Hollingshead, 1994, pp. 66–70). However, in this study, the nature of the task is the same across all groups, so task cannot be empirically examined. Also, the cross-sectional nature of this study limits our ability to study groups' evolution. Barley (1986) and DeSanctis and Poole (1994), to name a few, noted that technology use and technology structure vary over time and with use. Examination of these processes is beyond the scope of the current work.

Method

Sample and Procedure

We identified prospective subjects with three different methods. First, we asked the National Association of Investors Corporation (NAIC, the association guiding most investment clubs in the United States) for their support. The NAIC then provided us with the names of regional contacts for Arizona and Missouri. These contacts then provided us with the names of individual club presidents, who we then contacted and asked to distribute surveys at their next meeting. (Although many respondents had access to the Internet, we used a hard-copy survey to control for methods bias across the respondents.) Ninety-three surveys were obtained in this manner. The second method involved posting an electronic call for participation on the NAIC listserver. Interested parties contacted one of the authors via e-mail and were then mailed hard copies of the survey. Fifty-five surveys were obtained in this manner. The third method involved extracting e-mail addresses from every NAIC member club website. Calls for participation were e-mailed to this list of addresses, and hard-copy surveys were sent to those indicating an interest. Seventy-one surveys were obtained in this manner. All participants were offered the results of the study in return for their participation, as well as an opportunity to win $40 worth of lottery tickets in their home state.

Two hundred and nineteen investment club members completed surveys. From this group, we selected 76 respondents who were members of clubs that had existed for at least one year; provided full data on the study variables; met face-to-face at least once a month; and in case of multiple respondents from a particular club, had the longest tenure. The third hurdle resulted as respondents from only two clubs indicated that their club met without any face-to-face interaction. These represented pure virtual groups. Although very interesting, this small sample size prevented us from including them with the rest of the sample.

The clubs had an average of about 16 members (Standard Deviation = 7.31). Thirty-nine percent of the respondents were female, and the average age was about 47 (Standard Deviation = 13.82). While 100% of the clubs reported once a month face-to-face meetings, 88% indicated that they also used the telephone, 63% e-mail, 29% fax, and 33% the World Wide Web to conduct group business. Thus, 88% of the clubs fall into the "semivirtual" category in Figure 1, and 12% fall into the "traditional" category.

Measures

We measured the degree of virtualness by assessing all methods of communication used by the club in addition to their scheduled face-to-face meetings (recall that all respondents come from clubs who have one scheduled face-to-face meeting per month). Face-to-face, phone, e-mail, fax, and the World Wide Web were all offered as responses. Degree of virtualness is equal to the sum of the number of technologies group members reported using. Thus, a respondent from a club using only face-to-face communication would have a degree of virtualness = 1; a respondent from a club making use of all five listed forms of communication would have a degree of virtualness = 5.

As noted above, this research represents a conservative test of the hypotheses. Our measure of degree of virtualness does nothing to distinguish between uses of the technologies that are effective versus ineffective or sporadic versus constant; the level of information transmitted; or the richness the particular technology (channel) is perceived to have (e.g., Carlson & Zmud, 1999). The degree of virtualness measure does, however, provide an objective assessment of the complexity of the club's communication context. An ideal approach for this study (and many others) would be access to the full content of all communication between the group members. In this setting, that would have required full e-mail logs, tracks of Internet use, videotapes of club meetings, and recordings of all other communication. We chose, instead, to collect the data from real groups without in any way affecting their actions. This type of research has been called for (e.g., O'Mahony & Barley, 1999) to balance the wealth of excellent laboratory and e-mail studies, which allow access to the full content of group communication. The error variance in our approach should be unbiased, and the noise serves to decrease our likelihood of a significant result, making our results more robust. This is in contrast to other methods, where error variance

Table 1.   Adapted Ketrow (1991) Leadership Role Behavior Descriptions

Procedural1	Tries to keep the group's interaction focused on the agenda
Procedural2	Integrates the actions and contribution of others
Procedural3	Makes certain the discussion or meeting keeps moving
Procedural4	Restates ideas and suggestions of others for clarity
Socioemotional1	Encourages each participant to give his/her best effort
Socioemotional2	Encourages individuals to participate
Socioemotional3	Encourages people to work as a team
Task1	Amplifies ideas and comments when he/she thinks it is needed
Task2	Encourages participants to engage in the critical examination of ideas
Task3	Introduces information from qualified sources to confirm, dispute, or otherwise explore ideas being presented

might be biased toward one media or another (e.g., time spent communicating—typing takes longer than speaking; word counts—fewer in text versus oral media; or number of communications—a series of e-mails may in fact be one conversation).

We assessed socioemotional, procedural, and task leadership role behaviors using an adapted form of Ketrow's (1991) leadership role behavior descriptions (see Table 1). Ten behavioral descriptions (three socioemotional, four procedural, and three task) were presented on the questionnaires, and the respondents were asked to identify by name people in the club who best fit the given description. The survey indicated that "none" and "don't know" were also appropriate answers. Percentage of leadership role behavior coverage (that is, the number of behaviors occurring in a group) for each of the three categories was constructed by whether or not at least one person had been indicated for the behavior, divided by the number of behaviors represented in that leadership role behavior category. For example, percentage of socioemotional leadership role behavior coverage was created by adding the number of socioemotional leadership role behaviors attributed to group members (i.e., not left blank or answered with "none" or "don't know"), divided by three. We believe this measure of leadership role behavior coverage is the most conservative approach to assessing leadership role behaviors from a survey instrument. This approach is also consistent with the idea that different people in a group can perform leadership role behaviors, and that over time, such behaviors can rotate among group members (see for example, Zigurs, 2003). It is not necessary or even likely in many groups for just one person to do all the leadership behaviors. We measure whether or not the group member perceived others acting on the particular behavior, rather than asking the respondent to retrospectively speak to the number of behaviors, the quality of behaviors, etc.

Club age and number of members serve as control measures, as described below. Current portfolio value is a self-report measure, though a salient and objective one. All respondents provided data during the same three-month period (Spring 1997), during which time the S&P 500 Index grew 18% (760 to 900). We were not able to explicitly disentangle the portfolio value attributable to club dues versus stock appreciation, dividends, etc. However, we control for the number of members contributing dues (the only source of capital for these clubs) and club age (the number of years capital contributions have been made to the club's portfolio). (Specific levels of dues for each club were not measured, but are generally $25 to $50 per person per month) (O'Hara & Janke, 1996.) As the relationship between capital contributions and the study variables is a multiplicative one (current portfolio value = number of members × age of club × management of capital in terms of degree of virtualness and leadership role behaviors), we made a log transformation to enable analysis by ordinary least squares.[2]

Results

Provided in Table 2 are correlations and descriptive statistics. We conducted a multiple regression analysis to test for the hypothesized effects (see Table 3). As noted above, we used the number of members and the club's age as control variables to focus the examination on the part of portfolio value that was not a simple function of the deposit of club dues over time.

Table 2. Descriptive Statistics and Correlation Coefficients[a]

Variable	Mean sd	1	2	3	4	5	6
1. % Socioemotional Leadership Role Behaviors Covered	.80 .29						
2. % Procedural Leadership Role Behaviors Covered	.85 .26	.45					
3. % Task Leadership Role Behaviors Covered	.83 .25	.47	.54				
4. Degree of virtualness	3.13 1.08	.13	.29	-.01			
5. ln(Number of Members)	2.71 .43	-.01	.06	.04	.03		
6. ln(Club Age)	.99 .78	-.24	-.25	-.24	-.30	.07	
7. ln(Current Portfolio Value)	9.80 1.13	-.22	-.12	-.24	-.09	.44	.71

[a]N=76, critical value = .22 (p <.05, two-tailed).

Table 3. Regression Results

Variable	ln(CPV) $F(9, 66) = 21.69$ $p < .0001$ $R^2 = .75$ Adj. $R^2 = .71$
Constant[a]	5.70***
% Socioemotional Leadership Role Behaviors Covered	3.18***
% Procedural Leadership Role Behaviors Covered	-2.30
% Task Leadership Role Behaviors Covered	-.20
Degree of virtualness	.20
Degree of virtualness x % Social Leadership Role Behaviors Covered	-.94***
Degree of virtualness x % Procedural Leadership Role Behaviors Covered	.77*
Degree of virtualness x % Task Leadership Role Behaviors Covered	-.07
ln(Number of Members)	.89***
ln(Club Age)	1.11***

[a]Parameter estimates are non-standardized * p<.05   ** p<.01   ***p<.001

This is what the parameters of the resulting regression mean:

- For each percentage change in the number of members or the club age there is a predicted percentage change in current portfolio value

- For each unit change in the remaining terms, there is a predicted percentage change in current portfolio value

The overall model *F*-test for the log of current portfolio value (lnCPV) was significant. As a result, it was appropriate to test the separate hypotheses (Pedhazur, 1982). These results are presented in Table 3.

Hypothesis 1 proposed that the effect of socioemotional leadership role behavior coverage on group outcomes would be moderated by degree of virtualness. As shown in Table 3, the regression analysis revealed a significant negative interaction between degree of virtualness and socioemotional leadership role behavior coverage. Shown in Figure 2 is an illustration of these effects. Following from Cohen and Cohen (1983, pp. 320–325), the regression parameters are used to generate predicted scores for high and low values of the moderating variables. Mean scores are entered for all predictors except the moderators. High and low values of the moderators are created by adding or subtracting one standard deviation from the mean. By examining these predicted scores, it appears that percentage of socioemotional leadership role behavior coverage had a positive impact in groups with a low degree of virtualness but a negative one in groups with a high degree of virtualness.

Hypothesis 2 proposed that the effect of procedural leadership role behavior coverage on group outcomes would be positively moderated by degree of

Figure 2. Socioemotional Role Coverage by Virtualness Interaction

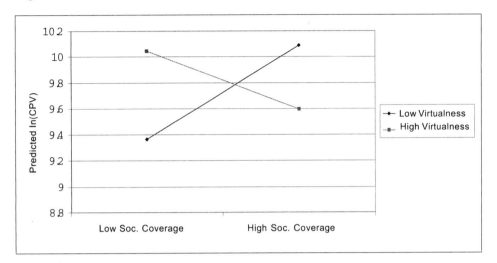

virtualness. As shown in Table 3, the regression analysis of lnCPV found a significant positive interaction for degree of virtualness and percentage of procedural leadership role behaviors covered. Shown in Figure 3 is an illustration of these effects. Examination of the predicted scores suggests that level of procedural leadership role behaviors had a positive impact in high degree of virtualness groups but a negative one in low degree of virtualness groups.

Hypothesis 3 proposed that the effect of task leadership role behavior coverage on group outcomes would be negatively moderated by degree of virtualness. Hypothesis 3 was not supported. Discussion of this, and the preceding results, follows.

Overview of Results

We asked three questions at the beginning of this chapter:

- What role does leadership play in the success of more virtual groups?
- Which leadership behaviors have which impacts?
- Why do these behaviors have the impacts they do?

In the following sections, we provide the answers suggested by our research in investment clubs.

Figure 3.   Procedural Role Coverage by Virtualness Interaction

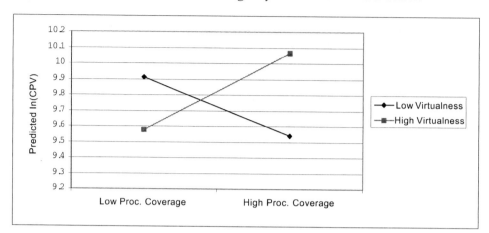

What role does leadership play in the success of more virtual groups? This has a complicated answer. We found opposite results for socioemotional (activities that motivate contribution and cooperation within the group) and procedural leadership role behaviors (activities that direct the group's actions). That is, we found that the more virtual a group was, the *less* socioemotional leadership behaviors benefited the group. Also, we found that the more virtual a group was, the *more* procedural leadership behaviors benefited the group's performance. Shown in Figures 2 and 3 are these results, and we discuss them more below. We found no clear effect for task leadership role behaviors (activities related to the generation and evaluation of information related to the task).

Which leadership behaviors have which impacts? As expected from some prior research, members in more traditional clubs (less virtual) had greater success when they performed more of the socioemotional leadership role behaviors. However, in more virtual clubs, these behaviors appear to hurt club performance. We anticipated the latter result, but nevertheless, it remains intriguing.

The results for procedural leadership role behaviors were also interesting. More virtual clubs with members who performed more procedural leadership role behaviors tended to be more successful in terms of portfolio value. However, in more traditional clubs, this variety of procedural leadership role behaviors tended to result in less successful performance.

Why do these behaviors have the impacts they do? Club members may be making informed decisions relating to the way they work. For example, in more virtual settings, they may have learned that fewer socioemotional leadership role behaviors are necessary to effectively perform. More virtual settings provide opportunities for all members to contribute. Requests for contributions beyond some perceived threshold may create information overload or other process losses. In less virtual settings, more traditional management of group communication may be required to obtain effective levels of contribution.

The results for procedural leadership role behaviors mean several things. First, analyzing and making decisions about stock investments with real money is a complex task, requiring interdependent work and access to large amounts of specialized data. Nearly a third of the respondents reported using the Web, and two thirds reported using e-mail to conduct club business. Because the 1996 NAIC guidelines (O'Hara & Janke, 1996) provide no advice on the use of electronic communication media in group work, group members must create protocols and cues to use these media well. If members do not pay attention to work procedures, then the group will likely be ineffective in sharing vital information and, therefore, make poor investment decisions. Or, they could make fewer decisions in a given time period and miss, at least in the bull market alive during this study, opportunities for substantial portfolio appreciation.

However, the negative effect in the less virtual clubs is surprising given prior research on group leadership roles and outcomes. The structure of the NAIC may again provide an explanation. Although the NAIC does not provide advice on how to run group work in more virtual clubs, it provides detailed advice on how to run face-to-face meetings (O'Hara, 1996). It may be that for less virtual clubs, high levels of procedural leadership role behaviors, in addition to the focus on running a meeting already provided by NAIC guidelines, may drive out opportunities for profitable work.

Recommendations

We found two clear managerial implications about leadership in semivirtual groups. First, more virtual groups benefit from less effort to motivate members' contributions and cooperation (socioemotional leadership behaviors). Less virtual groups benefit from more effort to motivate members' contributions and cooperation. This means that members and managers of semivirtual groups should gauge their attempts at facilitating contribution and cooperation based on their group's context. It may be that, at some point, greater use of technology provides ample opportunities for participation and cooperation, and beyond that point additional socioemotional leadership role behaviors just get in the way of productive action.

Second, more and less virtual groups also respond in opposite ways to procedural facilitation of the group. In the investment clubs studied here, more virtual groups benefit from more focus on procedure, while less virtual groups benefit from less focus on procedure. Members and managers of groups need to consider their virtualness if they are to perform to their highest potentials. More virtual groups, and their more complex contexts, may need additional efforts to maintain high levels of performance. These groups may need more standard operating procedures to manage the variety found in their work context.

The fact that more and less virtual teams respond in such different ways to basic management techniques is crucial to note. We are moving into uncharted organizational territory and must take into account the areas where our actions may need to adapt.

What Should Managers Consider in the Future?

Our research focused on groups doing real work, using a variety of evolving technologies and processes. This context provides a level of realistic complexity that may limit our ability to illustrate clear effects—such a world makes it hard for researchers to identify the "most" powerful impact on group success. We need additional study and practice with semivirtual groups in field settings to address the intricacies of the results documented here and to explain the lack of some expected outcomes. We suggest that future research and practice focus on elaborations of leadership role theory, as well as on more complex examinations of teams working in this continuum of virtual environments.

Elaboration of leadership role theory would be valuable in at least two areas. The first is a consideration of whether it is more appropriate to consider these as curvilinear effects. A curvilinear effect here means that, unlike a straight line effect that constantly moves in one direction, certain leadership behaviors are good up to a point, but after that, the effects are harmful. The results for socioemotional and procedural leadership role behaviors suggest the possibility that in certain settings, a group or its leaders can focus too much on leadership role behaviors. Our results can be explained by curvilinear effects, if we also consider a second elaboration—that of substitutes for these leadership behaviors.

Kerr and Jermier (1978) put forth the idea that characteristics of the people, the task, and the organization may act in place of, or substitute for, leadership behaviors. Here, we suggested that technology may substitute for socioemotional leadership role behaviors by creating opportunities and tools for group members to better contribute or by creating a situation in which group members are more likely to contribute without leadership support. We also suggested that the NAIC guidelines may be providing procedural support at a level that substitutes for procedural leadership role behaviors—in other words, standard operating procedures. These substitutes for leadership may provide support that renders further intervention (in the form of members performing more leadership behaviors) that is unnecessary and perhaps even harmful to the group's performance.

Further understanding of leadership role behaviors, and of situations that may play the role of substitutes for leadership, may help explain the lack of results for task leadership role behaviors. There may be resisting forces at work, or even leadership neutralizers (Kerr & Jermier, 1978), which limit the effectiveness of these behaviors in our context. While Kerr and Jermier (1978) raised the issues of substitutes and neutralizers of leadership, they did not break these forces down to the level of leadership role behaviors. Researchers and managers could pay more attention to the relationships between and across the types of leadership role behaviors. While Ketrow (1991) and other leadership role researchers suggested that these are separate concepts, it is also possible that behaviors interact in interesting ways.

Methodological advances may also be valuable for future research. This field study provided a unique opportunity to study a range of teams. Future research might benefit by greater focus on the intricacies of the team's work process and use of technology. Future research will need to consider the full continuum of communication context. In this study, technology provided added capabilities beyond the standard once a month, face-to-face meeting. Investment clubs or other groups that use complex communication capabilities to perform complicated tasks may find even stronger interactions between group leadership role behaviors and group outcomes when technology is used as an alternative, rather than a supplement, to face-to-face meetings.

Finally, the pattern of media use over time is an important aspect of technologically supported group behavior that has been insufficiently studied. Existing research, as discussed earlier, tends to dichotomize virtualness (face-to-face only or pure virtual only) or pit one medium against another (e.g., teleconferencing versus e-mail). (For an approach that considers location, time spent working apart, and technological support, see Griffith, Sawyer, & Neale, 2002.) More realistically, groups use combinations of media over time, and over tasks. Here, we only addressed groups that used technology in addition to a monthly meeting. More expansive research should vary the use and timing of periodic face-to-face meetings in more virtual groups as a way to attenuate any depersonalizing effect of mediated communication (e.g., Lakoff & Boal, 1995). Additionally, by looking at patterns of media use in virtual work, researchers may discover when face-to-face meetings augment electronically mediated work in order to enjoy the benefits provided by electronic media while minimizing the process losses created by them (Nohria & Eccles, 1992).

Conclusion

Semivirtual groups are an emergent and inevitable work structure in organizations. As the trends of globalization, technology proliferation, mergers and acquisitions, e-commerce, and project-oriented work continue, semivirtual groups will play an increasingly critical role. But more virtual groups can be as dramatically ineffective as many traditional groups have been. Managers and academics need to be aware of and understand the sometimes obvious, often subtle, impacts that leadership role behaviors play in semivirtual groups.

The investment clubs in this field study provide an interesting sample from which to study the effects of leadership in groups working more, or less, virtually. Leadership role behaviors certainly play a part in group success. However, the results presented here suggest an interaction among leadership role behaviors and the degree of virtualness. Leadership in these settings is complicated and must be sensitive to the needs of the group.

Acknowledgments

We thank the National Association of Investors Corporation and the hundreds of investment club members who participated in the formation and conduct of this research.

References

Barley, S. R. (1986). Technology as an occasion for structuring: Evidence from observations of CT scanners and the social order of radiology departments. *Administrative Science Quarterly, 31*, 78–108.

Carlson, J. R., & Zmud, R. W. (1999). Channel expansion theory and the experiential nature of media richness perceptions. *Academy of Management Journal, 42*(2), 153–170.

Cohen, J., & Cohen, P. (1983). *Applied Multiple Regression/Correlation Analysis for the Behavioral Sciences*. Mahweh, NJ: Lawrence Erlbaum.

Davenport, T. H., & Pearlson, K. (1998). Two cheers for the virtual office. *Sloan Management Review,* (Summer), 51–65.

DeSanctis, G., & Poole, M. S. (1994). Capturing the complexity in advanced technology use: Adaptive structuration theory. *Organization Science, 5*(2), 121–147.

Gibson, C. B., & Cohen, S. G. (eds.). (2003). *Virtual Teams that Work*. San Francisco, CA: Jossey-Bass.

Griffith, T. L., & Neale, M. A. (2001). Information processing in traditional, hybrid, and virtual teams: From nascent knowledge to transactive memory. In B. M. Staw & R. I. Sutton (Eds.), *Research in Organizational Behavior* (Vol. 23, pp. 379–421). Stamford, CT: JAI Press.

Griffith, T. L., Sawyer, J. E., & Neale, M. A. (2002). Virtualness and knowledge in teams: Managing the love triangle of organizations, individuals, and information technology. *Management Information Systems Quarterly, 27*(2), 265-287.

Hinds, P., & Kiesler, S. (eds.). (2002). *Distributed work: New research on working across distance using technology.*

Igbaria, M., Zinatelli, N., Cragg, P., & Cavaye, A. L. M. (1997). Personal computing acceptance factors in small firms: A structural equation model. *MIS Quarterly, 21*(3), 279–305.

Jarvenpaa, S. L., & Leidner, D. E. (1999). Communication and trust in global virtual teams. *Organization Science, 10*, 791–815.

Jarvenpaa, S. L., Knoll, K., & Leidner, D. E. (1998). Is anybody out there? Antecedents of trust in global virtual teams. *Journal of Management Information Systems, 14*(4), 29–64.

Jarvenpaa, S. L., Rao, V. S., & Huber, G. P. (1988). Computer support for meetings of groups working on unstructured problems: A field experiment. *MIS Quarterly, 12*(4), 645–666.

Kadlec, D. (1998, March 30). Jail the beardstown ladies! *Time, 151*, 54.

Kerr, S., & Jermier, J. M. (1978). Substitutes for leadership: Their meaning and measurement. *Organizational Behavior and Human Performance, 22*, 375–403.

Ketrow, S. M. (1991). Communication role specializations and perceptions of leadership. *Small Group Research, 22*(4), 492–514.

Lakoff, G., & Boal, I. A. (1995). Body, brain and communication. In J. Brook & I. A. Boal (Eds.), *Resisting the Virtual Life: The Culture and Politics of Information* (pp. 115–130). San Francisco, CA: City of Lights Books.

Locke, E. A. (1976). The nature and causes of job satisfaction. In M. C. Dunnette (Ed.), *Handbook of Industrial and Organizational Psychology* (pp. 1297–1349). Chicago, IL: Rand McNally.

Majchrzak, A., Rice, R. E., Malhotra, A., King, N., & Ba, S. (2000). Technology adaptation: The case of a computer-supported inter-organizational virtual team. *Management Information Systems Quarterly, 24*(4), 569–600.

Mannix, E. A., Griffith, T. L., & Neale, M. A. (2002). The phenomenology of conflict in distributed work teams. In P. Hines & S. Kiesler (Eds.), *Distributed Work: New Research on Working Across Distance Using Technology* (pp. 213–233). Cambridge, MA: MIT Press.

Maznevski, M. L., & Chudoba, K. M. (2000). Bridging space over time: Global virtual team dynamics and effectiveness. *Organization Science, 11*(5), 473–492.

McGrath, J. E. (1984). *Groups: Interaction and Performance.* Englewood Cliffs, NJ: Prentice Hall.

McGrath, J. E., & Hollingshead, A. B. (1994). *Groups Interacting with Technology: Ideas, Evidence, Issues, and an Agenda.* Thousand Oaks, CA: Sage.

Mowshowitz, A. (1997). Introduction to special issue on virtual organization. *Communications of the ACM, 40*(9), 30–37.

NAIC, & Easyware_Software. (1998, March 25). *Beardstown ladies and club accounting,* [Internet]. Available: http://www.better-investing.org/clubs/ladies.html [1999, May 18].

Nohria, N., & Eccles, R. G. (1992). Face-to-face: Making network organizations work. In N. Nohria & R. G. Eccles (Eds.), *Networks and Organizations: Structure, Form and Action* (pp. 288–308). Boston, MA: Harvard Business School Press.

Nunamaker, J. F., Jr., Briggs, R. O., Romano, N. C., Jr., & Mittleman, D. D. (1998). The virtual office work-space: Groupsystems web and case studies. In D. Coleman (Ed.), *Groupware: Collaborative Strategies for Corporate Lans and Intranets.* New York: Prentice-Hall.

O'Hara, T. E., & Janke, K. S., Sr. (1996). *Starting and Running a Profitable Investment Club.* New York: Times Books.

O'Mahony, S., & Barley, S. P. (1999). Do digital telecommunications affect work and organization: State of our knowledge. In R. I. Sutton & B. M. Staw (Eds.), *Research in Organizational Behavior* (Vol. 21, pp. 125–161). Stamford, CT: JAI Press.

Pedhazur, E. J. (1982). *Multiple Regression in Behavioral Research* (2nd ed.). New York: Holt, Rinehart, and Winston.

Postmes, T., Spears, R., & Lea, M. (2000). The formation of group norms in computer-mediated communication. *Human Communication Research, 26*(3), 341–371.

Pratt, M. G., Fuller, M. A., & Northcraft, G. B. (2000). The price of (media) richness: Group identification and the media selection dilemma in distributed groups. In M. A. Neale, E. A. Mannix, & T. L. Griffith (Eds.), *Research on Managing Groups and Teams: Technology* (Vol. 3). Stamford, CT: JAI Press.

Sproull, L., & Kiesler, S. (1991). *Connections: New Ways of Working in the Networked Organization.* Cambridge, MA: MIT Press.

Sproull, L. S., & Kiesler, S. (1986). Reducing social context cues: Electronic mail in organizational communication. *Management Science, 32,* 1492–1512.

Steiner, I. A. (1972). *Group Processes and Productivity.* New York: Academic Press.

Tidwell, L. C., & Walther, J. B. (2002). Computer-mediated communication effects on disclosure, impressions, and interpersonal evaluations. *Human Communication Research, 28*(3), 317–348.

Turoff, M. (1997). Virtuality. *Communications of the ACM, 40*(9), 38–43.

Venkatraman, N., & Henderson, J. C. (1998). *Real Strategies for Virtual Organizing* (98-01). Boston, MA: Systems Research Center, School of Management, Boston University.

Walther, J. B. (1995). Relational aspects of computer-mediated communication: Experimental observations over time. *Organization Science, 6*(2), 186–203.

Warkentin, M. E., Sayeed, L., & Hightower, R. (1997). Virtual teams vs. face-to-face teams: An exploratory study of a web-based conference system. *Decision Sciences, 28*(4), 975–996.

Webster, J., Trevino, L. K., & Ryan, L. (1993). The dimensionality and correlates of flow in human-computer interactions. *Computers in Human Behavior, 9,* 411–426.

Wiberg, M., & Ljungberg, F. (2001). Exploring the vision of "anytime, anywhere" in the context of mobile work. In Y. Malhota (Ed.), *Knowledge Management and Business Model Innovation* (pp. 153–165). Hershey, PA: Idea Group Publishing.

Zigurs, I. (2003). Leadership in virtual teams: Oxymoron or opportunity? *Organizational Dynamics, 31*(4), 339–351.

Zigurs, I., & Kozar, K. A. (1994). An exploratory study of roles in computer-supported groups. *Management Information Systems Quarterly, 18,* 277–297.

Endnotes

1   Electronic media includes these microprocessor-based technologies: e-mail, voice mail, fax, phone, bulletin boards, chat rooms, instant messaging, paging, and videoconferencing. We will use the terms electronic communication or communication technologies interchangeably.

2   Note that the above approach does not assess the internal rate of return, a widely recognized method for taking into account the amounts and the timing of the cash flows of an investment, and the measure of club performance suggested by the NAIC (1998). However, current portfolio value provides a measure that may be more reliable when asking for survey data from individual club members. Popular reports of the Beardstown Ladies investment club's bookkeeping errors support our more simple request for current portfolio value (Kadlec, 1998).

Chapter XI

Mediating Complexity: Facilitating Relationship Building Across Boundaries in Start-Up Virtual Teams

David J. Pauleen
Victoria University of Wellington, New Zealand

Lalita Rajasingham
Victoria University of Wellington, New Zealand

Abstract

Virtual teams are playing an increasingly important role in organizations. However, virtual teams' increasing team member interaction beyond traditional organizational boundaries has outpaced our understanding of their interpersonal dynamics and unique communication characteristics. Research shows that the development of interpersonal and group communications between team members is an important factor in effective working relationships; however, little research has been done on the effects of crossing organizational, cultural, and time and distance boundaries on relationship building in virtual teams. This chapter reports on a field study of New Zealand-based virtual team leaders working with boundary spanning virtual teams. From a team leaders' perspective, boundary-crossing issues (organizational, cultural, language, time and distance) can affect relationship building in many important ways. These effects are explored and the implications for practice and research are also discussed.

Introduction

In this chapter, we look at how virtual team leaders assess and respond to boundary crossing issues when building relationships with team members in start-up virtual teams. To give a sense of the revolutionary nature of virtual teams in this regard, similarities and differences with traditional colocated teams will first be examined. Virtual teams are a relatively new phenomenon, and by definition, are groups that work across time and distance via information and communications technology (ICT) (Townsend, DeMarie, & Hendrickson, 1998).

Groups are a basic human societal structure, heterogeneous, based on human communication, and associated with decision making. Cooperation becomes essential to achieve goals. Team creation and maintenance can be considered as a group communications system, subject to group dynamics. Teams are task oriented. Hirokawa and Poole (1996) suggested that the creation and mainte-nance of teams require rules and protocols, opinion leaders and gate keepers for decision making. With a complex communication process, even in a colocated environment with visual cues such as body language and gestures, in technology-mediated virtual environments, complexity assumes a greater dimension (Tiffin & Rajasingham, 1995, 2001). Sapir-Whorf's (1921, 1956) theory of linguistic relativity argues that the structure of a culture's language determines the behavior and habits of thinking of that culture and is an important consideration in building relationships across boundaries in virtual environments.

With rapid advances in information and communication technology allowing for alternatives to face-to-face communication, virtual teams are playing an increas-ingly important role in organizational life and are often assigned the most important tasks in an organization, such as multinational product launches, negotiation of mergers and acquisitions among global companies, and manage-ment of strategic alliances (Maznevski & Chudoba, 2000). However, their use has outpaced the understanding of their dynamics and unique characteristics (Cramton & Webber, 2000). This chapter adds to this understanding, particularly as related to leader-facilitated relationship building with team members.

The following section backgrounds relationship building, boundary crossing, and leadership in virtual teams. This is followed by a brief explanation of the grounded action learning methodology used in this study. The study's findings linking relationship building and boundary crossing are then presented, followed by the challenges and solutions section, in which key challenges faced by virtual team leaders are presented, highlighting the need for a higher level of communication skills by virtual team leaders. The chapter concludes with an overall strategy for team leaders working virtually as well as a call for more research in the area of virtual team leadership.

The Importance of Relationship Building in Virtual Teams

The link between team effectiveness and team member relationships is an important but still underdeveloped area of study in virtual teams. Research in group communication decision making in colocated teams is extensive. In their input-process-output general organizing group maintenance and conflict resolution model, Collins and Guetzkow (1964) argued that a task group or team faces two problems—the task and interpersonal obstacles. Relationships are connected to communication and cannot be separated from it, and the nature of the relationship is defined by the communication between its members. Usually defined implicitly rather than explicitly, relationships develop over time through a negotiation process between those involved (Catell, 1948).

Other relationship theorists such as Berger (1997), Bateson (1972), and Burgoon (1998), observed that messages are in two parts: content message and relationship message. The challenge for a team leader is to successfully interweave both aspects so that a desirable outcome is achieved. Fisher (1980) made useful contributions to the literature in his Interact Model of Decision Emergence, where he suggested that groups proceed through four phases in the process of reaching a consensus: orientation, conflict, emergence, and reinforcement. In a virtual team, this process again would pose new challenges for a leader.

While face-to-face meetings are the preferred way of building relationships and in general dealing with sensitive and complex situations, it is possible with the skillful and thoughtful application of virtual communication channels to effectively lead a completely virtual team. Research has found that computer-mediated teams share relational information and are likely to develop relational links over time (Chidambaram, 1966; Walther, 1997; Warkentin, Sayeed, & Hightower, 1997). However, because many virtual teams are project or deadline driven, there may not be the opportunity to allow relationships to develop over time. The idea of "swift trust" was put forth by Jarvenpaa, Knoll, and Leidner (1998) to describe how virtual team members may be able to accomplish tasks without first having developed relationships. This rational perspective centers on the view of "calculus of self interest," which weighs the cost and benefits of certain courses of action between team members. If a team member feels confident there will be a "payoff" for cooperating with and trusting a virtual team member, then they will do so. However, such trust is likely to be fragile and temporary.

The role of the team leader is to move the team toward its objectives by encouraging collaboration. This is done through a sustained process of relationship building, idea generation, prioritization, and selection. The particular challenge to virtual team leaders is to manage this process through electronically mediated interactions. In virtual team research, relational links have been associated with higher task performance (Warkentin & Beranek, 1999) and the effectiveness of information exchange (Warkentin et al., 1997). According to Lau et al. (2000), effective communication is the key to successful virtual teams, and one of the keys to effective communication is how well team members are able to build and maintain their personal relationships. According to Walther and Burgoon (1992), strong relational links are associated with enhanced creativity, and motivation, increased morale, better decisions, and fewer process losses. The building of relationships with virtual team members has been shown to be a fundamental concern for virtual team leaders (Pauleen & Yoong, 2001).

Communication is an essential element in virtual teams. Empirical studies support the important role communication plays in virtual teams (Robey, Khoo, & Poers, 2000). Many studies emphasized the importance of communication skills in accomplishing team requirements for coordination and efficient task execution (DeSanctis & Poole, 1997). One study showed that the impact of formal and informal communication on organizational commitment was greater for virtual employees than those in traditional offices (Whiting & Reardon, 1998, as cited in Robey et al., 2000). Jarvenpaa and Leidner (1999) found that communication was an important factor contributing to trust in global multicultural virtual teams.

Boundary Crossing in Virtual Teams

Boundary crossing is a defining characteristic of virtual teams. Contemporary organizations have highly permeable boundaries allowing substantial boundary-crossing communication (Manev & Sorenson, 2001). The concept of boundary crossing or spanning (Adams, 1976) suggests that individuals in one organization carry out extensive communication with members of an external organization. Boundary crossing is an important organizational activity that enhances the flow of information from the external environment. Those who engage in boundary-crossing activities, such as virtual team leaders, are likely to become more influential because of their ability to scan the environment and process this information (Tushman & Scanlon, 1981).

While traditional collocated teams may have members from different functions and cultures, sophisticated new synchronous and asynchronous organizational communication technologies make it easier than ever to form teams that consist of members from different functions, offices, organizations, countries, and cultures. Furthermore, virtual teams must function across time and distance, often with team members having never met. These conditions can present significant challenges to team leaders and members, team processes, and ultimately, team outcomes. Because virtual teams are still a relatively new organizational response to changing global realities, the challenges may be compounded by organizational policies that do not support or that may even hinder virtual team performance (Jackson, 1999; Vickery, Clark, & Carlson, 1999). These policies can include HR and IT policies, as well as general organizational and managerial attitudes.

Maznevski and Chudoba (2000) found that boundary crossing increases message complexity from simple, one-dimensional messages to complex, multidimensional messages. Assumptions and information tend to be shared within a single organization and also when location, culture, or professions are shared (Schein, 1984). In such shared contexts, messages may be simpler. However, in general, messages that cross boundaries are inherently more complex. In virtual teams, this problem is exacerbated where communication takes place exclusively through electronic channels. However, messages can be made simpler if members build strong, trusting relationships (Maznevski & Chudoba, 2000).

Structural characteristics of virtual teams can also affect relationship-building efforts. One study showed that more effective virtual teams used richer media when crossing boundaries and deliberately addressed relationship building to develop shared views and trust across all types of boundaries (Maznevski & Chudoba, 2000). These "boundary-spanning activities" were more frequent and intense, the greater the nature and number of boundaries. More boundaries between leaders and team members at the start of a virtual team will likely require higher levels of relationships with team members as well as more intensive relationship-building strategies.

Virtual Team Leadership

There has been long and extensive research on leadership in collocated teams and groups. A 1985 study counted more than 300 definitions of leadership (Bennis & Nanus, 1985). Typically, leadership can be viewed in a number of ways; for example, as a structured authoritative role (Hosking, 1988) or as the ability of individuals to intrinsically or extrinsically motivate followers (Bass, 1985). Generally, communication theorists agree that leadership involves social influence and the use of communication activities in motivating teams to achieve goals (Barge, 1996). Barge (1996) proposed leadership as mediation in order to overcome the variety of task and relational problems that may be encountered by a group and explained that leadership "entails devising a system of helping the group gets its work done, that is simultaneously stable and flexible and assists in managing the information shared among members and between the group and its external audience" (p. 319).

Virtual team leadership remains one of the little understood and often poorly supported elements in the success of virtual teams. Virtual team leaders are often the nexus of a virtual team, facilitating communications, establishing team processes, and taking responsibility for task completion (Duarte & Tennant-Snyder, 1999) and, as has been pointed out, doing so across multiple boundaries. In virtual teams, technology becomes the crucial and ever present link between team members (Lipnack & Stamps, 1997), one that team leaders must manage skillfully. Recent research (e.g., Kayworth & Leidner, 2001–2002) has begun to look at leadership issues in virtual teams. These studies suggest that the trend toward physically dispersed work groups necessitates further systematic inquiry into the role and nature of virtual team leadership.

One of the key skills in leadership in Barge's (1996) concept of leadership as mediation is that of relational management, which refers to the ability of leaders to "coordinate and construct interpersonal relations that allow an appropriate balance of cohesion, unity, and task motivation with a group" (p. 325). Cohesive teams tend to perform at higher levels and are more motivated to complete tasks. A central thread in this chapter is how team leaders can coordinate and construct interpersonal relations in a virtual environment across multiple boundaries that do not exist in traditional collocated teams.

In the following section, the grounded action learning methodology used in this study is briefly explained.

The Research

Grounded Action Learning

The research methodology used to gather the data presented in this chapter is derived from a combination of two research methodologies: action learning and grounded theory. In this case, an action learning program was used to gather data, while grounded theory techniques were used to analyze the detail.

Action Learning

Action learning is closely linked to action research and is cited as one of the several streams of action research (Lau, 1999). Action learning is described as the process by which groups of people work on real organizational issues and come up with practical solutions that may require changes to be made in the organization (Revans, 1982). Action learning is a practical group learning and problem-solving process, where the emphasis is on self-development and learning by doing. The group, known as the action learning set, meets regularly and provides a supportive and challenging environment in which members are encouraged to learn from experience, share that experience with others, have other members critique and advise, take that advice and implement it, and review with those members the action taken and the lessons learned (Margerison, 1988). The participants in this study were professional business people leading virtual teams within the larger context of their organizations and the rapidly evolving ICT environment. To ensure that participants had experiences to talk about, a specially designed action-learning-based virtual team training program was developed that provided participants with the knowledge and skills to implement and lead a virtual team as well as the opportunity to be able to reflect on and talk about them. These training programs functioned as learning spaces for the participants and the researcher, allowing for structured, yet flexible, training, semistructured interviewing, and freewheeling discussions. No particular hypothesis was tested in this research design, but the research question was directed at how virtual team leaders implement and manage virtual teams. The grounded theory approach was expected to produce a set of constructs and a description of their relationships relevant to the experiences of the participants.

Grounded Theory

Traditional grounded theory is a methodology for developing theory that is grounded in data, systematically gathered and analyzed, in which theory emerges during actual research through the continuous interplay between analysis and data collection (Strauss & Corbin, 1990). Central features of this analytic approach include the general method of (constant) comparative analysis, theoretical sampling, theoretical sensitivity, and theoretical saturation (Glaser & Strauss, 1967).

There have been recent studies in IS and communications that have made use of traditional grounded theory methods (e.g., Wright, 1999) and those that have used grounded theory approaches (e.g., Maznevski & Chudoba, 2000). A number of IS studies, particularly in interpretive inductive studies requiring the development of meaningful categories (e.g., Trauth & Jessup, 2000), have combined various elements of grounded theory with other research methods. The most commonly borrowed elements from traditional grounded theory are the grounded theory coding techniques (open, axial, and selective) used to analyze data. The grounded action learning approach used in this study was inspired by the grounded action research method introduced by Baskerville and Pries-Heje (1999), in which data gathered in an action research project were analyzed using grounded theory methods. This study follows a similar strategy, with data generated by an action learning training program being analyzed using grounded theory methods. The methods used here to analyze the data closely adhere to those set out by Glaser and Strauss (1967).

Data Collection and Analysis

Data were collected from a pilot study and two subsequent training programs involving a total of seven participants. The collection of research data took place over a period of three years. Several methods of data collection were used in this study. These include semistructured interviews and discussions between the researcher and the participants, and informal participant reports, as well as the researcher's journal, and to various degrees participant notes, organizational documentation, and copies of electronic conversations (e-mail). A large volume of data was collected, more than 250 pages of interviews and discussions were transcribed from the pilot project and two training programs. After these data were analyzed, it became clear that relationship building was the key basic social process (Glaser, 1978) that team leaders were concerned with as they initiated their virtual team. Other important conceptual categories also emerged from the data, including boundary-crossing issues.

In the following section, the relationship between boundary crossing and leader-facilitated relationship building with team members is discussed.

The Effects of Boundary Crossing on Relationship Building

The practical effect of working across a distance means that teams can and do effectively comprise members from different departments, offices (e.g., head and branch offices), and organizations, as well as different countries and cultures. Access to different organizational, functional, and cultural perspectives is one of the key reasons for using virtual teams (O'Hara-Devereaux &

Johansen, 1994). These "differences" represent an important set of conditions that a team leader will most likely have to assess and plan for before commencing a virtual team. The findings presented here focus on the boundary-crossing issues that concerned team leaders as they developed relationships with team members. According to the team leaders, the development of personal relationships between themselves and team members is an important prerequisite in establishing and maintaining virtual working relationships. Special attention will be drawn to the communication strategies leaders employed as they built these relationships. Illustrated in Table 1 are the different boundaries, as well as their organizational contexts, team membership, and virtual team tasks that the seven participants in this study needed to address in their virtual teams. As can be seen from the table, the team leaders in this study were managing teams that crossed boundaries of time, distance, culture, language, and organizations.

Table 1. Boundary Crossing in Team Leader's Virtual Teams

Participant/Positions	Organization & Project	Team	Boundaries
DW, Managing Director	NZ (New Zealand) advertising company -- part of an international partnership. Initiate a project within the international partnership.	Global, volunteer CEO membership; between four and eight members	Inter-organizational, cultural, language, time, distance
BC, Senior Policy Analyst	NZ Government Department. Long-term (> two years) treaty negotiation between government and indigenous group.	Representatives from government departments and claimant group; up to 20 core and extended members plus stakeholders	Inter-organizational, departmental, functional, cultural, language, distance
SC, Independent Contractor	NZ educational consulting company. Construct web page, followed by management of web-based assessment center.	Local, Wellington (NZ) based, independent contractors; fluid membership three to five	Organizational, functional, distance
RB, General Manager	NZ software and business development consulting company. Initiate virtual communication channels with branch office.	Members in NZ and Australia; five members	Intra-organizational, cultural, time, distance
RW, Managing Director	NZ-based political consultancy operating worldwide as a virtual organization. Manage a political campaign in California.	Members in NZ and California; three to four members	Inter-organizational, functional, cultural, time, distance
AR, Project Manager	NZ office of international consulting company. Develop and write a strategic plan for Southeast Asian government ministry.	Members in Southeast Asia. Australia and New Z; 12 core members plus stakeholders	Inter & intra-organizational, functional, cultural, language, time, distance
JJ, Project Analyst	Austral Asian trading company. Open and organize a branch office in Vietnam.	Members in Vietnam, NZ and Australia; three to four core members	Intra-organizational, cultural, language, time, distance

The collected data revealed a common concern among the team leaders with the effect of boundary crossing on the building and managing of virtual team relationships. Analysis of the data revealed three conceptual boundary-crossing categories: organizational boundary crossing, cultural/language boundary crossing, and time/distance boundary crossing. While organizational and cultural/language barriers exist in colocated teams, they are much more likely to be found in virtual teams and to have a more significant impact. Time and distance boundaries are unique to virtual teams.

Organizational Boundary Crossing

Organizational boundary crossing includes intra- and interorganizational boundaries. Different functions, departments, and organizations may have diverse work cultures, as manifested by deeply held core beliefs and assumptions (Kayworth & Leidner, 2000). For the team leaders in this study, who were working across organizational boundaries of at least one kind, the differences that tended to manifest in a significant way often had to do with issues of organizational culture and policies. Wiesenfeld, Raghuram, and Garud (1998) suggested that organizational identification would be the psychological tie that binds virtual workers together into an organization, preventing workers from thinking of themselves as independent contractors, operating autonomously. AR, who was leading a virtual team with members from a global consortium of organizations, saw clearly where things are heading with regard to organizational boundary crossing and the issue of identification. She said:

> *(AR) When you are within an organization, even though you may be in different countries, there is at least a general organizational culture, there are at least some norms you can relate to. They may be implemented differently in different parts of the world, but there are some rules. But when you're working interorganizationally, there can be a whole number of things that you have to sus out at the beginning. So in fact one employee in one organization could be working with different organizations at the same time each operating slightly differently in each of the different joint ventures.*

Having a strong organizational culture would appear to make a large difference in the level of relationship building that might be necessary in a team composed of members from within the same organization and in the level of team motivation, even if they are located in different countries. A strong organizational culture is exemplified by institution-based trust relationships (Nandhakumar, 1999; van der Smagt, 2000) and an anticipation of future association (Powell,

1990). AR illustrated this point when she commented on recruiting team members for her virtual team:

> *(AR) It is a sense of belonging to the same organization, collegiality that motivated them to join in and get the work done.*

The degree of relationship building necessary and the strategy for going about it are likely to be different when your team starts with this kind of collegiality. In this case, AR was able to use phone calls to develop a sufficient level of relationship with team members in different countries that led to the on-time completion of the project.

DW's case was somewhat unique. He was initiating a virtual team within a global partnership of independently owned and operated businesses, and the people he was trying to recruit as team members were busy CEOs from around the world. The favorable response he received to what was an e-mailed proposal indicates a high level of commitment to the partnership on the part of the independent operators. This was enough (along with the opportunity to experience something new) for DW to build a team on. Indeed, the basic degree of relationship needed to manage the team already existed.

BC's project highlights many of the issues involved when working across organizations. The project involved the negotiation of land treaty claims between the New Zealand government and an indigenous Maori group.[1] His team consisted of the claimants and other government departments and ministries. The claimants were different from the government members of the team. They comprised an indigenous cultural group with their own beliefs, values, and protocols. These differences affected team interaction. According to BC, the claimant group had definite preferences for certain communication channels, including face-to-face and formal letters. Whether these differences are considered cultural or organizational,[2] they still needed to be assessed by the team leader when building relationships. According to BC, the other members on the Government side of the team required varying degrees of boundary crossing. On the one hand, they were all part of the New Zealand government bureaucracy, as BC explained:

> *(BC) Government departments are used to working with each other and we can immediately assume that we can trust each other. We are all on the same side. And we could get a lot done without having to meet.*

On the other hand, they exhibited unique ministerial or departmental cultures, as BC further explained:

(BC) Definitely office cultures and protocols need to be sorted out in that they are of such importance. ....The Department of Conservation is particularly good at working virtually with e-mail. They respond quickly and actually say what they think and together we are getting a lot of work done that way. ....One Ministry's (anonymity requested) culture seems to be not e-mail based at all. I haven't seen an e-mail from them, I have not seen any paper from them (laughter). I don't know if my personal experience is typical but they seem to be "talking" people and they seem to have got quite a strange culture of people there.

The above quote from BC illustrates another aspect of organizational boundary crossing, which is the particular preferences of certain organizations for certain technologies, in this case, communication channels. Many of the participants recognized this factor, citing organizational or departmental preferences for e-mail or voice mail when leaving messages. RW experienced many difficulties trying to agree on common communication platforms with his team members, who were clients and independent consultants. He made this observation about the relative ease or difficulty of resolving this issue from an organizational perspective:

(RW) Obviously in an organization which is under single ownership you can work these issues out more easily than if you are all in separate ownerships.

As RW's and BC's cases show, team leaders may have to assess these preferences for particular communication channels at the organizational level.

Although it might appear obvious that organizational boundary crossing will increase the level of complexity and the time needed for a team leader to build relationships with team members, many of the findings discussed above were revealed to the participants only after careful reflection on and discussion of their leadership experiences.

Cultural/Language Boundary Crossing

Another important area of boundary crossing is cultural/language boundary crossing. This kind of boundary crossing will most likely take place in global virtual teams, however, it may also be a factor in national or even local virtual teams. The key point is whether a team leader is working with a team member from another nationality or ethnic culture. The effects of culture in team settings can be profound and can include, among other important issues, how individuals relate to each other (Kayworth & Leidner, 2000). Misinterpretations or distortions may occur as team members and team leaders interpret communications through their own cultural programming (Lewis, 1996), a challenge that is greatly complicated when attempted through virtual communication channels. The team leaders in this study had a number of experiences illustrating the importance of assessing culture as a key factor when choosing an appropriate degree of relationship and when creating relationship-building strategies, as well as the effect of communicating via ICT.

BC's case is a good example of a nationally based, culturally diverse team. His project concerned the negotiation of a land settlement case with an indigenous Maori group. Because of the cooperative nature of this government–claimant case, the claimants were considered to be on the team, rather than the opposing side. Although the claimant group members are New Zealand citizens, they retain their own cultural identity, and this tends to be group- and consensus-based, with a strong preference for face-to-face communication. Hence, negotiations with them were, to a great extent, cross-cultural. In any case, as members of the team, the team leader needed to assess cultural differences. Toward the end of the training program, BC was able to pinpoint some of the key factors that needed to be addressed in his interactions with the claimants. First and foremost was the need for the claimants to develop a close relationship with the Government team members before getting down to business. BC remembered that at the beginning of the negotiation process with the claimants, they went to Wellington and had a face-to-face meeting with BC's government office, although no meeting was required. They reported on what they had been up to and asked a few questions. In retrospect, BC concluded:

> *(BC) I guess they just wanted to meet with us. It was more than was required and more than what any other groups had done. But it built up some sort of rapport. It was just a little bit unusual at the very outset.*

The importance of melding different cultures when working together was a key learning point for BC. He explained:

> *(BC) There are two sorts of cultures that we need to bring together, between the claimant negotiators and the key Government negotiators, who are going to meet and be making hard judgments based on what we are telling them. And that requires a huge level of trust, which we are able to build up through a whole lot of face-to-face meetings over long periods of interaction, two years. We have got to the position where they can trust us as Government negotiators to be acting in their best interests. We are not going to be running them short, to try and*

get something from them. That requires a close cultural melding in a sense.

In BC's case, face-to-face was the only channel suitable for building relationships with the claimant group. In this case, it was the claimants who initiated the contact and the relationship-building process. There may be several reasons why this was so. A simple explanation may be the relative proximity of the two sides (about 150 km), which made it relatively easy to arrange face-to-face meetings. However, it is likely that a cultural preference for the use of face-to-face communication was the most significant reason. By the end of the training program, BC concluded:

> *(BC) Face-to-face was much more relevant than might otherwise have been the case. It's the way that Maori operate, by talking and looking at you.*

This conclusion is in line with Hall's (1976) theory of high- and low-context cultures, which states that for some cultures, communication is more about context then the actual verbal message. In high-context cultures, messages have little meaning without an understanding of the surrounding context, which may include the backgrounds of the people involved, previous decisions, and the history of the relationship. People from low-context cultures prefer more objective and fact-based information. The message is sufficient. As this case makes perfectly clear, the leader of a virtual team will need to take into account cultural preferences or even requirements for relationship building as well as preferences for communication channels when choosing a degree of relationship and a relationship-building strategy.

AR also experienced the effects of cultural boundary crossing in her team to a different effect. AR's virtual team consisted of New Zealand and Australian members, and Asians and an Englishman on location in Asia. She did not consider the New Zealanders (she is one herself), the Australians, or the Englishman to be culturally different from herself, and she thought that as a group she understood their communication styles. So when her e-mails on critical matters to the Englishman went unanswered time after time, rather than come down hard on this team member, she checked before she sent an "obnoxious e-mail," thinking that "maybe the guy's wife is sick." So AR consciously made an effort to keep the lines of communication open. Her "softly softly" approach yielded an "astonishing" reply:

> *(AR) I telephoned him. Please tell me if I have offended you in some way. He said, well I am a Yorkshireman and we go quiet when we're thinking. I was astounded by this. I felt like saying I don't care if you come from Mars, I need this stuff.*

This Englishman had been hired as the lead consultant on the project at the last minute, and AR had not attempted to build a relationship with him. She had assumed, until she learned otherwise, that she understood him, not only because he was an Englishman who spoke and wrote English, but also because he was a professional consultant like herself.

From previous experience, AR knew that Asians tended to respect authority by showing deference toward superiors, and she tried to communicate respect in her virtual communications with her Southeast Asian team members, for example, by writing "Dear Mr. Pang" rather than "hi" or "hello," as she did with her other colleagues. The cultural contrast between her Southeast Asian team members and the Australian and New Zealand members was pronounced, and AR was aware that the effect was greater then simply addressing e-mail. She recounted:

> *(AR) The Southeast Asian consortium partner and the clients have a different attitude toward authority. They were more respectful. In the West being critical doesn't necessarily mean negative criticism. Putting forward arguments can be positive, without being rude. The Southeast Asians have a very respectful attitude, which tends to minimize the open expression of differences.*

AR pointed out that communicating via technology was an added barrier when working across cultures. Working through a text-based or an audio channel does not provide the visual cues used to judge people's true feelings. Even using an audio channel, where you can judge the nuances and inflections of a voice and perhaps tell whether people are feeling frustrated or angry, the problem remains that you must know the person or their culture very well in order to form an accurate interpretation. AR explained:

> *(AR) In some cultures people will smile even when they're angry at you. Of course this is the problem of your only using one channel. If you're not getting the other cues, it makes things much more difficult. Some cultures may also get very excited when speaking while others may speak calmly and slowly. Each could be misinterpreted by the uninitiated.*

As with organizational boundary crossing, cultural differences would appear to be an obvious and important factor when leading virtual teams. However as AR's experience showed, even experienced team leaders can make wrong assumptions about culture. Cultural tolerance and empathy are basic conditions for communicative openness (Boutellier, Gassman, Macho, & Roux, 1998). AR's and BC's experiences crossing cultural barriers demonstrate the importance of cultural factors to any team leader wanting to build relationships across cultural boundaries. They will need to consider the degree of personal relationship necessary to get the working relationship underway, as well as the use of appropriate communication channels along with appropriate messages delivered in an appropriate manner.

Time and Distance Boundary Crossing

Crossing time and distance boundaries is what most obviously distinguishes virtual teams from colocated teams. The effect of distance on relationship-building strategies is proportional to how far the team leader and team members are from each other. The further away, the more difficult the use of face-to-face communication, which could be problematic in situations where face-to-face communication is the best or maybe the only option, as shown in BC's case. BC's case also demonstrated that when team members are close enough to get together for face-to-face meetings, it might be unnecessary to resort to technology. He related:

> *(BC) The other reason the claimants preferred face to face over a chat room or even video conferencing is that they're really not that far away and it doesn't really cost much for them to come down and talk to us.*

The effect of time on relationship-building strategies concerns the challenge of working across time zones. This may have little impact on the degree of relationship building that may be necessary but a large impact on creating strategies to build relationships, as the time differences can restrict the kinds of communication channels available to the team leader. If a team member is on the other side of the world, "12 hours away," synchronous communication using the phone or videoconferencing is bound to inconvenience one or both of the parties involved. This is probably not an issue that will make or break a virtual team of professionals, but it is one of the conditions that must be carefully and fairly assessed by the team leader before creating relationship-building strategies. As DW put it, "everybody has to be awake."

If asynchronous communication channels are used, such as e-mail, the problem of pacing communication exchanges can become a serious consideration. Response times between team leaders and team members may differ, constraining communications, causing uncertainty, and negatively impacting trust (Jarvenpaa & Leidner, 1999; Warkentin & Beranek, 1999). Time lags due to technical infrastructure and technological breakdowns, if not known by the people involved, can cause the team leader or team member to attribute noncommunication to lack of manners or conscientiousness, which can then seriously affect relationships (Cramton & Webber, 2000). These kinds of problems arose often in this study, as this comment shows:

> *(SC) I can never be sure when I will receive an e-mail reply. I think, have they got the message? Has it got there? And why haven't they replied? In other words they have the control over the reply. Why are they withholding it, why are they exerting this control? Why don't they just reply? It's not such a difficult request I sent them. It's a feeling of powerlessness.*

Another team leader echoed this sentiment:

> *(AR) From the start of the project, I kept a key person in Asia updated on the project. It was three weeks before I realized I hadn't heard anything from him....When working virtually it sometimes takes a long time before it filters through to you that something's wrong. And then all of a sudden you're kind of thinking where is that guy....When I called him, I found out he had not received any of my e-mails. He was somewhat upset, having thought I was ignoring him. Evidently the e-mails I was sending him were being forwarded to the wrong address. When I told him, I really did send him e-mails, he was, like, "yeah, yeah." It was not a great start to the relationship, but we sorted it out.*

The kinds of problems associated with crossing time and distance have the potential to greatly disrupt relationship building in a virtual team, particularly with inexperienced team members. It is necessary for the team leader to carefully assess these potential obstacles before creating relationship-building strategies, as well as respond in a fair and considered way should problems that may be caused by time and distance arise, much as AR did in the quote above, when she telephoned her team member.

Challenges and Solutions for Team Leaders and Organizations

Although exploratory in nature and limited to the experiences of seven team leaders, this study points to significant differences in colocated and virtual teams in leadership-led relationship building across boundaries. The greater number and variety of boundaries and their deeper impacts pose special challenges that virtual team leaders will need to mediate. Summarized in Table 2 are the key

Table 2. Mediating Complexity: Communication Challenges when Building Relationships with Virtual Team Members across Boundaries

| | **Types of Boundaries Crossed** | | |
	Organizational	**Cultural/Language**	**Time & Space**
Co-Located Teams	Shared organizational culture tends to support relationship building, although functional cultural can pose challenges.	Nonverbal cues can be understood by experienced leaders. Non-native speakers	The ability to regularly meet face-to-face generally supports relationship building across cultures of all types
Virtual Teams	Differing organizational policies can inhibit communication, as can organizational preferences for the use of different communication channels and ICT infrastructure. Lack of situational knowledge of team members can cause misunderstandings and mis-attribution leading to numerous potential difficulties.	Lack of nonverbal cues is difficult to overcome with most available communication channels. Cultural preferences for certain communication channels, often face-to-face	Building relationships across time and space require concerted efforts and more time than in co-located contexts. Arranging synchronous meetings or even phone calls across time zones is often problematic. Asynchronous channels face the problem of pacing communications. Dealing with "silence" is a particularly difficult challenge.

communication challenges faced by the team leaders in this study. Two of these challenges are discussed. First, virtual team leaders need to expand and hone their repertoire of skills in handling virtual communication channels. Second, what organizations can do to improve their team leaders' and members' virtual communication skills.

Colocated teams contain boundaries, often in the forms of ethnic and functional cultures, and team leaders must negotiate them to build relations with their team members. With regular face-to-face contact and a modicum of people-oriented skills, experienced team leaders can mediate these boundaries and build relationships with team members. But the process is significantly more complicated in virtual teams. Social presence is lacking and needs to be consciously developed through, often limited, electronic channels. Nonverbal communication cues are likewise unavailable or severely delimited in virtual contexts. Building relationships and trust in virtual environments requires strategic and skillful use of communication channels as well as the ability to mediate a host of boundaries and unseen elements. Virtual team leaders need to make adjustments in the content and frequency of team communications and the selection and use of communication channels when crossing boundaries. Leadership as mediation (Barge, 1996) must be conducted at a significantly higher level of sophistication than that in colocated teams.

Table 3. Mediating Complexity: Guidelines for Using Communication Channels to Build Relationships in Virtual Teams Across Cultural/Language Barriers

Preferred Communication Channels			
		Native Speakers	Non-native Speakers
High Context Cultures (relationship-oriented) (tend toward formality)	Media rich, Synchronous, Face-to-face, phone, video/audio	Media rich, synchronous, asynchrous	Face-to-face with interpretor, asynchronous written with editor
Low Context Cultures (task- oriented) (Tend toward informality with notable exceptions, e.g., Germans)	Flexible, as above, plus e-mail, fax, computer conferencing (on-line synchronous written chat, asynchronous discussion boards)	All channels -- synchronous and asynchronous	All channels with translator, interpreter or editor as required

Communication is a key element in a successful virtual team (Robey et al., 2000; Lau et al., 2000). Effective two-way communication or dialogue results in team socialization, improved cultural understanding, development of trust, and task completion (Kayworth & Leidner, 2000; Jarvenpaa & Leidner, 1999; Robey et al., 2000; Tan et al., 2000). As one team leader (AR) in this study recognized, assumptions and information tend to be shared within a single organization. In such shared contexts, messages may be simpler, less frequent, and delivered though "lean" communication channels. However, if boundaries must be crossed, then the development of strong trusting relationships based on shared views and developed through media-rich channels can lessen the need for more complex and frequent messages that would otherwise be required to accomplish the team's task (Maznevski & Chudoba, 2000). This contention that strong, trusting relationships are necessary in boundary-spanning teams seemed to be understood by most of the team leaders in this study.

The strategic use of communication channels is one critical skill that virtual team leaders will need to hone. Based on the findings from this study as well as the literature, illustrated in Table 3 are ways in which virtual teams leaders need to mediate cultural/language boundaries by consciously selecting the most appropriate communication channels. Higher-context cultures (Hall, 1976) will tend to require media-rich channels such as phone and videoconferencing to build relationships, at least until a sufficient level of trust has been developed. In contrast, lower-context cultures, which are more task-oriented, will tend to be more tolerant of a wider range of communication channels. By being task oriented, building relationships might be secondary to getting started on the task. Knowing the cultural composition of the team and team members' prior experiences working virtually and across boundaries in general are part of the complex web of factors that leaders need to determine and then mediate if they are to successfully build relationships with team members and, ultimately, complete team tasks.

The second challenge concerns organizational support structures. To improve virtual team leader and member skills, organizations will need to be willing to provide training and ongoing support to promote and develop effective boundary-crossing behaviors among virtual team members. Virtual team processes and dynamics are different from those of colocated teams and require special skills, particularly for first-time members. Virtual team activities are focused on networking and establishing links across boundaries (Duarte & Tennant-Snyder, 1999). Team members and, particularly, team leaders will often need to play multiple roles as negotiators (with customers), network and coalition builders (with other teams), lobbyists (with top management), and motivators (of team members) (Yan & Louis, 1999). A team leader's credibility is, in large measure, perceived to be directly related to the extensiveness of his or her network and the ability to obtain resources across traditional organizational lines (Duarte & Tennant-Snyder, 1999; Manev & Stevenson, 2001). To be effective, team leaders will need training in boundary crossing, networking, and relationship building skills (Yan & Louis, 1999). The findings of this study, as well as those of the research and practitioner literature, suggest that training in any number of other areas will be useful in building relationships in boundary-crossing contexts, including training in virtual team communication and virtual processes, ICT selection and use, and cross-cultural communication skills. Almost any training that increases team members' and leaders' flexibility and ability to mediate complexity will be valuable.

Conclusion

Realizing effective leadership in group, team, and multicultural interorganizational communications across diverse perspectives and global virtual environments today presents new, real and compelling challenges to team leaders, but they also present unparalleled opportunities for teams to expand on perspectives, approaches and ideas (Adler, 2002). Crossing organizational, cultural, and time and distance boundaries requires training, experience, and organizational support. These can go a long way in helping team leaders determine and work across the boundaries that may be present on their teams. In addition to their effects on building communication relationships, boundary-crossing differences can affect team processes and performance in many ways. To ignore them is to invite team failure. Leaders must learn to mediate the increased complexity inherent in virtual teams. A starting point for leaders to approach the complexity introduced by boundary crossing is to ask these two questions:

1.   What are the boundary-crossing influences of this situation?

2.   How can they be understood and worked with so that a good people-oriented environment of assurance and trust can be maintained and productivity can be enhanced?

Perhaps the ultimate challenge for team leaders, particularly in long-term or ongoing virtual teams, is to work to merge the individual cultures (functional, organizational, national, etc.) of the team members into a team culture. Commenting on the creation of organizational knowledge, Nonaka and Takeuchi (1995) stressed the importance of sharing tacit knowledge among multiple individuals with different backgrounds, perspectives, and motivations. They went on to say, "The individual's emotions, feelings, and mental modals have to be shared to build mutual trust" (p. 84).

Nonaka and Takeuchi (1995) suggested that this can be done by creating culturally appropriate metaphors and cognitive maps to guide team behavior, support relationships, and complete tasks. One of this study's team leaders, BC, referred to this as "cultural melding," and he understood that it required a high level of interpersonal and intercultural communications skills for relationship building.

In conclusion, there has been a pressing need for rigorous conceptual and empirical work to examine factors that influence virtual teams (Pare & Dube, 1999), and it is only in the most recent literature that there have been systematic attempts to look at how virtual team leadership can support virtual team success. This chapter has focused on issues related to team leader-facilitated relationship building across boundaries. Its results suggest directions for future research and practice, including the development of virtual leadership mediation and communication skills.

References

Adams, J. S. (1976). The structural dynamics of behavior in organizational boundary roles. In M. D. Dunnette (Ed.), *Handbook of Industrial and Organizational Psychology* (pp. 1175–1199). Chicago, IL: Rand McNally.

Adler, N. (2002). *International Dimensions of Organizational Behavior.* Cincinnati, IL: South-Western.

Barge, J. K. (1996). Leadership skills and the dialectics of leadership in group decision making. In R. Y. Hirokawa & M. S. Poole (Eds.), *Communication and Group Decision Making* (pp. 301–342). Thousand Oaks, CA: Sage.

Baskerville, R., & Pries-Heje, J. (1999). Grounded action research: A method for understanding IT in practice. *Accounting Management and Information Technologies, 9*, 1–23.

Bass, B. M. (1985). *Leadership and Performance Beyond Expectations.* New York: Free Press.

Bateson, G. (1972). *Steps to an Ecology of the Mind.* New York: Ballantine.

Bennis, W. G., & Nanus, B. (1985). *Leaders: The Strategies of Taking Charge.* San Francisco, CA: Harper Collins.

Berger, C. (1997). *Planning Strategic Interaction: Attaining Goals through Communicative Action.* Mahwah, NJ: Lawrence Erlbaum Associates.

Boutellier, R., Gassman, O., Macho, H., & Roux, M. (1998). Management of dispersed product development teams: The role of information technologies. *R and D Management, 28*, 13–26.

Burgoon, J. (1998). It takes two to tango: Interpersonal adaptation and implications for relational communication. In J. Trent (Ed.), *Communication from the Helm for the 21st Century* (pp. 53–59). Boston, MA: Allyn & Bacon.

Catell, R. (1948). Concepts and methods in the measurement of group syntality. *Psychological Review, 55*, 48–63.

Chidambaram, L. (1996). Relational development in computer supported groups. *Management Information Systems Quarterly, 20*, 142–165.

Collins, B., & Guetzkow, H. (1964). *A Social Psychology of Group Processes for Decision-Making.* New York: John Wiley & Sons.

Cramton, C., & Webber, S. (2000). Attribution in distributed work groups. In P. Hinds & S. Kiesler (Eds.), *Distributed Work: New Research on Working Across Distance Using Technology* (pp. 191–212). Cambridge, MA: MIT Press.

Davenport, T., & Pearlson, K. (1998). Two cheers for the virtual office. *Sloan Management Review, 130*, 51–66.

DeSanctis, G., & Poole, M.S. (1994). Capturing the complexity in advanced technology use: Adoptive structuration theory. *Organization Science, 5*, 121–147.

Duarte, N., & Tennant Snyder, N. (1999). *Mastering Virtual Teams: Strategies, Tools, and Techniques that Succeed.* San Francisco, CA: Jossey-Bass.

Fisher, A. (1980). *Small Group Decision Making: Communication and the Group Process.* New York: McGraw-Hill.

Glaser, B. (1978). *Theoretical Sensitivity: Advances in the Methodology of Grounded Theory*. Mill Valley, CA: The Sociology Press.

Glaser, B., & Strauss, A. L. (1967). *The Discovery of Grounded Theory: Strategies for Qualitative Research*. New York: Aldine De Gruyter.

Hall, E. T. (1976). *Beyond Culture*. New York: Doubleday.

Hirokawa, R., & Poole, M. S. (eds.). (1996). *Communication and Group Decision Making*. Thousand Oaks, CA: Sage.

Hosking, D. M. (1988). Organizaing, leadership and skilful process. *Journal of Management Studies, 25*, 147–166.

Jackson, P. J. (1999). Organizational change and virtual teams: Strategic and operational integration. *Information Systems Journal, 9*, 313–332.

Jarvenpaa, S. L., & Leidner, D. E. (1999). Communication and trust in global virtual teams. *Organizational Science, 10*, 791–815.

Jarvenpaa, S. L., Knoll, K., & Leidner, D. E. (1998). Is anybody out there? Antecedents of trust in global virtual teams. *Journal of Management Information Systems, 14*, 29–64.

Kayworth, T., & Leidner, D. (2000). The global virtual manager: A prescription for success. *European Management Journal, 18*, 183–194.

Lau, F. (1999). Toward a framework for action research in information systems studies. *Information Technology & People, 12*, 148–175.

Lau, F., Sarker, S., & Sahay, S. (2000). On managing virtual teams. *Healthcare Information Management Communications Canada, 14*, 46–53.

Lewis, R. D. (1996). *When Cultures Collide: Managing Successfully Across Cultures*. London: Nicholas Brealey Publishing.

Lipnack, J., & Stamps, J. (1997). *Virtual Teams: Reaching Across Space, Time, and Organizational Boundaries*. New York: John Wiley & Sons.

Manev, I. M., & Sorenson, W. B. (2001). Balancing ties: Boundary spanning and influence in the organization's extended network of communication. *The Journal of Business Communication, 38*, 183–205.

Margerison, C. (1988). Action learning and excellence in management development. *Journal of Management Development, 7*, 43–55.

Marsick, V., & O'Neil, J. (1999). The many faces of action learning. *Management Learning, 30*, 159–176.

Maznevski, M. L., & Chudoba, K. M. (2000). Bridging space over time: Global virtual team dynamics and effectiveness. *Organization Science, 11*, 473–492.

Nandhakumar, J. (1999). Virtual teams and lost proximity: Consequences on trust relationships. In P. Jackson (Ed.), *Virtual Working: Social and Organizational Dynamics* (pp. 46–56*)*. London: Routledge.

Nonaka, I., & Takeuchi, H. (1995). *The Knowledge-Creating Company*. New York: Oxford University Press.

O'Hara-Devereaux, M., & Johansen, R. (1994). *Global Work: Bridging Distance, Culture and Time*. San Francisco, CA: Jossey-Bass.

Pare, G., & Dube, L. (1999). Virtual teams: An exploratory study of key challenges and strategies. *Proceedings of the 20th International Conference on Information Systems* (pp. 479–483). Charlotte, NC.

Pauleen, D., & Yoong, P. (2001). Facilitating virtual team relationships via internet and conventional communication channels. *Internet Research: Electronic Networking Applications and Policies, 11*, 190–202.

Powell, W. W. (1990). Neither market nor hierarchy: Network forms of organization. *Research in Organizational Behavior, 12*, 295–336.

Revans, R. (1982). *The Origins and Growth of Action Learning*. Bromley: Chartwell-Bratt.

Robey, D., Khoo, H. M., & Poers, C. (2000). Situated learning in cross-functional virtual teams. *Technical Communication, 47*, 51–66.

Sapir, E. (1921). *An Introduction to the Study of Speech*. New York: Harcourt, Brace & World.

Schein, E. H. (1984). Coming to a new awareness of organizational culture. *Sloan Management Review, 25*, 3–16.

Strauss, A. L., & Corbin, J. (1990). *Basics of Qualitative Research: Grounded Theory Procedures and Techniques*. Thousand Oaks, CA: Sage.

Tan, B., Wei, K. K., Huang, W. W., & Ng, G. N. (2000). A dialogue technique to enhance electronic communication in virtual teams. *IEEE Transactions on Professional Communication, 43*, 153–165.

Tiffin, J., & Rajasingham, L. (1995). *In Search of the Virtual Class: Education in an Information Society*. London and New York: Routledge.

Tiffin, J., & Rajasingham, L. (2001). The hyperclass. In J. Tiffin & N. Terashima (Eds.), *Hyperreality: Paradigm for the Third Millennium* (pp. 110–125). London and New York: Routledge.

Townsend, A., DeMarie, S., & Hendrickson, A. (1998). Virtual teams: Technology and the workplace of the future. *Academy of Management Executive, 12*, 17–29.

Trauth, E. M., & Jessup, L. M. (2000). Understanding computer-mediated discussions: Positivist and interpretative analysis of group support system use. *Management Information Systems Quarterly, 24*, 43–79.

Tushman, M. L., & Scanlon, T. J. (1981). Characteristics and external orientations of boundary spanning individuals. *Academy of Management Journal, 24*, 83–98.

Van der Smagt, T. (2000). Enhancing virtual teams: Social relations v. communication technology. *Industrial Management and Data Systems, 100*, 148–156.

Vickery, C. M., Clark, T. D., & Carlson, J. R. (1999). Virtual positions: An examination of structure and performance in ad hoc workgroups. *Information Systems Journal, 9*, 291–312.

Walther, J. B. (1997). Group and interpersonal effects in computer-mediated interaction. *Human Communication Research, 23*, 342–369.

Walther, J. B. & Burgoon, J. K. (1992). Relational communication in computer-mediated interaction. *Human Communication Research, 19*, 50–88.

Warkentin, M., & Beranek, P. M. (1999). Training to improve virtual team communication. *Information Systems Journal, 9*, 271–289.

Warkentin, M. E., Sayeed, L., & Hightower, R. (1997). Virtual teams versus face-to-face teams: An exploratory study of a web-based conference system. *Decision Sciences, 28*, 975–996.

Whorf, B. (1956*). Language, Thought and Reality.* New York: John Wiley & Sons.

Wiesenfeld, B. M., Raghuram, S., & Garud, R. (1998). Communication patterns as determinants of organizational identification in a virtual organization. *Journal of Computer Mediated Communication, 3*, 4.

Wright, K. (1999). The communication of social support within an on-line community for older adults: A qualitative analysis of the Senior Net community. *Communication Quarterly, 47*, 33–44.

Yan, A., & Louis, M. R. (1999). The migration of organizational functions to the work unit level: Buffering, spanning, and bringing up boundaries. *Human Relations, 52*, 25–47.

Endnotes

[1]   This Maori group may be referred to as "Ngati Mea" to protect its anonymity.

[2]   It is supposed that a case could be made that the differences are either cultural or organizational or perhaps a combination of both, but this question is beyond the scope of this study and does not really affect the contention that boundaries are being crossed.

Chapter XII

Factors Contributing to Knowledge Sharing and Communication in a Large Virtual Work Group*

Olivia Ernst Neece
Claremont Graduate University, USA

Abstract

In this chapter, we discuss an eight-factor process model of large virtual groups. A team has been defined as a small group of people that work very closely on a project or process. We define a large work group as a larger group of people who are more loosely connected to one another than a team by a shared work process, project, or strategic goal. The eight factors are organizational support and purpose; egalitarian structure; team culture, trust, collaboration, and relationships; people—skills, expertise, and capabilities; motivation and rewards; communication processes; communication tools; and knowledge sharing. These factors to a greater or lesser degree have been shown to contribute to the effectiveness of communication in a large virtual work group during a two-phase study at Nortel Networks. Qualitative and quantitative results of this study are presented in the chapter. We discuss issues related to communication and knowledge sharing in the chapter as well as recommendations for successful organization and communication in large work groups.

Introduction

Firms have been using virtual-team-based structures to reduce costs as well as to share knowledge globally and to unleash innovation and creativity. Much research has been accomplished studying virtual teams. However, a hybrid organizational form exists in many organizations, where individuals or pairs of individuals do not actually work on a smaller team but are assigned to a large virtual work group. These groups do not appear to function in quite the same way as smaller teams function. While the literature on virtual teams has proliferated, there is little research on these larger hybrid organization types that are termed teams by management but actually function as large work groups. In this type of organizational form, team members (actually work group members) may work on their own or in pairs in remote offices. Members of virtual work groups may have little or sporadic contact with other members of the group. There is a gap in the research, where this type of relationship exists. The goal of this research was to provide a pilot study for research in this field. The concern here is for the firm to achieve the goals of knowledge sharing while retaining effectiveness in the completion of task objectives when groups are larger than those of normal team size. Further, it is the goal of this chapter to discuss the role-based performance self-efficacy of members of virtual group members during the completion of their work duties in relationship to a number of factors that exist within the firm. This chapter reviews the literature related to virtual teams, knowledge sharing, communication, and collaborative technologies from the fields of information sciences, technology and innovation, organizational behavior, organizational theory, and strategic management. It then reviews the findings of a two-phase case study of one large group of workers at Nortel Networks.

Nortel Networks, headquartered in Brampton, Ontario, Canada, has participated in major developments in the evolution of communications networks technology worldwide in more than 150 countries. A century ago, they began as a telephone manufacturer, supplying primarily the Canadian market. With revenues of $10.56 billion, they have become a leading mover in the next generation of communication technologies in four core businesses:

1.   Wireless networks supporting CDMA, CDMA2000, GSM, GPRS/EDGE, UMTS, and TDMA and delivering advanced multimedia communications to end users

2.   Wireline networks converging traditional voice with voice over Internet Protocol (IP), multimedia, and IP data services, including security, IP virtual private networks (VPN), and multiservice switching

3.   Enterprise networks focusing on a portfolio of solutions for businesses, including voice, high-powered data, IP virtual networking (IP VPN), security, multimedia applications, Internet Protocol (IP) telephony including convergence solutions, customer contact, and voice portal

4.   Optical networks providing storage connectivity, managed wavelength, and optical Ethernet services via technologies such as Photonics (DWDM and long-haul systems), next-generation SONET, and optical switching with integrated network management

Background

In this chapter, we discuss factors contributing to the effective functioning of communication in a large virtual work group. While a team was defined as a small group of people that work very closely on a project or process, we define a work group as a larger group of people who are more loosely connected to one another than a team by a shared work process, project, or strategic goal. They may be a loose grouping of teams that are connected to one another in a network of teams. Global groups are those that are located in more than one country. Virtual groups are defined as those that are primarily noncollocated and communicate through a variety of collaborative technologies (e-mail, synchronous and asynchronous white boards, teleconferences, videoconferences, virtual chat rooms, and Web meetings). In addition, there may be some face-to-face interaction, although this is often sporadic, and the entire group may not meet in a single place simultaneously.

Virtual Teams and Other Lateral Networks

Cross-functional and cross-domain project and process-oriented teams (Frost, 1996; Galbraith, 1994; Jassawalla & Sashittal, 1999) designed to encourage coordination and innovation, have become an established part of the structure of most firms. Some of these groups are permanent parts of the organization, others are organized for specific projects that may be of long or short duration, and still others come together for a short-term project. Any team or lateral organization network may be collocated or geographically dispersed. As narrowly defined by Townsend and Demarie (1998), virtual teams are groups that are "geographically and/or organizationally dispersed coworkers that are assembled using a combination of telecommunications and information technologies to accomplish an organizational task" (p. 18). The dispersion may be moderate, as in teams that are dispersed in several cities in close proximity, or it may be more extreme, where teams are in several time zones scattered across the globe (Lipnack & Stamps, 1997; Miles & Snow, 1986). In the most extreme version, team members remain on different continents in different countries, interact primarily through computer-mediated communication, and rarely or never see or speak to one another (Knoll & Jarvenpaa, 1995; O'Hara-Devereaux & Johansen, 1994). Some theorists broadened the definition of virtual teams to include teams that have some individuals who are collocated. Here, members use a combination of face-to-face interaction and communication via telecommunications links and collaborative technologies (Duarte & Snyder, 1999). Virtual teams often require fluid membership for group problem solving and decision making (Grant, 1995). The task may be temporary or adaptive to organizational and environmental change (Townsend & Demarie, 1998, p. 18). Intercommunal teams encourage synergistic, collective, and coherent knowledge development out of disparate areas of expertise and specialization. This furthers the creation of organizational "know-what" as well as organizational know-how (Brown & Duguid, 1998). Dorothy Leonard-Barton pointed out that embracing cross-community organization avoids isolation and furthers the prevention of turning core competencies into core rigidities (Leonard-Barton, 1995).

Teams, in general, have a myriad of organizational behavioral issues that may enhance or reduce effectiveness. Trust and leadership are two major issues confronting teams that affect their dynamics (Katzenbach & Smith, 1999; Lipman-Blumen, 1999; Pfeffer, 1994). These more complex governance forms may encounter greater problems during coordination due to mobility and complexity of communication (Dubé & Paré, 2001). Continual building on previous creative work requires an institutionalization of the knowledge transfer, reuse, and integration process, as well as development of a repository for the explicit and tacit knowledge developed by these innovators. Knowledge workers must be able to trust the firm and must be motivated and rewarded to encourage mentoring, documentation, and collaboration (Leonard-Barton & Deschamps, 1988; Szulanski, 2000).

Virtual teams may have problems beyond those of collocated teams due to dependence upon collaborative technology and the establishment of common ground (Grant, 1996; Majchrzak, Rice, Malhotra, King, & Ba, 2000). Although the use of an emergent and malleable collaborative technology may lead to enhanced communication within the group (Majchrzak, Malhotra, & King, 2000), issues of trust (Jarvenpaa, Knoll, & Al, 1998), collaboration, and leadership may be magnified due to communication and distance problems (Jassawalla & Sashittal, 1999) or governance issues (Duarte & Snyder, 1999). Further, the organization may have constraints of time and financial resources that inhibit knowledge sharing and communication (Neece, 2002b).

Eight Factors in Virtual Groups: Moderators and Resources

Two types of factors, found in the cross-disciplinary literature on virtual teams, influence the success of the process and the fulfillment of the project objectives. It is suggested that the same moderators and resources may affect the process of virtual work groups. The literature of virtual teams is cited here.

In this chapter, we study eight factors related to virtual groups. The term moderators is used for seven of the factors. Each of these factors moderate by directly or indirectly affecting performance. The seventh factor, communication tools, is actually a set of resources, including human- and electronic-based resources. The eight factors include the following:

1.   Organizational support and purpose
2.   Egalitarian structure
3.   Team culture, trust, collaboration, and relationships
4.   People
5.   Skills, expertise, and capabilities
6.   Motivation and rewards
7.   Communication processes
8.   Communication tools
9.   Knowledge sharing

Factor 1: Organizational Support and Purpose

Creative virtual teams work better under conditions of ambiguity and are inherently nonhierarchical (Katzenbach & Smith, 1999; Lipman-Blumen, 1999). Innovative teams, in order to develop into what Lipman-Blumen calls "Hot Groups," do not prosper in a hierarchical structure but need support from a corporate patron who will shield the group from the hierarchy. In firms with rigid strategic business unit (SBU) structure, innovative individuals are "imprisoned resources," because lateral communication and career path development are not encouraged. Individuals are retained in the same unit in the firm throughout their careers. Career path cross-development increases the ability of employees to see their core competencies in a new light. As Prahalad (1990) stated, "Competence carriers should be regularly brought together from across the corporation to trade notes and ideas" (p. 90).

Formal and informal communication structures and team-building interventions that improve the ability of team members to transfer, capture, and combine tacit knowledge into new knowledge forms may be a source of sustained competitive advantage (Bresman, Birkinshaw, & Nobel, 1999; Sherman & Lacey, 1999). While increased return on investment and increased efficiency have been the traditional measures of economic value, in the knowledge-creating firm, more qualitative factors are equally important (Nonaka, 1991). Such factors include the achievement of the firm's vision, aspirations, and strategic long-term goals. Knowledge hoarding (creating scarcity) is a cultural phenomenon. Down-sizing may artificially cause loss of knowledge by losing knowledge from previously unknown sources. Open meetings allow individuals to invade one another's boundaries and offer advice about a new perspective, encouraging knowledge creation, the antithesis of monopolistic thinking (Nonaka & Takeuchi, 1995). Companies that operate in frequently changing markets have been attempting to develop a more flexible structure and eliminated rigid business units. However, a new study found that even with flexible structures, the former organizational structure continued to shape the identity, beliefs, and social ties of employees well after the change. This study stressed the importance of forming a collaborative focus within the new group and the group leaders forging new links with other participants (Houston, Walker, Hutt, & Reingen, 2001).

Factor 2: Egalitarian Structure

Most theorists proposed that the structure of a virtual team should be egalitarian in order to provide a more fertile ground for innovative thinking and for open knowledge sharing. Critical competencies required for virtual team leaders include mentoring and coaching, having technological skills, encouraging the use of technological tools, networking, building trust, managing cross-culturally, developing careers, and developing team processes. Team members often take spontaneous leadership roles (shared leadership) at critical junctures in the project (Pearce & Sims, 2002).. Duarte and Tennant-Snyder suggested that virtual group leaders need to understand human dynamics in managing across cultures and use high-technology methods as their primary modes of communication (Duarte & Snyder, 1999). Establishment of purpose, values, goals, and objectives; the setting of policies and procedures; and a clear distribution of workload enable all team members to understand and work toward the same objective (Katzenbach & Smith, 1999; Lipman-Blumen, 1999). Senge (1990) stressed the fact that a true commitment to a "shared vision" brings people together to share a common vision and a common purpose (Senge, 1990).

Factor 3: Team Culture: Trust and Collaboration

Team culture is highly influenced by the frequency of communication (Cyert & Goodman, 1997) as well as the quality of communication. Hoopes (1999) found that teams that fully integrate and collaborate during the project process were more successful than teams that split the workload and integrated the product later in the cycle. Integration is critical to the success of projects and often results in a decrease in project completion time (Hoopes & Postrel, 1999). Integrated problem solving is also critical for successful process development (Pisano, 1994).

Trust is an issue that has been found to be of major importance in virtual teams (Gibson & Manuel, 2002; Jarvenpaa, Knoll, & Al, 1998). The global virtual-team context eliminates certain forms of social control, such as direct supervision, face-to-face contact during meetings, and close proximity for monitoring work progress (Jarvenpaa, Knoll, & Al, 1998). In new organizational structures such as networked organizations and teams, traditional social controls based on authority are traded for governance based on self-direction and self-control (Miles & Snow, 1992). Trust, under this loose form of governance, will promote open and substantive information exchange, increase the influence of communication, and improve confidence in the relationship (Earley, 1986; Yeager, 1978). Thus, trust can reduce transaction costs in the group interrelationships (Cummings & Bromiley, 1996; Handy, 1995). Paré and Dubé (1999) found in interviews with 20 virtual team leaders that early face-to-face meetings were considered essential in building vision, trust, and mutual accountability (Paré & Dubé, 1999). However, this early collocation may not always be possible.

All organizations are subject to political maneuvering. That is, they are subject to internal conflicts in relationships between people or groups in social or work situations based upon self-interest (Eisenhardt, 1989; Jensen & Meckling, 1996; Williamson, 1981). Because the introduction of an integrated knowledge management system and knowledge-sharing policies and processes will cause major change for many individuals, it is subject to such conflicts. Individuals will be more easily acculturated through the use of a shared language (common language, interpreters, or coding), a shared experience base, or some shared cultural norms (Clark, 1996; Szulanski, 2000).

Time constraints may also complicate communication and cause additional stress due to a limited notion of what is *productive* work. Some practitioners and academic researchers suggested setting a time or place for knowledge transfer, knowledge fairs, or chat rooms, to provide inducement to share (Davenport & Prusak, 1998).

Factor 4: People: Skills and Knowledge

Factor 4 is the combination of skills, expertise, knowledge, diversity, and capabilities of the individual team members (Ghoshal & Bartlett, 1997; Pfeffer, 1994). Virtual teams allow firms to build a structurally flat organization with optimized team membership, selecting from the best people regardless of their geographic location. Access to previously unavailable expertise, enhanced learning, enhanced cross-cultural understanding, increased knowledge transfer, reuse, and cross-functional/cross-domain interaction add to the benefits for the firm (Townsend & Demarie, 1998).

In regard to the fourth factor, "People: skills and knowledge," it is often easy to spot those who have the needed skills for a particular assignment. In the scientific community, particular individuals have expertise in astrophysics, fluid mechanics, biochemistry, semiconductors, or other specialized areas. In other areas, such as law, architecture, music, art, history, and literature, experts become known in the field and are sought for their expertise. Thus, the important members needed for a group are often known. At times, these group members will not be available to a firm, or a firm will need to be in a position to develop networks of expertise to tap this needed knowledge.

However, in more generalized process-oriented groups, there may be more latitude in selecting group members. An instrument and a learning system that can assist firms in determining the abilities needed for team members and training members is the Structure of Intellect System (SOI) founded by Dr. Mary Meeker. This protocol is based upon theories developed by J. P. Guilford (Guilford, 1967, 1977, 1982) and applied by Meeker (1969). Guilford identified 98 separate intellectual abilities through factor analysis, and Meeker developed methods for testing and strengthening these abilities in a wide range of age groups (Meeker, 1969; Meeker & Meeker, 2002). The primary application in industry is to define the profile or subset of abilities that correlate with success on specific jobs. The company can then select staff by testing those specific abilities in prospective employees. The company can also improve performance on the job by developing the abilities correlated with job success. The protocol was also used in outplacement for helping people move to new careers, and also by designing training to correspond to the abilities strongest in the employee demographic group.

Thus, it is believed that we can improve the performance of large virtual groups through selection and training. Firms can select and tailor learning and training systems to assist employees in making the transitions from collocated work to virtual work.

Factor 5: Motivation and Rewards

Motivation of team members and the rewards structure that encourages or discourages team performance are issues that have been the subject of debate since the Hawthorne experiments determined that people might be motivated by attention and recognition (Mayo, 1933). Negative motivation can discourage knowledge transfer and reuse (Hayes & Clark, 1985; Katz & Allen, 1982; Zaltman, Duncan, & Holbek, 1973). Szulanski, (2000) noted, "Lack of motivation may result in procrastination, passivity, feigned acceptance, sabotage, or outright rejection in the implementation and use of new knowledge" (p. 12). Effort and uncertainty are two major hurtles in locating distant knowledge. Simon and March used the term "satisficing" to describe the human tendency to settle for the knowledge or information that is adequate, but not ideal, in order to make a decision or for the immediate purpose at hand (March & Simon, 1958). According to Davenport and Prusak (1998):

> *Localness adds to market inefficiency because it causes people to make do with less than optimal knowledge while a much better "product" goes unsold or unused. In order to encourage knowledge owners to share, (firm's should) evaluate their performance and provide incentives based on knowledge sharing. (p. 41)*

Studies showed that the organizational context affects the motivation and the capability of individuals to practice knowledge transfer (Szulanski, 2000). In addition, the values and norms of the group and the organization (Kostova, 1999) and the directives or incentives (Leonard-Barton & Deschamps, 1988) as well as the counseling and support of management (Attewell, 1992) will either inhibit or encourage knowledge transfer and reuse. The ability to exploit knowledge transfer may be inhibited by the absorptive capacity of the receiver (Cohen & Levinthal, 1990). However, disincentives for reusing knowledge, such as rewards for invention and not for reuse or cultural norms such as "not invented here" may also hinder absorption. The challenges of abandoning past practices in favor of new methods can be significant, as shown in the innovation literature (Rogers, 1983), the planned organizational change literature (Glaser, Abelson, & Garrison, 1983), and organizational learning literature (Argote, 1999).

Factor 6: Communication Process

The use of collaborative technology cyberspaces for shared resources, digital libraries, access to instrumentation, and team communication, provide a platform for knowledge sharing among virtual team members. Ross-Flanigan (1998) discussed the potential loss of trust through lack of face-to-face interaction but suggested that the frequency and quality of virtual communication fosters rather than discourages interdisciplinary cooperation. The access to greater quantities of information and a wider cross section of participants allows team members to more easily bridge the gap between theory and experiment (Ross-Flanigan, 1998). With flexible distributed access, team members who have limited time for a project can check in when it is convenient and offer suggestions or modifications.

Factor 7: Communication Tools

Resources available to each team can be human, electronic, physical (e.g., prototypes, samples), or document-related resources and include some combination of data, information, explicit knowledge, and tacit knowledge. The availability and ease of locating resources are critical elements of project success. Resources should also contain contextual information for ease of searching (Majchrzak & Beath, 2001; Majchrzak, Neece, & Cooper, 2001).

Face-to-face interaction has been augmented by a variety of technological tools. Value is maximized in a system when hardware and software systems are integrated within and between enterprises (Kalakota & Whinston, 1997). Software should enable integration across varied hardware and operating system platforms. Systems can also be adapted to suit the team. For example, Majchrzak (2000) found that one virtual group changed their frequency of use and incrementally adapted an experimental collaborative tool to satisfy the group's needs (Majchrzak, Malhotra, & King, 2000). Global access will be required to take full advantage of the resources available. Because one of the main problems with international communication is cultural and language based, the deployment of real-time audio- and videoconferencing for development and brainstorming should enhance this interactive communication (Dubé & Paré, 2001).

Factor 8: Knowledge Sharing and Reuse

A wide variety of definitions have been offered for the terms, data, information, and knowledge. Further, distinctions have been made between tacit knowledge (that knowledge that defies simple codification) and explicit knowledge (knowledge that can be readily codified or written) (Hedlund, 1994; Kogut & Zander, 1992; Nonaka & Takeuchi, 1995; Polanyi, 1982). These definitions are less important here than the concept that all forms of data, information, and knowledge should be contextualized, shared, combined, and reused in order to create new knowledge. Creation of new knowledge and innovation is often dependent upon tapping the "tacit and often highly subjective insights, intuitions, and hunches of individual employees and making those insights available for testing and use by the company as a whole" (Nonaka, 1991, p. 3).

Knowledge transfer or sharing is the movement of knowledge from one source, the knowledge generator, to a knowledge receiver or knowledge reuser, either directly through personal contact or through an intermediary. Intermediaries include other persons, environmental resource planning systems (ERPs), knowledge management (KM) systems, other knowledge repositories or databases with search and retrieval capabilities, Centers of Excellence (Moore & Birkinshaw, 1998), papers, books, seminars, collaborative tools, people such as translators or knowledge brokers, contracts, plans, business processes, and person-to-person contact by telephone, letters, e-mails or meetings (Brown & Duguid, 1998). Knowledge reuse is adapting and synthesizing existing components, technologies, techniques, or procedures for use by a different person or group of people at a different time or location. It can be conceptualized as a communication problem: how to communicate information veridically between the two domains of the knowledge generator and knowledge reuser.

Clark's (Clark, 1996; Clark & Brennan, 1993) theory of language use suggests that veridicality of communication is more likely when both parties to the communication have a "common ground." Common ground can be defined as the beliefs, knowledge, and suppositions that the parties believe they share about the joint activity. Common ground can also be conceptualized as the set of shared norms and behaviors, defined as people behaving in ways expected by others (Ouchi, 1980; Tsoukas, 1996). Different communities have varying standards, different ideas of what is significant, different priorities, and divergent evaluating criteria (Brown & Duguid, 1991). For example, Hewlett Packard found that what looks like a best practice in California may not turn out to be the best practice in Singapore (Cole, 1999).

Role-Based Performance Scale

In order to determine if a particular mode of practice or process is valuable to a firm, it is important to assess the effectiveness of the people involved in the organization. In particular, organizations have begun to develop appraisal systems based on competency models. These focus on the skills people need to be effective in their current and future positions (Lawler, 1994).

Welbourne, Johnson, and Erez (1998) used role theory and identity theory to develop a generalizable measure of performance. Using role theory, they provided an explanation for why work performance should be multidimensional. Their model of work performance included several dimensions based upon identity theory, including the roles of job, career, innovator, team member, and organization citizen. The theory combines individual contributions within an organizational framework. The role-based performance scale (RBPS) assesses and measures these five unique components of behavior, many that are often overlooked in typical corporate performance appraisal instruments (Welbourne, Johnson, & Erez, 1998). In this study, we utilized this instrument in assessing a small subgroup of the Talent Acquisition Group. Then, the scale was used to assess the subgroup's self-assessment of effectiveness and process creativity in relationship to eight factors.

Issues and Problems

The eight factors discussed and reviewed above are issues that may affect the communications, knowledge sharing, and effectiveness of any large virtual work group. In general, the issues here concern factors that lead to overall effectiveness in large virtual work groups. More specifically, we are concerned with which of these factors are most highly correlated with knowledge sharing and reuse and which factors are most related to the effectiveness of communication. The goal of the researcher was to develop a process model of virtual work groups and then test this model at Nortel Networks in a pilot study. Nortel was most interested in this study, as they have a large number of people working in a virtual environment. Discussed in this chapter is a two-phase study of the virtual team process at Nortel Networks.

In Phase I, we conducted qualitative interviews and a detailed case study of one large work group, the "Talent Acquisition Team" (Nortel's title for the group), comprised of 340 members, in Canada and the United States. In Phase II, all members of this group were sent online surveys. The group leader was surveyed separately with additional questions, and her results were triangulated with the results of group members. In this study of Nortel Networks, group members shared a common task that involved more than 50% of their time at work. Some group members were collocated, while others were dispersed geographically throughout North America (United States and Canada). The group used a combination of face-to-face interaction and telecommunications and collaborative technologies, keeping in touch daily or weekly, depending upon the individual and his or her job description. Each work group member was involved in one or more tasks related to talent acquisition, including university recruitment, Nortel internal and external job Web sites; internal recruitment; and corporate recruiting, including locating, interviewing, and hiring potential applicants. Some work group members worked on several of these tasks simultaneously or rotated between tasks. Frequent changes in structure and assignment occurred during the case study.

The Talent Acquisition Team sponsor provided a set of informants from varying levels of the organization, and it appeared that preselection biases were not factors in the selection. Informants were contacted and interviewed by a single interviewer (preventing inter-rater reliability issues) by telephone or face to face. Interviewees were diverse in terms of their tenure at Nortel, gender, job descriptions, and levels of leadership in the firm.

Although there are many similarities between Canada and the United States, there are also many differences. According to some participants, the more spirited and less restrained personalities of Southern- and Texas-based American personnel were different than the personal habits of the more conservative Ottawa- and Toronto-based Canadians. This caused some friction in both directions. Further, Canadian personnel were particularly sensitive over the differences in cultural, economic, and political perspectives between our two nations. In addition, time changes and spatial distances for West-coast personnel, although only three hours and 3000 miles seemed to be troublesome in some cases. Although certainly not as extreme as those time and distance issues discussed by Sarker and Sahay, these issues still need to be actively addressed (Sarker & Sahay, 2002).

Questions included the formal and informal structure of the group, communication methods and frequency, motivation for group participation, incentives and disincentives, trust, collaboration, team environment, and the challenges of working in a virtual group. The participant was asked about the ways in which the group was most effective and least effective in reaching its goals and the goals of the firm. The interviewer fielded 20 interviews of 16 participants, each lasting for one to two hours. These resulted in 102 pages of typed verbatim notes taken by the interviewer. Notes from all interviews were organized by each question. The researcher assembled several tables to identify patterns across the interviews and coded these answers. These led to the development of the Virtual Group Process Model.

The following eight categories of factors were identified from these tables and included in a Virtual Group Process Model (Figure 1):

1.   Organizational support and purpose

2.   Egalitarian structure

Figure 1.   Process Model

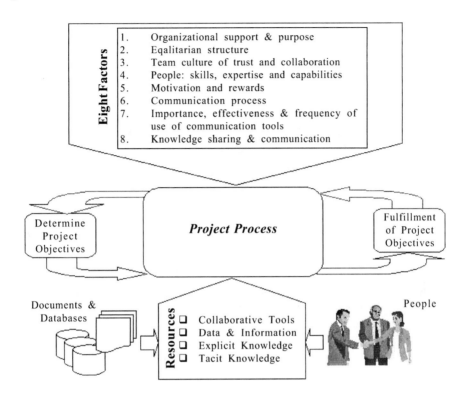

3.   Team culture of trust and collaboration

4.   Skills, expertise, and capability

5.   Motivation and rewards

6.   Communication processes

7.   Importance, effectiveness, and frequency of use of communication tools (including electronic technologies and nonelectronic communication)

8.   Knowledge sharing and communication

In Phase II, each member of the Talent Acquisition Team received a Web-based questionnaire. The response rate for questions 1–87 and 102–115 was 40.3%. Due to a random technical problem with Netscape, not all of the respondents received the entire Role-Based Performance Scale, and questions 88–101 were omitted for most participants. Thus, only 15.6% of the population assessed their own effectiveness, creativity, and general RBPS productivity using the Role-Based Performance Scale (Welbourne, Johnson, & Erez, 1998). However, this problem was random. It was determined that those who answered this portion were from all areas of the company and were widespread geographically. Therefore, we analyzed this information and report here the small sample it represents. The data will be used to assist in developing theory for future testing.

Scale Construction

Scales were developed to analyze the variables included in the model. In analyzing the data, principal components analysis (factor analysis) was used to identify variables that do not correlate well with other variables on the same metric. Questions with factor loadings of magnitude 0.40 or greater were included in the metric. In only a few cases was more than one question eliminated from the metric. Notably, however, the metric *Frequency of Communication Tools* had three questions that did not load well on a single factor; a single factor can only account for 27% of the variability in the data. Examinations of a two-factor solution indicate that the questions with low loadings can be considered a separate construct; two factors account for 48% of the variability. Due to this fact, *Frequency of Communication Tools* was eliminated from the model, and this factor was only included in the all communication tools metric. Metrics were constructed by adding response choices for each item with factor loadings with magnitudes greater than 0.40. Chronbach's Alpha was calculated for each metric. Pearson correlations were then calculated for each of the resulting metrics. Correlations can be seen in Table 1.

Solutions, Discussion, and Recommendations

The qualitative findings from Phase I (Neece, 2002a) include the results of the in-depth case study. From the literature and work group member interviews, a framework for studying large work groups was developed, based upon the daily process of services provided by service-oriented workers. In this framework, we examined the seven moderators of virtual work group behavior and the use of resources by this particular group. The Virtual Work Groups Process Model (Figure 1) may be useful for studying diverse types of large virtual work groups, organized for long-term or short-term projects. These groups may be involved in a variety of projects, including product innovation, process innovation, functional departmental projects, operational issues, and strategic development or imple-mentation. It is for this reason that the generalized term, project process, was

Table 1.   Pearson Correlation Scales

	KSHARE	IMPCOMTL	COMTOOL	FREQCOMA	FREQCOMB	HRBPSE	TEAMEFFC	CREATV	ALLCOM	COMPROC	CULTUR	EGALSTRC	MOTIVE	ORGSUP	PEOPLE		ALPHA
KSHARE	1	0.318	0.416	0.355	0.306	0.192	0.211	0.08	0.489	0.629	0.625	0.42	0.204	0.428	0.302		0.7683
IMPCOMTL	0.318	1	0.655	0.535	0.004	0.323	0.079	0.184	0.768	0.422	0.243	0.23	0.207	0.321	0.356		0.6401
COMTOOL	0.416	0.655	1	0.488	0.268	0.264	0.069	0.253	0.905	0.47	0.385	0.318	0.265	0.333	0.378		0.6879
FREQCOMA	0.355	0.535	0.488	1	0.055	0.235	0.101	0.019	0.543	0.32	0.306	0.311	0.197	0.319	0.171		0.636
FREQCOMB	0.306	0.004	0.268	0.055	1	0.03	-0.04	8E-04	0.311	0.331	0.365	0.307	0.029	0.219	0.201		0.4206
HRBPSE	0.192	0.323	0.264	0.235	0.03	1	0.792	0.772	0.272	0.462	0.343	0.502	0.36	0.361	0.22		0.9155
TEAMEFFC	0.211	0.079	0.069	0.101	-0.04	0.792	1	0.54	0.071	0.408	0.337	0.402	0.225	0.2	0.155		0.8224
CREATV	0.08	0.184	0.253	0.019	8E-04	0.772	0.54	1	0.242	0.324	0.143	0.232	0.119	0.091	0.169		0.8697
ALLCOM	0.489	0.768	0.905	0.543	0.311	0.272	0.071	0.242	1	0.565	0.453	0.377	0.248	0.384	0.439		0.8686
COMPROC	0.629	0.422	0.47	0.32	0.331	0.462	0.408	0.324	0.565	1	0.619	0.571	0.268	0.497	0.361		0.8371
CULTUR	0.625	0.243	0.385	0.306	0.365	0.343	0.337	0.143	0.453	0.619	1	0.692	0.321	0.483	0.374		0.8195
EGALSTRC	0.42	0.23	0.318	0.311	0.307	0.502	0.402	0.232	0.377	0.571	0.692	1	0.404	0.627	0.383		0.753
MOTIVE	0.204	0.207	0.265	0.197	0.029	0.36	0.225	0.119	0.248	0.268	0.321	0.404	1	0.5	0.38		0.6984
ORGSUP	0.428	0.321	0.333	0.319	0.219	0.361	0.2	0.091	0.384	0.497	0.483	0.627	0.5	1	0.328		0.5796
PEOPLE	0.302	0.356	0.378	0.171	0.201	0.22	0.155	0.169	0.439	0.361	0.374	0.383	0.38	0.328	1		0.5168

* For bold: Correlations larger than 0.29 (or smaller than -0.29) are significant at the 0.05 level

** For the rest: Correlations larger than 0.17 (or less than -0.17 are statistically significant)

*** see P values and sample sizes on the other worksheets herein used, rather than an explicit stepwise progression. The project process was addressed in a variety of contexts, and industries and models were developed for a variety of organizational forms that lead to theories of optimal project process. For example, Sanchez and Mahoney (1996) presented a modular model of product design where coordination is embedded into programmed innovation in an attempt to standardize component interfaces in a modular product architecture (Sanchez & Mahoney, 1996). Pisano (1994) explored the replication of new routines in projects designed to improve process development (Pisano, 1994). There is a need for a more general project process framework for firms to use to compare the process of groups involved in a variety of activities within the organization. While many of the segments of this model may seem familiar, what is new is the combination of a multidisciplinary approach to these model elements and their applications to larger work groups. They are important not only in an information science framework but also from the standpoint of organizational behavior, strategic management, organizational structure, productivity, and innovation. The model should provide understanding of the multidisciplinary effects of various process elements, moderators, and resources on group performance. The Virtual Work Groups Process Model (Figure 1) is such a framework.

There are three states in the model. The first state is the inception of the project or the development of the group, during which the project objectives are determined. In the Talent Acquisition Team, the project was an ongoing set of services provided to the entire firm. The process model may take place at varying levels of the organization depending upon the project purpose. In a product development process, the objectives may arise from customer requests or a perceived void in a product line. In some organizations, such as 3M, objectives may be introduced by anyone in the firm. In a government- or commercially-related bidding process, the project may develop to answer an announcement of opportunity (AO) or request for proposal (RFP). In a functional team, such as the Talent Acquisition Team at Nortel Networks, the purpose arises from administrative or strategic objectives.

The second state includes the actual process elements carried out by the team. This state includes a loop back toward establishment of project objectives, as these may need to be readdressed at any stage of the process. In addition, there is a feedback loop from the achievement of the objectives. The final state is the fulfillment of the project objectives. This state also has a feedback loop during which qualitative and quantitative analysis of team success in the fulfillment of project objectives should be communicated and discussed between the organizational actors, including managers, group leaders, and group members. In addition, group members should review their processes in order to improve their effectiveness in future projects. This review allows group processes to improve.

Variance Models

Based on analysis of the interview data and the literature survey, the researcher was able to develop two variance models for a modified set of moderators and resources. The first variance model (Figure 2) assists in identifying those factors that affect the following dependent variables: knowledge sharing and reuse, the importance of developing communication tools, and the effectiveness of existing communication tools. The factors include organizational support and purpose; egalitarian structure; team culture, trust, collaboration, and relationships; people, skills, expertise, and capabilities; motivation and rewards; and communication processes (see Figure 2).

In the second variance model (Figure 3), a different set of dependent variables included: the high Role-Based Performance Self-Efficacy scale (RBPS), team effectiveness (a subset of RBPS), and team creativity (a subset of RBPS). These were also tested with knowledge sharing and reuse and an all communications tools variable added as an independent variable. In the following section, we will discuss the empirical results as well as a few of the participant comments regarding each of these issues. These interview discussions provide a richness of perspective that data alone cannot provide.

Figure 2. Virtual Team Moderators and Resources Variance Model

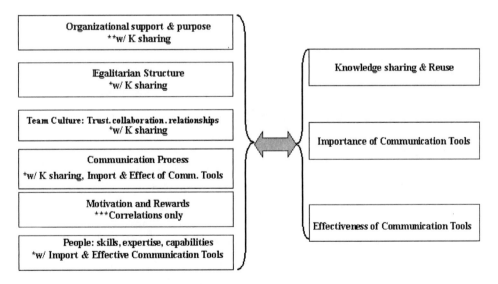

* Factors with positive regression coefficients at .05
** Factors with positive regression coefficients at .10
*** Note: All factors had statistically significant correlations; strongest correlations are noted by * or **

Figure 3.   Virtual Team Role Based Performance Self-Efficacy and Team Effectiveness

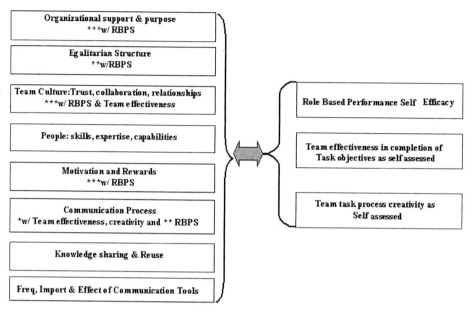

* *Factors with positive regression coefficients at .05*
** *Factors with positive regression coefficients at .10*
*** *Note: All factors had statistically significant correlations; strongest correlations are noted by * or ***

Role-Based Performance Self-Efficacy Scale and Team Leader Measurement of Effectiveness

The Role-Based Performance Self-Efficacy scale is a highly tested measure of performance in four major roles: job, career, innovator, team member, and organization citizen (Welbourne, Johnson, & Erez, 1998). The theory combines individual contributions within an organizational framework. This scale has an interquestion reliability of 0.9155. The subsets of team effectiveness and creativity have reliabilities of 0.8224 and 0.8697, accordingly.

The RBPS correlated with the scales of organizational support, egalitarian structure, team culture, motivation and rewards, and communication process. Findings in the regression were statistically significant for communication process and egalitarian structure, both of which were at the 0.10 level. Findings in the regressions for the subsets of effectiveness and creativity were statistically significant at the 0.05 levels for communication process only.

The team leader was asked to assess the effectiveness of the entire group on a five-point Likert Scale from 1 "strongly disagree" to 5 "strongly agree." Her assessment of group effectiveness was as follows:

3.47 = *The group is working hard enough to get the task done well, on time, and within the budget.*

3.40 = *Members have the diverse expertise required to accomplish the task.*

3.33 = *Members use their knowledge efficiently.*

4.20 = *The task requires members to use a variety of high-level skills.*

4.73 = *The group task has meaningful and visible outcomes.*

3.93 = *The group has autonomy in deciding how the work is done.*

3.07 = *The group gets regular feedback on how well the group is performing.*

2.93 = *The group developed an approach to the work that is fully appropriate for the task.*

2.80 = *Assess how well the group is implementing the strategy that you planned for the group.*

3.54 = *Average effectiveness score*

Group members scored themselves quite high on the RBPS (Table 1) at 82.4082, with an average score of 4.15 per item. On the effectiveness scale, the mean was 20.25 on a five-item scale for an average score of 4.05. They scored themselves similarly on the creativity scale, with an average score of 4.02. What is interesting here is that the group leader scored them very high on meaningful and visible outcomes, higher than they scored themselves. This measure may be the most meaningful to the team, as it is a concrete measure and triangulates fairly closely with the group leader's perception. The group leader scored them low on appropriate approach to the work and strategic implementation. Unfortunately, many members of organizations, especially those at lower levels, fail to grasp the concepts of strategic implementation of long-term corporate goals. With frequent changes in management and their own position in the organization, it is difficult to find fault with employees who score low in these areas. For example, at the time of the study, the group leader had not met with all 340 members to discuss the strategy of the Talent Acquisition Team. Some members, in interviews, expressed that they did not know what the company planned to do in the long term. Further, although she had viewed the work of many in the major centers, she may not have visited all the smaller remote outposts, where only one or two people were working alone to assess their approach to the work. It is unfortunate that within one year after the study, more than half of the employees who were included left the firm, including the leader of the group. This is, of course, due to the fact that the current state of the economy has taken its toll on talent acquisition activities.

Results of the Study: Discussion of the Eight Factors

The following discussion considers the quantitative results of the study as well as the qualitative comments of study participants in regard to the eight factors discussed in this chapter. Pearson correlations can be found in Table 1.

Factor 1: Organizational Support and Purpose

The organization needs to provide special support for virtual groups. Such support includes the perception of equal opportunities, adequate technological and physical infrastructure, and support for virtual functionality. Nortel Networks provides excellent technological support for virtual groups and extensive access to electronic and telephonic means of interaction. The corporation accepted telecommuting and remote intranet access by many employees. One project manager commented:

> *I feel strongly that virtual teams work and enjoy working for this company because it is accepted by the company. It is a definite advantage. It allows us to open up the diversity and incorporate other people rather than forcing them to show up on site every day.*

The same project manager was also concerned about the tendency for the firm to outsource "noncore services" and to automatically lay off the "bottom 10%" of employees. He said:

> *There is an inkling in the back of my head that some day I will be outsourced and laid off. It is fourth quarter and people are being laid off (in accordance with the) talent segmentation process, doing away with the bottom 10%. I agree with this but it is disheartening...*

Leadership issues include the establishment of purpose, communication of values, and coordination and development of an enabling culture. The group sponsor discussed the team purpose:

The main mission of the group is to get the right talent in the company at the right time and put them in the right place. Each group has a talent plan...what vehicles we use to attract the talent, how do you get them interviewed, hired and embedded as a Nortel employee?

The timing of the study was difficult for many team members. Several were just told that there would be a new team sponsor of the Talent Acquisition Team, and the group was undergoing a reorganization. Since the study completion, the entire team disbanded. While most interviewees seem to take leadership and job changes in stride, one participant discussed the disruptive nature of this particular change:

(The team sponsor) moving to another group was pretty shocking without any notice...(there are) a lot of changes going on and there is no communication.

Factor 2: Egalitarian Structure

Nortel has been proud of its goal of an egalitarian structure or flat organization. This was discussed by one of the group leaders:

Formal structure...not a lot of hierarchy. Priming the activity you have myself. As my peers you have the talent strategists and my counterpart at Europe, but I would be the centralized information gatherer. Ultimately I am responsible for driving that activity. So ultimately I have overall responsibility for recruiting for global ops. For each of those locations you ideally have a project leader and recruiters...It is more like a leadership relationship rather than managing behaviors and that sort of thing. As far as the resources I have, they are expert contributors.

However, although the structure is stated as egalitarian, there are still "bosses," and the virtuality of the workspace poses an issue for some individuals who assume they will be penalized for being "invisible":

It's hard for you to prove to your boss in another location that you can do the job and that you are a high performer. A poor performer will not be seen as much—taking longer lunches— getting away with more stuff.

Factor 3: Team Culture—Trust, Collaboration, and Relationships

Cultural issues such as encouraging trust, collaboration versus competition, developing working relationships, and team spirit contribute to team effectiveness. The challenges of virtual teams were discussed by one team leader:

> *You have to work smarter to make a virtual team work well. If you take people working in different time zones and then you take some of the challenges and magnify these, time zones and cultural differences, you understand how challenging coordination is.*

While Nortel supports a virtual team culture, project managers noted that some people are less capable of producing while off site. One project manager discussed this:

> *Most of the people are dependable and do a good job, but it takes a special person that can handle being on their own in another location.*

There were individual differences in capabilities for collaboration rather than competitive behavior, as was noted by the following comments by two participants in different subteams:

> *(One team member) looks at the other recruiters as being his competition. But the other folks are more collaborative...potential leaders are more collaborative.... (However) the majority of recruiters are highly competitive...When they come into this collaborative environment it is a complete shock.*

People will discuss who can be trusted. (The) team was not perfect because of this. They (recruiters) are used to being paid on volume and commission and they are competitive and do not help each other out. That has had an impact on our team.

Factor 4: People—Skills, Expertise, and Capabilities

Essential factors concerning people are developing or acquiring team members with the appropriate skills, expertise, and capabilities. It is also important to deal sensitively with diversity (age, gender, national origin, ethnicity, culture, location) and personality issues. Nortel Networks uses the Talent Acquisition Team for finding qualified and creative employees, but team members also search for qualified employees for their team. Individuals found that the participatory nature and friendships with other people were important enablers. One participant commented:

> *Doing a job well, feeling I contribute by maximizing quality and quantity of hires. Self-actualization, learning more as I am doing it. Competing with myself...a customer focused approach. Friendships are a big part.*

The quality of work done by individuals from outsourced firms was seen as a problem by several team members:

> *The most frustrating (part) is that once an offer is made, the drafting of the documents is done by another group and the mistakes that happened generated frustrations...a lot of time was spent putting out fires.*

Several subteam leaders and managers discussed challenges evinced by the flatter, more virtual, organization:

> *You are having to affect other people even though they do not report to you. But it requires even better relationship building skills.*

Team members should be selected for depth of knowledge resources and contacts and breadth of knowledge resources and networks. Nowhere is this more evident and critical than in talent acquisition. Coff (1999) mentioned that the development of extensive internal networks should enhance the firm's capabilities (Coff, 1999). The frequent job rotation at Nortel Networks appears to create a greater number of weak ties in the organization, as confirmed by interviewees who often mentioned that Nortel hired many independent recruiters who had a larger variety of contacts.

Factor 5: Motivation and Rewards

Organizations and teams should reward sharing—group rewards enable collaboration, while pay for performance and individual rewards encourage hoarding and monopolies. Among the recruiters, there seems to be an internal conflict between organizational motivation (extrinsic rewards) and psychic rewards (intrinsic motivation). One recruiter mentioned both:

> *There is a contradiction between what was desirable and what was stated. This was regardless of the objective criteria. (Rewards are) both volume-based (and for) thinking outside the box and*

being customer driven. In spite of this, people want to be number one and have as many hires as possible. Some enjoy the adrenaline.

The problem stems from the basic corporate financial reward structure as the team sponsor concluded:

There is quite a bit of competition among the groups. The Nortel structure rewards individuals, not team efforts. I came in brand new...there was a lot of competition for them to prove themselves to me. We have these silos, since we reward the individual approach.

Factor 6: Communication Process

Many in the virtual community mentioned the loss of face-to-face interactions. While some loners prefer the independence of a remote office, most people were vocal and open about their loss of personal contact. For example, one manager said:

We needed a clear goal at the beginning that we would communicate weekly or have some big meetings at the beginning to jump-start the task. It is hard when you are not collocated to have collaboration that is as rich. You have to have frequent face-to-face meetings. But since we were on a time schedule we had to keep to our agenda and meet goals and objectives rather than allowing the natural ease of idea exchange.

Another comment was as follows:

What I miss most and why I would be hesitant to do another virtual team. I miss the interactions where you get to collaborate more. In a virtual team people must have a more circumscribed role. I won't say we didn't share some of these back and forth, but it is more so when you are collocated. But it is kind of lonely just working on your own.

With this in mind, it is all the more important to improve the communication tools that are provided for this virtual work in order to ease the task and provide a more natural setting.

Factor 7: Communication Tools

The all communication tools scale had an interitem reliability of 0.8686, importance of communication tools, 0.6401, and effectiveness of communication tools 0.6879. Empirical results yielded some difficulty with the subcategory of frequency of use of communication tools due to some problems with individual questions failing to meet the requirements of factor analysis, even after splitting the category in two. Therefore, we chose to drop this separate category and included the remaining questions in the all communication tools category used in Model 2. In general, these three scales were positively correlated with all other scales. In the Model 1 regression, people—skills and capabilities and communication processes were both statistically significant in relationship to the importance and the effectiveness of communication scales, with corresponding R squares of 0.2498 and 0.2537.

At Nortel, a combination of electronic, human, physical, and document-related resources are available to team members. These resources may contain data, information, explicit knowledge, tacit knowledge, or a combination of any of these. Human resources quality and quantity seemed to vary from group to group. Keeping up with high-quality personnel needs is difficult with the high growth planned by Nortel Networks. Some individuals complained that there was insufficient manpower to drive the talent acquisition process:

Where you are hiring 10,000 people in one year, we may have had a lot of little leaks, but then you turn up the volume and you really see where the leaks are.

Other individuals were pleased with the available resources:

As far as the resources I have, I have expert contributors. I have someone who is assigned to me in talent marketing...someone in competitive intelligence...someone from talent acquisition. It's a pretty cool infrastructure. You have...everything you need in a recruiting organization. If you looked at all of the elements you need, we've pretty much got it.

Extensive use of e-mail and voice mail for interaction was found among all personnel, especially those who were not collocated. However, e-mail saturation was a common complaint. Weekly teleconferences are popular. However, difficulty in getting everyone to join the call was cited as the biggest hurdle. Visual information is sent via e-mail prior to the call to enhance communication. It was interesting that none of the interviewees mentioned collaborative technologies such as virtual white boards for real-time visual access during discussions. These technologies can be used in real time or asynchronously and are more collaborative than e-mails. Also, considering that this is a high-technology firm, it was surprising that only the team sponsor used videoconferences. Desktop video capability is not provided. The problem may be the lack of facilities or the quality of the technology. One manager mentioned quality:

> *I have participated in videoconferences. It's not a refined technology. In fact, it can almost impede communication. If you get there and cannot connect, you have to improvise. I would not give it a glowing recommendation just yet....We don't make the video-conference systems, we make the infrastructure it travels on.*

The lack of immediate response and visual impressions were two problems cited in relation to virtual communication. Travel for face-to-face meetings may assist remotely located employees in feeling more connected. One project manager in Canada noted that some off-site group members felt that they were out of the loop. Disenfranchisement of solitary home-based workers in remote locations was found to be a problem with certain team members. As said, "We do have a new employee who wants to come up here every week from Orlando, Florida."

Factor 8: Knowledge Sharing

This scale had an interitem reliability of 0.7683. Empirical results for knowledge sharing and reuse found all other scales to be correlated with this scale. In examining knowledge sharing as a dependent variable in Variance Model 1, regression results found statistically significant relationships at the 0.05 level between knowledge sharing and team culture, egalitarian structure, and communication process, and at the 0.10 level with organizational support. The R square for this model was 0.5099. Knowledge sharing was not found to be statistically significant in relation to the RBPS, effectiveness, or creativity.

Knowledge sharing and communication skills are enabled through skill development, education, and training. In addition, the culture of sharing should be supported at all levels of the organization. In knowledge markets, there are knowledge sellers (also known as the experts) and knowledge buyers. Three issues cause knowledge markets to operate inefficiently (Davenport & Prusak, 1998). One cause is the incompleteness of information and guides for buyers and sellers, including explicit information about price structure. As a project manager mentioned:

(One team member) was to divide up his workload, but for a month he had not shared his knowledge and workload with (a second team member).

A second cause is the asymmetry of knowledge—abundant knowledge in one department and a shortage somewhere else. Knowledge feasts and famines have more to do with information patterns and distribution systems than absolute scarcity, as discussed by the team sponsor:

There is not enough knowledge sharing...the fact that we are a virtual team (and are located) all over the world has its downside.

The third reason for inefficiency of knowledge sharing is the localness of knowledge. In fact, due to lack of trust, face-to-face interaction is often the best way to procure knowledge. Reliable information about more distant knowledge sources is often unavailable. A participant discussed this problem:

(Only about) 50% of the people share information with others. Maybe it is because they have never met face-to-face.

There are several pathologies that explain nonoptimal behavior regarding knowledge transfer. The first of these is a knowledge monopoly (knowledge hoarding). Among those interviewed, knowledge hoarding was rarely mentioned. In fact, one team member mentioned, "I don't see anyone keeping resumes to themselves." Trade barriers in the knowledge market may be caused by unwillingness to accept knowledge from outside sources (not invented here). An organization may lack a knowledge-transfer infrastructure or effective market mechanisms, or there may be a perception of inadequate quality of available information. One interviewee commented:

Some of the ideas some people have are not that good. So it would depend upon who told me the idea, or how much thought had gone into the idea that was presented to me.

Recommendations

From this study, it was found that several factors were important in encouraging knowledge sharing and communication in this large work group. The importance of the eight-factor process model was confirmed through the study. Discussed in the following table are these factors, their scope, and the recommendations of the researchers for practitioners (see Tables 2a, b). We believe that these

Table 2a: Recommendations

Factor	Scope	Recommendation
Organizational support & purpose	Communicate Purpose and importance of each individual	Communicate firm's values to everyone, but especially to those not in the central office.
	Ensure adequate communication facilities	Provide good resources to assure a flow of communication (e.g. videoconference, teleconference, virtual collaboration tools).
Egalitarian structure	Support for individuals as leaders of their portion of the task & organizational group.	Group members should be considered as expert contributors to increase self-motivation and decrease "satisficing".
		Provide a clear structure, whether flat or hierarchical. Confusion regarding structure and reporting relationships leads to problems
Team culture, trust, collaboration and relationships	Assists in the development of group culture & relationships during virtual work.	Select people for the abilities in terms of collaboration, ability to work on their own, flexibility, and skills with technology. Use leadership instruments such as Achievement Styles Inventory (ASI)[1] to assess leadership capabilities.
		Awareness of the challenges that people face regarding time zones, working alone, cultural differences, and communication issues. Help the group build the culture and trust through team building exercises.
People their skills, expertise and capabilities	Ensures selection of appropriate group members.	Selection of those with abilities matched to particular skills, expertise and capabilities needed for the group (e.g. astrophysics, biochemistry, maritime law, high-rise architecture, semi-conductors)
		Develop knowledge networks to fill gaps in group's knowledge or to add group members.
		Use of testing instruments such as the Structure if Intellect (SOI)[2] to match abilities and individual skills and to assist training.
Motivation and rewards	Ensures fullest participation of each individual.	Use both psychic rewards (positive reinforcement) as well as financial rewards.
		Discourage competitions, these restrain communication and cause gaps in the information flow. Contrary to popular opinion competitions do not increase productivity they curtail it by causing mistrust among group members.
		Build and reward a collaborative environment where there is shared leadership with group rather than individual rewards.

recommendations can assist organizations in improving their virtual work group process by increasing knowledge sharing, improving collaboration, and assisting the communication process within and between virtual work groups.

Conclusion and Future Study

In conclusion, this study was limited, as it is a case study of only one firm and subteams involved in only one functional area of the firm. During this study, we

Table 2b. Recommendations

Factor	Scope	Recommendation
Communication process	Provides a fertile environment for sharing knowledge, collaboration and reuse	All information should be shared information. Do not use one individual as a filter. Share ideas and encourage everyone, no matter what their position is to share their ideas.
	Loss of face-to-face interaction is a fact of life in virtual groups. Mitigate this loss through some rules of the road.	1. Set communication goal (e.g. once a week, with full participation and no one leaving during a teleconference. 2. Teleconferences should be short. 3. Set an agenda in advance for all meetings. 4. Videoconference is preferable (if available) 5. Send work product in advance to all participants before meeting
Communication tools	Provides resources needed for virtual and face-to-face communication	The following resources are required for virtual groups: • Email with high speed internet connections • Remote teleconference capabilities • Ability to share documents, drawings and images asynchronously (non-simultaneously
		The following resources are advantageous for virtual groups: ♦ Collaborative groupware or intranet capability ♦ Virtual group meeting rooms with the ability to share drawings, documents and ideas synchronously (simultaneously). ♦ Videoconferences, mitigating the loss of face-to-face contact ♦ Palm or hand-held computer data access
Knowledge sharing	Involves all of the other seven factors and is the value added of group work	Open up the gates of communication, develop the culture, and train the knowledge sharing skills in order to make virtual groups into efficient groups

found empirical and qualitative evidence to support many of the eight factors in the empirical model. However, there is evidence to support additional study of the Work Group Process Model and Variance Model 1 and Variance Model 2. Case studies as well as empirical studies are required in a variety of organizations, in other functional and operational areas, and in various domains, in order to confirm the generalizability of these findings. There were many questions left unanswered following this study. It was clear that there was significant disenfranchisement with individuals who worked alone in remote locations. There was also evidence that calling a large work group a "team" confuses members of the group. Some individuals thought they were members of the Talent Acquisition Team, and others thought that they were members of a smaller team that had no official title, such as "Dave's group." Further, constant change in responsibilities and positions led to further structural confusion and an inability to exchange important knowledge and information. It was unclear as to whether the problems of large work groups are greater than those of smaller virtual teams. A comparison study of large work groups and small teams within one organization may assist in shedding light on this issue. During such studies, we may find additional moderators of work group process or differences in how these moderators affect different types of firms or functions within firms. In particular, it will be of import to delve further into the relationship between the eight factors and the Role-Based Performance Self-Efficacy Scale and other types of effectiveness instruments.

It is valuable, however, to consider the multidimensional and multidisciplinary view of the work group process that was presented in this chapter. Such studies should prove interesting to academics and will provide assistance to practitioners in the future.

References

Argote, L. (1999). *Organizational Learning: Creating, Retaining, and Transferring Knowledge*. Norwell, MA: Kluwer.

Attewell. (1992). Technology diffusion and organizational learning: The case of business computing. *Organization Science, 3*(1), 1–19.

Bresman, H., Birkinshaw, J., & Nobel, R. (1999). Knowledge transfer in international acquisitions. *Journal of International Business Studies, 30*(3), 439–462.

Brown, J. S., & Duguid, P. (1991). Organizational learning and communities of practice: Towards a unified view of working, learning, and innovation. *Organization Science, 2*, 40–57.

Brown, J. S., & Duguid, P. (1998). Organizing knowledge. *California Management Review, 40*(3), 90–111.

Clark, H. (1996). *Using Language*. Cambridge, UK: Cambridge University Press.

Clark, H., & Brennan, S. (1993). Grounding in communication. In R. M. Baecker (Ed.), *Readings in Groupware and Computer-Supported Cooperative Work*. San Francisco, CA: Morgan Kaufmann.

Coff, R. (1999, August). *Who reaps the gains from social capital? Appropriating rent from dynamic capabilities*. Paper presented at the Academy of Management Meeting, Chicago, Illinois, USA.

Cohen, W., & Levinthal, D. (1990). Absorptive capacity: A new perspective on learning and innovation. *Administrative Science Quarterly, 35*(1), 128–152.

Cole, R. E. (1999). *Managing Quality Fads: How American Business Learned to Play the Quality Game*. New York: Oxford University Press.

Cummings, L. L., & Bromiley, P. (1996). The organizational trust inventory (OTI): Development and validation. In R. M. Kramer & T. R. Tyler (Eds.), *Trust in Organizations: Frontiers of Theory and Research* (pp. 302–330). Thousand Oaks, CA: Sage Publications.

Cyert, R. M., & Goodman, P. S. (1997). Creating effective university–industry alliances: An organizational learning perspective. *Organizational Dynamics, 1997*, (Spring), 45–57.

Davenport, T. H., & Prusak, L. (1998). *Working Knowledge: How Organizations Manage What They Know*. Boston, MA: Harvard Business School Press.

Duarte, D. L., & Snyder, N. T. (1999). *Mastering Virtual Teams: Strategies, Tools, and Techniques that Succeed*. San Francisco, CA: Jossey-Bass.

Dubé, L., & Paré, G. (2001). Global application of collaborative technology in collaborative teams. *Communications of the ACM, 44*(12).

Earley, P. C. (1986). Trust, perceived importance of praise and criticism, and work performance: An examination of feedback in the United States and England. *Journal of Management, 12*(4), 457–473.

Eisenhardt, K. M. (1989). Agency theory: An assessment and review. *Academy of Management Review, 14*, 57–74.

Frost, C. F. (1996). *Changing Forever: The Well-Kept Secret of America's Leading Companies*. East Lansing, MI: Michigan State University Press.

Galbraith, J. R. (1994). *Competing with Flexible Lateral Organizations* (2nd ed.). Reading, MA: Addison-Wesley.

Ghoshal, S., & Bartlett, C. A. (1997). *The Individualized Corporation: A Fundamentally New Approach to Management* (1st ed.). New York: HarperCollins.

Gibson, C., & Manuel, J. (2002). *Building trust: Effective multi-cultural communication processes in virtual teams*. Unpublished manuscript, Los Angeles, CA.

Glaser, E. M., Abelson, H. H., & Garrison, K. N. (1983). *Putting Knowledge to Use*. San Francisco, CA: Josey-Bass.

Grant, A. W. H. (1995). Realizing your company's full profit potential. *Harvard Business Review*, (September/October).

Grant, R. M. (1996). Toward a knowledge-based theory of the firm. *Strategic Management Journal, 17*, 109–122.

Guilford, J. P. (1967). *The Nature of Human Intelligence*. New York: McGraw-Hill.

Guilford, J. P. (1977). *Way Beyond the IQ: Guide to Improving Intelligence and Creativity*. Buffalo, NY: Creative Education Foundation.

Guilford, J. P. (1982). Cognitive psychology's ambiguities: Some suggested remedies. *Psychological Review, 89*, 48–59.

Handy, C. (1995). Trust and the virtual organization. *Harvard Business Review, 73*(3 May/June), 40–50.

Hayes, R. H., & Clark, K. B. (1985). *Exploring Productivity Differences at the Factory Level*. New York: John Wiley & Sons.

Hedlund, C. (1994). A model of knowledge management and the N-form corporation. *Strategic Management Journal, 15*, 73–90.

Hoopes, D. G., & Postrel, S. (1999). Shared knowledge, "glitches," and product development performance. *Strategic Management Journal, 20*, 837–865.

Houston, M. B., Walker, B. A., Hutt, M. D., & Reingen, P. H. (2001). Cross-unit competition for a market charter: The enduring influence of structure. *Journal of Marketing, 65 April 2001*(2), 19–34.

Jarvenpaa, S. L., Knoll, K., & Al, E. (1998). Is anybody out there? Antecedents of trust in global virtual teams. *Journal of Management Information Systems, 14*(4), 29–65.

Jassawalla, A. R., & Sashittal, H. C. (1999). Building collaborative cross-functional new product teams. *Academy of Management Executive, 13*(3), 50–63.

Jensen, M. C., & Meckling, W. H. (1996). Theory of the firm: Managerial behavior, agency costs and ownership structure. In J. M. Shriftz & J. S. Ott (Eds.), *Classics of Organization Theory* (4th ed.). Belmont, CA: Wadsworth.

Kalakota, R., & Whinston, A. B. (1997). *Electronic Commerce, A Manager's Guide*. Reading, MA; Harlow, UK; Menlo Park, CA: Addison-Wesley Longman.

Katz, R., & Allen, T. J. (1982). Investigating the not invented here (NIH) syndrome: A look at the performance, tenure and communication patterns of 50 R & D project groups. *R&D Management, 12*(1), 7–19.

Katzenbach, J. R., & Smith, D. K. (1999). *The Wisdom of Teams: Creating the High-Performance Organization*. New York: HarperCollins.

Knoll, K., & Jarvenpaa, S. L. (1995, January). *Learning virtual team collaboration*. Paper presented at the Hawaii International Conference on Systems Sciences Proceedings, Honolulu, Hawaii, USA.

Kogut, B., & Zander, U. (1992). Knowledge of the firm, combinative capabilities, and the replication of technology. *Organization Science, 3*, 383–397.

Kostova, T. (1999). Transnational transfer of strategic organizational practices: A contextual perspective. *Academy of Management Review, 24*(2), 308–324.

Lawler III, E. E. (1994). From job-based to competency-based organizations. *Journal of Organizational Behavior, 15*(1), 3–15.

Leonard-Barton, D. (1995). *Wellsprings of Knowledge: Building and Sustaining the Sources of Innovation.* Cambridge, MA: Harvard Business School Press.

Leonard-Barton, D., & Deschamps, I. (1988). Managerial influence in the implementation of new technology. *Management Science, 34*(10), 1252–1265.

Lipman-Blumen, J. (1996). *The Connective Edge: Leading in an Interdependent World.* San Francisco, CA: Jossey-Bass.

Lipman-Blumen, J. (1999). *Hot Groups.* New York: Oxford University Press.

Lipman-Blumen, J. (2000). *Achieving styles inventory.* Retrieved on 4/28/2002 from: http://www.achievingstyles.com/instruments/info.asp.

Lipnack, J., & Stamps, J. (1997). *Virtual Teams: Reaching Across Space, Time and Organizations with Technology.* New York: John Wiley & Sons.

Majchrzak, A., & Beath, C. (2001). Beyond user participation: A process model of learning and negotiation during system development. In A. Segars, J. Sampler & R. Zmud (Eds.), *Redefining the Organizational Roles of Information Technology in the Information Age.* Minneapolis, MN: University of Minnesota Press.

Majchrzak, A., Neece, O. E., & Cooper, L. P. (2001). Knowledge reuse for innovation—the missing focus in knowledge management: Results of a case analysis at the Jet Propulsion Laboratory. *Academy of Management Best Paper Proceedings 2001*, Washington, D.C.

Majchrzak, A., Rice, R. E., Malhotra, A., King, N., & Ba, S. (2000). Computer-mediated interorganizational knowledge-sharing: Insights from a virtual team innovating using a collaborative tool. *Information Resources Management Journal, 13*(1), 44–59.

March, J. G., & Simon, H. A. (1958). *Organizations.* New York: John Wiley & Sons.

Mayo, E. (1933). *The Human Problems of an Industrial Civilization.* Boston, MA: Harvard University Graduate School of Business Administration.

Meeker, M. (1969). *The Structure of Intellect: Its Interpretation and Uses.* Columbus, OH: Merrill.

Meeker, M., & Meeker, R. (2002). *Bridges to learning.* From: http://www.bridgeslearning.com/Programs/research_statistics.cfm.

Miles, R. E., & Snow, C. C. (1986). Organizations: New concepts for new forms. *California Management Review, 18*(3, Spring), 62–73.

Miles, R. E., & Snow, C. C. (1992). Causes of failures in network organizations. *California Management Review, Summer*, 53–72.

Moore, K., & Birkinshaw, J. (1998). Managing knowledge in global service firms: Centers of excellence. *Academy of Management Executive, 12*(4), 81–92.

Neece, O. E. (2002a). Moderators and resources enabling effective virtual team communication: A case study at Nortel Networks. *Proceedings of the Americas Conference on Information Systems 2002*, Dallas, Texas, USA.

Neece, O. E. (2002b). A strategic systems perspective of organizational learning: Development of a process model linking theory and practice. In E. Szewczak & C. Snodgrass (Eds.), *Managing the Human Side of Information Technology.* Hershey, PA: Idea Group Publishing.

Nonaka, I. (1991). The knowledge-creating company. *Harvard Business Review* (November/December), 2-9.

Nonaka, I., & Takeuchi, H. (1995). *The Knowledge-Creating Company.* New York: Oxford University Press.

O'Hara-Devereaux, M., & Johansen, B. (1994). *Global Work: Bridging Distance, Culture, and Time.* San Francisco, CA: Jossey-Bass.

Ouchi, W. G. (1980). Markets, bureaucracies, and clans. *Administrative Science Quarterly, 25*, 129–141.

Paré, G., & Dubé, L. (1999, January). *Virtual teams.* Paper presented at the Proceedings of the 20th International Conference on Information Sciences.

Pearce, C. L., & Sims, H. P. (2002). Vertical versus shared leadership as predictors of the effectiveness of change management teams: An examination of aversive, directive, transactional, transformational and empowering leader behavior. *Group Dynamics: Theory, Research, and Practice, 6*(2), 172–197.

Pfeffer, J. (1994). *Competitive Advantage Through People: Unleashing the Power of the Work Force.* Boston, MA: Harvard Business School Press.

Pisano, G. P. (1994). Knowledge, integration, and the locus of learning: An empirical analysis of process development. *Strategic Management Journal, 15*, 85–100.

Polanyi, M. (1962). Personal Knowledge. Chicago, IL: University of Chicago Press.

Prahalad, C. K. A. G. H. (1990). The core competence of the corporation. *Harvard Business Review* (May/June), 79-90.

Rogers, E. (1983). *The Diffusion of Innovation (3rd Ed.)*. New York: Free Press.

Ross-Flanigan, N. (1998). The virtues (and vices) of virtual colleagues. *Technology Review, 101*(2, March/April), 52–59.

Sanchez, R., & Mahoney, J. T. (1996). Modularity, flexibility, and knowledge management in product and organization design. *Strategic Management Journal, 17*(Winter), 63–76.

Sarker, S., & Sahay, S. (2002). *Information systems development by U. S.– Norwegian virtual teams: Implications of time and space.* Paper presented at the Proceedings of the 35th Hawaii International Conference on System Sciences, Honolulu, Hawaii, USA.

Senge, P. M. (1990). The leader's new work: Building learning organizations. *Sloan Management Review, 32*(1, Fall), 7–23.

Sherman, W. S., & Lacey, M. Y. (1999, August 9). *The role of tacit knowledge in the team building process: Explanations and interventions.* Paper presented at the Academy of Management Meeting, Chicago, Illinois, USA.

Szulanski, G. (2000). The process of knowledge transfer: A diachronic analysis of stickiness. *Organizational Behavior and Human Decision Processes, 82*(1, May), 9–27.

Townsend, A., & Demarie, S. (1998). Virtual teams: Technology and the workplace of the future. *Academy of Management Executive, 12*(3), 7–29.

Tsoukas, H. (1996). The firm as a distributed knowledge system: A constructionist approach. *Strategic Management Journal, 17*(Winter), 11–25.

Welbourne, T., Johnson, D. E., & Erez, A. (1998). The role-based performance scale: Validity analysis of a theory-based measure. *Academy of Management Journal, 41*(5), 540–555.

Williamson, O. (1981). The economics of organization; the transactions-cost approach. *American Journal of Sociology, 87*, 548–577.

Yeager, S. J. (1978). Measurement of independent variables which affect communication: A replication of Roberts and O'Reilly. *Psychological Reports*, 1320–1324.

Zaltman, G., Duncan, R., & Holbek, J. (1973). *Innovations and Organizations*. New York: John Wiley & Sons.

Endnotes

[1] The Achieving Styles Inventory (ASI) studies an individual's connective leadership profile that includes the following styles: vicarious (mentors), contributory (helps), collaborative (joins forces), entrusting (empowers), social (networks), personal (persuades), power (takes charge), competitive (out-performs), and intrinsic (excels) (Lipman-Blumen, 1996, 2000). This inventory can assist in predicting whether an employee will excel as a "shared leader" in a virtual work group.

[2] The Structure of Intellect System, (SOI) protocol, founded by Dr. Mary Meeker, is based upon theories developed by J. P. Guilford (Guilford, 1967, 1977, 1982) and applied by Meeker (1969). Guilford identified 98 separate intellectual abilities through factor analysis, and Meeker developed methods of testing for and strengthening these abilities in a wide range of age groups (Meeker, 1969; Meeker & Meeker, 2002). The primary application in industry is to define the profile or subset of abilities that correlate with success on specific jobs and to improve performance through training.

[*] The author wishes to express special thanks to Kathryn Armentrout, Helen Sims and Joel Middleton, in appreciation for their assistance on this chapter.

Chapter XIII

Trust, Rationality and the Virtual Team

Peter Murphy
Victoria University of Wellington, New Zealand

Abstract

Virtual teams need trust in order to function. Trust is an efficient way of gaining group cooperation. Online, trust is more effective than instruction or authority or status in getting people who are largely strangers to one another to work together. But trust is not a simple quality. The kind of trust that is the cement of distance relations of a global or virtual kind is different from the type of trust that binds face-to-face interactions and from the procedural kind of trust that operates in regional or national organizations of a traditional managerial kind. This study looks at the ways in which trust between virtual team members is generated. "Trust between strangers" is optimally generated when persons are allowed to self-organize complex orders and create objects and processes of high quality. Also looked at are the kinds of personalities best suited to working in a virtual collaborative environment. The study concludes that persons who prefer strong social or procedural environments will be less effective in a virtual environment. In contrast, self-steering ("stoic") personality types have characteristics that are optimally suited to virtual collaboration.

Introduction

Trust is a crucial medium for organizational action. It facilitates cooperation and coordination of organizations and their agents without them having to rely on more costly and time-consuming legal, managerial, and budgetary arrangements. Trust, however, must be built. Conventional ways of creating trust reflect the nature and rationality of conventional organizations. Such organizations are based on personal hierarchy or impersonal procedures or a mix of both. Trust is created in them through rituals of social interaction or through perceptions of procedural fairness and reliability. By this standard, organization of a virtual kind is not conventional. Work or collaboration at a distance mediated by e-mail is difficult to structure using the means of social contact or formal rules. Underlying this difficulty is the fact that the organization of distance interactions, to be effective, relies on ethical, organizational, personality, and interactive assumptions that often are at odds with other widely practiced managerial and administrative styles.

Entrenched management metaphors, like that of "teams," have limited applicability in the world of virtual organization. Virtual behavior requires us to think differently about human interaction and association and about the nature of trust. Conventional means of trust building work poorly in a virtual context. Yet, paradoxically, virtual organizations rely on trust to an even greater extent than do face-to-face organizations. In virtual organizations, the actions and intentions of coworkers are often invisible, opaque, or difficult to validate.

To escape the "trust is difficult to establish/trust is more necessary than ever" antinomy[1] in virtual organizations, we need to think of virtual teams or groups as a different genre of organization. In particular, the senior managers who set up virtual organizations need to be conscious of the specific nature of virtual bodies. If they are not, they will misjudge what these bodies can and cannot do. Members of virtual organizations and groups are less amenable and less responsive to conventional management techniques. Virtual collaborators acting at a distance are not in a position to respond to the logic of "we know this person well" or to the procedural rationality of rules, deadlines, Gantt chart milestones, or contractual targets. What they respond to is pattern-based self-organizing collaboration. This is the model of persons working together to create objects and processes, relying on a minimum of rules or social interaction to do so. "Trust between strangers" is generated by their success in creating objects and processes of high quality.

Such collaboration will not suit all personalities in a working environment. Persons who prefer strong social or procedural environments will be less effective in a virtual environment. In contrast, self-steering ("stoic") personality types have characteristics suited to such an environment. Awareness of personality constraints is crucial for middle managers who select personnel for work in virtual environments. Mismatching of personality to virtual role sets up conditions for poor staff performance.

Which Trust? Whose Trust?

Trust is an elegant and efficient way of coordinating organizational action. Imagine how cumbersome it would be if such action had to be mediated by managerial instruction or contractual terms, let alone by rules or courts, all of the time. If persons and organizations trust each other, lots of routine barriers to getting things done disappear, and actors can spend a lot less time worrying about whether their collaborators and peers will do what they promised to do. Trust also inspires confidence, and confidence inspires energy, activity, and commitment.

Human beings do not automatically trust each other. Sometimes they never trust each other. In the best of circumstances, trust takes time to establish. The ways in which actors and their organizations go about incubating trust reflect the natures of different organizations. The most common forms of organization are those based on personal hierarchy or impersonal procedure or a mix of both. Personalized forms of organization rely heavily on the rituals of social interaction to achieve goals. More impersonal forms of organization rely on rules and rule-like qualities (such as targets) to get things done. Conventional organizations often mix social and procedural motivations. Trust is created in conventional organizations through face-to-face social interaction or through the operation of a culture of rules. Through the medium of social interactions, actors form and test bonds of trust. They establish that they can or cannot rely on each other. In more formal settings, actors appraise the capacity of each other to execute and apply rules—or rule-like qualities such as contractual deadlines—in ways that are not arbitrary or chaotic. If we sense through social interaction that a coworker will be disloyal, unreliable, or evasive, we will not trust that person. If we observe rule application or implementation that is arbitrary, contradictory, or impulsive, the same applies. We withdraw trust from the person responsible.

An organization that is virtual, however, is not conventional. It is based on collaboration at a distance mediated (primarily) by e-mail.[2] Participants in virtual organizations are geographically spread apart, often across the world; they meet rarely if at all; even communication by voice or image tends to be rare, or at the very least disembodied. Virtual organizations typically lack a common professional or procedural basis for working together. Participants are drawn from different offices, organizations, and disciplines. They are the spiritual opposites of the "organization men" who filled the technostructures of mid-20th-Century Fordist managerial capitalism (Chandler, 1977; Galbraith, 1978 [1969]; Whyte, 1956). These factors mean that normal workplace or office social interaction is not available to virtual coworkers. They do not have the means of body language, watching, playing, collegiality, or socializing usually available to collocated work partners. Distance collaborations invariably bring together coworkers with different cultures of rule interpretation and implementation (some loose, some strict). Because collaborations are usually temporary, an atmosphere of authoritative rule interpretation and implementation is difficult to establish.[3] Virtual actors at a distance—no matter how frequent their e-mail correspondence—find it difficult to build trust on the basis of "I know this person well" or "I know the expectations of the organization well" or "I understand the disciplinary basis for this person's way of working." In the case of working together virtually, actors are relative strangers, and the organization of their interaction is time limited.

The Organization as a City

The economist Friedrich Hayek observed that the origins of capitalism lay in the capacity of human beings to generate long-distance order between unknown persons (Hayek, 1989). Hayek believed that they did this via the medium of markets and contracts. He was both right and wrong. Long-distance traders created the most spectacular forms of economic organization dating back to the ancient world. Whether it was at Athens, Rome, Florence, Venice, Amsterdam, London, Chicago, or New York, these traders pioneered the most advanced forms of capital in their time. They did this by being proficient at understanding the nature of self-organizing systems (Jacobs, 2000; Johnson, 2002). These are forms of order that emerge between agents, not on the basis of rules but patterns. Such agents may be anonymous. Traders in a stock market, for instance, are largely unknown to each other. Agents may also be virtual persons who have limited knowledge of each other or each other's circumstances. The type of order that coalesces between such agents is of a particular type. It is an emergent order. Under conditions of emergent order, agents do not have to know each other or know much about each other, and they do not have to share (very many) rules, in order for a complex pattern of interaction to emerge between them.

Hayek imagined that contracts were the basis of the emergent order of long-distance markets. But contracts, like rules, only have a limited validity in such contexts. Contracts, like regulatory policies, are at best a secondary driver of the complex interactions that develop between unknown persons or between virtual persons at a distance. This is why virtual collaborations can easily come unstuck. Attempts to run virtual collaborations on the basis of contracts and rules are liable to be self-defeating. Yet, to do otherwise means adapting to a very different kind of organizational logic. Many actors, not least of all managers, are resistant to this.

If organization is partly a matter of rationality and partly a matter of personality, then effective virtual collaboration supposes forms of rationality and personality markedly different from those inscribed in organizations based on strong social or procedural foundations. In a virtual organization, it is assumed that peers and managers can act without dense webs of social connections, rules, or contract specifications. When new communicative technologies were spun off from research organizations in the 1990s and became part of the mainstream of doing business and governance, this tacit assumption was often violated. As computer-mediated communication technology spread, so did the idea of virtual teams or collaborations—and so did misunderstandings about their natures. The instinct of managers and participants was to assume that computer-mediated communication is just "another channel" without any structural "bias."[4] But, in point of fact, it has a powerful "bias," reflective of its origins. It is stamped with the character of the world of the intellectual capital organization where it originated. In this world, interaction and production, relations and outcomes are routinely achieved by means of pattern recognition and emergent order.

The logic of virtual organization undermines many of the most powerful tacit images of organizations.[5] The screen organization—where persons interact through their computer screens—is not a social body, it is not a legal-rational entity where everyone agrees on "the rules," "team" metaphors are near useless to explain it, and project managers rarely find any way of getting virtual partners to follow detailed contractual datelines or specifications (see Chapter 2 by Fernandez, in this book). Virtual organizations, where they are effective, operate much more like the classic example of emergent order—the city (Jacobs, 2000; Johnson, 2002). Cities, especially great cities, embody an astonishing array of complex interactions in which rules (planning) or contracts (written agreements) play a surprisingly small role. Cities have a public life—a commons—that is a kind of anonymous collective order. Nobody prescribes that order. It is order between strangers, rather than familiars. Yet it orchestrates a dense combination of shopping, manufacturing, socializing, governing, communicating, and transporting. This order is implicit. Most people, most of the time, participating in it, figure it out without knowing much about each other and without having to read large prescriptive documents. It is order based on the city dweller's sense of pattern and rhythm.

Pattern Thinking

Consider the question: How are cities possible? "Super managers" do not create them. It is generally agreed that planned cities are disappointing in reality. On the other hand, cities are not supervillages or superclubs, and they are not supercontractual associations. Rather, city denizens—in a vast multitude of roles ranging from gardeners, shoppers, and builders to manufacturers, film-goers, and teachers—cooperate without knowing much about each other. They can do so because the city is one of those things that we call a commons—or more accurately, it is a composite of many different kinds of commons. Commons function as bridges between human beings. Commons are objects, spaces, or processes that strangers have a mutual stake in and that bind these strangers in tacit cooperation and trust.

What kind of objects, spaces, and processes attract strangers and bring them into cooperation? This question is best answered by thinking of the example of great trading cities like Piraeus in the ancient world, Constantinople, Venice, Amsterdam, Chicago, and New York. These are places, at their height, filled with unknown persons dealing in long-distance relations. These same cities are also successful at creating order by design. High levels of artistic, technological, or scientific forms characterize them. It is form or pattern that strangers most easily share. Cities that create a climate conducive to pattern thinking are cities in which tacit, almost invisible, bonds of trust and cooperation emerge between unknown persons. This can happen on all levels. Whether it is stacking boxes in a row, digging a garden bed, negotiating rush-hour traffic, tooling a piece of machinery, or writing copy for an advertisement, all human beings act on, adapt, modify, copy, and create patterns. At its highest, pattern thinking is architectonic or morphogenetic. It is responsible for the creation or discovery of new or innovative patterns.

A city is a vast mosaic of intersecting and overlapping forms and patterns. Nobody prescribes or negotiates this overlap and intersection. It just happens. It is part and parcel of pattern thinking. It is achieved almost without comment, because human beings have an intuitive, perhaps even hard-wired, sense of beauty, elegance, economy, efficiency, proportionality, symmetry, rhythm, periodicity, and other pattern-generating "norms." Strangers feel comfortable cooperating with one another if the common things between them have these kinds of characteristics. This is why a poorly designed "built environment" will generate crime, fear, and mistrust, while an environment that is beautiful, even if it is only a beaten-up, weathered beauty, will generate confidence and trust and cooperative behavior. Exactly the same applies to organizations. Agreements or rules of the game, contracts, and teams are much less powerful devices for coordinating the actions of unknown persons or little-known persons working on multidisciplinary projects over vast distances than are forms of emergent order. In a business environment, as soon as a working group of marketers, systems engineers, product developers, business analysts, client managers, sales people, and lawyers—spread across multiple time zones—is created, you have a division of labor that is unlike a social village or an interdepartmental committee and is much more like the stranger city of the mercantile cosmopolis. Its peculiar mosaic does not work on the basis of the social familiarity of "the team" or "the family," or the rules and agreements of "the contract" or "the institution."

"Team" metaphors are especially misleading. The conditions and logic of virtual collaborators require the participants in the virtual group (peers and managers) to have a civic motive. Civic motives allow strangers or persons with little knowledge of each other to cooperate. Civic motives appear when persons use or produce objects (spaces, things, processes) in between themselves, despite having few rules and little to do with one another. Patrons at a theatre rarely meet the actors who perform, yet the anonymous space shared between audience and actor constitutes the theatrical experience. The same applies to tradespersons and clients, shop assistants and customers, and captains of vessels and their passengers. Long ago in cities, people learned to short circuit interactions and rely on their pattern sense of beauty, rhythm, proportion, efficiency, and the like. If the shop assistant works efficiently, customers will cooperate and stand in a queue. If not, they will storm off. If the dancers' performance is beautiful, or the captain's handling of the vessel is smooth, the audience and the passengers will return again.

This is also what makes complex virtual interactions possible. It is what sustains electronic commerce, for instance. Electronic commerce is a form of silent trade. What primarily binds vendor and purchaser are not social ties or rules or agreements. These may be present, but they are not dominant. This is why multimedia design is a major component in most forms of electronic commerce. Multimedia design functions like the architectural design of great department stores. In these sorts of cases, design becomes the media of commercial transaction, as important as—indeed often more important than—contacts, rules, or contracts. What binds the vendor and the purchaser is the beauty, rhythm, and efficiency of the space between them.

Trust at a Distance

Where civic motives exist, relative strangers are much more likely to form bonds of trust and cooperation. They will form these bonds through participation in the cocreation of objects, spaces, or processes that have the salient characteristics that draw strangers together. When they start to create, share, or transact things that have the morphogenetic power of simplicity, lucidity, symmetry, rhythm, elegance, and efficiency, they will have moved a long way toward overcoming the relative absence of corporeal presence and the relative ineffectualness of discursive rules and agreements that other, "closer to home," kinds of organization rely upon.

At the core of knowledge economies are neither market nor command relations but various kinds of commons based on civic motives. These unite unknown persons in extended orders. The members of a virtual commons are bound together by the objects that they create, transact, or share. The object, or rather its qualities, is a kind of *third party* between the parties. The designers of a superior piece of software will probably work for a firm with a command structure. They will also possess marketable skills that they contracted to that firm for a price (and could contract to another firm). But the bonds among them, stimulated by the object that they are designing, govern their work as a group. The effectiveness of their collaboration is conditioned by what they design. Such object-orientated feelings are no different in principle from those felt by users, consumers, manufacturers, or vendors of a designed object. The object-orientated bonds that design cultures produce are different from personalized loyalty bonds or bureaucratic procedural bonds of hierarchical organizations.

Societies, cities, and regions with a strong ethos of design dominate knowledge economies. The emergence of design cultures mediating relations between strangers cannot be explained by the determinism of communications or communications technology. Rather, designed objects are their own media of communications and interaction. Object-orientated communications—communicative interaction about objects with strong design qualities—employ the communicative media and technologies of their day. But that which made Florence or Venice the great economic powers of the 15th and 16th Centuries, or that made San Francisco's Silicon Valley the driver of late 20th Century American economic power, was the capacity to design fabrics (in one case) and operating systems and software applications (in the other case). To the extent that Silicon Valley replicated the peer-based production of the Renaissance artisan, and to the extent that its global reach was defined by horizontal-type "projects" and "alliances" rather than the command structures of firms, and by design-driven markets relying on high interactivity between supplier, manufacturer, retailer, and customer, rather than by low-interactivity staples markets, these characteristics were *not* produced by networked communications. Networked communication is just as likely to advance the interests of loyalty and functional hierarchies as anything.

We see this, for example, in the way that "electric age" communications, from the telegraph to the networked computer, allowed organizations to begin to act as if distance did not exist. One of the consequences of this was, in many cases, to facilitate a move from high-trust organizations to low-trust organizations. In a high-trust organization, the basic assumption is that those in an official position can be relied upon to carry out their roles or functions effectively by self-steering. Technologies of virtual contact often encourage the replacement of self-steering with regulation and policy direction. Head offices come to believe that they can enforce rules and strategies by telephone and fax rather than leave it to "the person on the spot."

In such cases, it is believed that technology will serve to conquer distance. The conquest of distance acts as a force and a mythology that reduces trust. This scenario conforms to the commonplace view that trust is a product of face-to-face relations (O'Hara-Devereaux & Johansen, 1994; Nohria & Eccles, 1992), and that "trust needs touch" (Handy, 1995, p. 46). Trust, it is supposed, requires the kind of social discussion and social intimacy that is only possible on the part of those who work and interact in the same physical location. Self-disclosure and personal relationships create trust. A kind of intimacy, symbolized by interpersonal warmth and social support, is crucial to build trust. A variation of this argument is the proposition made, for instance, about the Japanese corporation model (Fukuyama, 1995), that an organization can be considered a high-trust organization where interaction is not depersonalized and where face-to-face relations remain central to its functioning.

If we were to accept these assumptions, we would conclude that trust is a variant of loyalty. It arises where agents are loyal to their superiors, peers, and subordinates. Trust is a media of interaction in place of rules. It arises in environments where people define themselves as being interested in serving others. Trust requires signals of understanding and readiness to help others. Trust on this account is a highly "social" medium of interaction. The existence of trust is confirmed and underwritten by social friendliness, warmth, and intimacy.

Distance would seem antithetical to trust. Prima facie, distance would appear to make social warmth between organizational peers, subordinates, and superiors difficult to achieve. There is, however, a counterargument to this. This begins with the proposition that computer-mediated communication between relative strangers—Internet relay chat and e-mail, in particular—can be friendly in the hands of many communicants. The argument is that this is a powerful medium for creating intimacy between strangers. This is so especially under conditions in which communicative partners have time to exchange and accumulate information about themselves, and where they can anticipate further encounters (Walther, 1996). Persons will disclose things to an e-mail confidant that they would never disclose to, say, a close colleague that they work with in the same physical location. But, one should not assume that this is a replication of face-to-face trust. In fact, it is opposite. Self-disclosure is a sign of trust in face-to-face relations, because those relations are governed by shame culture (even if only residually today). Even in the most individualized societies, where conscience rather than shame is the dominant moral emotion, persons in face-to-face settings typically remain reticent about disclosure. The moral sense of shame (or its demoralized version, embarrassment) creates circumspection in people in social settings. Thus, those who disclose to others something personal are indicating that they trust the other person not to abuse the confidence or retail that confidence to others. This is a way of saying "I know you'll be loyal to me." These kinds of exchanges help create organizational patterns based on loyalty.

If a person discloses a confidence in the anonymous medium of computer-mediated communication, the shame affect does not apply. Face-to-face disclosure always risks the disapproving facial expression or stare of the other person. In virtual communication, that risk disappears. So, persons are often more willing to talk about themselves to partners online. But this is not a mark of trust, or at least not in the same degree were those parties to be in the same physical room. Doubtless, to retail a personal communication to third parties is an act of disloyalty, but we should not assume that such an act would be felt, in terms of moral affect, to be as mortifying as if someone had retailed a confidence told to them face-to-face.

A Different Kind of Trust

So what are we saying? That trust is a function of face-to-face relations?—not at all. Rather, what we are saying is that trust can underpin long-distance relations, but this trust is not the same kind as the social trust that is the cement of face-to-face loyalty relations. There is a fundamental difference between social trust and distance trust. These two types of trust are readily confused. The confusion arises from the assumption that interaction at a distance and interaction at close proximity have the same or similar operating premises. This confusion is frequently made, despite the fact that geographical distance is such a palpable and *sui generis* force. One of the great late-20th-Century myths was the idea of the abolition of distance. Anyone who has suffered a long-haul air-flight should be disabused of this myth. Yet, it persists. Computer-mediated communications reinforced the myth of the abolition of distance. The spread of the power of close-to-instantaneous transmission of e-mail messages around the world brought with it an avalanche of false prognostications that the tyranny of distance could be eliminated.

One of the consequences of organizations acting "as if distance did not exist" was to encourage the illusion that, even though agents and officers of an organization are geographically distributed, they could be treated "as if" they are present in one physical location. This illusion afflicts contemporary organizations that encourage employees to work together by e-mail. This is not a new illusion. We see the same kind of technology-driven chimera afflicting shore commands when they began to use wireless telegraphy and radio to instruct navy vessel captains.[6] Distance, on some level, is never conquerable. A radio message is not a face-to-face communication. If we think it is, a paradox is invariably created. If trust fails in distance relations, we ask ourselves how to fix it. If we rely on conventional explanations of trust, we will say that what is needed is "better social relations" or "better rule-governed predictability." Yet, the paradox is that such expectations may be the *cause* of failing trust. Ship captains resisted the radio revolution because it ate into their autonomy and authority. Looked at from the standpoint of the shore, mistrust was the suspicion created when seaward parties did not respond to instruction in "social" ways, or did so only with grim truculence. From the standpoint of the vessel, captains looked for a procedure (a "process") that would bury the unwanted commands. Expectations of trust bred mistrust.

Distrust in organizations often rests on confusion about the nature of trust. The confusion rests on the assumption that trust is a generic medium. Yet, in reality, in distance relationships that do not work, the problem is not absence of generic trust. Rather, the problem is that the power of geography cannot be erased, and face-to-face relations cannot be simulated at a distance.[7] Also, rules cannot create an effective order on a large scale, especially on a scale that crosses state and national borders (the borders that most commonly defined classic office-based organizations). All of this means that the kinds of trust or confidence bonds to be found in face-to-face associations and rule-based organizations cannot be replicated at a distance. To attempt to do so is a self-fulfilling prophecy of failure.

In such problematic cases—and they are common—rather than look for the kind of trust that is proper to distance relations, actors in distributed organizations or systems are encouraged to look for signs of trust of a social or procedural type. They are tempted to look for something that simply cannot be replicated at a distance. Naturally, they end up disappointed. At the same time, they are subtly discouraged from looking for the kind of trust that is pertinent to long-distance or large-scale order.

What kind of trust is this? First, it is the kind of trust that allows the agents in long-distance organizations to be relatively self-steering. Yes, big organizations have hierarchies and rules. Hierarchies and rules are standard ways of creating order. Yet, hierarchies are most effective if the extent of the organization is local or relations between agents can be personalized, as when intraorganizational or interorganizational relations are conducted face-to-face. Rules, on the other hand, work reasonably well on a medium scale. For example, as organizations (firms and government departments) evolved in the 19th Century away from familial and patrimonial models, and as they scaled to national dimensions, one of the devices employed in this evolution was to take a load off hierarchy and place more load on procedure as a way of running organizations.[8] This was relatively successful with national organizations, although there remained debates (which continue to the present day) as to whether personalized hierarchies or impersonal rules were the most effective for meeting contingent situations requiring adaptive flexibility. Where national organizations were relatively stable over the long term and could insulate themselves from the forces of larger-scale order/disorder, "proceduralism" worked quite well. That is to say that rule-based order works best on a medium scale, where personal relations lose effectiveness, yet where the abstractions of large-scale, global order or disorder do not make themselves felt strongly.

Personality Type and Self-Steering Capacity

The wider the extent of an organization, the more distributed its nature. The greater the intersection between it and long-distance orders (such as global markets or global regulatory bodies, or continental customs unions), the less effective are hierarchies or rules. If an organization works across countries, or continents, or regions, or even between cities, especially where those cities are world cities, the greater will be the importance of emergent order and patterns, autonomous judgment, and self-steering capacity. Consequent upon this, a distance system (which is virtual in the strongest sense of the word) needs agents who have initiative. These are "intelligent agents" who, once given a task or objective, do not need to be told what to do and do not constantly refer "up the chain" or to the "policy manual" to be directed through each step of their operations. At a distance, *less communication is more*.

Hierarchies and rules continue to play a role in any large organization in setting terms and conditions for action. But notably, for "action at a distance," such rules and roles need to be substantially supplemented with interpersonal initiative from above, sideways, or below. This is the intangible asset of "leadership." Without leadership initiative, groups cannot act effectively, because the alternative steering mechanisms (hierarchies and rules) are ineffective at gluing together collaborative action at distance, or even more simply, at directing action at a distance. Rules are difficult to enforce in virtual circumstances, and the response to authority can simply be "who are you?"

Autonomous judgment and leadership initiative in virtual contexts must be approached with care, however. Both can be carried out in arbitrary and irrational ways. This destroys trust. Judgment and attempts at leadership can be egotistical, inconsistent, self-dramatizing, imperious, confused, or confusing. The genres of corporate writing introduced in America in the late 19th Century had many vices but one particular virtue: self-restraint.[9] They were "telegraphic." This is a virtue important for all distance transactions. Eloquence at close-hand is bombast at a distance.[10] Distance magnifies, and the group functions like an echo chamber. Leading or directing behavior quickly becomes exaggerated, and group members exposed to such behavior quickly begin to feel like subjects in a tyranny. The "tyrannical" leader and the "enthusiastic" egotist in a group erode trust between group members. So does the "mercurial" personality who can never be pinned down to anything, and the "adventurer" who wants to "move on" constantly in search of risk and thrill. In retrograde cases, self-steering may be nothing more than melodramatic self-assertion or an attempt to claim the center of attention in order to be "noticed." Trust relies on consistency in action. The enthusiast and the tyrant are inconsistent and unpredictable. They generate uncertainty of a destructive kind. In contrast, agents who do not panic—who are calm, cool, sanguine—create trust. This is not the type of trust created by the loyal person in organizations with a strong service-loyalty ethic or the conscientious person in procedure-governed organizations. But it is a powerful form of trust all the same.

Personality Types

From these considerations, we can begin to draw conclusions about the kinds of personalities that work well under virtual conditions. What is assumed here is that the efficacy of distance communications and collaborations depends on personality types. Not all personality types are equally suited or adaptable to working virtually, or to interacting with unknown persons in extended orders. As summarized in Table 1, virtual trust has a strong affinity with a distinctive personality type, and this type arises under specific organizational and interactive conditions.

The Social Personality Type

"Social" personality types will find virtual conditions difficult. These are personalities for whom "relationships" are the primary focus of interest. These personalities flourish in organizational settings, where face-to-face interaction is the basic driver of organizational behavior. The ideal-type "social" personality prefers company, is cooperative, is respectful of authority, is deferential to

Table 1. Trust and Personality Types

Kinds of Trust	Organizational Form	Principal Personality Traits	Mode of Interaction
Social Trust	Service hierarchy Familial enterprise Household-style Bond	Respectful of authority Loyal Self-sacrificing Paternalistic	Personal Face-to-face
Procedural Trust	Managerial capitalism Legal-rational Office-based teams	Rule-following Conscientious Methodical Process-driven	Impersonal
Distance "Stoic" Trust	Virtual Long-distance Self-organizing Commons-based	Autonomy Self-steering Object-oriented Pattern-thinking	Interaction between strangers

others, and promotes social harmony. Correspondingly, the social personality thinks of others and is self-sacrificing and loyal. The leadership style of the social personality type is consensual and paternalistic. These ideal typical characteristics are conducive to building trust. However, in distance relations, the possibilities of signaling understanding, loyalty, deference, or respect are limited to explicit messages. The all-important dimension of physical and unspoken communication—a tap on the shoulder, going to dinner together, and so on—is absent and cannot be replicated. The consensus formation that is necessary to the functioning of organizations with a pronounced service-loyalty ethos requires high levels of socioemotional communication (Walther, 1996). Under virtual conditions, the possibility of socioemotional communication is reduced significantly.

The Procedural Personality Type

The "procedural" personality will be equally out of water in a virtual setting. This person views order not as a product of relationships but of method. Procedural personalities are prudent in their interactions and careful in their dealings. They rely on a certain distance between their self and others. They are "good fits" for the impersonal middle scale of the national- or regional-size rule-based organization. They induce trust in others, because they communicate a strong sense of fidelity that is associated with impersonality. This fidelity may pertain to the overall good of the organization or to specific rules of the organization. The ideal type of procedural personality is dedicated. One particular form of dedication is conscientiousness. This means doing things "right" or "the right way." It means acting methodically, with attention to detail, in a careful, cautious, and prudential manner. The procedural personality is good at creating regularity. Such persons tend to feel comfortable with habit and routine and prefer steady state organizations. Routine sets an organizational tone of impersonality. The preference for impersonality means that such personalities will tend to be socially reserved and polite and will exhibit self-restraint in interactions. Because of their attention to detail, the procedural personality is good at identifying irregularity and is observant of departures from the norm. In some organizational settings, this evolves into a management style that sets high store on surveillance and oversight and the search for trustworthy employees (Kipnis, 1996).

Because of their attention to detail (not least of all, the detail of rules), procedural personalities can be poor at conceiving the big picture. This makes them unsuited to virtual acting. The virtual conditions of extended orders are conducive to sketchiness. They are accompanied by the invisibility of many specific operational details. At the point where hierarchies and rules can no longer effectively domesticate distance, those who act at a distance find themselves with little detailed information about the circumstances of the agents and agencies they are working with or the multiple environments that they are working across. To fill in the gaps with explicit information of the kind that one finds in an organizational file would be too costly and too cumbersome. Tacit information, of the kind acquired through presence and face-to-face interaction, is also out of reach. Virtual partners therefore need to be able to ignore a lot of specifics. Because of this, procedural personalities, who are dominant in medium-scale rule-based organizations, are much less effective at working in large-scale contexts that cross boundaries, borders, offices, cultures, and rule sets. Process cannot be the primary or driving consideration in distance collaboration. Organizations (offices, field commands, logistic warehouses, laboratories, and so on) in different locations will have different rules, expectations, and rule interpretations. They will weight the importance of rules differently.

Even more crucial, under the virtual conditions of extended orders, interaction time is limited. In process-driven organizations, committee time is key. Committee time can be simulated in distance collaborations but only in a limited way. Virtual actors consult. They do this individually and collectively. Consultation is most effective between individuals. Networked communications can facilitate this. Individuals can consult synchronously (chat and telephone) and asynchronously (e-mail, threaded discussion). Groups can consult asynchronously (e-mail). Synchronous group communication (video- or audioconferencing) becomes the substitute for the committee meeting. The virtual conference is most effective for executive meetings where the emphasis is on specific, executable decision making. Where there is drawn-out committee-style discussion of processes, schedules, rules, legal implications, fine detail, and the like, the absence of shared tacit knowledge of rules or roles becomes an impediment to progress. Process is a poor driver of action across disparate organizations spread over large distances. The virtual conference, because it can be voice-based, replicates some of the important aspects of face-to-face meetings, thereby simulating some of the otherwise missing social dimension of interactive time, while eliminating some of the distracting social cues and responses that fritter away meeting time. But if the aim of virtual meeting is to drive a project through rules, it is pointless.

The Stoic Personality Type

What this underlines is that neither social nor procedural models are appropriate for collaboration or action at a distance in extended orders populated by either virtual or unknown persons, and conditioned by virtual or unknown circumstances. This begs the question then: what personality type is most suited to these conditions? The answer is a type with a high capacity for self-steering.[11] Let us call this personality type the "stoic" type (Murphy, 1999). The stoic type is self-directed and independent. The stoic does not need constant company and is comfortable being alone or working independently. In the face of uncertainty, the stoic is calm, dispassionate, and unflappable. The stoic type prizes intelligence rather than social feedback or procedural neatness. This is not an absolute but a matter of degree. There are different kinds of intelligence. One kind is ingenuity, the problem-solving kind of intelligence. Another kind of intelligence is more abstract and speculative. Both are creative in nature.

We have seen how social feedback and rule fidelity build trust. What about the case of intelligence? Why do we trust an intelligent agent? We trust them first because of their capacity for self-steering. We trust their ability to get the job done with a minimum need for either positive reinforcement or procedural supervision. Such intelligence is highly correlated with creativity. One of the principle traits of creative personalities is their persistence. In solving a problem, they will work long hours and very hard, and will not surrender easily to the problem. This is not obstinate behavior. They will simply reapproach the problem from different angles until they reach a solution. At the higher levels of creative action this is crucial, for these personalities will persist against the odds, when everyone else thinks that "the idea is stupid" and there is little chance of it finding an audience or an application (Staw, 1995). Without persistence, the risk-averse "social average" of inherited solutions and ideas would dominate economic and social institutions. Persistence is a stoic quality. It is a word for a stoic kind of rationality. Persistence combines the idea of enduring the pain of an unsolved problem together with a faith in intelligence in the face of social pressure to desist. Stoics combine a strong sense of autonomy that permits them to resist social pressure, together with the rational drive to repeat and to readdress operations or ideas until they work.

Self-steering is not selfish behavior. Autonomy is not the antithesis of cooperation. What is key is the manner in which autonomy produces cooperation. It does not rely on social or procedural motives. Self-steerers cooperate through their sense of pattern. They interact through the abstractions of rhythm, beauty, efficiency, economy, and the like. They adapt to each other without heavy reliance on roles or rules. The advantages of this for interactions over long distances are numerous.

In large-scale systems, where the reach and, consequently, the power of hierarchies and rules are inherently weaker, self-steered action is at a premium.[12] Steerage is not an accidental metaphor. Maritime companies are the longest established long-distance organizations.[13] They always relied on the self-determination of their captains and pilots at sea. Even in the era of satellite communications and instantaneous global positioning information, it still remains impossible to navigate a vessel from the head office. For land-bound organizations, however, the perceived risk of self-steering is that such action will be unilateral. But, in fact, steerage is a constant adjustment to an environment. Navigators take cues from the environment and use documents (charts), but they do so in combination with their judgment, in order to reach their destination. Judgment compensates for the scarcity of information or the unexpected event (the contingencies of the sea) that the navigator must deal with. In turn, judgment rests on something more fundamental—the navigator's internal sense of emergent order. Even under chaotic conditions, seas manifest patterns. The elements of this order include sea currents, winds, short-term weather, long-term climate, political conditions (like war and piracy), and the law of the sea. The ability to discern the "the design of nature" among all of these elements makes a navigator skilled. Pattern recognition under conditions of volatility and contingency is essential to effective self-steering.

Skilled navigators earn a reputation for reliability. We trust their ability to get the job done under conditions of uncertainty. The same applies to action under the virtual conditions of extended order. All organized action contains elements of uncertainty—both endogenous and exogenous contingencies. Where organized action occurs at a distance, with limited means for communicative feedback, and across borders, regions, nations, and cultures, successful interaction or collaboration requires a high level of capacity to create structure and order (a "stable system"), where conventional means to do so (roles and rules) are scarce.

Successful members of virtual groups are good at creating order, not by social or procedural means but by abstract or architectonic means (Murphy, 2001b).[14] Intelligence is another word for this capacity. It is the ability to make seemingly unrelated things fit. It is this capacity that makes intelligent agents not only good at fulfilling tasks but also at working collaboratively. They quickly find a good rhythm, a symmetrical division of labor, an elegant fit, and a time economy for acting together. Of course, if the real objective of the virtual collaboration is social or procedural, such agents will probably not work well together, because roles and rules will get in the way. But if the organization is sympathetic to forms of patterned interaction, then the probability is that the intelligent agents will act well in tandem. Intellectual capital organizations are particularly good at achieving this. Good science, technology, or art is never produced by roles or rules. The great intellectual capital organizations know this. They encourage creation and interaction through patterns. They allow the act of creating elegant and beautiful objects or lucent and efficient systems to be the primary motivator of cooperation.

Rationality

The predominant form of communicative interaction between intelligent agents is neither interpersonal nor impersonal but what might be described as hyperpersonal (Walther, 1996). Long-distance and asynchronous communication reduces the number of social cues and procedural directions that an agent can receive. This can be constructive.[15] Standing outside of the flow of organizational instructions and policy—and being relatively immunized against the panoply of nonverbal hierarchical status cues and signaling of social presence that chews up working time—can be liberating for the life of the mind. Walther talks of the possibility for communicants to construct ideal imagery. By this, he means images of others based on skimpy, often paralinguistic clues (i.e., how bad their spelling is). But, opportunities to create ideal imagery, caused by a partial release from social and procedural demands and time constraints, are more fundamental than this suggests. It is from such imagery that intelligent systems and beautiful objects are created. Such imagery is the product of puzzling about how a package of isolated fragments fits together. Speculating about something as crude as paralinguistic evidence—"what does this persons' tortured e-mail syntax tell me about their character?"—is a parlor game version of more fundamental mental processes of association, inference, deduction, and pattern creation.

Figuring out a person from minimal clues is a puzzle. Analogously, intelligent agents look at the world as if it is a jigsaw puzzle. If the puzzle is simply a pile of pieces on a table, they ask themselves how the pieces fit together. This kind of attitude to the world gives them a high level of toleration for uncertainty. For the intelligent agent, uncertainty is not chaos but an opportunity to create order. The response of the intelligent agent to contingency—a condition that large-scale orders by their nature are especially prone to—is not panic or anxiety, which only exacerbates uncertainty. Rather, the response is one of curiosity. The intelligent agent sets about figuring out what kind of systemic forces or patterns are present alongside the contingencies and how order can be created by taking into account those contingencies. This attitude means that intelligent agents are also able to cope well with multiple contingencies that arise when organized groups cross the strong boundaries of office, city, region, nation, and culture. Those boundaries exist to define systems and create certainties. Whatever their origins, these are preestablished systems that over time have come to manage internal and environmental uncertainties by defining strong social solidarities or procedural conventions. If uncertain or threatened, organizations assert their family-like or law-like identities. Boundary crossers have no such luxury. They have to create their own systemic order. Indeed, their forte is system design or order creation.

Boundary crossers, however, cannot expect to create their own substitute strong boundaries. For one thing, the interactions of these boundary crossers by and large are temporary (Meyerson, Weick, & Kramer, 1996), and in cases where they become permanent, they succeed precisely because they do not rely on the strong markers of hierarchies and rules. While debarred from conventional techniques of dealing with uncertainty, boundary crossers, like any group or organizational unit, are subject to internal and external uncertainties. This is especially so in large-scale orders. It is most especially so for temporarily created groups that work across local, regional, and national scaled boundaries. As we move from local to medium to large scale, the number of unpredictable or uncontrollable forces increases. Like the individual stoic actor, the intelligent group searches for rationality in the forces that impinge on it. The underlying expectation of the stoic is optimistic—the assumption is that there is rational behavior on the part of organizations, markets, administrations, and jurisdictions on a global scale. These expectations are not always met, or at least not prima facie. But effective virtual groups are those that are good at identifying or fashioning architectonic solutions. That is, they are good at defining or finding the elements of order that exist in chaotic, highly contingent, or unexplored situations. They do not add to the uncertainty by panic behavior. They do not seek to reduce uncertainty simply by constructing reassuring social narratives or by legislating rules. Like the best virtual collaborators, the best virtual groups are stoic. Where contexts are chaotic, they search for rationality.

This rationality can be called the rationality of patterns. Rationality supposes that certain actions or events repeat. What has happened in the past is a guide to what will happen in the future. However, not all consistency in action and events is good. Imagine a tap that leaks. It goes drip-drip for a sustained period. This kind of consistency or repeatability is nightmarish. In contrast, rationality is a product of the kind of repeatability that one finds in patterns. Patterns are composed of repetition and differences. Motifs in a pattern are repeated. On a printed page, for example, black text and white space create pattern repetition. Paragraph indents, page breaks, and borders introduce difference, a repeating difference that provides variance from the more monotonous repetitions. These combined patterns create a rhythmic order for eye and mind. Rationality "looks" something like an artfully designed printed page. It provides structure that we interact with perhaps thousands of time per month, but we never tire of it. It is elegant and attractive, economic and efficient.

Rationality is a powerful medium for the coordination of action. Organizations habitually try to simulate rationality through roles and rules. They tap the power of virtues like loyalty and of norms like regularity. In the case of virtual groups, however, roles and rules have limited efficacy. In such circumstances, rationality has to be embodied directly in functions like pattern recognition and pattern creation. Such functions are analogous to the art of design. They involve the capacity to recognize and create systemic, aesthetic, technological, commercial, and other kinds of order. Creativity is not an ethical virtue like loyalty and it is not a social norm like regularity. It is the capacity to put the pieces together, to think in *kosmopoietical* or order-making terms (Murphy, 2001a).

The rationality of the virtual group embodies a kind of *cognitive virtue*. It rests on cognitive abilities to discern and create patterns. Trust and cooperation are engendered between virtual actors, because human beings feel comfortable with, and are attracted to, patterned structures. Trust and cooperation are not the faithfulness of the loyal person or the predictability of the regular guy of the Fordist managerial era. Rather, virtual trust arises from the rhythm of those who work together, act together, transact, and manufacture together through the medium of artful design. Objects, spaces, things, and processes that are well designed inspire trust between their makers, users, and consumers. This is true of any beautifully designed system or object. We have an intuitive sense, when we look at it or hold it, that it will work well, and we can rely on it. Its symmetries and its proportions, its scale and its rhythms, express a spirit that inspires in us the sense of faith that a gothic church does, the sense of sublime regularity that a great clockwork mechanism does, and the sense of harmonic resolution of a wonderful piece of music.

Conclusion

Distance relations are difficult to organize. Historically, a relative handful of societies—in the main great city portals from London and Amsterdam to New York and Los Angeles—have been truly successful at managing them. With the explosion of computer-mediated communications in the 1990s, there followed the expectation that electronic portals would spring up everywhere, and the dominance of a handful of world cities in distance commerce would fade. But this did not happen. Indeed, if anything, the power of portal cities was enhanced. The map of Internet traffic looks much like the maps of maritime and land transport. The key sites of 20th Century computer industries were the U.S. West Coast sea portals, Seattle and San Francisco. These were places with a long history of dealing with distance.

One of the reasons for the failure to create alternative portals is the anxiety that attaches itself to distance. Only some cities and some organizations—and these are strongly correlated—are good at forging relations between unknown persons. Once we get beyond the consideration of its abstract potential, the technology of virtual collaboration is not a short-cut to creating deep relations between unknown persons. Technology is governed by its context. Anxieties that attach to acting at a distance encourage organizations to replicate that which is less anxiety provoking. They fall back on familiar social and procedural routines. However, in an age in which wealth is increasingly intellectual in form (Stewart, 1997), and in which the generation of wealth rests increasingly on the contribution of science, technology, aesthetics, symbolic communications, and systems development, those who are able to act at a distance are fundamentally advantaged. For intellectual capital is, and always has been, intimately bound up with distance collaboration. To manage distance relations well is increasingly a condition of the creation of wealth. Human anxieties in the face of the abyss of distance remain fundamental barriers to many, perhaps most, organizations being successful participants in the organization of distance. Success in this domain is measured not by the accumulation of social capital or by meeting deadlines, but by the objects and processes cocreated by relative strangers working together at a distance and united by the powerful symmetries and elegant economies of the virtual common place of their distributed organization.

Old habits die hard. Organizations that concede, in principle, the importance of internationalization and globalization often, in practice, undermine their own affirmations in their fundamental management structures and in their everyday administration. Virtual organization is a litmus test of this. It represents a fundamental challenge to senior and middle managers. The challenge for the former is to understand *where* virtual groups fit into their organization. The challenge for the latter is to understand *how* these groups work and *who* is suited to working in them. Those who figure out the "where, how, and who" of virtual structures, and how these structures and their pattern natures best complement social and procedural modes of organization, will find themselves with an enhanced capacity to act across distance. But achieving this requires more than rhetoric or policy—and more than just preparedness to implement new technologies. Above all, it requires new, unmapped ways of working, trusting, and thinking.

References

Ablate, J. (1999). *Inventing the Internet*. Cambridge, MA: MIT Press.

Castells, M. (2000). *The Rise of the Network Society*. Oxford: Blackwell.

Chandler, A.D. (1977). *The Visible Hand: The Managerial Revolution in American Business*. Cambridge, MA: Harvard University Press.

Clegg, S. (2000). Globalizing the intelligent organization. In J. Garrick & C. Rhodes, (Eds.), *Research and Knowledge at Work*. London: Routledge.

Duarte, D., & Snyder, N. (1999). *Mastering Virtual Teams*. San Francisco, CA: Jossey-Bass.

Friedman, K. (1998) Cities in the information age: A Scandinavian perspective. In M. Igbaria & M. Tan (Eds.), *The Virtual Workplace*. Hershey, PA: Idea Group Publishing.

Fukuyama, F. (1995). *Trust: The Social Virtues and the Creation of Prosperity*. New York: Free Press.

Galbraith, J.K. 1978 [1969]. *The New Industrial State*. Boston, MA: Houghton Mifflin.

Grimshaw, D., & Kwok, S. (1998). The business benefits of the virtual organization. In M. Igbaria & M. Tan (Eds.), *The Virtual Workplace*. Hershey, PA: Idea Group Publishing.

Handy, C. (1995). Trust and the virtual organization. *Harvard Business Review*, 73(3).

Hayek, F. (1989). *The Fatal Conceit*. Chicago, IL: University of Chicago Press.

Innis, H. (1950). *Empire and Communications*. Oxford: Clarendon Press.

Innis, H. (1951). *The Bias of Communication*. Toronto: University of Toronto Press.

Jacobs, J. (2000). *The Nature of Economies*. New York: Vintage.

Jenkins, R. (2001). *Churchill*. London: Macmillan.

Johnson, S. (2002 [2001]). *Emergence: The Connected Lives of Ants, Brains, Systems and Software*. Harmondsworth: Penguin.

Kipnis, D. (1996). Trust and technology. In R. M. Kramer & T. R. Tyler (Eds.), *Trust in Organizations*. Thousand Oaks, CA: Sage.

Knoll, K., & Jarvenpaa, S. (1998). Working together in global virtual teams. In M. Igbaria & M. Tan (Eds.), *The Virtual Workplace*. Hershey, PA: Idea Group Publishing.

Lebow, I. (1995). *Information Highways and Byways: From the Telegraph to the 21st Century*. Piscataway, NJ: IEEE Press.

Lipnack, J., & Stamps, J. (2000). *Virtual Teams: People Working Across Boundaries with Technology.* New York: John Wiley & Sons.

Meyerson, D., Weick, K., & Kramer, R. M. (1996). Swift trust and temporary groups. In R. M. Kramer & T. R. Tyler (Eds.), *Trust in Organizations.* Thousand Oaks, CA: Sage.

Murphy, P. (1999). The existential stoic. *Thesis Eleven*, 60.

Murphy, P. (2001a). *Civic Justice.* Amherst, NY: Humanity Books.

Murphy, P. (2001b). Architectonics. In P. Murphy & J. Arnason (Eds.), *Agon, Logos, Polis,* (pp. 207–232). Stuttgart: Franz Steiner Verlag.

Naughton, J. (1999). *A Brief History of the Future: The Origins of the Internet.* London: Weidenfeld & Nicolson.

Nohria, N., & Eccles, R. G. (1992). Face-to-face: Making network organizations work. In N. Nohria & R. G. Eccles (Eds.), *Networks and Organizations: Structure, Form, and Action.* Boston, MA: Harvard Business School Press.

O'Hara-Devereaux, M., & Johansen, R. (1994). *Global Work: Bridging Distance, Culture, and Time.* San Francisco, CA: Jossey-Bass.

Ray, D., & Bronstein, H. (1995). *Teaming Up: Making the Transition to a Self-Directed, Team-Based Organization.* New York: McGraw-Hill.

Rice, R. E., & Love, G. (1987). Electronic emotion: Socioemotional content in a computer-mediated network. *Communication Research*, 14.

Stafford, L., & Reske, J. R. (1990). Idealization and communication in long-distance premarital relationships. *Family Relations*, 39.

Staw, B. M. (1995) Why no one really wants creativity. In C. M. Ford & D. A. Gioia (Eds.), *Creative Action in Organizations.* London: Sage Publications.

Stern, S., Porter, M. E., & Furman, J. L. (2000). *The determinants of national innovative capacity.* Accessed: September 2002 from: http://web.mit.edu/jfurman/www/Innovative%20Capacity.pdf.

Stewart, T. A. (1997). *Intellectual Capital: The New Wealth of Organizations.* New York: Doubleday.

Walther, J. B. (1996). Computer-mediated communication: Impersonal, interpersonal and hyperpersonal interaction. *Communication Research*, 14.

Whyte, W. (1956). *The Organization Man.* New York: Simon and Schuster.

Yates, J. (1989). *Control through Communication: The Rise of System in American Management.* Baltimore, MD: Johns Hopkins University Press.

Endnotes

1   An antinomy is a pair of contradictory statements, both of which are true.

2   In Asia today, mobile/cell phone text messaging is emerging as an alternative to office-based and computer-based e-mail. In part, this reflects the greater reliance on personal contact in Asia for the conduct of business. It also reflects the origin of e-mail in office-based activity. Text messaging and e-mail are conducive to distance interaction, yet both bear the marks of their originating cultures: one in the world of personal affiliation, the other in the world of the procedural office.

3   As Lipnack and Stamps (2000) remarked: "Strategic alliance teams comprise people from different companies. They lack common reporting structures or policies because people in them come from different hierarchies. In cross-functional teams (the best known virtual teams), no common authority figure may tie everyone together until they reach the CEO level" (p. 146).

4   The "bias" of different communicative media was first systematically drawn attention to by Harold Innis (1950, 1951).

5   As Lipnack and Stamps (2000) observed, we can go back to the 1950s to find the genesis of a distinction made between two types of organizational leader—the social leader and the task leader. Social leaders focus on group identity, status, and attractiveness. Task leaders focus on expertise and accomplishment. In virtual working, however, it is difficult to communicate rank online. Expertise, in the sense of knowledge, is a more viable definer of leadership in virtual settings. However, even in this case, titled or bureaucratically defined expertise is just as difficult to assert anonymously online as is status. The person who leads socially and the person whose expertise is defined by their office require some kind of face-to-face interaction, or some kind of visible presence, to underline their authority. Thus, there remains a strong need in conventional organizations for face-to-face meetings, even if they are not functionally necessary. At the same time, there are strong pressures that operate against this. As Knoll and Jaravenpaa observed in 1998: "Although global virtual teams consisting of 'strangers' might be a rare business arrangement today" such arrangements are also "a glimpse of the future. Today, many organizations fly people to face-to-face (FtF) meetings. Yet in a future of compressed time windows coupled with dwindling margins and budgets, when ad hoc teams will be formed overnight to solve problems, and the next day, people will be unable to materialize physically from the far corners of the earth" (p. 3). If you were a traditional industrial company—say, a food processor, like

Rank Hovis, with 11 flour mills scattered through the United Kingdom—and managers were spending two to three days in order to go to a face-to-face meeting, the potential economic benefits of virtual management are obvious (Grimshaw & Kwok, 1998, p. 53). Accordingly, Duarte and Snyder observed (1999): "The business justification for virtual teams is strong. They increase speed and agility and leverage expertise and vertical integration between organizations to make resources readily available. Virtual teams also lessen the disruptions of people's lives because people do not have to travel to meet" (p. 9).

That may be all true, however, at the same time, technology does not solve the problems of strangers, or relative strangers, working together, and the deep levels of anthropological and social readjustment needed to make such interactions work.

[6]   As Irwin Lebow (1995) observed: "Old traditions die hard, and the autonomy of the ship's captain is one of the oldest. The problem of making the operating navy (as opposed to the Washington navy) enthusiastic, or at least comfortable, with wireless was analogous to that of making the field army accepting of the telegraph when it was first introduced. If anything, the problem was greater with the navy, and vestiges of it still remain almost 100 years later" (p. 81). This is what retired Admiral Lucien Capone referred to as the *Nelsonian syndrome* when he wrote in 1979: "We demand instant, rapid, reliable, and secure communication with our subordinates—but we prefer to hear from higher authority once a year by slow mail."(ibid.) A number of failures of the British navy in sea battles against the Germany navy early in the First World War can be attributed to Winston Churchill's over-use of wireless telegraphy to send instructions to operational ships from London. (See Roy Jenkins, 2001, pp. 244–246.)

[7]   Geographic distance denotes space–time differences. However, the same kind of issue appears in the case of organizational distance—the distance represented by cross-functional or interorganizational collaboration (Lipnack & Stamps, 2000, p. 62).

[8]   On the long-term historic shift from patrimonialism to proceduralism in government organization, see Murphy (2001a).

[9]   On the development of the genres of corporate communications, see Yates (1989).

[10]   If you doubt this, think of the effect of radio or television broadcast on congressional or parliamentary rhetoric. What sounds convincing in a face-to-face chamber sounds inflated when broadcast. The sound-bite of broadcast media is just another variant of the telegraphic imperative of all distance communication.

11   Self-management in organizations predates virtual collaboration. For a study of the application of self-direction in traditional organizations, see Ray & Bronstein, 1995. The authors (p. 22) define the idea of self-direction in the following way: "A self-directed work team is a group of interdependent, highly trained employees who are responsible for managing themselves and the work they do. They set their own goals, in cooperation with management, and the team plans how to achieve those goals, and how their work is to be accomplished. The central organizing fact of a team is that it has a common purpose and measurable goals for which the team can be held accountable, independent of its individual members. Employees on a self-directed team handle a wide variety of functions and work with a minimum of direct supervision" (p. 22).

12   Or as Lipnack and Stamps put it: "Cooperation requires independence...To a significant degree, virtual teams self-manage. For them to succeed, people must be independent and capable of making quick yet thoughtful decisions. Virtual people need to known more, decide more, do more" (p. 170).

13   As Ken Friedman (1998) noted: "The shipping industry has always been something of a virtual workplace, with companies outsourcing services and projects to each other, trading and brokering everything from information to risk to cargo capacity to ship management and ships themselves." The tendency of shipping companies historically to adopt something akin to a virtual logic is a product of the fact that sea regions have been the great incubators of economic interactions between strangers, and continue to be so today. For the same reason, sea regions have been the historic incubators of intellectual capital. That also remains the case today, with the Mediterranean (Italy), the North Sea (Britain and Netherlands), the Baltic (Finland, Denmark, Sweden, and Norway), the Tasman Sea (Australia and New Zealand), the China Seas (Japan), and thalassic North America (the Great Lakes-Hudson, Houston and California coast regions) producing the vast majority of the world's intellectual capital. Second-ranked IP nations (Singapore, Taiwan, South Korea, Ireland, and Israel) replicate this pattern as well. See Stern, Porter, and Furman (2000).

14   Architectonics refers to the capacity for thinking and acting as a good architect does, that is, not according to rules and procedures but according to shapes and patterns, mathematical ratios, geometrical proportions, structural rhythms, and so on. The general gravitation of knowledge economies toward abstraction, and its permeating influence, is well-captured by Stewart Clegg (2000) when he observed: "Increasingly, technology in the postmodern era is a source of abstract events, for which the hallmark is neither reliability nor efficiency but their *representation*. One aspect of new technologies is the essentially invisible material process

that unfolds in their application…Operating a lathe through feel, rhythm and visual cues as extensive sensory data is a very different operation to reading from a computer graphic…Abstract events require a kind of learning without environmental stimuli as cues…" (p. 85).

[15] An argument against virtual communication is that it filters out social cues and thereby reduces information "richness." However, reducing socioemotional contents may be a positive, and a positive even from the standpoint of the emotions. A reduction in socioemotional communication may open possibilities for an increase in cognitive emotional communication. Stafford and Reske (1990) pointed to the positive correlation between reduced-cue, asynchronous communication, and intimacy. They use the traditional example of letter writing, but their evidence can be extrapolated to computer-mediated communication as well. Stafford and Reske studied premarital partners, some of whom lived with or near-by each other, the others in long-distance relationships. The conclusion of their study was that couples rated highest for martial adjustment, communication, and idealization who used face-to-face communications least, while the percentage of asynchronous communication exchanges in the form of letters positively correlated with good adjustment, communication, idealization, and with one additional factor: love. This is not a surprising result, given what else we observed about the relation between virtual communication, trust, and rationality.

About the Authors

David J. Pauleen is a Senior Lecturer at the School of Information Management and Director of the MCA/Honours Program in IS at Victoria University of Wellington, New Zealand. He received his PhD in Information Management from Victoria University of Wellington, his MA in Intercultural Management from the School for International Training, and his BA in Oriental Languages from the University of California. His current research interests include virtual teams and related issues, particularly information and communication technologies, intercultural communication and cultural biases in the development and use of communications technologies, team leadership and facilitation, and knowledge management of team processes and outcomes. His work has appeared in *Internet Research — Electronic Networking Applications and Policy, Journal of Information Technology, Leadership and Organizational Development Journal, Journal of Global Information Management,* and *Journal of Knowledge Management.*

*   *   *   *

Ann Frances Cameron is a PhD student of MIS and Organizational Behavior at Queen's University, Kingston, Canada. Previous degrees include a Master of Science in Management, also from Queen's University, and a Bachelor of Information Systems, from St. Francis Xavier University in Nova Scotia, Canada. She spent some time in practice, working as an application analyst.

Working for Imperial Oil Ltd. at various Canadian sites, her responsibilities included onsite training and coordinating global distribution of an in-house developed application. Currently, her main areas of research are the use of technology in virtual teams, as well as the unintended and unexpected consequences of emerging communication technologies.

Stacey L. Connaughton (PhD, University of Texas at Austin) is an Assistant Professor in the Department of Communication at Rutgers University, USA. Her research interests include identity, identification, and leadership, particularly as they relate to virtual organizations and political parties. She facilitated workshops and wrote guidebooks for corporate, governmental, educational administrative, and student groups in the areas of leadership, team-building, and work relationships.

John A. Daly is the Liddell Professor of Communication and the TCB Professor in the Management Department at the University of Texas at Austin, USA. He published a number of books and articles on topics involving communication. He also consulted with a number of companies worldwide on issues tied to improving communication effectiveness.

Line Dubé is an Associate Professor in the Department of Information Technologies at HEC Montréal , Canada. She holds a master's degree in Project Management from Université du Québec à Montréal and a PhD in Business Administration from Florida International University. She is mainly interested in the organizational impacts of information technology. Her current research projects focus on virtual teams and on knowledge management through the implementation of virtual communities of practice. Her work has been published in several journals, including *Communications of the ACM* and *Information and Organization*, and presented at major academic and professional conferences.

Schahram Dustdar is an Associate Professor at the Distributed Systems Group, Information Systems Institute, Vienna University of Technology, Austria. He received his MSc (1990) and PhD degrees (1992) in Business Informatics from the University of Linz, Austria. His work experience includes several years as the founding head of the Center for Informatics (ZID) at the University of Art and Industrial Design in Linz (1991–1999), Austrian project manager of the MICE EU-project (1993–1997), and director of Coordination Technologies at the Design Transfer Center in Linz (1999–2000). While on sabbatical leave, he was a postdoctoral research scholar (Erwin-Schrödinger scholarship) at the

London School of Economics (Information Systems Department) (1993 and 1994) and a visiting research scientist at NTT Multimedia Communications Labs in Palo Alto, California, during 1998. Since 1999, he works as the founder and chief scientist of Caramba Labs Software AG (CarambaLabs.com) in Vienna, a venture-capital-funded software company focused on software for collaborative processes in teams. Caramba Labs was nominated for several (international and national) awards: World Technology Award in the category of Software (2001); Top-Startup companies in Austria (Cap Gemini Ernst & Young) (2002); and MERCUR Innovationspreis der Wirtschaftskammer (2002).

Walter D. Fernández is a Senior Project Manager specializing in major IT projects. He is currently working for a major corporation in the telecommunications industry. He has more than 15 years of experience designing and implementing innovative information systems. Over the last six years, Walter has been working on multiple-firm and multiple-teams IT development and implementation projects. He has a Bachelor of Business (Computing) degree and a Master of Information Technology degree from the Queensland University of Technology, Australia, where he is in the final stages of completing a PhD degree focusing on management issues in metateam projects

Terri L. Griffith (BA, Psychology, UC Berkeley; MS and PhD, Organizational Psychology and Theory, Carnegie Mellon University) is a Professor of Management in the Leavey School of Business. Her research and consulting interests include the implementation and effective use of new technologies and organizational practices, most recently focusing on virtual teams and "negotiated implementation." Her recent field research includes sites within the Sutherland Group, a major imaging company, and two major high-techs. She is a Senior Editor for *Organization Science,* and recently coedited the book, *Research on Managing Groups and Teams: Technology* (2000, JAI Press).

Tammie D. Hertel is a Program Manager for Collaboration and Virtual Team Projects at a large, global semiconductor manufacturing company, where she is also a master trainer and designer of effective virtual teams courses. Tammie is also President of TeamAbilities (USA) (www.TeamAbilities.com), a company that provides instructor-led online training and content development designed to develop and establish high-performing effective virtual teams. She received a BA in Management and a master's degree in E-Education from the University of Phoenix in addition to other graduate-level studies in Information Technology. Her research interests include asynchronous technologies, reward systems, user interface design, and next-generation collaboration technologies.

Andrea Hornett, Assistant Professor of Business at The Pennsylvania State University's Delaware County campus near Philadelphia (USA), teaches strategy, leadership, and research, often employing virtual teams to prepare students for global business. She began studying virtual teams in 1995. She is linking that endeavor to aspects of knowledge sharing and extending research she began at The George Washington University's doctoral program in organizational learning. She has 30 years of management and consulting experience in a variety of environments and claims that her role in the 1972 Hurricane Agnes recovery involved a virtual team using a fax machine transmitting one page every six minutes!

David K. Meader is on the faculty in the Department of MIS at the University of Arizona, USA. He received his PhD in MIS, his MA in Organizational Psychology, and his BS in Computer Science from the University of Michigan. He received his MBA from the University of North Carolina–Chapel Hill. Prior to entering his PhD program, he worked six years as a systems analyst and systems consultant in San Francisco for companies such as Chevron, Bank of America, and Teknekron. He has given numerous presentations to corporate and academic groups on the effective use of information technology in business. His current research investigates eLearning technologies and strategies.

Peter Murphy is Senior Lecturer in Communications, School of Information Management, Victoria University of Wellington, New Zealand. He is the author of *Civic Justice* (Humanity Books, 2001) and of more than 40 scholarly articles on ethics, politics, urbanism, and communication. Murphy coedited *The Left In Search of a Center* (University of Illinois Press, 1996), edited the special issue of *South Atlantic Quarterly* (Duke University Press, 1998) on friendship, and coedited *Agon, Logos, Polis* (Franz Steiner, 2000). Among his appointments, he has been visiting professor of Philosophy in the Graduate Faculty of the New School for Social Research in New York City and visiting professor in Political Science at Baylor University, Texas. He has also worked in the Internet search directory industry, where he experienced virtual team life first-hand.

Olivia Ernst Neece is the Director of Operations of The Ernst Group, investors in commercial real estate and marketable securities. She is a Researcher and Teaching Assistant at the Claremont Graduate University, USA. Previously, she held the posts of assistant professor at California State University Northridge, vice president of Project Administration for Hirsch Bedner Associates, vice president of Operations and Development of Design Services AIRCOA, and president of Olivia Neece Planning and Design. She earned her BS, Business/

Finance from University of Southern California and an MBA from the Anderson School–University of California Los Angeles. She is a member of Beta Gamma Sigma, Academy of Management, and Institute for Operations Research and Management Sciences, and she is a Founder of the Los Angeles Music Center.

Guy Paré is an Associate Professor of MIS at HEC Montréal , Canada, and a Research Fellow at CIRANO. He also serves as Associate Editor on the *MIS Quarterly* editorial board. He received his PhD in Business Administration from Florida International University. His current research interests focus on IT in healthcare, IT staffing and career issues, IT change agentry, and virtual teams. Journals and conference proceedings where his publications have recently appeared include *Communications of the ACM, European Journal of Information Systems, International Journal of Medical Informatics, Health Services Management Research, Journal of Medical Systems*, and *Proceedings of ICIS and SIGCPR.*

Lalita Rajasingham is Senior Lecturer and Director of Master and PhD programs in Communications Studies, at Victoria University of Wellington, New Zealand. Her long and varied career in communications includes radio and television broadcasting experience in Malaysia, Australia, Britain, and New Zealand. She is consultant with a number of international organizations, including the Asia-Pacific Institute of Broadcasting Development, the Commonwealth of Learning, and the World Bank. Since 1986, her area of research and teaching is in the application of information technology to human communications and education. She is widely published nationally and internationally. Her coauthored book titled *In Search of the Virtual Class: Education in an Information Society* helped to pioneer future directions in education on the Internet for the 21st Century. She is currently coauthoring a sequel on the virtual university.

D. Sandy Staples, PhD, is an Associate Professor in the School of Business at Queen's University, Kingston, Canada. His research interests include exploring the enabling role of information systems for virtual work and knowledge management and assessing the effectiveness of information systems and IS practices. He published articles in various journals and magazines, including *Organization Science, Information & Management, Journal of Strategic Information Systems, Journal of Management Information Systems, Communications of the Association of Information Systems, International Journal of Management Reviews, Business Quarterly, Journal of End-User Computing, OMEGA*, and *KM Review*. He is currently an Associate Editor of *MIS Quarterly* and serves on the editorial boards of other journals.

Ian K. Wong is an undergraduate commerce student at Queen University, School of Business, Canada. His research interests are in organizational behaviour and, in particular, to issues related to volunteer work and volunteer motivation. Ian has published in the journal *Information & Management*.

Index

NEW from Idea Group Publishing

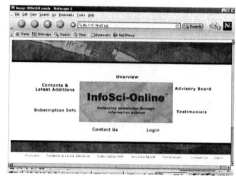